SCARECROW AUTHOR BIBLIOGRAPHIES

1. John Steinbeck—1929–71 (Tetsumaro Hayashi). 1973. *See also nos. 64 and 99.*
2. Joseph Conrad (Theodore G. Ehrsam). 1969.
3. Arthur Miller (Tetsumaro Hayashi). 2nd ed., 1976.
4. Katherine Anne Porter (Waldrip & Bauer). 1969.
5. Philip Freneau (Philip M. Marsh). 1970.
6. Robert Greene (Tetsumaro Hayashi). 1971.
7. Benjamin Disraeli (R. W. Stewart). 1972.
8. John Berryman (Richard W. Kelly). 1972.
9. William Dean Howells (Vito J. Brenni). 1973.
10. Jean Anouilh (Kathleen W. Kelly). 1973.
11. E. M. Forster (Alfred Borrello). 1973.
12. The Marquis de Sade (E. Pierre Chanover). 1973.
13. Alain Robbe-Grillet (Dale W. Frazier). 1973.
14. Northrop Frye (Robert D. Denham). 1974.
15. Federico García Lorca (Laurenti & Siracusa). 1974.
16. Ben Jonson (Brock & Welsh). 1974.
17. Four French Dramatists: Eugène Brieux, François de Curel, Emile Fabre, Paul Hervieu (Edmund F. Santa Vicca). 1974.
18. Ralph Waldo Ellison (Jacqueline Covo). 1974.
19. Philip Roth (Bernard F. Rodgers, Jr.). 2nd ed., 1984.
20. Norman Mailer (Laura Adams). 1974.
21. Sir John Betjeman (Margaret Stapleton). 1974.
22. Elie Wiesel (Molly Abramowitz). 1974.
23. Paul Laurence Dunbar (Eugene W. Metcalf, Jr.). 1975.
24. Henry James (Beatrice Ricks). 1975.
25. Robert Frost (Lentricchia & Lentricchia). 1976.
26. Sherwood Anderson (Douglas G. Rogers). 1976.
27. Iris Murdoch and Muriel Spark (Tominaga & Schneidermeyer). 1976.
28. John Ruskin (Kirk H. Beetz). 1976.
29. Georges Simenon (Trudee Young). 1976.
30. George Gordon, Lord Byron (Oscar José Santucho). 1977.
31. John Barth (Richard Vine). 1977.
32. John Hawkes (Carol A. Hryciw). 1977.
33. William Everson (Bartlett & Campo). 1977.
34. May Sarton (Lenora P. Blouin). 1978. Out of print. See no. 104.
35. Wilkie Collins (Kirk H. Beetz). 1978.
36. Sylvia Plath (Lane & Stevens). 1978.
37. E. B. White (A. J. Anderson). 1978.
38. Henry Miller (Lawrence J. Shifreen). 1979.
39. Ralph Waldo Emerson (Jeanetta Boswell). 1979.
40. James Dickey (Jim Elledge). 1979.

A. L. Rowse at All Souls College, Oxford, July 1976

A. L. Rowse

A Bibliophile's Extensive Bibliography

Sydney Cauveren

Scarecrow Author Bibliographies, No. 103

The Scarecrow Press, Inc.
Lanham, Maryland, and London
2000

SCARECROW PRESS, INC.

Published in the United States of America
by Scarecrow Press, Inc.
4720 Boston Way
Lanham, Maryland 20706
http://www.scarecrowpress.com

4 Pleydell Gardens, Folkestone
Kent CT20 2DN, England

British Library Cataloguing in Publication Information Available

Library of Congress Cataloging-in-Publication Data

Cauveren, Sydney, 1947–
    A. L. Rowse : a bibliophile's extensive bibliography / Sydney Cauveren.
       p.   cm. — (Scarecrow author bibliographies ; no. 103)
    Includes bibliographical references and index.
    ISBN 0-8108-3641-6 (alk. paper)
    1. Rowse, A. L. (Alfred Leslie), 1903– Bibliography.   2. English
literature—History and criticism Bibliography.   3. Great Britain—History
—Tutors, 1485–1603 Bibliography.   4. Shakespeare, William, 1564–1616
Bibliography.   I. Title.   I. Title: Alfred Leslie Rowse.   III. Series.
Z8763.67.C38 1999
[PR6035.084]   99-15195
016.828′91209—dc21   CIP

To John
and our shared
admiration of and devotion to
our friend Leslie

Contents

Preface

> Reasonably enough there is no end to research: one is always finding something later that might, perhaps should, be in the book. No matter: the account must be closed, if only temporarily, and the book should be an organic whole.
>
> A. L. Rowse, *Historians I Have Known*

This is the first comprehensive bibliography on the work of A. L. Rowse, the great British historian, Shakespearean scholar, and ambivalent man of letters.

It is addressed not only to students of literature and history but also to bibliophiles and collectors on both sides of the Atlantic. Oddly enough, it has been compiled in Australia, further testifying to the international reputation of A. L. Rowse.

An immensely prolific and controversial writer and researcher, A. L. Rowse is never dull. His books and articles are weighted with scholarship while peppered with a spirited prose style that makes his work leap forth with life for his readers. This is particularly so in his chief area of expertise, the Elizabethan age. He draws his readers in, to expose that age to them unlike any other historian has managed to accomplish before him. And, for nearly fifty years, A. L. Rowse never ceased to give his public new and illuminating insights and discoveries into that age and about its most famous writer, William Shakespeare.

I think this is an essential work. Every major writer—indeed Cornwall's premier man of letters this century—should have a bibliography compiled. And preferably before the cost of such an exercise becomes insurmountable.

This bibliography provides unparalleled exposure of A. L. Rowse's career. Given, herewith, as a labor of love! Ideally, a university or college grant or scholarship helps finance a project that is five years in the making. Indeed I have noticed that many bibliographers give grateful acknowledgment to a benefactor. I only have to thank my own dogged determination to succeed. Thankfully this has prevailed against all adversity!

It is a sad reflection on the publishing industry today that not a single British publisher of Rowse's major works was interested in his bibliography, not even in seeing a single word of it. All were ready to profit from the author in the past but had no interest in putting anything back in, for the record or to further aid the cause of scholarship. But I feel very sure A. L. Rowse would be pleased to know that this work is being published in the United States. As he once candidly observed to me, "The generosity of the Americans seems inexhaustible."

A. L. Rowse proved a perfect subject for a bibliographer, full of interest! This reference source should prove useful to researchers in the following subjects: Elizabethan history; William Shakespeare, his life and plays and the solutions to the sonnets; Christopher Marlowe, the rival poet; historians of the twentieth century; Sir Winston Churchill and the history of the Churchill family; politics of the twentieth century; leading figures of Rowse's generation, both literary and political, at Oxford, in England and in America; Cornwall and Oxford, historical and geographical; poetry, particularly Rowse's poems about Cornwall and the American landscape; reviews, both by A. L. Rowse on the most significant books on history and literature published over the past seventy years, and reviews of A. L. Rowse's books.

Section A includes a rich cross-section of reviews of A. L. Rowse's books to illustrate the wide critical and often controversial reception his historical and other works received both in England and in America.

In sections D and F, letters and items from newspapers like *The Times,* in London, have been expanded upon by giving an excerpt of contents. These items were difficult to cite in the original, and without the facility to photocopy for my records. Where warranted, subheadings are added to further clarify contents. Also, where applicable in section D, every effort has been made to cross-reference entries with known reprintings, either in other periodicals or in book-form publications.

The massive research I conducted over the past three years on journals and newspapers, as well as my quest for print-run numbers from publishers, offered both delightful discoveries and annoying frustration. In the process, I acquired a potency of patience previously unknown to me!

A number of A. L. Rowse's publishers did not respond to any of my inquiries. The following could not provide print-run numbers: Weidenfeld & Nicolson, Thames & Hudson, Sphere, Batsford, and Michael Joseph. Some other companies had with the years either merged or gone out of business with the trail of past records lost. Therefore, where not provided, print-run numbers were unobtainable.

But I would like to record herewith my appreciation for information, as well as for help received in other ways, from the following: John Handford, archivist at Macmillan for print-run numbers; Michael Bott, archivist at the University of Reading Library for Jonathan Cape print-run numbers and further assistance; Catherine Halliday at Duckworth for print-run numbers; Elizabeth James at the British Library for further information on books by Macmillan; Duvall Y. Hecht of Books on Tape, Inc., New Port Beach, California, for audio books information; Walter H. Annenberg for details about *Westminster Abbey*; the Folio Society, Pat West of the Members Room; John Bodley, for Faber & Faber print-run numbers; Alexandra Erskine, librarian, *The Daily Telegraph*, London; R. Jones, the library, *Evening Standard*, London; BBC Written Archives Centre, Reading, for data on radio and television broadcasts and scripts. I also thank the executors of the estate of the late Dr. A. L. Rowse for permission to use extracts from his correspondence.

For translations, I wish to thank the following libraries: Narodni Knihovna, National Library of Prague, Czech Republic; Det Kongelige Bibliotek, Copenhagen, Denmark; Koninklyke Bibliotheek, The Hague, Holland; Bibliotheque Nationale de France, Paris, France; Die Deutsche Bibliothek, Frankfurt am Main, Germany; Universitets Biblioteket, Oslo, Norway; Biblioteka Narodowa, Warsaw, Poland; National Library of Russia, St. Petersburg, Russia; Biblioteca Nacional, Madrid, Spain; Kungliga Biblioteket, Stockholm, Sweden.

I also acknowledge assistance from humanities librarians in Australia, at the Fisher Library, Sydney University, particularly Mary Rothe for introducing me to the electronic Periodicals Contents Index and Jillian Brown of the Audio Visual Department; State Library of New South Wales; La Trobe University Library, Melbourne; State Library of Victoria; State Library of South Australia; the British Library in London and the Cornish Studies Library, Redruth, Cornwall—Terry Knight, principal librarian, Cornish Studies. I also thank Richard Ollard, Dr. Rowse's biographer, for his guidance and encouragement. And special gratitude to Phyllis Cundy and Pat Julian for much Cornish information.

I am particularly grateful for Dr. Rowse's personal encouragement, which is amply exemplified through the marvelous, lengthy interview that he specifically gave in his ninetieth year in order to introduce this work. In it he discusses all aspects and facets of his long literary career.

I am most indebted to the kindness of Mr. John R. Walde—to whom this book is dedicated—for constantly being there, creating order out of chaos over the long duration, and then keyboarding most of the manuscript into a computer file for presentation to the publisher.

Last, with all the good will and desire in the world, this first bibliography of A. L. Rowse, though aimed at being extensive and comprehensive, cannot be definitive. Unfortunately, restrictions placed on the Rowse papers at Exeter University prevented me from consulting this massive archive. I suspect these could yield further material, as A. L. Rowse was an immensely prolific writer who also published his letters and poems and articles in obscure and local-area publications difficult to trace, as well as with all the internationally known

presses. I would therefore welcome any omissions being brought to my attention for inclusion in future editions. I trust that one of my main aims will have
been fulfilled, that this "dedicated foundation stone" will have opened up the
floodgates!

Introduction

A. L. Rowse in Conversation
with Sydney Cauveren

I ought to give you a copy of the bibliography that has so far been done by this expert at the University of Sheffield I think [Gordon L. Hunt, an incomplete chronological listing]. And I think I ought to give you some names and addresses because you know there is a terribly distinguished scholar who is writing my biography. He's called Richard Ollard. He's a very good historian and he wants to do my biography. There are several people who want to do it. He's the best. He's a terribly good writer and an awfully nice man and I can't stop it. Of course an awful lot of distinguished writers have very much wanted not to have their biography written and some people have stopped it, as Thackeray did. T. S. Eliot wanted to stop it, but you can't stop it you see. So you might as well cooperate a bit because it's going to be done anyway, even though you don't like it.

You have written eighty-nine books. That's one book for every year. How many more do you hope to write?

Well, if I really lived till I was a hundred and still possessed my faculties and wasn't completely ga-ga, there are several subjects that I am sorry I haven't had time to do. For instance, I wrote, as you know, the family history of the Churchills. I think the point is that it sets a good model of family history because family histories before that tended to be very genealogical and awfully boring, whereas I hope my book is really alive.

To go on with the point of family history, I should really very much like to have written the family history of the two most fascinating Cornish families. One the Godolphins and secondly the Killigrews. But I shall never live to do those two you see.

Why not?

Well, it involves a great deal of research. One thing that rather disappoints me and also rather amuses me, wryly, is the way in which academics don't really have the sense to chose really interesting subjects. There are any number of interesting biographies that ought to be written and they go on rewriting the same old subjects. I've just had to review a really rather boring academic biography of Elizabeth I. Well, who wants another?

What order do you place your work in? You want to do these biographies on the families—the Killigrews and the Godolphins—but you are doing a book on the Regicides at present. How do you work out the order of things?

Well, I was asked to write that *[The Regicides]*. I shouldn't really have thought of writing that if it hadn't been suggested to me. But I think, Sydney, you know already that I really began life as a poet. You see I was writing poetry when I was a schoolboy and it was even published when I was a schoolboy. I didn't know how you published anything. It was my headmaster who really put me in for writing essays that won national prizes and all that. Of course I really didn't know a thing about it. Nor did my people who were comparatively illiterate. You know they weren't hardly able to read and write. I've rather over compensated that, don't you think?

But don't you think they did something right in producing you?

Well, they did their best according to their lights. But their lights were really rather dim. Anyway, I was writing poetry and I won, you see, an open scholarship in English Literature at Christ Church and I really expected to do the English literature course. But the dons at Christ Church made me do history. And I was really equally interested in history. The two things actually go together. English literature and English history. These have been the two great interests of my life.

Wouldn't history be much more difficult and academic to write than literature?

Yes, I think that was true. I think you are quite right. I found doing historical research was a tremendous uphill job. And I also had rather an inferiority complex about research. People used to make a tremendous song and dance about research. When I was young at Oxford, they made so much fuss about it that they never got on with writing their own books. I remember when quite young having to go to Cambridge. All those clever academics were all very clever about how difficult it was to write history. Well, I rather kept mum for once and hugged myself with the thought—well, I at any rate am trying to write history.

But you are writing history that lives. That is the big difference between you and other historians that I have read. They are so stodgy and stale. It is impossible to bring it out, whereas you bring people straight in!

Well, it's rather wonderful how dull they can make it if they get up very early in the morning and try very hard. I think that to some extent they owe that to the kind of academic climate they live in. They think that they ought not to be very interesting.

But you lived in that climate!

Well, I think they are not very interesting in themselves. You see, I have always been inspired from the time I was a very small boy. I always wanted to know. I think I was very inquisitive. Very curious to know and of course my rather stupid parents were always engaged in saying little boys should be seen and not heard. Well, silly fools. I must have been a very interesting small child. But what I found was that ordinary people were never capable of giving you any answers and that really made me very resentful. It made me look down on them, but then of course all ordinary people are very stupid and very uninteresting. So I was really rather reduced to living my own kind of mental life by myself and I was always reading and also observing and watching. Some of the members of my family were rather more interesting, especially a very old great-uncle who was rather lively. I was always asking him what the life of the village was like when he was young. Well, the result of that was that I got to know what was going on in the village a hundred years before me. And that was how my best-known book, *A Cornish Childhood,* was started.

It didn't start as an autobiography. It really started as a sort of social history of the village because I've been keeping notes about that for quite a long time. I remember I was writing away the social history of the village where I was born and then when I came up to the point at which I was born I felt distinctly shy. Oh, my goodness me, I've got to start in on me! So, I've been writing about me ever since. Several autobiographical books.

Would *A Cornish Childhood* be the biggest seller you have had? It is still in print—must have sold millions?

Yes, it sold half a million copies. The book is very, very living. Of course, it was also very easy to write because before it, I had a very terrible illness. I had a couple of duodenal operations and I was so desperately ill in the University College Hospital in London that I couldn't even read. So I lay there remembering all the things that had given me pleasure and thinking about bathing on the Cornish beaches because I was having a very high temperature and all that. When I began to get stronger and to recover, I found that the book was all there ready in my head. Just write it out, easily.

Is that how books are created, in your head? Or, as you have suggested to me, one should keep a notebook to write things down, or is that how a book is triggered off?

You really need to do both. But rather the same thing has happened only this year because I've been asked by the publishers to write a book that is not an autobiography, but it's naturally partly autobiographical, called *All Souls in My Time*. Well, I've written again that book, out of my head—out of my memory.

How long did it take to write that book, for example?

Well, I wrote it really, again, rather quickly because I did not consult my diaries. And I've been reading one of my All Souls diaries since, you know, and of course I find all sorts of things that are interesting in the diaries, which I couldn't very well put into the book because *All Souls in My Time* is really written about All Souls, not me. I come in to it, but it really is a picture of that famous Oxford college.

And the characters?

And some of the very important historical characters whom I knew there, like Archbishop Lang, who was the archbishop at the time of the abdication of the Duke of Windsor. And I knew Lord Halifax, who was foreign secretary, and Lord Simon . . .

But you weren't impressed with Halifax, were you? He is in your book *All Souls and Appeasement*.

He had been viceroy of India. He was rather a silent man who was not really very communicative. Some of these rather public figures were really more willing to talk than others and I find records of their conversations and things that they told me in my diary.

In 1932 you wrote *Politics and the Younger Generation*, which is a book you don't talk about these days.

Well, because it's a very juvenile book.

But wasn't it a valuable experience?

I don't really want to talk about that book because I've grown very much older since then. When I reread that book a year or two ago, I thought it wasn't really quite so bad as I thought. But I don't really want to talk about that book. It is very unimportant, so forget it.

After that, you wrote *The Question of the House of Lords*.

Well, I don't want that mentioned either. Don't mention these books that I'm not interested in and that I've completely outgrown. I think you might begin with the book that you've got the manuscript of—*On History*. That is much more important to talk about because though it was the very first little book that I ever wrote—and you so kind as to buy the manuscript, not from me because I had given it, as you know, to the London library to help their funds when it was auctioned. But the importance of that little book, that you've got the manuscript of, is this. That really, very surprisingly, gives you the program of what I ultimately was to fulfil in my historical writing, and that's much more worth talking about. Because one doesn't want to talk about political books written by a young man because politics really is an adult subject and really it's only the opinions of people who are experienced and older in politics that are really worth taking notice of.

Of course there is a very important intellectual point about politics. You probably do not know the work of the most distinguished intellect alive in England in this century on the subject of politics. It was a man called Michael Oakeshott. And it is absolutely characteristic that you've never heard of him because he was really the most distinguished brain writing on the subject. Well, of course, in the sort of filthy democratic society people never know those minds that are of the greatest importance. They've all heard of Bertrand Russell and what he wrote about politics was absolute rubbish. His judgment was frightfully bad and he's not really worth taking notice of. Whereas Michael Oakeshott was a real genius on the subject. I didn't know him personally, but I completely agree with his view about it.

Though he was the professor of politics at the London School of Economics, he really thought that politics was a very second-rate occupation. And if you look at what goes on in the world, of course, politicians occupy the headlines in the newspapers, but they are hardly worth attending to. Intellectually they are apt to be second-rate. Of course, that was not true of a really great man like Churchill or a really great woman like Margaret Thatcher. But they are liable not to be properly appreciated by third-rate brains, so we don't really have to bother about them.

When I was young, I couldn't help being interested in politics then, because it was the last period in which this small country could exercise an influence in world affairs. Our affairs in Britain were conducted by a lot of thoroughly second-rate people in Baldwin and Neville Chamberlain who were completely wrong about appeasing Hitler and appeasing Germany and of course, a really great man like Winston Churchill, who knew how wrong they were.

Well, I was quite young, but I knew Germany and I knew German history and I knew that it was absolute rubbish. Well, I was right about all that. And I did write a tract that is still very much noticed called *All Souls and Appeasement*. Because it happened that three or four of the leading fellows of All Souls were involved in it. But the college as a whole was very much against it. And of course, I was one of the people sticking my neck out and it was very unpopular because the whole country was really with Neville Chamberlain. How wrong they were! Well, you can't go by the minds of ordinary people because they never understand anything. They were certainly wrong about appeasement and now people realize it.

But I think one reason for it was that in the First World War so many of the very ablest young men of that generation had all been killed by the bloody Germans who made the war. And, I think the result of it was that both Britain and France lost some of their very best young men who really would have conducted the affairs of Britain and France much more effectively if they had remained alive. Well, I was aware of all that, and that is one of the good points that remains true in that early book of mine, *Politics and the Younger Generation*. I was right about that.

The second point is that the first German war had been such a terrible experience for both Britain and France that the great bulk of the people were absolutely bent on peace. Well, of course they wanted peace. But Hitler didn't. He always meant the war. He meant the war against Russia in the first instance because he intended to get on top in the whole of Eastern Europe. Well, if he had succeeded we would have been at his mercy. And all these second-rate people who were conducting our affairs never saw that. You don't get peace, as a matter of fact, by being pacific when you're dealing with a tiger, or when you're dealing with a militarist country like Germany.

Well, I was a political candidate, which really kept me on the opposition side as a Labour man. I have always been in a sense on the opposition side. On the unpopular side. I am now again rather on the unpopular side because everybody really wants to take the line of least resistance. They, all of them, want the country to spend, spend, spend and never really think about saving for a rainy day. They want, as a matter of fact, to spend all the capital on consumer goods. It's a consumer society—a consumption society—everywhere, because of course, the great mob electorate never really knows what's the best thing for the country.

Hopefully they are buying some of your books in the process!

Well, I don't really expect anything from them.

What topic do you enjoy writing about most? Of course, you have the poetry, the history, the politics, the biographies, the autobiographies, and the reviews.

Yes, well, this is a very good point to raise. Of course, the history books that I wrote were research books because I was a research fellow of All Souls College. That was my job. But I was always very much hipped on the Elizabethan age. In some ways that was the greatest and the most exciting age in England's history because it was really the beginning of everything when we were a very small country of only 5 million in population that really defeated the Spanish empire—the Spanish world empire, and I think that the inspiration of that really led to the most marvelous epoch in our literature with our very greatest writer, Shakespeare. So it was ultimately, absolutely natural that I should want to write the biography of the greatest writer in the Elizabethan age. There was nothing remarkable about that.

But that again was not particularly popular because an awful lot of the English Lit. people really thought of me as just a mere historian and they had a sort of trade union feeling that I was engaged in trespassing in their sphere.

How do you feel about the fact, doing the biography and so much other work on Shakespeare, without any original material to go on?

There is a great deal of original material to go on. There's the whole of Shakespeare's work. And the whole of Shakespeare's work expresses in it his experience of the age. In addition to that there's the whole documentation of the Elizabethan age. Well, most of the people writing about William Shakespeare really write about him in only one dimension—the literary. I wrote about him in two dimensions, in both the literary and also the history. So I think you might say that I really had rather an unfair advantage. And that made them damned envious. I think to do them justice, I think they genuinely did not have the imagination to realize that in order to understand the life's work of the greatest writer in the Elizabethan age, you really have to know about the age. And therefore an awful lot of the books written about William Shakespeare are really not worth reading. You can save time and cut them out.

As the result of my detective work, I was able really to solve most of the problems of Shakespeare's biography. Who was the rival poet? Well, the obvious man—Christopher Marlowe. But I never expected that I should discover who Shakespeare's young mistress—the Dark Lady—was. I was given that by providence from on high for sticking to my guns and never giving up, and not listening to the third-rate.

So you see Sydney, I think that we can look at my writing in three divisions. I've already mentioned to you, there's my research work mostly on the Elizabethan age, as a research fellow of All Souls. There are all those volumes giving you a complete portrait of the Elizabethan age—four volumes.

The England of Elizabeth sold well over 300,000. And there are the sequels to that. *The Expansion of Elizabethan England*, and then there are two volumes on the Elizabethan renaissance. Then there are my Elizabethan biographies. The first research work that I did was a rather difficult biography of the famous *Sir Richard Grenville of the Revenge*. That's my first research biography.

That I followed up with a portrait of *Tudor Cornwall*. That's a portrait of sixteenth-century society, when you look at it in miniature, in detail for a small area. Well, if I hadn't done that first, I wouldn't have been able to cope with a portrait of the whole of Elizabethan England, which followed. And then there are the further Elizabethan biographies. I did a kind of biography of Sir Walter Ralegh. I had the great advantage there of discovering the secret of Sir Walter Ralegh's marriage and the birth of a son who was never known to history. That all came from my highlighting the diary of Sir Walter Ralegh's brother-in-law, Sir Arthur Throckmorton. So all that was a new contribution to history.

And then I did these Shakespeare biographies. The best edition of that is the revised edition of *Shakespeare the Man* because I kept on making new discoveries from studying Shakespeare's work, and also the documents in the Bodleian Library at Oxford—the case books of Simon Forman, where I discovered the Dark Lady—the Elizabethan figure Emilia Bassano, Mrs. Lanier, who was also a poet in her own right and who had been mistress of the patron of Shakespeare's company, Lord Hunsdon. Well, you couldn't get closer than that. She is the Dark Lady. And of course, they don't really like to think that I've discovered it, but in fact, it's unanswerable. It never will be answered.

I also did a biography of Christopher Marlowe and a biography of Shakespeare's young patron, the earl of Southampton, who is of course the young man in Shakespeare's sonnets. You see, nobody had noticed before I did that the dedication of Shakespeare's sonnets to Mister W. H. was not William Shakespeare's but was the publisher's, the very well-known publisher, Thomas Thorpe. "T. T."—Thomas Thorpe—and Mister W. H. was not the young man in Shakespeare's sonnets who is, of course, his patron, the earl of Southampton. Everybody had been mixed up about that until I really worked at it and until I worked out the whole problem.

Well, perhaps that's enough about my research work. Because that is what I was working at in Oxford and later on at the Huntington Library in California. This was pure research work. And I've carried on research work since I retired because that book I've given you called *Court and Country* is quite an important book in that it's all based on original research. That's a research book.

Well, I needed a bit of recreation from all that hard research work and therefore I wrote quite a lot of literary books, very often in vacations at home in Cornwall or, when I happened not to be researching, on holiday in America. When I was at University College in Virginia, for instance. So there are quite a lot of literary books like the autobiographies *A Cornish Childhood*, or, *A Cornishman at Oxford*, or, *A Cornishman Abroad*, or, *A Man of the Thirties*. And then quite a lot of literary essays. I can't remember the names of all of them, but some of them are essays about people that I've known like *Memories of Men and Women*, and *Glimpses of the Great*, and so on.

Well, the third division is very important because it's the poetry. Strangely enough, I have continued to write poetry all my life. I began as a poet and I've gone on writing poetry, and the poetry really represents the private inner life that I've lived, as against the public life and the external life that's really in the history and the essays and the politics books. Therefore I attach more importance in a way to my poetry because the whole of my secret life is really in the poetry. I still write poems. One of the best I've written, as you know, quite recently, is about the funeral of my brother at St. Dennis, and I think you've got that.

Of course it's a very queer thing in literary life that people think because you are really best of all known as a historian, that your poetry needn't be taken notice of. They think it's all right that you can write poetry and at the same time write plays; or you can be a novelist and you can write poetry; or you can be a critic and write poetry, but they haven't noticed that it's a very rare thing to be both a historian and a poet. Macaulay was a great historian and also a very good poet. In the Elizabethan age, Samuel Daniel was a very good poet and also, secondarily, a historian. Most people never notice anything and never understand anything.

But I think people who read your work, in the magnificent prose that you write, can detect poetry in the very work!

Well, I think that's why the history is alive, and not really dead. But maybe, you see, they don't notice what a rare combination it is to be both a historian and a poet. Literary life is so compartmentalized that I always get described in the papers as the historian Rowse.

I've just noticed that my name appears in this Churchill book. I hadn't really noticed that before. I've only just been reading this new book about Sir Winston Churchill as a painter [*Winston Churchill, His Life As a Painter* (1990) by his daughter, Mary Soames]. Well, it is rather an interesting example because Sir Winston Churchill's painting is really very much downgraded simply because he was such a great man as a politician. And again an awful lot of people don't realize what a very fine historian he was simply because he was a politician.

Well, this is because people are so compartmentalized. There's a very great deal of specialization in modern life and they don't understand, I think, someone who really straddles both worlds and both subjects. They don't realize what a very good historian Churchill was. Of course, I did. I've read all his historical work. And they don't now realize what a very good painter he was. And I think similarly, they don't realize what a good poet I am.

I am interested to learn a few secrets about your methods of work—the research—the drafting of a book, all in long hand, I believe and then how long it takes before it gets to the typist!

Yes, I do as a matter of fact, Sydney, write all longhand. I am not clever enough to be able to type. And I am not really in favor of dictated work. Churchill, you know, dictated an awful lot of his books and that tends to make them a bit long-winded and rhetorical. I am in favor really of writing out longhand. And I console myself when I think that William Shakespeare wrote everything out longhand, as Erasmus did.

Well now, with regard to method of work, I think that quite consistently we can adhere to those same three divisions that I have already mentioned. You see, with regard to research work, there's a great deal of drudgery involved. You can't help drudgery. A historian has really got to stick at it and read the best of what's written about the period he is studying. The printed work first, and then second he goes on to the documents that are printed and third he goes really right on to the original manuscripts and the documents themselves. At that I've done a good deal of work in the Public Record Office in early years and also at the Bodleian Library, and in the British Museum, and in the Huntington Library in California.

What documents have moved you most to touch in the original?

Well, I was most excited when I was young and came upon the documents in the Public Records Office that showed that young Richard Grenville, before he came of age, was involved in a typical Elizabethan affray in which he killed a man! Well, I was cold with excitement at discovering that because nobody had known anything about that since the day it happened. He was pardoned because he was underage, and it was an affray in which they were all of them fighting in the typical Elizabethan way. Just like Christopher Marlowe, that's what Elizabethans were like. All, except William Shakespeare. He was a very prudent, gentlemanly, upper-class type of man, who behaved much better.

Well you see, when you have assembled all the material like that, then you have the business of licking it into shape. The business of composition. And there, what is very important, I learned when I was very young, you must have a skeleton. You must have a scheme. Even this really laps over into your literary work. I always realized that even when I was writing only an essay, you ought to begin with introduction, one, two, three, four, five points—conclusion. And, if you don't really work out a scheme, you're all over the place.

Now, for example, many, many years ago, I thought of compiling *A Cornish Anthology*. You know that book, Sydney. Well, an awful lot of people like that book. It was rather a favorite bedside book of my friend, the warden of All Souls, John Sparrow. He liked that book. Well, for many years I simply couldn't do it. I couldn't really get the hang of it. I collected material, but it wasn't until I thought out a proper scheme of constructing the book that I could really bring it all together. So it wasn't until twenty years after I thought of it that I managed to do that book. And, you know, that book has just had a new edition. I am waiting to see it. I haven't seen that yet.

But there you are. Of course, that's far more important when you're doing a really big research book like *Tudor Cornwall*. I mean, that book, you see, starts at the bottom of society with the land and then the industries—the mineral and the tin industry—and then how people worked on the land. The land is the absolute foundation, so that really is the beginning. Then, on the basis of that, you come to the villages, the towns, and then the social structure and then the people and then the cultural life, which is the top. The sort of crest of the wave.

Well, you see the same thing works out with my biggest book, which is the four volumes on the Elizabethan age. It begins with *The England of Elizabeth*, then it goes on to the expansion of that society, and then in the end it comes to the cultural expansion in Elizabethan drama, and Elizabethan literature and architecture and music and painting. You've got to think out the structure. The bone structure comes first. You see, that's the important thing with a play. It's no good really writing all over the place.

Well, when you come to write your literary works I think that the same method maintains but you really must follow your hunch. You must write about what it is that you have an inner feeling for. Here again I'm rather surprised at the dull academics because very often they are writing about something that they've got no particular yen to write about.

Well, I have always been writing about the Tudor period and the sixteenth century, and the Elizabethan age and Shakespeare because that's what I am interested in. It stands to reason that you will write best about what you really have a feeling for. Well now, the same applies to the second division of your literary work. I mean I've written essays about those people who really interest me. I've always been interested in Jonathan Swift, so I wrote a biography of Jonathan Swift. I've always been interested in Matthew Arnold, so I wrote a biography of Matthew Arnold.

What about doing a whole biography about Thomas Hobbes?

Well, he's the leading figure in this latest book of mine called *Four Caroline Portraits*. I've not written a biography of him. I've written really a study of his thought. But I've also written a literary biography of Quiller-Couch, who was my mentor and a great patron of mine when I was young.

When you come to the writing of poetry, this is a much more difficult and much more subtle subject. I think that a lot of professional poets really work at their poetry as I should work say, at historical research. Now, that is not my idea of poetry. I only really write poetry when I feel emotionally moved. And I think that is a better idea. Thomas Hardy wrote his poetry like that. Of course a lot of people have really tried to define poetry, which is almost impossible to do, but Hardy said that it was really words that were arranged rhythmically because they sprang out of the movements of your heart and mind in such a way as to move other hearts and minds. And my friend Phillip Larkin thought exactly the same thing; that that's all that you need to know about poetry. It really is writing that moves your heart and therefore it moves other peoples hearts.

Now, I think a great deal of the rubbish that's written today and is supposed to be poetry doesn't move anybody's heart. It's bogus. And, to make a joke, it's genuinely bogus. And it isn't any good. And it won't live. And I think that the best of my poetry will live because I think it springs from the heart. And I've usually written it only when I've been moved. Some people find my poetry rather sad and I think that the reason is that when I am moved by a friend's death or unhappiness or I'm rather unhappy myself that I find poetry a consolation. It's a great consolation, so I don't regard poetry as work.

There's a very funny thing about poetry. John Betjeman, my great friend, knew this, that very often you're given a first line. One of the greatest modern French poets, whom I've met, Paul Valery, knew this. He said—this is a *dono*—this is something that is given to you. And I've nearly always found what John Betjeman found, that a first line is given to you from on high. It actually really springs up from your subconscious. And, you go on from that. And that is really the way that real poetry is written.

My great friend T. S. Eliot didn't really have quite that idea. His idea was a more intellectual one. He thought that you ought really to work at poetry and he wrote once that he really wrote his poetry as a kind of solution to a problem. And therefore his poetry, I think, is much more intellectual. And there's quite a lot of T. S. Eliot's poetry that is rather dull. It's intellectual and rather prosaic. And I think what really contradicts his own attitude about poetry is that his best poetry is personal. And it is emotional.

In relation to methods of work, if you are doing a big project, like *Four Caroline Portraits*, do you work in the morning?

I do now. I think its best to work when your brain is at its best in the morning and then I very often have a rest in the afternoon, just as Mr. Churchill did, and then I can write again very often inspired by tea. I am a great drug fiend. I'm a tremendous tea druggist, like Dr. Johnson, and I am rather like Dr. Johnson in another respect. You know he was an awful bully with a warm heart and he was rather a good poet. And most people really tend to ignore his poetry, simply because he was such a great prose writer. And they tend to ignore the poetry of Jonathan Swift, again because he really was a writer of prose.

Well, I find I'm rather pepped up after drinking tea. I don't drink as much tea as Dr. Johnson did, but you are very kind in pepping me up from Australia along with John (Walde), sending me some Earl Grey, which is my favorite tea as you know. I'm not quite so keen on China tea as perhaps I ought to be.

Another writing time is from tea until supper. When I was younger, I used to be able to write after dinnertime and go on writing until quite late. Winston Churchill did an awful lot of his work late at night. Well, I've never been keen on that. I've always been keen on preparing at night the work that I am going to do next morning.

I learned that trick quite young, from a very distinguished poster artist who had a flat in the same house where I had a flat in London. Afterwards it was completely destroyed by a beastly German bomb. The whole house was destroyed and a great deal of the square wrecked. And that poster artist said to me, you know, when I'm all worked up at night, and I'm full of ideas, I very often just jot down a sketch so that when I come to my work next morning, I'm not faced with that terrible cold blank white page. There is something for me to work on. Now, I've taken that tip. And very often at night when I'm rather worked up and full of ideas, I jot down a few notes so that next morning when rather coldly I've got to face the writing pad, there are the ideas for me to work on. And I think that is really a very good tip that I've very often handed on to other people.

People very often, you know, suffer a writing block. Even T. S. Eliot had a writing block. He told me sometimes he couldn't write a poem for several years. Well, I think that Eliot was much too conscious in his work. He was a very, very clever man, but poetry really doesn't come out of your cleverness. That's subsidiary. You're quite right. It comes out of the subconscious, it comes out of the deepest part of the man and then you use your cleverness to sharpen up your inspiration.

That's like William Shakespeare, who was a damned clever man. But we don't think of William Shakespeare as cleverness in the first instance. We think of his inspiration. It's absolutely wonderful the ideas that he was inspired by. And the characters that came to life in his mind. Of course he was a clever man who then worked it up and criticized his plays. We know that because you see, he sometimes worked over an early play of his and improved it.

And we know something about Shakespeare's working method. I've spotted this, as some people have never noticed it. But William Shakespeare never completed a play called *Timon of Athens*. When you go in to that play and properly study it, you will see that some of the first act is finished and some of the last act is finished and some of the middle of the play is only just roughed out. Now that shows you how he worked. William Shakespeare didn't write a play beginning at the beginning and then going straight on until the end. He imagined a scene as it was and then he wrote that.

Of course, when you are writing a research work you begin at the beginning and you do go straight forward until you come to the end.

When you're writing a poem it may not be entirely like that because some lines may be given to you that you can really work into the poem afterward. You see the whole business of writing a poem is very subtle, psychologically. I think that it's rather a queer and rather an abnormal process. And one thing I am absolutely certain about here is, I think one ought not to be too self-conscious about it. It's no good digging down, digging up the roots to see how the plant is getting on. That kills it. I think you must have a certain kind of conscious confidence to let your subconscious do it for you.

And that I think is again true. When I was only a schoolboy I found out that if you had to learn lines of poetry for the next day, if you learned them in the evening before you went to bed, when you woke up next morning, there they were ready for you. I think that people aren't aware of the importance of the subconscious. You ought never to play with it. You ought to let it have its run.

A very great English writer knew that. That was Rudyard Kipling. He was a marvelous genius. And he is underrated by the third-rate, who really aren't worthy to do up his shoelaces. Rudyard Kipling wrote a very interesting autobiography about the way you write. And he said, when I am writing there's a little imp that comes on the end of my pen and he takes charge of it and he writes the thing for me. And if I dare to interrupt him and stop him, I can't go on. Now that's very important. I find that. When I'm writing, and I take up a pen, I very often get ideas given to me that I think I never thought of. And a sentence, or a thought, will come into my mind.

In that review of mine of a new biography of Shakespeare that really makes a great deal of use of my work, I'm glad to say, because it means that the young writer has got it right. But he begins with the usual nonsense about how is it that this humble actor, you see, really developed into the greatest of English writers. Well of course, he never was a humble actor. And it suddenly came into my head to say, he was no more a humble actor than Sir John Gielgud is a humble actor. Well, I know Gielgud, who is a marvelous actor. He isn't humble, any more than I am. We know our own value. So we don't take any notice of what third-rate people think.

There's a very funny thing about third-rate people, why it is they like to depreciate the first-rate. I think it's partly envy. But it's also partly genuine. They simply can't get there. They simply can't understand it. I've just been writing this morning, a letter to Sir Winston Churchill's daughter who has just sent me this wonderful book about Sir Winston Churchill's painting. And I said to her what I said to a mere museum man at All Souls, who was running down Sir Winston Churchill's painting, and I was so angry. I said to him, "that's always what third-rate people say about the first-rate." He didn't like that much. But you see, that's true, first-rate people are capable of appreciating first-rate work. And they are apt to be much more generous.

I got wonderful encouragement from the greatest historians who were writing in my time, G. M. Trevelyan in England and Samuel Eliot Morison in America. And I was always encouraged in my poetry by T. S. Eliot. Well, if my poetry was good enough for T. S. Eliot, it's damn well good enough for the third-rate people who can't write poetry for toffee! You see? I said that in my letter to Winston Churchill's daughter this morning. It's a curious thing that it's the third-rate who really depreciate and denigrate first-rate work. I think it's partly genuine. They can't understand it. They can't get there, but they should bloody well try. You see the look on my face? They should try. And second they should have a sense of humor, and know their own rating. And third, if they don't know it, I am prepared to tell them. You're very third-rate, aren't you? Why don't you try to understand? So you must never take any notice of what they say or think.

That brings me to a further point that may be very important for you, Sydney. An awful lot of people in the literary or artistic or theater snake pit have got an instinct to frustrate you. If they can't do it themselves, they don't like you to be able to do it. You must never pay any attention to them. They will discourage you if they can. The great historian G. M. Trevelyan one day said to me, "you know, I have the impression here at Cambridge, that all these medieval historians are looking over each other's shoulders." That was absolutely true.

My greatest friend at Oxford, K. B. McFarlane, could never get his own books written. He was a first-class medieval historian, but because he couldn't write his own books, he was mad about my books. I one day gave him *The Expansion of Elizabethan England*. When I wrote that book the top boy in the Elizabethan age was then Sir John Neale. And Sir John Neale wrote me a letter and he said, "You have written, and I must tell you, a great book." When I gave McFarlane, my greatest friend, a copy of that book, he sent it back to me. I took Neale's letter down to him and I said to him, "Look, you very much respect Sir John Neale, as the top boy in my field. This is what Sir John Neale says, you have written, and I must tell you, a great book. If my book is good enough for John Neale, it's certainly good enough for you!" My god, he turned absolutely pale. And he said, "I suppose you think that we are rather second-rate." Well, I made rather a mistake, and I said I suppose that's really what I do think. But he wasn't second-rate. He was first-rate but he had a psychological block and the only book he ever wrote was the book that I bullied him into writing for my series. And he never wrote any of his own medieval books. They all had to be put together from his notes by his pupils after he died.

Well, it wasn't my fault that he couldn't write his own bloody books. But this is what you have to put up with from ordinary people. And I'm not very good at putting up with ordinary people. And don't you ever allow yourself to be discouraged. First-rate people will always encourage. I was always encouraged by Sir John Neale and by G. M. Trevelyan and by T. S. Eliot and by Edith Sitwell and so on. First-rate people do their best to help others. You know that! I don't help third-rate people who are no good at doing it. And you know it was very queer that even my nearest friends at Oxford, like McFarlane, they could never learn anything from me. They couldn't take it. I learned hand over fist from them. Silly idiot!

I had another great friend, Richard Pares, at All Souls. I was always learning about the eighteenth century from him, but he wouldn't learn how to write a book from me. Academicism, a certain amount of envy, and when Richard Pares wrote his first big research book, it was just a heap. Three hundred thousand words. It wasn't a book. I said to him, "My dear Richard, a book has to have an organic life." And out of his book, Namier and G. N. Clark excavated two books and a couple of absolutely first-class research articles.

Years later Richard Pares wrote a book that was a family history. And he said to me, "My dear professor (he always used to call me professor for fun because he knew that I didn't think very highly of professors), I think you would approve of this book." And I said, "How's that then Richard?" And he said, "Because it has got a beginning, a middle, and an end." It's got structure. It's an organic book.

Well, they could have learned any amount about how to write from me. But they didn't know, so I didn't tell them. Serve them right, for being like that. Now that's just like Thomas Hardy. Thomas Hardy, like me, had to work his way up from the very bottom, very simple people. And one day, when he became very famous, and he'd written all his books and poems, and so forth, he was in a literary party in London, with a man I knew, Desmond McCarthy. The old boy really stayed in a corner by himself. And when he met Desmond McCarthy, Thomas Hardy said, "Do you tell all these people your ideas, because I don't!" Shrewd old peasant.

Well, I'm quite generous in telling people how to work, if they want to know. If they don't want to learn from me, that's their loss.

Every writer has to deal with publishers. What publishers have been best to you? Macmillan, Cape, Weidenfeld and so on.

Well, I really began, you see, with Faber because Geoffrey Faber was a fellow of All Souls. And I knew T. S. Eliot and Eliot was a director of Faber's and they really produced my first book. They produced that book, *Politics and the Younger Generation*. And, they published the first three or four volumes of my poetry. And T. S. Eliot wrote the actual blurbs on the jackets, you know. He was a great writer of blurbs, Eliot was.

Well, when I came to my first work of historical research, I terribly wanted that book vetted by the top boy, Sir John Neale, in the Elizabethan age, and so I took that book to Cape because he was the reader for Cape. And Sir John Neale was tremendously helpful. He made me cut 10,000 words out of the beginning. And I had to revise the book and, of course, I never looked back after that. I learned how to do it. An awful lot of these academic writers don't know how to slim their books. They simply don't know how to cut. Well, it always improves a book to cut, and slim it. I think it would improve me to slim my figure a bit, Sydney!

So then I went to Cape. Cape published several of my books and they published also *A Cornish Childhood*. But old Jonathan Cape was rather mean about royalties and Macmillan gave me a very much better offer. And so I went to Macmillan, not only because they gave me a very big offer but it was the first time in my life that I'd ever seen a check for £1,000, you see, but I also wanted to be published in America by the Macmillan Company. So then they published a lot of my books you see.

Actually, with regard to publishing, I again had rather a consistent idea because I've always been a bit of a planner, planning my books and so forth. I wanted Faber to publish my poetry because they were the best, you know, publishers of poetry. I wanted Cape to publish my autobiographical books, like *A Cornishman at Oxford* and *A Cornishman Abroad* and I wanted Macmillan to deal with my heavy books, which I really wanted published on the Elizabethan age in both England and America.

I think it really worked out rather well. When it came to rather more popular, illustrations books, you mentioned Weidenfeld. Well, they really wanted me to write, they suggested to me, a popular illustrated book. Well Sydney, I know some of my limitations, you may not think so, but I've never been an illustrations man. I tend rather to leave that to the publishers.

And Weidenfeld were very good on illustrations and therefore they published a whole series of what I call illustrated books. They wanted me to write a sort of short view of English history for the great big public they had in mind. They wanted me to write a book on the Tower of London, and another on Windsor Castle. All those are short texts and the illustrations are in some ways the most important thing.

That was especially true in regard to a magnificent but terribly expensive rare book, *Westminster Abbey*. And that was how I began illustrated books. The

American ambassador over here, Walter Annenberg, noticed that there wasn't a really good, big, illustrated book on the Abbey and so he financed, with Weidenfeld, an absolutely magnificent book that he wanted written up by all the specialists. He got a specialist to do the sculpture. He got a specialist to do the stained glass. He got a specialist to do the architecture and he got me to write the main core of the book, which was the history of the Abbey.

That's an absolutely magnificent book. You haven't got it? I think I'll show you a copy of that book. We'll go down in a minute to the library and I'll show you that book. Of course there's never been a cheap edition of it. I've sometimes thought of picking out my history of Westminster Abbey and publishing that separately. But I've never got round to that. I've always been too hard at work.

After Weidenfeld, and so forth, you have also published with a lot of local publishers. You're supporting the Cornish industry there!

Well, we've never really talked about that. But of course, I am a very patriotic Cornishman. I've tried to encourage other people to write. I've got a friend of mine whom I've encouraged to write several books about the Cornish in Australia. Because it's very remarkable—the Cornish contribution. You know, there's a Cornish area in South Australia where the Cornish miners went. But it is very nice to think that your great Prime Minister Menzies was half Cornish. He told me so himself. On his mother's side, Menzies was Cornish. Well, Bob Hawke is Cornish on both sides. I don't think he's a bit interested in Cornwall. But Menzies was much more interested in the wider world and was a greater man.

I encouraged people also to write about the Cornish miners in America. One fellow was so slow in writing it up that I took my pen in hand and went around to all the mining areas where the Cornish people were and I wrote a book that has just only recently been republished, called *The Cornish in America*. And that's been republished by a Cornishman down here in Cornwall. And then I did the *Cornish Anthology* and I encouraged another friend of mine to do a Devon anthology. In America I encouraged a great friend of mine to do a Virginia anthology. I think she also did a Maryland anthology. And another friend of mine did an Indiana one. But you know, they don't have the imagination to take this up. There ought to be an anthology for every state in the American union.

How would you like to be remembered?

Well, just as a writer. As a poet and as a historian. You can put in a Cornishman if you want to. That's enough, isn't it?

You are far more extraordinary than ... "just a writer"!

Well, that's all right. A poet and historian. Some people have rather wondered which ought to come first. J. B. Priestley, I knew quite well. He wasn't sure whether I was a poet writing history or whether I was a historian writing poetry. Well, I'm both. I'm rather in favor of ambivalence.

What do you think is your greatest achievement among all your books. It must be some eighty-nine books. If someone said you can take just one to a desert island?

I don't really believe that number. I think that's just titles.

Well, which one would you take, if they said you could only keep one?

I think the *Collected Poems* called *A Life*. Because that really gives you the clue. It gives you the key. Of course I should be very pleased, if you really were generous enough, to select one from each of the three divisions. So then, you could take *A Cornish Childhood*. Then you could take *Tudor Cornwall* and then you could take *Shakespeare the Man*. But I think if you take my *Collected Poems—A Life*, you've really got the clue. Because you see, there's my inner life there. And, there's my American life. I've written more American poems than any English poet has ever written about America. Because English poets have really not been very much inspired by American landscape.

I always look for whom books are dedicated. How do you decide? You dedicated *Discovering Shakespeare* to your readers, which was very generous. But others are dedicated to specific people.

Well, I think that the line I have in mind is who is the appropriate person . . .

[At this point, two sharp whistle blows from below interrupted A. L. Rowse's reply. It drew, however, his spontaneous and exhilarating response: "That's lunch!" That was Phyllis, his housekeeper, giving the signal from her pantry that lunch was on the table and that we were expected downstairs! It also abruptly concluded this interview, given in the author's ninetieth year and recorded at Trenarren House, Trenarren, St. Austell, Cornwall, on the morning of Saturday, September 11, 1993.]

Reference Sources Consulted

PRINT SOURCES

1. The British Library Catalogue
2. The National Union Catalogue (USA)
3. The English Catalogue (Books), 1926–1965
4. British Books in Print, 1971–1986
5. Whitaker's Books in Print, 1990–1996
6. Social Sciences and Humanities SOURCE Index
7. British Humanities Index
8. Readers Guide to Periodical Literature (USA)
9. The Catholic Periodical Index
10. Biography Index, 1946–1992 (17 volumes)
11. Writings on British History, 1901–1974
12. Essay and General Literature Index, 1900–
13. Comprehensive Index to English-Language Little Magazines, 1890–1970
14. The Guardian Index, 1986–
15. The Observer Index, 1991–
16. The Times Index, 1922–
17. The Times Literary Supplement Index (TLS)
18. The Christian Science Monitor Index, 1983–
19. The New York Times Index
20. Personal Name Index to the New York Times Index, 1975–1989
21. The Wall Street Journal Index, 1972–
22. Social Sciences and Humanities CITATION Index
23. The American Humanities Index, 1976–1996
24. Humanities Index, 1974–1996
25. Book Review Digest

26. Book Review Index
27. Who's Who (UK)—A. L. Rowse first listed in 1938
28. International Who's Who (USA)
29. The Writers Directory, 1994–1996, St. James Press, London, 1994
30. The Oxford Companion to English Literature, 5th edition, OUP, 1985
31. Combined Retrospective Index to Book Reviews in Humanities Journals, 1802–1974
32. Combined Retrospective Index to Book Reviews in Scholarly Journals, 1886–1974
33. An Index to Book Reviews in the Humanities, vols. 1–31, 1960–1990

ELECTRONIC SOURCES

1. *MLA International Bibliography* [computer file]. (Published for the Modern Language Association by H. W. Wilson)
2. *Historical Abstracts on Disk.* (ABC-Clio)
3. *Periodicals Contents Index Computer File.* (Chadwyck-Healy)
4. *ATLA Religion Database on CD-ROM.* (American Theological Library Association)
5. *Catholic Periodical and Literature Index on CD-ROM.* (American Theological Library Association)

Chronology

1903	Alfred Leslie Rowse born in Tregonissey, Cornwall, 4 December
1922	Douglas Jerrold Scholar at Christ Church College, Oxford
1925	First Class, Modern History School
1925	Prize Fellowship at All Souls College, Oxford
1927	*On History: A Study of Present Tendencies* (first history book)
1927–1930	Lecturer at Merton College, Oxford
1929	M.A.
1931–1935	Lecturer at London School of Economics
1931, 1935	Labour Candidate for Penryn–Falmouth, Cornwall
1931	*Politics and the Younger Generation* (first political book)
1934	*The Question of the House of Lords* (Hogarth Press)
1937	*Sir Richard Grenville of the 'Revenge'* (first Elizabethan biography)
1941	*Tudor Cornwall* (first Tudor history)
1941	*Poems of a Decade* (first poetry book)
1941	Awarded the Jenner Medal for *Tudor Cornwall*
1942	*A Cornish Childhood* (first volume of autobiography; best-seller)
1946	*The Use of History* (best-seller)
1950	*The England of Elizabeth* (first volume of Elizabethan trilogy; best-seller)
1952	D. Litt., Oxford University
1952	Fellow, Royal Society of Literature
1952–1953	President of the English Association
1952–1953	Millar Visiting Professor, University of Illinois, Urbana
1957	Raleigh Lecturer, British Academy
1958	Fellow of the British Academy
1958	Trevelyan Lecturer, Cambridge University

1959–1960	Visiting Professor at University of Wisconsin, Madison, and Lynchburg College, Virginia
1960	D. Litt., University of Exeter (Honorary Degree)
1960	D.C.L., University of New Brunswick, Fredericton, Canada
1962–1969	Senior Research Associate at Huntington Library, California
1963	Beatty Memorial Lecturer, McGill University, Montreal, Canada
1963	*William Shakespeare: A Biography* (first book on Shakespeare; best-seller)
1964	*Shakespeare's Sonnets* (resolves question of dating the sonnets)
1971–1972	President of the Shakespeare Club, Stratford-Upon-Avon
1972	Elected to the Athenaeum
1973	In January, announces his discovery and identity of Shakespeare's "Dark Lady"
1974	*Simon Forman: Sex and Society in Shakespeare's Age* (from the diaries that would ultimately yield the "Dark Lady")
1975	Emeritus Fellow of All Souls
1981	*A Life: Collected Poems*
1982	Awarded the Silver Benson Medal, Royal Society of Literature, for poetry and services to literature
1988	*Shakespeare the Man,* revised edition (summarizes twenty years of research on William Shakespeare—the definitive biography)
1996	Companion of Honour
1997	Dies at Trenarren House, St. Austell, Cornwall, 3 October

A

Books and Pamphlets by A. L. Rowse, and Associated Reviews

A1. *On History: A Study of Present Tendencies* **(1927)**
First edition. London: Kegan Paul, Trench, Trubner, October 1927. 2s.6d. 102 pp, Fcap 8vo. Psyche Miniatures. General Series, no. 7.

First American edition. *Science and History: A New View of History.* New York: Norton, 1928. US$1. 87 pp. The New Science Series. There were reprints of the 1927 first English edition *On History: A Study of Present Tendencies.* Folcroft, Pa.: Folcroft Library Editions, 1975. US$12.50. 102 pp, 23 cm. Philadelphia: R. West, 1977.

Reviews. Clark Lectures at Cambridge: *Aspects de la biographie,* Andre Maurois.

A2. *Politics and the Younger Generation* **(1931)**
First edition. London: Faber & Faber, October 1, 1931 (nil record of print-run numbers). 5s 0d. 303 pp, 8vo.

Further printing. February 22, 1934 (a cheap edition, probably the remainder of the first printing, rejacketed to clear the stock).

Reviews. *Times Literary Supplement,* October 15, 1931 (Anon.). *Criterion,* January 1932 (Charles Smyth). *Political Quarterly,* January-March 1932 (Leonard Woolf).

A3. *Extempore Memorial (For C. H.)* **1933**
First edition. Oxford: Privately printed, 1933. Unpaginated, 8 pp, 9" x 5 3/4". Dark green paper wrappers printed in black.

Contents. A poem in memory of Charles Henderson.

Note. Reprinted in *New Oxford Outlook,* November 1935, pp. 264–266; *Poems of a Decade* (1941); *A Life: Collected Poems* (1981).

1

A4. *The Question of the House of Lords* **(1934)**
First edition. London: Hogarth Press, Leonard and Virginia Woolf, October 1934 (2,000 copies). 1s 6d. 64 pp, crown 8vo, 7 1/4" x 4 3/4". Blue paper wrappers printed in black. Day to Day Pamphlets, no. 19.

A5. *Queen Elizabeth and Her Subjects* **(with G. B. Harrison) (1935)**
First edition. London: George Allen & Unwin, February 12, 1935 (1,500 copies). 5s 0d. 139 pp, crown 8vo, 7 3/4" x 5", 8 plates.

Contents. Introduction plus six (of 10) essays by A. L. Rowse. Originally delivered as a series of talks for the BBC in spring 1934: Queen Elizabeth, William Cecil, Lord Burghley, The Earl of Essex, Sir Walter Ralegh, Cardinal Allen, The Elizabethan Age.

First American edition. Freeport, N.Y.: Books for Libraries Press, 1970. 139 pp, 23 cm (Essay Index Reprint Series). There was a further printing by Ayer in 1977 (Essay Index Reprint Series).

Reviews. *London Mercury,* April 1935 (Anon.). *Quarterly Review* (UK), July 1935 (Anon.). *History* (UK), March 1936 (R.B.W.).

A6. *Mr. Keynes and the Labour Movement* **(1936)**
First edition. London: Macmillan, October 1936 (3,000 copies). 2s 6d. 68 pp, crown 8vo, 7 1/2" x 5".

Contents. On the political implications of *The General Theory of Employment, Interest, and Money.*

Reviews. *New Statesman and Nation*, October 24, 1936 (Anon.). *Spectator*, October 30, 1936 (Anon.). *London Mercury*, November 1936 (Anon.). *Economic Journal*, March 1937 (Barbara Wootton). *International Affairs* (UK), March 1937 (D. A. Routh). *Giornale Degli Economisti e Rivista Di Statistica* (Italy), May 1937 (G.D.V.). *Political Quarterly*, April-June 1937 (Colin Clark). *Rivista Internazionale Di Scienze Sociali* (Italy), July 1937 (A. Fossati). *Manchester School* 1937 (G. W. Daniels). *Zeitschrift für Sozialforschung* (Germany) 1937 (Baumann).

A7. *Sir Richard Grenville of the "Revenge": An Elizabethan Hero* **(1937)**
First edition. London: Jonathan Cape, June 11, 1937 (1,960 copies ordered in April 1937). 12s 6d. 365 pp, 8vo, 9" x 5 1/4", 8 plates, 1 map, Grenville crest on binding. Second impression, September 1937. Further printings were published on October 11, 1940 (2,000 copies) (1,750 quires transferred to the Bedford Historical Series 9) (ordered in September 1937). The Bedford Historical Series 9, June 13, 1949 (1,500 copies ordered January 1949). July 16, 1962 (2,000 copies ordered Dec 1961). Jonathan Cape, Paperbacks Series 3, September 23, 1963 (5,000 copies ordered March 1963). Reissued by Jonathan Cape, February 3, 1977 (1,500 copies) and by the Book Club Associates Edition, September 1976 (2,000 copies). Also a paperback edition by Jonathan Cape in 1963, no. JCP3.

First American edition. Boston: Houghton Mifflin Company, June 11, 1937 (1,040 copies). US$3.50. 365 pp, 8vo, 9" x 5 1/4".
Reviews. *Times (London)*, June 11, 1937 (Anon.). *Times Literary Supplement*, June 12, 1937 (Anon.). *Spectator*, June 18 1937 (Isaac Foot). *New Statesman and Nation*, June 19, 1937 (David Garnett). *Manchester Guardian*, June 22, 1937 (E.H.). *Sunday Times*, June 1937 (J. E. Neale). *Book Society News*, June 1937 (Edmund Blunden). *Christian Science Monitor*, July 7, 1937 (V. S. Pritchett). *Night and Day* (UK), July 8, 1937 (Evelyn Waugh). *London Mercury*, July 1937 (W. M. Childs). *Saturday Review of Literature*, September 25, 1937 (C. D. Abbott). *Books*, September 26, 1937 (C. J. Finger). *New York Times*, September 26, 1937 (Percy Hutchison). *Boston Transcript*, October 16, 1937 (B. C. Bowker). *Canadian Forum*, November 1937 (D. J. McDougall). *Punch* 192, 1937 (Anon.). *History*, March 1938 (J. A. Williamson). *American Historical Review*, April 1938 (Fulmer Mood). *Books and Bookmen*, June 1977 (Philip Mansel).

A8. *Tudor Cornwall: Portrait of a Society* (1941)
First edition. London: Jonathan Cape, September 5, 1941 (1,500 copies). 18s 0d. There were further printings ordered in November 1941 (1,000 copies). Third impression was ordered in September 1942 (1,325 copies, published in 1943), fourth impression in May 1947 (1,000 copies, reissued October 27, 1947), fifth impression ordered in November 1948 (1,000 copies, published in 1949), and sixth impression ordered in May 1957 (1,000 copies reissued November 4, 1957, in the Bedford Historical Series). Out of print February 22, 1966.

New English edition. London: Macmillan, June 1969 (2,000 copies + 3,000 Scribner imprints ordered January 13, 1969). 462 pp, 8vo, illustrated. Also a paperback edition by Redruth, Cornwall, Dyllansow Truran, December 1990.

First American edition. New York: Scribner's, October 16, 1969 (3,000 copies). US$8.95. 462 pp, 22 cm, illustrated, maps (new edition).

Reviews. *Spectator*, September 12, 1941 (David Mathew). *New Statesman and Nation*, September 13, 1941 (Raymond Mortimer). *Listener* (UK), September 25 1941 (Anon.). *Times Literary Supplement*, September 27, 1941 (Anon.). *Observer*, September 28, 1941 (G. M. Trevelyan). *Book Society News* (UK), September 1941 (Edmund Blunden). *Life and Letters To-day* (UK), December 1941 (Ernest Hudson). *Dublin Review*, January 1942 (R. Weiss). *Scrutiny* (UK), January 1942 (Vera Mellers). *Punch*, July 8, 1942 (J.K.). *Economic History Review* 12, 1942 (Christopher Morris). *Journal of Economic History* (USA), November 1943 (Frederick C. Dietz). *Punch*, June 25, 1969 (Lewis Bates). *Times Literary Supplement*, July 10, 1969 (Anon.). *Concordia Theological Monthly* (USA), May 1970 (Carl Stamm Meyer).

A9. *Poems of a Decade* (1931–1941)
First edition. London: Faber & Faber, September 18, 1941 (1,000 copies). 6s 0d. 111 pp, demy 8vo.

Contents. 65 poems with (uncredited) dust jacket blurb by T. S. Eliot. Presented in three parts: I. Earlier Poems (18); II. The Decade (31); III. Poems of War-Time (16).

Further printing. Second impression, February 1942 (nil record of print-run number).

Reviews. *New Statesman and Nation*, October 4, 1941 (Raymond Mortimer). *Times Literary Supplement*, October 4, 1941 (Anon.). *Spectator*, October 31, 1941 (Kathleen Raine). *Dublin Review*, January 1942 (Charles Williams). *Dublin Magazine*, January-March 1942 (W.P.M.).

A10. *A Cornish Childhood* (1942)
First edition. London: Jonathan Cape, June 15, 1942 (3,000 copies ordered in April 1942). 12s 6d. 282 pp, 8vo.

Contents. First volume of autobiography.

Further printings. Ordered in July 1942 (2,000 copies, published in August 1942). Third impression ordered in August 1943 (2,000 copies, published in September 1943). Readers Union edition (20,000 copies) ordered in February 1944). Fourth impression ordered in May 1945 (2,000 copies). Fifth impression ordered in May 1946 (3,200 copies). Sixth impression ordered in December 1955 (1,000 copies, published in 1956). Seventh impression ordered in February 1965 (1,000 copies). New impression ordered in October 1973 (1,500 copies for reissue, April 18, 1974). Paperback (Arrow Books/Imprint Hutchinson Group, London 1962). Paperback (Cardinal by Sphere Books, London, April 1975). Paperback (Anthony Mott/*Cornish Library*, no. 2, London, March 1982). Reprinted in 1983, 1988, 1990, and 1993.

First American edition. New York: Macmillan, 1947. US$4. 282 pp, 8vo. There were further printings by Clarkson N. Potter, distributed by Crown Publishers, New York (the Cape reissued format, hardcover, 282 pp.), 1974, 1979.

Note. A. L. Rowse in an interview: *New Yorker,* October 19, 1963: "My autobiography *A Cornish Childhood,* which took me up to eighteen, has sold a hundred thousand copies in England."

Reviews. *Punch*, June 17, 1942 (H. Kingsmill). *Times Literary Supplement*, June 27, 1942 (Anon.). *Sunday Times*, June-July 1942 (Raymond Mortimer). *Country Life* (UK), July 3, 1942 (Howard Spring). *Spectator*, July 10, 1942 (H.W.H.). *Observer*, July 19, 1942 (Stephen Spender). *Listener* (UK), July 30, 1942 (Anon.). *Book Society News* (UK), July 1942 (Edmund Blunden). *Life and Letters To-day* (UK), August 1942 (Winifred Bryher). *Time and Tide*, September 12, 1942 (Renée Haynes). *New York Times*, October 5, 1947 (Herbert Lyons). *Booklist*, November 15, 1947 (Anon.). *School and Society*, November 22, 1947 (Anon.). *New York Herald Tribune*, November 23, 1947 (G. W. Johnson). *Christian Science Monitor*, December 8, 1947 (R.B.). *Commonweal*, January 23, 1948 (E.V.R. Wyatt). *Times (London)*, May 15, 1975 (Anon.). *Publishers Weekly* (USA), August 20, 1979 (Anon.). *Library Journal* (USA), October 1, 1979 (Nancy C. Cridland). *Wall Street Journal*, December 24, 1979

(Edmund Fuller). *Times Educational Supplement,* April 23, 1982 (Charles Thomas). *Times Literary Supplement,* May 28, 1982 (Charles Causley).

A11. *The Spirit of English History* (1943)

First edition. London: Jonathan Cape, October 25, 1943 (3,000 copies ordered in July 1943). 7s 6d. 150 pp, crown 8vo, six maps.

Further printings were ordered in December 1943 (5,500 copies). Third impression ordered in May 1944 (5,650 copies). Fourth impression ordered in December 1944 (7,450 copies, published in 1945). Fifth impression ordered in January 1947 ((5,150 copies, published in 1947). Sixth impression ordered in March 1957 (2,000 copies). Out of print August 7, 1967. Longman's, Green, and C/L, London, November 1, 1943, for the British Council: Paperback and hardcover editions. AB Ljus Forlag, Stockholm 1944, Ljus English Library, Volume 23. Paperback.

First American edition. New York: Oxford University Press, 1945. US$2. 158 pp, maps, 20cm.

Reviews. *Punch* (UK), November 3, 1943 (H. Kingsmill). *Listener,* November 25, 1943 (Anon.). *Observer,* November 28, 1943 (Dr. Ernest Barker). *Life and Letters To-day* (UK), November 1943 (Winifred Bryher). *Times Literary Supplement,* December 4, 1943 (Anon.). *Manchester Guardian,* December 10, 1943 (A. J. P. Taylor). *Spectator,* December 17, 1943 (Anon.). *Christian Science Monitor,* February 26, 1944 (Harold Hobson). *School and Society,* August 5, 1944 (Anon.). *Book Week,* October 21, 1945 (J. T. Frederick). *Springfield Republican,* October 27, 1945 (Anon.). *New York Times,* October 28, 1945 (Isaac Anderson). *Nation* (USA), November 24, 1945 (Keith Hutchison). *Weekly Book Review,* December 30, 1945 (H. S. Commager). *Thought* (USA), March 1946 (Grover Cronin Jr.). *American Historical Review,* April 1946 (F. M. Marcham). *Scrutiny* (UK), Summer 1946 (A. J. Woolford). *Yale Review,* Winter 1946 (Wallace Notestein)

A12. *Poems Chiefly Cornish* (1944)

First edition. London: Faber & Faber, February 4, 1944 (1,302 copies). 6s 0d. 78 pp, 9" x 5 1/4".

Contents. 43 poems with (uncredited) dust jacket blurb by T. S. Eliot.

Further printings. There were further printings in March 1944 (2d impression), January 1945 (3d impression), and February 1946 (4th impression; nil record of print-run numbers).

Reviews. *Times Literary Supplement,* February 19, 1944 (Anon.). *Listener* (UK), April 13, 1944 (Anon.). *Punch,* April 19, 1944 (J.K.). *Book Society News,* April 1944 (Edmund Blunden).

A13. *The English Spirit: Essays in History and Literature* (1944)

First edition. London: Macmillan, December 1944 (10,000 copies ordered August 29 1944). 12s 6d. 275 pp, 8vo.

Contents. 38 essays: Mr. Churchill and English History; The Rhythm of English History; The Historical Tradition of British Policy; The English Spirit;

Drake's Way; The Idea of Patriotism; The Spirit of Adventure; Seamen and Empire; Pageant of London; St. Thomas of Chelsea; Erasmus and England; The Tudor Character; The Elizabethan Exhibition; Elizabeth at Rycote; Elizabethan Subjects; The Old Music School at Oxford; The Spanish College at Bologna; Trinity, Cambridge; The Caroline Country Parson: George Herbert; The English Revolution; John Hampden; Falkland; John Pym; Conservative Revolutionary Clarendon's "Life"; Pictures in a Deanery; Jonathan Swift; Sarah Churchill in Old Age; Horace Walpole and George Montagu; The *Letters of Junius*; William and Dorothy Wordsworth; The Young Froude; Carlyle's *Past and Present*; Macaulay's *Essays*; Kilvert's Diary; The Public Records; The Use of History; Oxford in War-Time; Three Americans on England.

Further printings. There were further printings in 1945 (twice, 5,000 copies ordered December 5, 1944 and 5,000 copies ordered February 13, 1945). In 1946 (5,000 copies ordered January 3, 1946) and 1950 (2,000 copies ordered January 23, 1950). Second edition (revised and reset) in 1966 (3,000 copies ordered April 19, 1966).

First American edition. New York: Macmillan, 1945. US$2.75. 275 pp, 22 1/2 cm.

Further printings. There were further printings in 1946. New York: Funk & Wagnalls/Minerva Press M18, August 15, 1967. 276 pp, 8vo, paperback. Revised edition, 1966.

Contents. 25 essays: The Personality of Shakespeare; The Problem of Shakespeare's Sonnets Solved; The Shakespeare Exhibition; Queen Elizabeth I and the Historians; Sir Winston Churchill As an Historian; Erasmus and England; The Tudor Character; An Elizabethan Exhibition; Elizabeth at Rycote; The Spanish College at Bologna; The Old Music School at Oxford; The Caroline Country Parson; Three Civil War Figures; Clarendon's Life; Pictures in a Deanery; Swift As Poet; Sarah Churchill in Old Age; Horace Walpole and George Montagu; The *Letters of Junius*; Carlyle's Past and Present; Macaulay's Essays; The Neglected Froude; Kilvert's Diary; Rudyard Kipling; Three Americans on England.

Reviews. *Punch*, November 15, 1944 (H. Kingsmill). *New Statesman and Nation*, November 18, 1944 (V. S. Pritchett). *Time and Tide*, November 18, 1944 (C. V. Wedgwood). *Observer*, November 26, 1944 (B. I. Evans). *Times Literary Supplement*, December 2, 1944 (Anon.). *Spectator*, December 8, 1944 (Ernest Barker). *Manchester Guardian*, December 27, 1944 (B. I. Evans). *Christian Science Monitor*, December 30, 1944 (Harold Hobson). *Spectator* 173, 1944 (E. Barker). Time, February 5, 1945 (Anon.). *New Yorker,* February 17, 1945 (Anon.). *Saturday Review of Literature*, February 24, 1945 (Leonard Bacon). *Journal of Modern History* (USA), June 1945 (G. H. Guttridge). *Booklist*, July 1, 1945 (Anon.). *New York Times*, September 30, 1945 (Clare Howard). *Nation*, November 24, 1945 (Keith Hutchison). *Weekly Book Review*, December 30, 1945 (H. S. Commager). *The Times*, August 18, 1966 (Anon.). *Punch*, September 7, 1966 (Peter Dickinson). *Cornish Review*, Autumn 1966

(E. W. Martin). *New Yorker,* April 6, 1968 (Anon.). *Choice* (USA), July 1968 (Anon.).

A14. *West-Country Stories* (1945)

First edition. London: Macmillan, November 1945 (12,000 copies ordered June 19, 1945). 8s 6d. 222 pp, crown 8vo.

Contents. 21 narratives both of fact and fiction: The Wicked Vicar of Lansillian; The Stone That Liked Company; All Souls' Night; The Beneficent Shoes; Restinnes? Restinnes?; Cornish Conversation Piece; How Dick Stephens Fought the Bear; Pageant of Plymouth; The Duchy of Cornwall; Rialton: A Cornish Monastic Manor; The Story of Polruddon; Cornwall in the Civil War; John Opie and Harmony Cot; Kilvert in Cornwall; The Sentimental Journey; Our Local Heritage; Three Great Travellers on St. Austell; Tribute to a China-Clay Worker; In the Gyllyngdune Gardens; West-Country Journey; Charles Henderson.

Further printings. There were further printings in 1946 (Macmillan, 5,000 copies ordered November 2, 1945).

First American edition. New York: Macmillan, 1946. US$2.50. 222 pp, 19 cm.

Reviews. *Observer*, November 11, 1945 (J. C. Trewin). *Spectator*, November 16, 1945 (Anon.). *Punch*, November 21, 1945 (H. P. Eden). *Manchester Guardian*, November 28, 1945 (G.T.). *Times Literary Supplement*, December 8, 1945 (Anon.). *New Statesman and Nation*, January 26, 1946 (Philip Toynbee). *New Yorker*, February 9, 1946 (Anon.). *New York Times*, February 10, 1946 (Struthers Burt). *Book Week,* February 17, 1946 (John Norcross). *New Republic* (USA), March 11, 1946 (Denis Plimmer). *Saturday Review of Literature*, March 16, 1946 (J. P. Wood).

A15. *The Use of History* (1946)

First edition. London: Hodder & Stoughton for the English Universities Press, May 1946. 4s 6d. 247 pp, crown 8vo.

Contents. The key volume in the Teach Yourself History Library. General Editor, A. L. Rowse. (See part B for details.)

Further printings. 2d impression (August 1946), 3d impression (June 1947), 4th impression (March 1948). Revised edition, London: Men and Their Times Series, English Universities Press, 1963, 213 pp. Revised edition, Men and Their Times Series, London: English University Press, March 1970. Revised edition, Harmondsworth: Penguin, Pelican Books, May 1971, 172 pp.

First American edition. New York: Macmillan, 1948. US$2. 247 pp, 18 cm.

Further printings. Men and History Series, New York: Collier Books, 1963, 1965, 160 pp, 18 cm. History and Historiography, no. 27, New York: Garland, 1985.

Reviews. *Observer*, July 7, 1946 (Harold Nicolson). *Punch*, July 10, 1946 (H. Kingsmill). *Time and Tide*, July 13, 1946 (C. V. Wedgwood). *Times Liter-*

ary Supplement, August 17, 1946 (Anon.). *New Statesman and Nation*, September 28, 1946 (Kingsley Martin). *Spectator*, September 6, 1946 (Phoebe Pool). *Cambridge Review*, October 1946/June 1947 (Dr. F. J. E. Raby). *International Affairs* (UK), October 1947 (Martin Wight). *School and Society*, May 1, 1948 (Anon.). *Christian Science Monitor*, June 22, 1948 (E.S.P.). *Saturday Review of Literature*, July 3, 1948 (Asher Brynes). *New York Times*, July 11, 1948 (Hans Kohn). *Christian Century*, September 15, 1948 (Anon.). *History* (UK), October 1948 (H. Butterfield). *William and Mary Quarterly* (USA), October 1948 (H. M. Tinkcom). *American Historical Review*, January 1949 (Rushton Coulborn). *Times Literary Supplement*, April 5, 1963 (Anon.)

A16. *Poems of Deliverance* (1946)
First edition. London: Faber & Faber, December 6, 1946 (4,026 copies). 7s 6d. 94 pp, demy 8vo.

Contents. 56 poems with (uncredited) dust jacket blurb by T. S. Eliot. Two sections: I. Poems of War and Peace. 34; II. Poems between Two Wars, 22.

Reviews. *Time and Tide*, January 4, 1947 (Renée Haynes). *Times Literary Supplement*, February 8, 1947 (Anon.). *Listener*, February 13, 1947 (Anon.). *Spectator*, January 3, 1947 (Richard Church).

A17. *The End of an Epoch: Reflections on Contemporary History* (1947)
First edition. London: Macmillan, November 1947 (5,000 copies ordered July 22, 1947). 15s 0d. 324 pp, 8vo, 8 3/4" x 5 1/2".

Contents. 23 essays on politics of the time: Apology by Way of Preface; British Foreign Policy: A *Times* Correspondence; The Tradition of British Policy; Reflections on the European Situation; The End of an Epoch; Reflections on Lord Baldwin; The World and U.S. Policy; Democracy and Democratic Leadership; The Prospects of the Labour Party (1937); What Is Wrong with the Civil Service?; The Dilemma of Church and State; Socialism and Mr. Keynes; The Rise of Liberalism; The Debacle of European Liberalism; What Is Wrong with the Germans?; Germany: The Problem of Europe, France: The Third Republic; The Literature of Communism: Its Theory; The Theory and Practice of Communism; Marx and Russian Communism; An Epic of Revolution: Reflections on Trotsky's *History*; Questions in Political Theory; Marxism and Literature.

Further printings. London: Macmillan, 1948 (3,000 copies ordered December 8, 1947).

First American edition. New York: Macmillan, 1948.

Reviews. *Punch*, November 26, 1947 (H. Kingsmill). *New Statesman and Nation*, November 29, 1947 (R. H. S. Crossman). *Manchester Guardian*, December 2, 1947 (Anon.). *Spectator*, December 19, 1947 (D. W. Brogan). *Observer*, December 21, 1947 (T. E. Utley). *Times Literary Supplement*, January 10, 1948 (Anon.). *New York Herald Tribune*, February 29, 1948 (H. B. Parkes). *International Affairs* (UK), April 1948 (T. H. Minshall). *Political Quarterly*

(UK), April-June 1948 (Anon.). *American Academy of Political and Social Science Annals* 257, May 1948 (Preston Slosson). *American Political Science Review,* June 1948 (E. G. Lewis). *New York Times,* August 15, 1948 (Hans Kohn). *American Historical Review,* October 1948 (Preston Slosson). *Current History* (USA), October 1948 (Anon.). The Journal of Politics (USA), November 1948 (R. K. Gooch). *Spectator,* December 1947–January 1948 (D. W. Brogan). *International Journal* 4, 1950 (Underhill).

A18. *The West in English History* (1949)
First edition. London: Hodder & Stoughton, November 1949. 10s 6d. 190 pp, 8 1/4" x 5 1/2".

Contents. A selection of essays originally broadcast on the BBC West Regional Network. Edited throughout by A. L. Rowse with his "Note" and "Introductory" and essays: VII, Tudor Cornwall; XVIII, The West in English History.

Further printing. January 1950.

Reviews. *Times Literary Supplement,* December 30 1949 (Anon.). *Cornish Review,* Spring 1950 (R. Glynn Grylls).

A19. *The England of Elizabeth: The Structure of Society* (1950)
First edition. London: Macmillan, November 1950 (10,000 copies ordered September 15, 1950). 25s 0d. 547 pp, 8vo, 24 plates.

Contents. First volume of trilogy on the Elizabethan age.

Further printings. London: Macmillan, 1951 (5,000 copies ordered December 8, 1950). Macmillan, 1951 (5,400 copies ordered January 10, 1951). Macmillan, 1959 (2,000 copies ordered January 27, 1959). Macmillan, 1961 (3,000 copies ordered April 14, 1961). Macmillan, 1962 (3,000 copies ordered August 3, 1962). Macmillan, 1964 (10,000 copies ordered March 24, 1964). Macmillan, 1964 (2,000 copies ordered June 15, 1964). Macmillan, April 1981 (Papermac) (5,000 copies). Reprint Society London 1953, 1957, 605 pp, 8vo. Cardinal by Sphere Books, September 1973.

Note. The exact breakdown of hardcover versus Papermac 1961–1964 is uncertain.

First American edition. New York: Macmillan, 1951. US$6.50. 547 pp, 25 cm.

Further printings. Macmillan, 1951. New York: Collier Books, 1966. Madison: University of Wisconsin Press, 1978 (reprint of 1951 edition published by Macmillan).

Note. A. L. Rowse in an interview in the *New Yorker,* October 19, 1963: "My book *The England of Elizabeth* has sold 120,000 copies in England, hard covers alone."

Reviews. *Listener,* December 7, 1950 (Maurice Ashley). *Observer,* December 10, 1950 (C. V. Wedgwood). *Spectator,* December 15, 1950 (J. B. Black). *Times Literary Supplement,* December 15, 1950 (Anon.). *Country Life* (UK),

December 29, 1950 (Howard Spring). *Economist* (UK), December 30, 1950 (Anon.). *Sunday Times*, circa December 1950 (G. M. Trevelyan). *New Statesman and Nation*, January 13, 1951 (H. P. Trevor-Roper). *History Today,* February 1951 (Alan Bullock). *Kirkus,* February 1, 1951 (Anon.). *Manchester Guardian*, March 6, 1951 (R. H. Tawney). *Library Journal*, March 15, 1951 (Katherine Tappert Willis). *Christian Science Monitor*, April 5, 1951 (Harold Hobson). *Chicago Sunday Tribune,* May 27, 1951 (Edward Wagenknecht). *Christian Science Monitor*, June 6, 1951 (Leila Flower). *San Francisco Chronicle,* June 10, 1951 (C. W. Weinberger). *Nation* (USA), June 16, 1951 (Alfred Harbage). *New York Herald Tribune*, June 24, 1951 (S. C. Chew). *Commonweal* (USA), June 29, 1951 (G. B. Harrison). *Dublin Magazine*, April-June 1951 (Anon.). *Canadian Historical Review,* June 1951 (J. B. Conacher). *New York Times*, July 8, 1951 (Thomas Caldecot Chubb). *Booklist*, July 15, 1951 (Anon.). *New Yorker*, July 28, 1951 (Anon.). *Saturday Review of Literature*, July 28, 1951 (Garrett Mattingly). *William and Mary Quarterly,* July 1951 (Conyers Read). *School and Society*, August 25, 1951 (W. H. Beyer). *Current History* (USA), August 1951 (Anon.). *American Historical Review*, October 1951 (Louis B. Wright). *English Historical Review,* October 1951 (Gladys Scott Thomson). *Kenyon Review* (USA), Autumn 1951 (Paul Goodman). *History* (UK), February 1952 (J. E. Neale). *Revue Historique* (French review), circa 1951. *Revue d'Histoire Ecclesiastique* (France) 46, 1951 (Dom Hubert Daupin). *American Academy of Political and Social Science, Annals* 280, March 1952 (B. Wilkinson). *Journal of Higher Education* 1952 (Harold R. Walley). *South Atlantic Quarterly,* January 1952 (William B. Hamilton). *John O'London's Books of the Month* (UK), October 1965 (Jacob Faithfull).

A20. *The English Past: Evocations of Persons and Places* (1951)

First edition. London: Macmillan, September 1951 (5,000 copies ordered May 30, 1951). 15s 0d. ix pp + 245 pp, 8vo.

Contents. 12 essays: All Souls (1945); Bisham and the Hobys; Hillesden in Buckinghamshire; Dear Dr. Denton; The Milton Country; Swift at Letcombe; Afternoon at Haworth Parsonage; Thomas Hardy and Max Gate; John Buchan at Elsfield; Nottingham: A Midlands Capital; D. H. Lawrence at Eastwood; Alun Lewis: A Foreword.

Further printings. Macmillan, October 1951 (3,000 copies ordered October 3, 1951). Revised edition, Macmillan, September 2, 1965 as *Times, Persons, Places: Essays in Literature* (3,000 copies ordered December 22, 1964).

Contents. 10 essays: D. H. Lawrence at Eastwood; Nottingham: Lawrence's City; John Buchan at Elsfield; Thomas Hardy and Max Gate; Haworth Parsonage; Swift at Letcombe; The Milton Country; Doctor Denton: A Seventeenth-Century Gentleman; Hillesden in Buckinghamshire; Bisham and the Hobys.

First American edition. New York: Macmillan, 1952. US$3.75. 245 pp, 22 cm.

Reviews. *Observer*, October 7, 1951 (Harold Nicolson). *Manchester Guardian*, October 9, 1951 (Norman Shrapnel). *Times Literary Supplement*, October 19, 1951 (Anon.). *Punch* 221, 1951 (H. P. Eden). *New York Times*, January 20, 1952 (Herbert F. West). *New York Herald Tribune*, January 27, 1952 (DeLancey Ferguson). *Chicago Sunday Tribune*, February 3, 1952 (A. C. Ames). *Listener*, February 14, 1952 (Anon.). *Christian Science Monitor*, February 21, 1952 (Ruth Chapin). *New Republic* (USA), March 10, 1952 (Willard Thorp). *San Francisco Chronicle*, March 16, 1952 (Anon.). *New Yorker*, March 22, 1952 (Anon.). *Springfield Republican*, March 23, 1952 (Anon.). *Dublin Magazine*, January-March 1952 (Anon.). *Booklist*, April 15, 1952 (Anon.). *Bookmark*, May 1952 (Anon.). *The Times*, September 9, 1965 (Anon.).

A21. *A New Elizabethan Age?* (1952)

First edition. London: Oxford University Press, August 18, 1952. 5s 0d. 14 pp, med. 8vo.

Contents. English Association presidential address 1952.

A22. *The Spirit of the Elizabethan Age* (1953)

First edition. Glasgow: Glasgow Junior Chamber of Commerce, 1953. 16 pp, 23 cm.

Contents. Being an address delivered to the Glasgow Junior Chamber of Commerce and members of the public on Thursday, May 28, 1953.

On cover. Glasgow Junior Chamber of Commerce. Coronation 1953.

A23. *A History of France* (by Lucien Romier) (1953)

First edition. London: Macmillan, 1953. 487 pp, 8vo, 8 plates, 3 maps.

Contents. Originally published in France under the title *L'ancienne France: Des Origines a la Revolution,* stopping at 1789. Translated and completed by A. L. Rowse.

Further printings. Macmillan, 1955, 1959, 1960. Macmillan, 1962 Papermac 40 series, 487 pp. 21s 0d (3,100 copies ordered December 14, 1961). Macmillan, 1964 (Papermac 40 Series, 2,000 copies ordered October 22, 1963). Macmillan, 1966.

Note. Extract Macmillan Editions Book 28: 1,000 Papermac covers. 21/-. 1,000 Papermac covers. US$4.95 (New York: St. Martin's Press). 442 Papermac covers 21/-. 3,150 jackets 30/- ordered March 21 1962. (Precise details of hardcover versus Papermac breakdown are uncertain.)

First American edition. New York: St. Martin's Press, 1953. US$6.50.

Further printings. New York: St. Martin's Press, 1966.

Reviews. *Kirkus* (USA), September 15, 1953 (Anon.). *Chicago Sunday Tribune*, November 1, 1953 (Gilbert Twiss). *Library Journal*, November 1, 1953 (F. E. Hirsch). *Times Literary Supplement*, November 13, 1953 (Anon.). *Manchester Guardian*, November 17, 1953 (A. J. P. Taylor). *Booklist*, December 1, 1953 (Anon.). *New York Herald Tribune Book Review*, December 13,

1953 (Geoffrey Bruun). *Current History,* December 1953 (Anon.). *Dublin Review* 228, 1954 (Outram Evennett). *English* 10, 1954 (D. M. Stuart).

A24. *An Elizabethan Garland* (1953)

First edition. London: Macmillan, September 25, 1953 (3,000 copies ordered May 22, 1953). 15s 0d. 162 pp, 8vo, 8 plates.

Contents. 13 essays: Coronations in English History; The Coronation of Queen Elizabeth I; Queen Elizabeth I and the English Historians; Elizabethan Christmas; The Royal Palaces; The Queen's Canaletto; In Pursuit of Elizabethan Ireland; Sir Francis Drake and British Enterprise; Prehistory for Historians; Beginnings of the Commonwealth; Impressions of America; Churchill on the Grand Alliance; A New Elizabethan Age?

Further printings. London: Macmillan, 1953 (2,000 copies ordered September 25, 1953).

First American edition. New York: St. Martin's Press, 1953. US$3. 162 pp, 23 cm.

Further printings. New York: St. Martin's Press, 1954. New York: AMS Press, 1972. 162 pp, 23 cm.

Reviews. *Punch*, October 7, 1953 (J. Richardson). *Times Literary Supplement*, October 23, 1953 (Anon.). *Tablet,* October 24, 1953 (J. J. Dwyer). *Listener*, October 29, 1953 (Anon.). *Economist* (UK), October 31, 1953 (Anon.). *Time and Tide*, October 31, 1953 (C. V. Wedgwood). *New York Times*, November 11, 1953 (Orville Prescott). *The Month,* January 1954 (Anon.).

A25. *The Expansion of Elizabethan England* (1955)

First edition. London: Macmillan, October 7, 1955 (10,000 copies). 30s 0d. xiii pp + 450 pp, 8vo, 27 plates.

Contents. Second volume of trilogy on the Elizabethan age.

Further printings. London: Macmillan, 1971 (1,000 copies). Macmillan Papermac 31, 1963 (2,000 copies ordered August 28, 1962). Macmillan Papermac, November 1981 (not found). London: Reprint Society, 1957, 475 pp. London: Cardinal by Sphere Books, September 1973 (paperback).

First American edition. New York: St. Martin's Press, 1955. US$5.75. 450 pp, 23 cm.

Further printings; Toronto: Macmillan Company of Canada, 1955. New York: Harper & Row, 450 pp, 21 cm, 1965. New York: Scribner's, September 1, 1972. US$3.95 The Scribner Library Lyceum editions.

Reviews. *Listener*, October 6, 1955 (G. R. Elton). *Time and Tide*, October 8, 1955 (Jack Simmons). *Observer*, October 9, 1955 (C. V. Wedgwood). *Country Life,* October 27, 1955 (Howard Spring). *The Times,* October 27, 1955 (Anon.). *Spectator*, October 28, 1955 (Philip Magnus). *Times Literary Supplement*, October 28, 1955 (Anon.). *Tablet,* November 5, 1955 (J. J. Dwyer). *Economist* (UK), November 12, 1955 (Anon.). *New Statesman and Nation*, November 12, 1955 (Michael Howard). *New Yorker*, November 12, 1955

(Anon.). *Chicago Sunday Tribune,* November 13, 1955 (Edward Wagenknecht). *New York Herald Tribune,* November 13, 1955 (S. C. Chew.). *Library Journal,* December 1, 1955 (Lee Ash). *Christian Science Monitor,* December 8, 1955 (Eric Forbes-Boyd). *Renaissance News* (USA), Winter 1955 (Caroline Robbins). *New York Times,* December 18, 1955 (Robert L. Schuyler). *History Today,* December 1955 (Oliver Warner). *Encounter,* January 1956 (Angus Wilson). *Booklist,* March 1, 1956 (Anon.). *American Academy of Political and Social Science, Annals* 304, March 1956 (E. S. Beller). *American Historical Review,* April 1956 (David Harris Willson). *Current History* (USA), June 1956 (Anon.). *William and Mary Quarterly* (USA), July 1956 (William B. Willcox). *Canadian Historical Review,* September 1956 (J. B. Conacher). *Review of Politics* (USA), July 1956 (William R. Trimble). *Manuscripta* (USA), February 1957 (M. B. McNamee).

A26. *The Early Churchills: An English Family* (1956)

First edition. London: Macmillan, November 1956. 36s 0d. 420 pp, 8vo, 16 plates, genealogical table.

Contents. First volume of biography of the Churchill family.

Further printings. London: Macmillan, 1959 (1,500 copies ordered October 28, 1958). Harmondsworth: Penguin Books, October 1969 (paperback). Reprinted 1969.

First American edition. New York: Harper & Brothers, September 19, 1956. US$6.50. 378 pp, 25 cm.

Further printings. Westport, Connecticut: Greenwood Press, 1974 (reprint of the 1956 Harper edition). Dorset Classic Reprints Society, Marboro Books, January 17, 1991.

Reviews. *Kirkus* (USA), June 15, 1956 (Anon.). *Christian Science Monitor,* September 20, 1956 (W. H. Stringer). *New York Herald Tribune,* September 23, 1956 (C. V. Wedgwood). *New York Times,* September 23, 1956 (Geoffrey Bruun). *Chicago Sunday Tribune,* September 30, 1956 (A. C. Ames). *Library Journal,* October 1, 1956 (J. D. Marshall). Time, October 1, 1956 (Anon.). *Saturday Review of Literature,* October 6, 1956 (L. B. Wright). *The Times,* November 8, 1956 (Anon.). *Manchester Guardian,* November 9, 1956 (John Carswell). *Observer,* November 11, 1956 (Roger Fulford). *Times Literary Supplement,* November 16, 1956 (Anon.). *New Statesman and Nation,* November 24, 1956 (John Rosselli). *San Francisco Chronicle,* November 25, 1956 (Anon.). *Springfield Republican,* December 2, 1956 (Richard McLaughlin). *Listener,* December 13, 1956 (Anon.). *Spectator,* December 14, 1956 (Christopher Hill). *Economist* (UK), December 22, 1956 (Anon.). *Current History,* December 1956 (Anon.). *American Historical Review,* October 1957 (Willson H. Coates). *Economic Journal,* September 1957 (N. G. Annan). *English Historical Review,* October 1957 (Gladys Scott Thomson). *Nation* (USA), April 26, 1958 (Raymond Postgate). *History* 43, 1958 (Mark A. Thomson). *Sunday*

Times, circa November-December 1956 (Sir Arthur Bryant). *Observer*, circa November-December 1956 (Roger Fulford).

Note. The *Spectator* review for December 14, 1956, states that "Dr. Rowse's book has been selected as the Daily Mail Book of the Month."

A27. *The Later Churchills* (1958)

First edition. London: Macmillan, June 12, 1958 (8,000 copies). 35s 0d. 528 pp, 8vo, 12 plates, genealogical table.

Contents. Second volume of biography of the Churchill family.

Further printings. Harmondsworth, U.K.: Penguin Books, October 1971 (paperback). London: Reprint Society published a combined one-volume edition, *The Early and the Later Churchills* in 1959, 420 pp + 528 pp (hardcover). London: Macmillan, 1966 (Papermac P152), *The Churchills: The Story of a Family* (Abridged edition) (15,000 copies ordered May 4, 1966). London: Book Club Associates, 1970, *The Churchills: The Story of a Family* (abridged edition), 577 pp (hardcover).

First American edition. *The Churchills: From the Death of Marlborough to the Present.* New York: Harper & Brothers, 1958. US$7.50. 430 pp, 23 cm.

Further printings. Toronto: Macmillan Company of Canada, 1958, as *The Later Churchills.* New York: Harper & Row, May 24, 1967, as *The Churchills: The Story of a Family* (abridged edition). Westport, Connecticut: Greenwood Press, February 25, 1974 as *The Churchills: From the Death of Marlborough to the Present.*

Reviews. *Kirkus* (USA), February 1, 1958 (Anon.). *Nation* (USA), April 26, 1958 (Raymond Postgate). *Chicago Sunday Tribune,* April 27, 1958 (C. L. Mowat). *New York Herald Tribune,* April 27, 1958 (C. V. Wedgwood). *New York Times,* April 27,1958 (Geoffrey Bruun). *Springfield Republican,* April 27, 1958 (Anon.). *Christian Science Monitor,* May 1, 1958 (W. H. Stringer). *Saturday Review of Literature,* May 3, 1958 (L. B. Wright). *Time,* May 12, 1958 (Anon.). *Library Journal,* May 15, 1958 (John David Marshall). *San Francisco Chronicle,* May 20, 1958 (William Hogan). *The Times,* June 12, 1958 (Anon.). *Observer,* June 15, 1958 (Harold Nicolson). *Times Literary Supplement,* June 20, 1958 (Anon.). *Listener,* June 26, 1958 (Anon.). *New Statesman and Nation,* June 28, 1958 (John Raymond). *Time and Tide,* June 28, 1958 (Robert Greacen). *Spectator,* July 4, 1958 (D. W. Brogan). *National and English Review* (UK) 151, 1958 (Eric Gillett). *History* 44, 1959 (Mark A. Thomson). *Canadian Historical Review,* June 1959 (Anon.). *English Historical Review,* April 1960 (Asa Briggs). *American Historical Review,* April 1962 (Stanley Pargellis). *Books and Bookmen,* March 1972 (Cecil Roberts).

A28. *Poems Partly American* (1959)

First edition. London: Faber & Faber, January 30, 1959. (1,000 copies) 12s 6d. 71 pp, demy 8vo.

Contents. 36 poems that fall mostly into three sections—Oxford, Cornwall, and America: I. Mostly Oxford (16); II. America (11); III. Cornwall (9).

Reviews. *Spectator*, January 30, 1959 (G. D. Klingopulos). *Listener*, March 26, 1959 (Francis King). *Times Literary Supplement*, May 29, 1959 (Anon.). *Current History* (USA), July 1959 (Anon.).

A29. *The Elizabethans and America*: The Trevelyan Lectures at Cambridge, 1958 (1959)

First edition. London: Macmillan, 1959 (7,500 copies ordered May 29, 1959). 25s 0d. 222 pp, 8vo, 8 plates.

Contents. Eight essays, a compilation of the First Trevelyan Lectures, which A. L. Rowse was asked to deliver on their foundation in 1958. They also form a pendant to *The Expansion of Elizabethan England*. The Conflict for the New World: Spaniards, Portuguese, French, English; Queen Elizabeth I and America; Ralegh, Hakluyt, and Colonisation; Virginia; Sir Ferdinando Gorges and New England; Pilgrims and Puritans: The Elizabethan Element; Newfoundland, Nova Scotia, and the North-West Passage; America in Elizabethan Literature, Science and the Arts.

Further printings. London: Macmillan, January 21, 1965. London: Greenwood Press, November 1978.

First American edition. New York: Harper & Brothers, October 20, 1959. US$4. 222 pp, 22 cm.

Further printings. Toronto: Macmillan Company of Canada, 1959. New York: Harper & Row, Harper Colophon Books, no. 52, 1965. Paperback. Westport, Connecticut: Greenwood Press, 1978 (reprint of the 1959 Macmillan edition).

Reviews. *Kirkus* (USA), September 1, 1959 (Anon.). *Listener*, October 15, 1959 (Joel Hurstfield). *Spectator*, October 16, 1959 (Christopher Hill). *Observer*, October 18, 1959 (G. R. Elton). *The Times,* October 22, 1959 (Anon.). *Times Literary Supplement*, October 23, 1959 (Anon.). *Tablet,* October 31, 1959 (J. J. Dwyer). *Library Journal*, November 1, 1959 (R. R. Rea). *Economist* (UK), November 7, 1959 (Anon.). *Chicago Sunday Tribune,* November 15, 1959 (S. W. Halperin). *New York Herald Tribune*, November 15, 1959 (Garrett Mattingly). *New York Times*, November 15, 1959 (Henry Commager). *Christian Science Monitor*, November 18, 1959 (J. N. Goodsell). *New Statesman and Nation*, November 28, 1959 (R. W. B. Lewis). *Saturday Review of Literature*, December 12, 1959 (Richard B. Morris). *Booklist*, December 15, 1959 (Anon.). *Nation*, December 19, 1959 (Louis B. Wright). *Book of the Month Club News* (USA), January 1960 (Roger Pippett). *Western Humanities Review* (USA), January-March 1960 (Philip C. Sturges). *American Historical Review*, April 1960 (Louis B. Wright). *Virginia Magazine of History and Biography,* April 1960 (Wesley F. Craven). *Library Review* (Scotland), Spring 1960 (Esmond Wright). *Mississippi Valley Historical Review,* June 1960 (Caroline Robbins). *New England Quarterly* (USA), June 1960 (Willard M. Wallace). *San Francisco*

Chronicle, July 17, 1960 (C.W.W.). *Journal of Southern History,* August 1960 (Charles F. Mullett). *Geographical Journal* (UK), September 1960 (A. H. W. Robinson). *Canadian Historical Review,* December 1960 (W. B. Willcox). *History* 45, 1960 (David B. Quinn). *English Historical Review,* January 1961 (J. W. Blake). *William and Mary Quarterly* (USA), January 1961 (Darrett B. Rutman).

A30. *St. Austell: Church, Town, Parish* (1960)

Subscribed edition. 719 copies. St. Austell: H. E. Warne, 1960. £1.25. 94 pp, 4to, map of the historic parish. Photographs by Charles Woolf.

Contents. Celebrates the 700th anniversary of the dedication of the parish church of St. Austell, Cornwall.

Further printings. First public edition, 1960.

Note. Text only, reprinted in *The Little Land of Cornwall,* 1986.

Reviews. *Times Literary Supplement,* October 21, 1960 (Anon.). *The Times,* November 3, 1960 (Anon.). *Economist,* March 18, 1961 (Anon.). *History Today,* April 1961 (A.H. [Alan Hodge]). *Geographical Journal* (UK), September 1961 (E. W. Gilbert). *English Historical Review,* January 1962 (W. G. Hoskins).

A31. *All Souls and Appeasement: A Contribution to Contemporary History* (1961)

First edition. London: Macmillan, 1961 (5,000 copies ordered January 16, 1961). 18s 0d. 122 pp, crown 8vo, 7 plates.

Contents. Provides an insider's view of leading political figures at All Souls and their disastrous policy of appeasement with Hitler.

First American edition. New York: St. Martin's Press, 1961. 122 pp, 21 cm.

Further printings. New York: Norton, November 20, 1961, as *Appeasement: A Study in Political Decline, 1933–1939.* New York: Norton, 1963 (The Norton Library, N1 39).

Reviews. *The Times,* April 20, 1961 (Anon.). *New Statesman and Nation,* April 21, 1961 (David Marquand). *Spectator,* April 21, 1961 (James Joll). *Times Literary Supplement,* April 21, 1961 (Anon.). *Observer,* April 23, 1961 (Sir William Hayter). *Listener,* April 27, 1961 (C. P. Snow). *Time and Tide,* April 27, 1961 (Martin Gilbert). *Economist,* May 13, 1961 (Anon.). *Punch,* May 17, 1961 (B. A. Young). *Contemporary Review,* August 1961 (Anon.). *New York Herald Tribune,* November 21, 1961 (Maurice Dolbier). *New York Herald Tribune,* December 3, 1961 (G. A. Craig). *New York Times,* December 7, 1961 (William C. Fitzgibbon). *Springfield Republican,* December 10, 1961 (F. L. Spencer). *Chicago Sunday Tribune,* December 24, 1961 (S. W. Halperin). *New York Times,* December 24, 1961 (C. P. Snow). *Australian Quarterly,* December 1961 (F. G. Stambrook). *Canadian Forum,* December 1961 (Denis Smith). *International Review of Social History* 6, pt. 2, 1961 (Anon.). *Christian Science Monitor,* January 4, 1962 (Harold Hobson). *Saturday Review of Litera-*

ture, January 13, 1962 (Frank Altschul). *New Yorker*, January 20, 1962 (Anon.). *Mississippi Valley Historical Review*, March 1962 (Anon.). *New Leader* (USA), April 30, 1962 (Stephen R. Graubard). *Foreign Affairs* (USA), April 1962 (Henry L. Roberts). *Virginia Quarterly Review*, Spring 1962 (Anon.). *International Journal*, Spring 1962 (Gordon A. Craig). *Political Science Quarterly*, June 1962 (George Woodbridge). *American Historical Review*, July 1962 (Oron J. Hale). *World Affairs* (USA), Fall 1962 (Donald Armstrong).

Note. American edition, *Appeasement: A Study in Political Decline, 1933–1939* only, carries on dust jacket major blurbs by historians Henry Steele Commager and Allan Nevins.

A32. *Ralegh and the Throckmortons* (1962)

First edition. London: Macmillan, April 5, 1962 (5,000 copies ordered November 23, 1961). 35s 0d. ISBN: 333 09157 4. xii pp + 348 pp, demy 8vo, 14 plates.

Further printings. London: Macmillan, 1962 (5,000 copies ordered April 11, 1962). London: Reprint Society, 1964.

First American edition. *Sir Walter Ralegh: His Family and Private Life.* New York: Harper & Brothers, June 6, 1962. US$6.95 348 pp, demy 8vo. Illustrated.

Further printings. New York: St. Martin's Press, 1962, as *Ralegh and the Throckmortons*. Toronto: Macmillan Company of Canada, 1962, as *Ralegh and the Throckmortons*. Greenwood, Connecticut: Greenwood Press, 1975.

Reviews. *Economist*, March 31, 1962 (Anon.). *The Times*, April 5, 1962 (Anon.). *Manchester Guardian*, April 6, 1962 (Joel Hurstfield). *Listener*, April 12, 1962 (G. R. Elton). *New Statesman and Nation*, April 13, 1962 (Lawrence Stone). *Spectator*, April 13, 1962 (Christopher Hill). *Observer*, April 15, 1962 (Harold Nicolson). *Times Literary Supplement*, April 20, 1962 (Anon.). *Tablet*, April 21, 1962 (Patrick McGrath). *Punch*, April 25, 1962 (R. G. G. Price). *Kirkus* (USA), May 1, 1962 (Anon.). *Books of the Month* (UK), May 1962 (Hugh Ross Williamson). *New York Herald Tribune*, June 3, 1962 (Garrett Mattingly). *Christian Science Monitor*, June 7, 1962 (Harold Hobson). *New York Herald Tribune*, June 7, 1962 (Maurice Dolbier). *Saturday Review of Literature*, June 9, 1962 (John Clive). *Chicago Sunday Tribune*, June 10, 1962 (R. P. Stearns). *New York Times*, June 11, 1962 (Orville Prescott). *New Yorker*, June 30, 1962 (Anon.). *Booklist*, July 1, 1962 (Anon.). *New York Times*, July 1, 1962 (Charles W. Ferguson). *Springfield Republican*, July 1, 1962 (F. L. Spencer). *America*, July 21, 1962 (John J. O'Connor). *Bookmark*, July 1962 (Anon.). *Library Journal* (USA), July 1962 (Robert R. Rea). *San Francisco Chronicle*, August 12, 1962 (Nancy Griffin). *Nation* (USA), September 1, 1962 (Michael Lewis). *Canadian Historical Review*, September 1962 (John F. H. New). *Month*, September 1962 (Richard Blundell). *North Carolina Historical Review*, Autumn 1962 (Mattie E. E. Parker). *History*, October 1962 (Wallace T. MacCaffrey). *American Historical Review*, January 1963 (W. Gordon Zeeveld). *Journal of Southern History* (USA), February 1963 (Lacey Baldwin Smith). *Virginia*

Magazine of History and Biography, April 1963 (R. A. Skelton). *William and Mary Quarterly,* April 1963 (David B. Quinn). *English Historical Review,* July 1964 (Patrick Collinson).

A33. *William Shakespeare: A Biography* (1963)
First edition. London: Macmillan, October 3, 1963 (15,000 copies ordered April 29, 1963). 45s 0d. ISBN: 333 04725 7. xiv pp + 485 pp, 8vo, 23 plates.

Further printings. London: Macmillan, 1963 (6,500 copies ordered September 30, 1963). London, New English Library, September 1967. New edition paperback, Mentor Books no. 5011.

First American edition. New York: Harper & Row, January 6, 1964 (1963 in book). US$6.95. 478 pp, 8vo. Illustrated.

Further printings. Toronto: Macmillan Company of Canada, 1964. New York, Pocket *Books* 1965. Marboro Books, May 1995.

Note 1. An interview with A. L. Rowse in the *New Yorker,* October 19, 1963, states: "It's the sole Book-of-the-Month Club selection for that month" [January 1964].

Note 2. A. L. Rowse to Ava, Viscountess Waverley in a letter from the Huntington Library, California, dated October 24, 1965: "My Shakespeare biography is nearing 200,000 in hard covers."

Reviews. *The Times,* October 3, 1963 (Ivor Brown). *Time and Tide,* October 3, 1963 (Hugh Ross Williamson). *Daily Telegraph,* October 4, 1963 (J. I. M. Stewart). *New Statesman and Nation,* October 4, 1963 (William Empson). *Observer,* October 6, 1963 (Terence Spencer). *Sunday Telegraph,* October 6, 1963 (M. C. Bradbrook). *Sunday Times,* October 6, 1963 (Cyril Connolly). *Punch,* October 9, 1963 (J. Bowle). *Listener,* October 10, 1963 (Christopher Ricks). *Spectator,* October 11, 1963 (Philip Brockbank). *Evening Standard,* October 15, 1963 (Malcolm Muggeridge). *Economist,* October 19, 1963 (Anon.). *Yorkshire Post,* October-November 1963 (Kenneth Muir). *Tablet* (UK), November 2, 1963 (Robert Speaight). Books of the Month (UK), November 1963 (Burnett James). *Library Journal* (USA), December 15, 1963 (James Sandoe). *Times Literary Supplement,* December 26, 1963 (Anon./John Crow). *Book of the Month Club News* (USA), December 1963 (Clifton Fadiman). *Contemporary Review,* December 1963 (William Kean Seymour). *London Magazine,* December 1963 (John Lehmann). *Arizona Quarterly,* Winter 1963 (Richard Hosley). *Poetry Review* (UK), Winter 1963 (John Smith). *Dalhousie Review* (Canada), Winter 1963–1964 (G. P. V. Akrigg). *Book Week,* January 5, 1964 (G. B. Harrison). *Chicago Sunday Tribune,* January 5, 1964 (H. Buckmaster). *New York Times,* January 5, 1964 (Edward Hubler). *Newsweek,* January 6, 1964 (Anon.). *New York Times,* January 6, 1964 (Orville Prescott). *New York Herald Tribune,* January 7, 1964 (A. Pryce-Jones). *New York Review of Books,* January 9, 1964 (Frank Kermode). *Time,* January 10, 1964 (Anon.). *Saturday Review of Literature,* January 11, 1964 (Bernard Grebanier). *America,* January 25, 1964 (P. Albert Duhamel). *Nation* (USA), January 27, 1964 (Christopher Sykes). *Month* (UK), January 1964 (J. F. X. Harriott, S.J.). *Quarterly Review* (UK), January 1964 (Anon.). *San Francisco Sunday Chronicle,* February 2, 1964 (R. E. Fitch). *Atlantic Monthly* (USA), February 1964 (William Barrett). *Canadian Forum,* February 1964 (Hugh Maclean). *Critic* (USA), February 1964 (Fallon Evans). *National Review* (USA), March 24, 1964 (G. Wills). *New Leader* (USA), March 30, 1964 (R. Shahani). *Christian Century,* April 15, 1964 (P. Elmen). *English* (UK), Spring 1964 (R. A. Foakes). *Virginia Quarterly Review,* Spring 1964 (R. C. Bald). *English Language Notes* (USA), June 1964 (Leonard F. Dean). *Meanjin Quarterly* (Australia), June 1964 (David Bradley). *Kenyon Review* (USA), Summer 1964 (Ronald Berman). *Southerly* (Australia) 3, 1964 (Gerald Alfred Wilkes). *Reporter,* September 24, 1964 (David Littlejohn). *Sewanee Review* (USA), Autumn 1964 (Charles T. Harrison). *College English* (USA), October 1964 (J. L. Barroll). *Hudson Review* (USA), Winter 1964–1965 (Patrick Cruttwell).

A34. *Shakespeare's Sonnets* (1964)

First edition. London: Macmillan, February 27, 1964 (5,000 copies ordered October 22, 1963). 42s 0d. ISBN: 333 02411 7. xxxvii pp + 319 pp, 8vo, 1 frontispiece plate.

Contents. Edited, with an introduction and notes by A. L. Rowse.

Further printings. London: Macmillan, 1964 (985 copies + 515 paperback copies ordered August 11, 1964). 2d edition 1973 as *Shakespeare's Sonnets—The Problems Solved* (750 copies + 1,500 paperback copies). Reprinted 1976 (750 paperback copies). 3d edition (revised) 1984 (650 copies + 750 paperback copies). Reprinted 1985 (500 paperback copies). Reprinted 1991 (510 paperback copies). Reprinted 1993 (525 paperback copies). Reprinted 1994 (306 paperback copies).

First American edition. New York: Harper & Row, April 24, 1964. US$5.

Note. A. L. Rowse to Ava, Viscountess Waverley, in a letter dated October 24, 1965, writes that Harper's Perennial Classics has sold 65,000 copies.

Further printings. New York: Harper & Row, August 2, 1973, 2d edition as *Shakespeare's Sonnets—The Problems Solved.*

Reviews. *The Times,* February 27, 1964 (Anon.). *Observer,* March 1, 1964 (Ivor Brown). *Sunday Telegraph,* March 1, 1964 (M. C. Bradbrook). *Sunday Times,* March 1, 1964 (Christopher Ricks). *Times Literary Supplement,* March 12, 1964 (Anon.). *New Yorker,* March 18, 1974 (G. Steiner). *Listener,* April 23, 1964 (Laurence Lerner). *Books of the Month* (UK), April 1964 (John Connell). *New York Times,* May 3, 1964 (Kenneth Muir). *Quarterly Review* (UK), July 1964 (Anon.). *Punch* 246, 1964 (P. Dickinson). *Times Educational Supplement,* June 15, 1973 (J. H. P. Pafford). *Spectator,* July 14, 1973 (Richard Luckett). *Tablet,* July 21, 1973 (Francis Berry). *Times Literary Supplement,* August 10, 1973 (Anon.). *Wall Street Journal,* August 21, 1973 (Edmund Fuller). *New York Times,* September 23, 1973 (David L. Stevenson). *Choice* (USA), January 1974 (Anon.). *Shakespeare Quarterly,* Winter 1974 (Susan Snyder).

A35. *Christopher Marlowe: A Biography* **(1964)**
First edition. London: Macmillan, 1964 (5,850 copies ordered February 25, 1964). 35s 0d. xi pp + 220 pp, 8vo, 8 plates.

Further printings. London: Macmillan, February 1981, Papermac (with alterations).

First American edition. *Christopher Marlowe: His Life and Work.* New York: Harper & Row, 1964. US$5.95. xi pp + 220 pp, 23 cm.

Further printings. New York: Harper & Row, January 25, 1965. New York: Grosset & Dunlap, 1966 (Grosset's Universal Library, UL198).

Reviews. *The Times*, September 3, 1964 (Anon.). *Times Literary Supplement*, September 3, 1964 (Anon.). *Spectator*, September 4, 1964 (C. B. Cox). *Economist*, September 5, 1964 (Anon.). *Observer*, September 6, 1964 (Christopher Ricks). *Sunday Telegraph*, September 6, 1964 (M. C. Bradbrook). *Sunday Times*, September 6, 1964 (John Russell Brown). *New Statesman and Nation*, September 18, 1964 (Frank Kermode) *Punch*, September 30, 1964 (John Bowle). *John O'London's Books of the Month* (UK), September 1964 (Eileen Marlow). *Listener*, October 1, 1964 (Terence Spencer). *Tablet*, October 24, 1964 (Robert Speaight). *Contemporary Review,* November 1964 (Gavin Thurston). *Library Review* (Scotland), Winter 1964 (James A. Michie). *New York Times*, January 11, 1965 (Eliot Fremont-Smith). *Best Sell,* January 15, 1965 (J. J. Clarke). *Christian Science Monitor*, January 21, 1965 (Eric Forbes-Boyd). *Book Week*, January 24, 1965 (John Simon). *New York Times*, January 24, 1965 (G. B. Harrison). *America,* January 30, 1965 (P. A. Duhamel). *New Yorker*, January 30, 1965 (Anon.). *Quarterly Review* (UK), January 1965 (Anon.). *Nation* (USA), February 1, 1965 (Anthony Burgess). *Library Journal*, February 15, 1965 (James Sandoe). *Atlantic Monthly* (USA), March 1965 (Phoebe Adams). *Critic* (USA), April 1965 (Anon.). *English* (UK), Spring 1965 (Hermann Peschmann). *Canadian Forum*, June 1965 (W. F. Blissett). *College English* (USA), November 1965 (Irving Ribner). *Sunday Times*, February 1, 1981 (Anon.).

A36. *A Cornishman at Oxford: The Education of a Cornishman* **(1965)**
First edition. London: Jonathan Cape, January 14, 1965. 5,000 copies (ordered in September 1964). 30s. 319 pp, demy 8vo. Frontispiece portrait.

Contents. Second volume of autobiography.

Further printings. London: Cape, April 18, 1974, 1,500 copies (ordered in December 1973).

New Impression. London: Anthony Mott, March 1983, Cornish Library paperback.

First American edition. New York: Hillary House, 1965. 319 pp, demy 8vo.

Further printings. Mystic, Connecticut: Lawrence Verry, 1965. US$6.

Reviews. *New Statesman and Nation*, January 15, 1965 (Frank Kermode). *Spectator*, January 15, 1965 (Patrick Anderson). *Economist*, January 16, 1965 (Anon.). *Observer*, January 17, 1965 (Francis Hope). *Sunday Telegraph*, January 17, 1965 (John Hale). *Sunday Times*, January 17, 1965 (J. W. Lambert). *Times Literary Supplement*, January 21, 1965 (Anon.). *Tablet*, January 23, 1965 (D.W.). *Punch*, February 10, 1965 (R. G. G. Price). *Listener*, February 18, 1965 (Maurice Ashley). *New York Times*, April 11, 1965 (Anthony Burgess). *New York Review of Books,* June 17, 1965 (Noel Annan). *Christian Science Monitor*, October 7, 1965 (Harold Hobson). *American Historical Review*, October, 1965 (Charles F. Mullett).

A37. *Shakespeare's Southampton: Patron of Virginia* (1965)
First edition. London: Macmillan, 1965 (5,000 copies ordered June 10, 1965). 45s. ISBN: 333 09849 8. xii pp + 324 pp, demy 8vo. 16 plates.

First American edition. New York: Harper & Row, January 25, 1966 (1965 in book). US$6.95. xii pp + 324 pp, 25 cm.

Reviews. *Tablet*, October 9, 1965 (Patrick McGrath). *The Times*, October 14, 1965 (Anon.). *Economist*, October 16, 1965 (Anon.). *Observer*, October 17, 1965 (Ivor Brown). *Sunday Telegraph*, October 17, 1965 (John Hale). *Spectator*, October 22, 1965 (Martin Seymour-Smith). *Sunday Times*, October 24, 1965 (John Russell Brown). *Punch*, November 3, 1965 (John Raymond). *New Statesman and Nation*, December 3, 1965 (K. G. Davies). *Contemporary Review,* December 1965 (William Kean Seymour). *Library Journal* (USA), January 1, 1966 (P. W. Filby). *Times Literary Supplement*, January 20, 1966 (Anon.). *Best Sell,* February 1, 1966 (J. J. Murray). *New York Times*, March 6, 1966 (Bernard Grebanier). *Book Week*, March 27, 1966 (G. B. Harrison). *Choice,* May 1966 (Anon.). *American Historical Review*, July 1966 (Theodore K. Rabb). *Virginia Magazine of History and Biography,* July 1966 (P. L. Barbour). *English Historical Review,* April 1967 (Penry Williams).

A38. *Bosworth Field: And the Wars of the Roses* (1966)
First edition. London: Macmillan, November 1966 (6,000 copies ordered July 28, 1966). 45s. ISBN: 333 00345 4. xiv pp + 317 pp, 8vo. 16 plates. Genealogical chart Houses of Lancaster and York. 2 maps.

Further printings. London: History Book Club, 1967 (3,500 copies ordered from Macmillan, July 28, 1966). London: Panther Books, October 1968. London: Granada Publishing, Panther Books, 1971. Ware, Hertfordshire: Wordsworth Editions, 1998. Paperback.

First American edition. *Bosworth Field: From Medieval to Tudor England.* The Crossroads of World History Series. Garden City, N.Y.: Doubleday, May 6, 1966. US$5.95. ISBN: 66 14930. 317 pp, 24 cm.

Reviews. *Library Journal* (USA), May 1, 1966 (R. R. Rea). *New York Times*, May 2, 1966 (Eliot Fremont-Smith). *New Yorker*, May 28, 1966 (Anon.). *Christian Science Monitor*, June 26, 1966 (Eric Forbes-Boyd). *New York Times*, September 18, 1966 (Charles W. Ferguson). *Choice* (USA), September 1966 (Anon.). *Observer*, November 27, 1966 (J. P. Kenyon). *Sunday Telegraph*, November 27, 1966 (Rivers Scott). *Sunday Times*, November 27, 1966 (Paul Murray Kendall). *Kenyon Review* (USA), November 1966 (Russell Fraser).

Tablet, December 10, 1966 (T. Charles-Edwards). *Times Literary Supplement*, December 22, 1966 (Anon.). *Economist*, December 31, 1966 (Anon.). *History Today*, February 1967 (Alan Rogers). *Spectator*, March 3, 1967 (David Knowles). *New Statesman*, August 4, 1967 (K. G. Davies). *Northern History* (UK) 3, 1968 (N. Pronay). *History* 54, 1969 (C. D. Ross).

A39. *Poems of Cornwall and America* (1967)
First edition. London: Faber & Faber, April 6, 1967. (1,000 copies) 21s 0d. 70 pp, demy 8vo.

Contents. 39 poems; author's fifth volume of poetry: I. largely American (26); II. largely Cornish (13).

Reviews. *Times Literary Supplement*, June 22, 1967 (Anon.). *Spectator*, July 28, 1967 (C. B. Cox). *Poetry Review* (UK), Autumn 1967 (G. Nevin). *Contemporary Review*, November 1967 (William Kean Seymour). *English* (UK), Spring 1968 (Howard Sergeant). *English Studies* (The Netherlands), June 1968 (Michael Thorpe).

A40. *Cornish Stories* (1967)
First edition. London: Macmillan, April 1967 (3,000 copies ordered October 20, 1966). 25s 0d. ISBN: 333 05221 8. viii pp + 152 pp, crown 8vo.

Contents. 12 stories. The first three stories were published in *West-Country Stories*, 1945. How Dick Stephens Fought the Bear; The Wicked Vicar of Lansillian; All Souls' Night; Death of a Principal; Trespettigue's Vote; The Curse upon the Clavertons; The Advowson of Lambethow; The Squire of Reluggas; The Recluse of Rescorla; The Choirmaster of Carluddon; The School-Mistress of Tregwedna; Tredynham's Folly.

Further printings. London: Macmillan, 1968, reprinted (1,000 copies).

Note. A. L. Rowse to Richard Church in a letter from All Souls College, Oxford, dated June 2, 1967: "*Cornish Stories* . . . has sold nearly 3,000 in a month *without* a review!"

Reviews. *Times Literary Supplement*, July 20, 1967 (Anon.). *The Times*, September 7, 1967 (Anon.). *Cornish Review*, Spring 1967 (Frank Baker)

A41. *A Cornish Anthology* (1968)
First edition. London: Macmillan, November 1968 (4,000 copies ordered August 1, 1968). 45s 0d. ISBN: 333 01502 9. 300 pp, demy 8vo.

Contents. 239 selections over 11 chapters, including Thomas Hardy, R. L. Stevenson, Shakespeare, Southey, D. H. Lawrence, Matthew Arnold, John Betjeman, and A. L. Rowse. Edited and compiled by A. L. Rowse. I. Prologue; II. Places; III. People; IV. History and Events; V. Travellers and Travelling; VI. Occupations and Callings; VII. Folklore, Charms, and Inscriptions; VIII. Birds, Beasts, Flowers, and Gardens; IX. Customs and Beliefs; X. Victoriana; XI. Epilogue.

Further printings. Penzance, Cornwall: Alison Hodge, April 1982. Paperback. Penzance, Cornwall: Alison Hodge, October 1990. Paperback.

Reviews. *Sunday Telegraph*, November 17, 1968 (Derek Sumpter). *The Times*, November 30, 1968 (Ray Gosling). *Times Literary Supplement*, February 13, 1969 (Anon.).

A42. *The Cornish in America* (1969)
First edition. London: Macmillan, June 1969 (2,000 copies ordered March 19, 1969). 70s 0d. xi pp + 451 pp, 8vo.

Contents. Includes appendix of Cornish surnames.

Further printings. Redruth, Cornwall: Dyllansow Truran, June 1991.

First American edition. *The Cousin Jacks: The Cornish in America.* New York: Scribner's, March 17, 1969. US$8.95. ISBN: 68, 57082. 451 pp, 22 cm.

Reviews. *Publishers Weekly* (USA), January 27, 1969 (Anon.). *Library Journal*, April 1, 1969 (Jack Goodwin). *Wall Street Journal*, April 15, 1969 (Anon.). *Times Literary Supplement*, July 10, 1969 (Anon.). *Cornish Review,* Winter 1969 (E. W. Martin). *American Historical Review*, December 1969 (Wilbur S. Shepperson). *Choice* (USA), December 1969 (Anon.). *Journal of American History,* December 1969 (Francis P. Weisenburger). *History Today,* February 1970 (F. L. Harris). *Pacific Northwest Quarterly,* April 1970 (Herman J. Deutsch). *American Quarterly,* Summer 1970 (John J. Appel). *Historian* (USA), August 1970 (Norman O. Forness). *Pacific Historical Review,* November 1970 (William S. Greever). *Wisconsin Magazine of History,* Winter 1970–1971 (James E. Wright). *International Migration Review* (USA), Fall 1971 (Robert D. Cross). *English Historical Review,* October 1971 (P. A. M. Taylor).

A43. *The Contribution of Cornwall and Cornishmen to Britain* (1969)
First edition. Newton Abbot/Bristol: Seale-Hayne Agricultural College/South Western Electricity Board, 1969. 12 pp, 22 cm.

Contents. The George Johnstone Lecture for 1969.

Note. Reprinted in *The Little Land of Cornwall* (1986).

A44. *The Elizabethan Renaissance: The Life of the Society* (1971)
First edition. London: Macmillan, October 14, 1971 (10,000 copies). £3.50. ISBN: 333 12534 7. x pp + 294 pp, demy 8vo, 8 plates (16 illustrations).

Contents. Volume 3, book 1 of trilogy on the Elizabethan age.

Further printings. History Book Club, 1971 (2,000 copies). London: Sphere Books, Cardinal Paperback, August 1974.

First American edition. New York: Scribner's, April 28, 1972. US$12.50. ISBN: 0 684 12682 6. xiv pp + 336 pp, 24 cm. Illustrations.

Further printings. Scribner Library, 1973. Paperback. US$4.95.

Reviews. *The Times*, October 14, 1971 (Joel Hurstfield). *New Statesman and Nation*, October 15, 1971 (Paul Johnson). *Economist*, October 16, 1971 (Anon.). *Observer*, October 17, 1971 (Anon.). *Sunday Telegraph*, October 17, 1971 (Nigel Dennis). *Tablet*, October 23, 1971 (Patrick McGrath). *Times Literary Supplement*, October 29, 1971 (Anon.). *Spectator*, November 6, 1971 (G. R. Elton). *Listener*, December 16, 1971 (K. H. D. Haley). *History Today,* December 1971 (Alan Haynes). *Books and Bookmen,* January 1972 (Cecil Roberts). *Library Journal,* February 15, 1972 (John Burmaster). *Publishers Weekly,* March 6, 1972 (Anon.). *Wall Street Journal,* May 8, 1972 (Edmund Fuller). *Book World,* May 21, 1972 (John Kenyon). *New Yorker,* May 27, 1972 (Anon.). *America,* June 24, 1972 (Albert J. Loomie). *Choice* (USA), September 1972 (Anon.). *Historian* (USA), November 1972 (John R. Rilling). *Economic History Review* (UK) 4, 1972 (Robert Ashton). *American Historical Review,* February 1973 (Maurice Lee, Jr.). *History* 58, 1973 (Glanmor Williams). *Publishers Weekly,* January 28, 1974 (Anon.).

A45. *The Elizabethan Renaissance: The Cultural Achievement* (1972)
First edition. London: Macmillan, September 1972 (8,000 copies). £3.95. ISBN: 333 13788 4. x pp + 386 pp, 16 plates (27 illustrations).

Contents. Volume 3, book 2 of trilogy on the Elizabethan age.

Further printings. History Book Club, 1972 (6,000 copies). London: Sphere Books, Cardinal Paperback, December 1974.

First American edition. New York: Scribner's, December 1, 1972. US$12.50. ISBN: 0 684 12965 5. 412 pp.

Reviews. *New Statesman and Nation,* September 8, 1972 (Jonathan Keates). *Economist,* September 9, 1972 (Anon.). *Observer,* September 24, 1972 (John Kenyon). *The Times,* September 28, 1972 (Anon.). *Spectator,* October 21, 1972 (John Buxton). *Publishers Weekly,* October 30, 1972 (Anon.). *Books and Bookmen,* November 1972 (Francis Sheppard). *Times Literary Supplement,* December 1, 1972 (Anon.). *Library Journal,* December 15, 1972 (William H. Magee). *New York Times,* December 15, 1972 (Thomas Lask). *Wall Street Journal,* December 19, 1972 (Edmund Fuller). *New Yorker,* December 23, 1972 (Anon.). *Nation* (USA), January 15, 1973 (Seymour Kleinberg). *Commonweal* (USA), April 27, 1973 (Mark Taylor). *Choice* (USA), April 1973 (Anon.). *American Historical Review,* June 1973 (W. Gordon Zeeveld). *Virginia Quarterly Review,* Winter 1973 (Anon.). *History* 60, 1975 (Lindsay Boynton).

A46. *Strange Encounter* (1972)
First edition. London: Jonathan Cape, June 15, 1972 (1,500 copies ordered in February 1972). £1.25. ISBN: 0 224 00699 1. 54 pp, demy 8vo.

Contents. 32 poems. Sixth volume of poetry.

Reviews. *Spectator,* July 22, 1972 (Christopher Hudson).

A47. *Westminster Abbey* (1972)
First edition. London: Annenberg School Press/Weidenfeld & Nicolson, 1972. (10,000 copies approx.). £10. ISBN: 0 297 99535 9. 264 pp, folio. Numerous color and b/w plates, illustrations, and charts. Printed in Italy by Amilcare Pizzi. The main body of text is a historical perspective of the abbey by A. L. Rowse.

Contents. Page 5, dedication by Ambassador Walter Annenberg; p 13, foreword by Dean Eric Abbott; pp 15–35, prologue by John Betjeman; pp 37–145, "The Abbey in the History of the Nation," by A. L. Rowse; pp 147–195, "The

Art and Architecture," by George Zarnecki; pp 197–254, "The Tombs and Monuments," by John Pope-Hennessy; pp 255–258, epilogue by Kenneth Clark.

Benefactor. Walter H. Annenberg, U.S. ambassador to the Court of St. James. Further printings. Radnor, Pa: Annenberg School Press; New York: Doubleday. Second impression. 6,000 or 8,000 copies. US$35.

Note. Walter H. Annenberg in a letter to Sydney Cauveren, dated October 9, 1996: "There were approximately 10,000 copies printed initially, and there was a second printing of 6,000 or 8,000. The connection of Weidenfeld & Nicolson was indeed helpful in the publication of the book . . . they were of important assistance."

Reviews. *The Times*, November 30, 1972 (Anon.). *Economist*, January 6, 1973 (Anon.). *Guardian Weekly,* January 6, 1973 (David Piper). *Books and Bookmen*, February 1973 (Francis Sheppard). *New Republic* (USA), November 17, 1973 (Doris Grumbach).

A48. *The Tower of London: In the History of the Nation* (1972)

First edition. London: Weidenfeld & Nicolson, August 31, 1972. £3.25. ISBN: 0 297 99540 6. 280 pp, royal 8vo. Illustrations.

Further printings. Cardinal paperback, April 1974.

First American edition. *The Tower of London in the History of England.* New York: Putnam, 1972. US$12.95. ISBN: 0 399 11040 2. 280 pp, 26 cm. Illustrations.

Reviews. *The Times*, August 31, 1972 (Anon.). *Best Sell,* November 15, 1972 (W. B. Hill). *Library Journal*, November 15, 1972 (R. C. Hoffmann). *Books and Bookmen*, November 1972 (Francis Sheppard). *Times Literary Supplement*, December 1, 1972 (Anon.). *Choice* (USA), April 1973 (Anon.)

A49. *Shakespeare the Man* (1973)

First edition. London: Macmillan, April 1973 (4,000 copies). £4.95. ISBN: 333 14494 5. xi pp + 284 pp, 8vo. 16 plates (24 illustrations).

Further printings. London: Literary Guild/Book Club Associates, 1973 (4,000 copies). London: Macmillan, reprinted with alterations 1973 (1,500 copies). Frogmore, St. Albans: Paladin, September 1976. Paperback. London: Macmillan. Revised edition, January 1988 (1,500 copies).

First American edition. New York: Harper & Row, July 25, 1973. US$10. ISBN: 0 06 013691 X. 284 pp, 22 cm. Illustrations.

Further printings. New York: St. Martin's Press. Revised edition, 1989.

Reviews. *Sunday Times*, February 4, 1973 (Hugh Trevor-Roper). *Publishers Weekly*, April 23, 1973 (Anon.). *The Times*, April 26, 1973 (Michael Ratcliffe). *New Statesman and Nation*, April 27, 1973 (Paul Johnson). *Times Literary Supplement*, April 27, 1973 (Anon.). *Spectator*, April 28, 1973 (John Bowle). *Observer*, April 29, 1973 (Bernard Levin). *Sunday Times*, April 29, 1973 (John Raymond). *Listener*, May 3, 1973 (John Carey). *Economist*, May 5, 1973 (Anon.). *Library Journal*, May 15, 1973 (William H. Magee). *Books and Bookmen,* May 1973 (John Bayley). *Times Educational Supplement*, June

15, 1973 (J. H. P. Pafford). *Drama: The Quarterly Theatre Review* (UK), Summer 1973 (Ivor Brown). *History Today,* July 1973 (Alan Haynes). *New York Times*, August 3, 1973 (Anatole Broyard). *Christian Science Monitor*, August 15, 1973 (W. N. Knight). *Wall Street Journal*, August 21, 1973 (Edmund Fuller). *Atlantic Monthly,* August 1973 (Phoebe Adams). *Contemporary Review,* August 1973 (William Kean Seymour). *English* (UK), Autumn 1973 (Michael Hattaway). *New York Times*, September 23, 1973 (David L. Stevenson). *Critic* (USA), September-October 1973 (Bernard Levin). *Esquire,* November 1973 (Anon.). *Dalhousie Review* (Canada), Winter 1973–1974 (A. R. Young). *Choice* (USA), January 1974 (Anon.). *New Yorker*, March 18, 1974 (George Steiner). *Southern Humanities Review* (USA), Fall 1974 (L. M. Robbins). *Encounter,* April 1989 (Eric Sams).

A50. *Windsor Castle: In the History of the Nation* (1974)

First edition. London: Weidenfeld & Nicolson, February 1974. £3.95. ISBN: 0 297 76712 7. 254 pp, royal 8vo. Illustrations.

Further printings. London: Book Club Associates, 1974.

First American edition. *Windsor Castle in the History of England.* New York: Putnam, 1974. US$14.95. ISBN: 0 399 11352 5. 254 pp, 26 cm. Illustrations.

Reviews. *Sunday Telegraph*, March 3, 1974 (Patrick Morrah). *Sunday Times*, March 10, 1974 (Anon.). *Spectator*, March 23, 1974 (Elizabeth Jenkins). *Times Literary Supplement*, April 12, 1974 (Anon.). *Times Educational Supplement*, April 19, 1974 (P. E. Clarke). *History Today,* April 1974 (Alan Haynes). *Publishers Weekly*, May 13, 1974 (Anon.). *Books and Bookmen,* May 1974 (Robert Beddard). *Library Journal*, July 1974 (S. R. Herstein).

A51. *Simon Forman: Sex and Society in Shakespeare's Age* (1974)

First edition. London: Weidenfeld & Nicolson, April 4, 1974. £4.50. ISBN: 0 297 76741 0. xiii pp + 315 pp, 23 cm. Plates, maps.

Contents. Drawn from the Elizabethan doctor and astrologer's voluminous papers and case books at the Bodleian Library in Oxford.

Further printings. London: Picador/Pan Books. Paperback 1976: *The Case Books of Simon Forman: Sex and Society in Shakespeare's Age.*

First American edition. *Sex and Society in Shakespeare's Age: Simon Forman the Astrologer.* New York: Scribner's, 1975. US$9.95. ISBN: 0 684 14051 9. xiii pp + 315 pp. 23 cm. Plates, maps.

Further printings. New York: Scribner's, 1976. US$12.50.

Reviews. *The Times*, April 4, 1974 (Derek Parker). *Observer*, April 7, 1974 (John Kenyon). *Sunday Telegraph*, April 7, 1974 (Anthony Quinton). *Sunday Times*, April 7, 1974 (Anthony Storr). *Punch*, April 10, 1974 (Mary Edmond). *New Statesman and Nation*, April 12, 1974 (Paul Johnson). *Spectator*, April 13, 1974 (Richard Luckett). *Manchester Guardian Weekly*, April 20, 1974 (Anon.). *Times Literary Supplement*, June 7, 1974 (Anon.). *History Today,* June 1974 (Alan Haynes). *Sunday Times*, July 21, 1974 (Anon.). *Encounter,* July 1974

(Philip Brockbank). *Times Educational Supplement*, August 16, 1974 (J. H. P. Pafford). *Sunday Times*, December 1, 1974 (Anon.). *Publishers Weekly*, December 9, 1974 (Anon.). *New Humanist*, circa 1974 (Roger Manvell). *Library Journal*, February 1, 1975 (Dorothy E. Litt). *New Republic* (USA), February 22, 1975 (O. B. Hardison). *Review of English Studies*, November 1975 (Joan Rees). *Time*, January 19, 1976 (Paul Gray). *New Yorker*, February 16, 1976 (Anon.). *New York Times*, February 21, 1976 (Thomas Lask). *Virginia Quarterly Review,* Spring 1976 (Anon.). *The Times*, September 4, 1976 (Peggy Miller). *Choice,* November 1976 (Anon.). *Books and Bookmen*, November 1977 (Roger Prior). *Notes and Queries,* October 1978 (R. E. Alton).

A52. *Peter: The White Cat of Trenarren* (1974)

First edition. London: Michael Joseph, April 1974. £2.25. ISBN: 0 7181 1228 8. 103 pp, 23 cm. Plates.

Contents. The first of A. L. Rowse's cats to be put under the loving microscope of the author, who considers cats "perfect writer's animals."

Further printings. London: Weidenfeld & Nicolson, March 8, 1979, 115 pp, as *Three Cornish Cats:* part 1—Peter, the White Cat of Trenarren; part 2—Chalky Jenkins, a Little Cat Lost; part 3—Tommer, the Black Farm Cat. As *A Quartet of Cornish Cats,* April 1986, 132 pp, adding part 4—Flip, My Last Cat. Redruth, Cornwall: Dyllansow Truran, August 1992, 132 pp, as *A Quartet of Cornish Cats.*

Reviews. *Sunday Times*, April 7, 1974 (Sue Read). *Observer*, April 28, 1974 (Anon.). *New Statesman and Nation*, May 3, 1974 (Arthur Marshall). *The Times*, May 9, 1974 (Anon.). *Sunday Telegraph*, May 19, 1974 (Neville Braybrooke). *Books and Bookmen,* July 1974 (Beverley Nichols). *New Statesman and Nation*, March 23, 1979 (Arthur Marshall). *Sunday Telegraph*, April 1, 1979 (H.L.). *Observer*, May 25, 1986 (Chaim Bermant). *Country Life,* June 12, 1986 (Marghanita Laski).

A53. *Victorian and Edwardian Cornwall: From Old Photographs* (with John Betjeman) (1974)

First edition. London: Batsford, July 1974. £3. ISBN: 0 7134 3167 9. 116 pp, 4to. 160 b&w illustrations.

Contents. Introduction and commentaries by A. L. Rowse. Acknowledgments vi; introduction vii–x; 1. The North Coast Illustrated, pp. 6–15; 2. The South Coast Illustrated, pp 16–35; 3. Fishing, Wrecks, and Lifeboats, pp 36–52; 4. Inland, pp 53–68; 5. Farming and Mining, pp 69–86; 6. Occupations and Livelihoods, pp 87–99; 7. Schools, Recreations, Law, and Order, pp 100–118; 8. Railways and Royal Visits, pp 119–129; 9. Characters and Entertainments, pp. 130–149; 10. The Scilly Isles, pp. 150–160.

Further printings. Second Impression 1976. £3.50. Third Impression 1977. Paperback. £2. Reprint, Fitzhouse Books, 1990. £10.99.

Reviews. *The Times*, July 25, 1974 (Ion Trewin). *Sunday Times*, August 4, 1974. Photo and caption. (Anon.)

A54. *Discoveries and Reviews: From Renaissance to Restoration* **(1975)**
First edition. London: Macmillan, June 19, 1975. (2,000 copies + 1,000 Barnes
& Noble imprints). £6.95. ISBN: 333 18392 4. xi pp. + 283 pp, demy 8vo.

Contents. A collection of 55 essays, addresses, and reviews, largely 16th and
17th centuries. Discoveries, Simon Forman and the Dark Lady. I. The Recep-
tion of My *William Shakespeare*; Popular Misconceptions about William
Shakespeare; Southampton's Quatercentenary: What Shakespeare Owed to
Him; Mr. W. H. and Who He Was; Shakespeare's Landlady in Silver Street;
Shakespeare, Bacon, Marlowe, Oxford, and Sex; The True Story of Mary Fitton;
Shakespeare at Work; The Shakespeare Industry; The Shakespeare Trade Union;
Shakespeare Trade Unionists and Others; A Master on Marlowe. II. The Popu-
larity of History; McFarlane on the Fifteenth Century; Private Lives of Tudor
Monarchs; Henry VIII; Cardinal Wolsey; Thomas Cromwell As Reformer;
Utopia versus Realism; Erasmus—Great European; The Reformation Parlia-
ment; Tudor Politics; The Court of Henry VIII; Anne Boleyn; Katherine Parr,
an Amateur View; Doctrinaire Academics; Elizabethiana; John Stow As an
Historian; Fulke Greville; Ralegh As Writer; Computer's History; Thomas
Hariot: Elizabethan Scientist; Elizabethan Magus: John Dee; Elizabethan Song-
Writer: John Dowland; Mediterranean Epic. III. The Iron Century; The Prot-
estant Mind; Two Caroline Officials; Durham in Transition; What Did the Civil
War Settle?; Civil War Facts and Fantasies; Civil War Cheshire; Somerset Con-
flict; Levellers' Nonsense; The Fifth Monarchy Men; Oliver Cromwell; The
Rump; Puritan Administrators; Wenceslas Hollar in Perspective; Country Life
in Restoration Northamptonshire; Pepys in History; Pepys and His Oxford
Friends; Langbaine and the English Dramatists.

First American edition. New York: Barnes & Noble Books, 1975. (1,000 copies) US$20. ISBN: 0 06 496009 9. xi pp. + 283 pp. 23 cm.

Reviews. *Sunday Times*, June 15, 1975 (Anon.). *Contemporary Review*, Au-
gust 1975 (R. C. Churchill). *Tablet*, August 30, 1975 (Roger Sharrock). *Choice*
(USA), October 1975 (Anon.). *Booklist*, November 1, 1975 (Anon.). *Books and
Bookmen*, November 1975 (Roger Prior). *Modern Language Review*, June-
December 1975 (E. D. Pendry). *Scotsman*, June-December 1975 (Harry Reid).
Shakespeare Studies 11, 1978 (Alice-Lyle Scoufos)

A55. *Oxford in the History of the Nation* **(1975)**
First edition. London: Weidenfeld & Nicolson, June 1975. £4.50. ISBN: 0 297
76939 1. 256 pp, 4to. 96 illustrations (16 in colour).

Further printings. London: Book Club Associates/Weidenfeld & Nicolson
1975. London: Weidenfeld & Nicolson, June 20, 1985. Large paperback edition.

First American edition. *Oxford in the History of England.* New York: Putnam,
1975. US$15.95. ISBN: 0 399 11570 6. 256 pp. 26 cm. Illustrations, some in
color.

Reviews. *The Times*, June 12, 1975 (January Morris). *New Statesman and Nation*, June 13, 1975 (John Carey). *Observer*, June 15, 1975 (Philip Toynbee). *Sunday Telegraph*, June 15, 1975 (Joanna Richardson). *Sunday Times*, June 15, 1975. (Anon.). *Spectator*, June 21, 1975 (Hugh Lloyd-Jones). *Economist*, July 26, 1975 (Anon.). *Times Literary Supplement*, October 17, 1975 (Roger Fulford). *Books and Bookmen*, November 1975 (John Betjeman). *New York Times*, December 7, 1975 (Charles L. Mee, Jr.). *Wall Street Journal*, December 9, 1975 (Edmund Fuller). *Christian Science Monitor*, December 10, 1975 (Robert Nye). *New Yorker*, January 12, 1976 (Anon.). *Choice*, February 1976 (Anon.). *Sunday Times*, July 4, 1976 (Harold Hobson).

A56. *Jonathan Swift: Major Prophet* (1975)
First edition. London: Thames & Hudson, November 1975 (out of print 1981). £5.95. ISBN: 0 500 01141 9. 240 pp, Med 8vo.16 plates (25 illustrations).

Contents. A biography of Swift.

First American edition. New York: Scribner's, April 30, 1976 (1975 in book). US$8.95. ISBN: 0 684 14561 8. 240 pp. 24 cm. Illustrations.

Further printings. New York: Scribner's, 1976. US$10.

Reviews. *Daily Telegraph*, November 6, 1975 (Margaret Lane). *Observer*, November 9, 1975 (John Kenyon). *The Times*, November 13, 1975 (Kay Dick). *New Statesman and Nation*, November 14, 1975 (Matthew Hodgart). *Spectator*, November 15, 1975 (Pat Rogers). *Manchester Guardian Weekly*, November 23, 1975 (Anon.). *Sunday Times*, November 23, 1975 (Michael Gearin-Tosh). *Sunday Telegraph*, November 30, 1975 (Stephen Vizinczey). *Books and Bookmen*, January 1976 (Joanna Richardson). *History Today*, February 1976 (Joanna Richardson). *Publishers Weekly*, March 8, 1976 (Anon.). *Times Literary Supplement*, March 12, 1976 (Clive Probyn). *Library Journal* (USA), March 15, 1976 (Arthur E. Jones, Jr.). *Saturday Review of Literature*, May 1, 1976 (Russell Fraser). *Wall Street Journal*, May 14, 1976 (Edmund Fuller). *Atlantic Monthly*, May 1976 (Phoebe-Lou Adams, initialed "PLA"). *Christian Science Monitor*, June 21, 1976 (Eve Ottenberg). *New York Review of Books*, June 24, 1976 (Irvin Ehrenpreis). *New Yorker*, August 2, 1976 (V. S. Pritchett). *Choice*, October 1976 (Anon.). *Thought*, December 1976 (William R. Siebenschuh). *Philological Quarterly*, Fall 1976 (William Kupersmith). *Scriblerian* (USA), Fall 1976 (Leland D. Peterson). *Journalism Quarterly* (USA), Autumn 1976 (William White). *AUMLA* (Journal of the Australasian Universities Language and Literature Association), November 1976 (I. H. Legg). *Critic* (USA), Winter 1976 (John Deedy). *Arbor* (Spain), March 1977 (Pilar Hidalgo). *Sewanee Review*, April 1977 (A. Norman Jeffares). *Modern Language Review* (UK), October 1977 (Jenny Mezciems).

Note. The review by V. A. Pritchett in the *New Yorker* was also published as an essay, "Jonathan Swift: The Infantilism of Genius," in *The Tale Bearers: Essays on English, American, and Other Writers*, by V. S. Pritchett (1980).

A57. *Robert Stephen Hawker of Morwenstow: A Belated Medieval* (1975)
First edition. St. Germans, Cornwall: Elephant Press, 1975. £1.20. ISBN: 0 904
931021. 33 pp, 24 cm. Illustrations.
　　Contents. Essay. (Republished in *The Little Land of Cornwall,* 1986.)
　　Reviews. *The Times,* November 6, 1975 (Anon.).

A58. A *Cornishman Abroad* (1976)
First edition. London: Jonathan Cape, March 25, 1976 (4,000 copies ordered
November 1975). £5.95. ISBN: 0 224 01244 4. 318 pp, demy 8vo.
　　Contents. Third volume of autobiography.
　　Reviews. *Listener,* March 25, 1976 (Patricia Beer). *Economist,* March 27,
1976 (Anon.). *Spectator,* March 27, 1976 (Beverley Nichols). *Observer,* March
28, 1976 (Philip Toynbee). *Sunday Telegraph,* March 28, 1976 (John Lehmann).
Sunday Times, March 28, 1976 (J. W. Lambert). *Daily Telegraph,* April 1, 1976
(David Holloway). *The Times,* April 1, 1976 (Derek Parker). *Tablet,* April 10,
1976 (Douglas Woodruff). *Books and Bookmen,* June 1976 (Christopher Sykes).
Contemporary Review, June 1976 (Anon.). *London Magazine,* December 1976–
January 1977 (Patric Dickinson).

A59. *Brown Buck: A Californian Fantasy* (1976)
First edition. London: Michael Joseph, June 1976. £3.40. ISBN: 0 7181 1456
6. 72 pp, 23 cm. Illustrations.
　　Contents. A story of many different animals observed in the Huntington Li-
brary and Garden in California. Drawings by John Ward, R.A.
　　Reviews. *Times Educational Supplement,* September 10, 1976 (Edward
Blishen). *Books and Bookmen,* October 1976 (Charity Blackstock). *Junior
Bookshelf* (UK), December 1976 (Anon.).

A60. *Matthew Arnold: Poet and Prophet* (1976)
First edition. London: Thames & Hudson, September 1976 (out of print, 1981).
£6.50. ISBN: 0 500 01163 X. 208 pp, med. 8vo. 16 plates (24 illustrations).
　　Contents. Biography of Matthew Arnold.
　　First American edition. Lanham, Maryland: University Press of America, Au-
gust 1986. US$18.75. ISBN: 0-8191-5120-3. 208 pp, 24 cm. Illustrations.
　　Reviews. *Sunday Times,* September 26, 1976 (Christopher Ricks). *Observer,*
October 3, 1976 (Bernard Bergonzi). *Sunday Telegraph,* October 3, 1976 (C.
B. Cox). *The Times,* October 7, 1976 (David Williams). *Times Literary Supple-
ment,* October 8, 1976 (Phyllis Grosskurth). *Economist,* October 9, 1976
(Anon.). *Spectator,* October 9, 1976 (Roy Fuller). *New Statesman and Nation,*
October 22, 1976 (John Carey). *Times Educational Supplement,* November 26,
1976 (David Wright). *Books and Bookmen,* November 1976 (Jack Simmons).
Arizona Quarterly, Autumn 1978 (Patrick McCarthy).

**A61. *Homosexuals in History: A Study of Ambivalence in Society,
　　　　Literature, and the Arts* (1977)**
First edition. London: Weidenfeld & Nicolson, April 21, 1977. £7.95. ISBN:
0 297 77299 6. xiii pp + 346 pp, 25 cm. 16 plates (36 illustrations).

Contents. A thought-provoking look at homosexual men of genius through the ages, and their contributions to society, politics, literature, and the arts.

First American edition. New York: Macmillan, 1977. US$12.95. ISBN: 0 02 605620 8. xiii pp + 346 pp, 25 cm. Illustrations.

Further printings. New York: Carroll & Graf, 1977, 1983. Paperback. New York: Carroll & Graf, 1997. Paperback. U.S.$14.95. New York: Dorset Press, 1977, 1983.

Reviews. *Publishers Weekly*, February 14, 1977 (Anon.). *Spectator*, April 23, 1977 (Robert Skidelski). *Observer*, April 24, 1977 (Phyllis Grosskurth). *Sunday Times*, April 24, 1977 (Anthony Storr). *Sunday Telegraph*, May 1, 1977 (Jonathan Sumption). *Times Literary Supplement*, May 13, 1977 (Arthur Calder-Marshall). *Library Journal*, May 15, 1977 (Neal R. Shipley). *Economist*, June 18, 1977 (Anon.). *The Times*, July 14, 1977 (Giuliano Dego). *The National Times* (Australia), July 25–30, 1977 (Anthony Storr). *Books and Bookmen,* July 1977 (H. Montgomery Hyde). *The Christian Century*, November 16, 1977 (William Muehl). *American Historical Review*, December 1977 (Arthur N. Gilbert). *Historian,* February 1978 (Vern L. Bullough). *Religious Humanism* (USA), Spring 1989 (Daniel Ross Chandler). *Library Journal*, October 1, 1995 (Reilly Reagan).

Note. The review by Reilly Reagan in the *Library Journal* is of the audio version: *Books on Tape,* 1995 (3738), 12 cassettes, unabridged, 18 hours. $US96.

A62. *Shakespeare the Elizabethan* (1977)

First edition. London: Weidenfeld & Nicolson, May 19, 1977. £4.95. ISBN: 0 297 77254 6. 128 pp, 4to. Plates (some in color).

Contents. Eight chapters and epilogue: 1. Stratford Beginnings; 2. Shakespeare and His Patron, Southampton; 3. The Rival Poet and the Dark Lady; 4. The Lord Chamberlain's Company; 5. Success; 6. The Fall of Essex and Southampton; 7. Jacobean Plays; 8. Last Years.

First American edition. New York: Putnam, 1977. US$14.95. ISBN: 0 399 11889 6. 128 pp, 29 cm. Illustrations.

Reviews. *Sunday Times*, May 29, 1977 (Geoffrey Grigson). *Publishers Weekly*, September 12, 1977 (Anon.). *Books and Bookmen,* September 1977 (Elizabeth Jenkins). *Library Journal*, November 15, 1977 (Emily T. Berges). *Choice,* April 1978 (Anon.).

A63. *Milton The Puritan: Portrait of a Mind* (1977)

First edition. London: Macmillan, October 13, 1977 (3,500 copies). £5.95. ISBN: 0 333 21850 7. 297 pp, demy 8vo.

Contents. Milton was above all an intellectual. This is a study of his thought and of the stand he took on the bitterly divisive issues of his time that led to civil war.

First American edition. Lanham, Maryland: University Press of America, 1985. ISBN: 0 8191 4778 8. 297 pp, 8vo. Paperback.

Reviews. *Times Educational Supplement*, October 28, 1977 (Lois Potter). *Sunday Times*, November 13, 1977 (Hugh Trevor-Roper). *History Today*, December 1977 (Alan Haynes). *Month*, February 1978 (Douglas Woodruff). *Contemporary Review*, March 1978 (R. C. Churchill). *Sewanee Review*, July 1978 (G. K. Hunter). *Christianity and Literature* (USA) 28, 1979 (Leland Ryken). *Milton Quarterly* (USA), May 1980 (Roy Flannagan).

A64. *The Tower of London* (1977)

First edition. London: Michael Joseph/Folio Miniatures, October 1977. £1.95. ISBN: 0 7181 1544 9. 32 pp, small 8vo. 16 pp color lithographic plates.

Contents. Celebrates the 900th anniversary of the foundation of the White Tower: the very heart of the Tower of London.

Reviews. *Times Literary Supplement*, October 28, 1977 (George Speaight). *Books and Bookmen*, December 1977 (Auberon Waugh).

A65. *Heritage of Britain* (1977)

First edition. London: Artus (for Marks & Spencer), 1977. 184 pp, royal 4to. Illustrations in color.

Contents. Six chapters: 1. Prehistory and Early Influences; 2. Capitals and Regional Centres; 3. City and Country Landmarks; 4. Defences and Dwellings; 5. Seats of Prayer and Learning; 6. Technology and the Arts.

Further printings. London: Weidenfeld & Nicolson, July 3, 1995. Hardback. £7.99. ISBN: 1 8987 9936 9.

Note. A. L. Rowse in a letter to Sydney Cauveren, dated March 1978: "Marks & Spencer ordered 30,000 of my 'Heritage of Britain', sold out before Xmas, & have ordered another 30,000."

First American edition. New York: Putnam, 1977. US$14.95. ISBN: 0 339 12012 2. 184 pp. 31 cm. Color illustrations.

Further printings. New York: British Heritage Press, 1983. Distributed by Crown.

Reviews. *Christian Century*, December 14, 1977 (Anon.).

A66. *The Road to Oxford* (1978)

First edition. London: Jonathan Cape, March 1978 (1,000 copies ordered November 1977). £2.95. ISBN: 0 224 01573 7. 86 pp, demy 8vo.

Contents. 47 poems, including five children's verses. Seventh volume of poetry.

Further printings. Second impression 1978 (500 copies ordered, May 1978).

Reviews. *Country Life*, April 6, 1978 (Kathleen Raine). *Books and Bookmen*, June 1978 (John Betjeman). *Sunday Telegraph*, August 20, 1978 (Shirley Toulson). *Sydney Morning Herald*, September 9, 1978 (Clement Semmler).

A67. *The Byrons and the Trevanions* (1978)

First edition. London: Weidenfeld & Nicolson, October 5, 1978. £8.50. ISBN: 0 297 77548 0. 212 pp, demy 8vo. 8 plates (16 illustrations).

Contents. Examines the succession of intermarriages and extramarital relationships between the Byron and Trevanion families.

Further printings. Devon: Reader's Union Limited, 1978. Newton Abbot: Reader's Union, 1979.

First American edition. New York: St. Martin's Press, 1979. US$11.95. ISBN: 0 312 11135 5. 212 pp, demy 8vo. 8 plates (16 illustrations).

Reviews. *The Times*, October 19, 1978 (Stewart Perowne). *Publishers Weekly*, November 20, 1978 (Anon.). *Books and Bookmen*, December 1978 (Elizabeth Longford). *Library Journal*, January 1, 1979 (Nancy C. Cridland). *New Yorker*, March 12, 1979 (Anon.). *Wall Street Journal*, May 21, 1979 (Edmund Fuller). *Atlantic Monthly*, June 1979 (Phoebe-Lou Adams). *Choice*, June 1979 (Anon.). *Virginia Quarterly Review*, Autumn 1979 (Anon.).

A68. *The Poems of Shakespeare's Dark Lady: Salve Deus Rex Judaeorum* (1978)

First edition. London: Jonathan Cape, November 16, 1978 (4,000 copies, including 1,500 for Clarkson N. Potter). £4.95. ISBN: 0 224 01631 8. xiii pp + 144 pp, 8vo. 12 plates (13 illustrations).

Contents. Preface and introduction: Shakespeare's Dark Lady, pp 1–37, by A. L. Rowse. Salve Deus Rex Judaeorum by Emilia Lanier [The Dark Lady of the Sonnets!], pp 39–144 (originally published in 1611).

First American edition. New York: Clarkson N. Potter, 1979 (1,500 + 8,500 first order increase, reprinted). Distributed by Crown Publishers. US$10. ISBN: 0 517 53745 1. xiii pp + 144 pp. 8vo. 12 plates (13 illustrations).

Reviews. *Tablet*, January 13, 1979 (Francis Berry). *New York Times*, May 20, 1979 (R. A. Sokolov). *Choice*, November 1979 (Anon.)

A69. *The Annotated Shakespeare* (1978)

First edition. London: Orbis Books, 1978. £35. ISBN: 0 85613 073 7. Boxed set. Three volumes in a slip case: 752 pp + 800 pp + 912 pp. 4to. Illustrated throughout.

Contents. An enormous work that *Time* magazine called "an extravagant three-volume work that has no precedent and is not likely to have successors." A. L. Rowse is general editor and has provided the introductions throughout. Volume 1, The Comedies. Volume 2, The Histories, Sonnets, and Other Poems. Volume 3, The Tragedies and Romances.

Further printings. Second edition, 1979.

First American edition. New York: Clarkson N. Potter, 1978 (50,000 sets). Distributed by Crown Publishers. US$60. Includes 240 copies on vellum, signed by the author. ISBN: 0 517 53509 2. Boxed set. Three volumes in a slip case: 752 pp + 800 pp + 912 pp. 4to. Illustrated throughout.

Contents. A. L. Rowse is general editor and has provided the introductions throughout. Volume 1, The Comedies. Volume 2, The Histories, Sonnets and Other Poems. Volume 3, The Tragedies and Romances.

Further printings. New York: Greenwich House, 1988 (three vols. in one), 2,461 pp.

Reviews. *Time,* November 13, 1978 (Stefan Kanfer). *Sunday Telegraph,* December 24, 1978 (Francis King). *New Republic,* January 13, 1979 (Nona Balakian). *New York Times,* February 4, 1979 (Michael Goldman). *Atlantic Monthly,* February 1979 (Phoebe-Lou Adams). *Sydney Morning Herald,* March 3, 1979 (David L. Frost). *Shakespeare Quarterly,* Winter 1979 (Jeanne Addison Roberts). *Library Journal,* April 15, 1979 (E. Pearlman).

A70. *A Man of the Thirties* (1979)
First edition. London: Weidenfeld & Nicolson, August 23, 1979. £7.95. ISBN: 0 297 77666 5. 215 pp, 8vo.

Contents. Fourth volume of autobiography.

Reviews. *Economist,* August 25, 1979 (Anon.). *Observer,* August 26, 1979 (Kathleen Nott). *Sunday Telegraph,* August 26, 1979 (Rebecca West). *Spectator,* September 8, 1979 (Stephen Koss). *London Magazine,* December 1979–January 1980 (Peter Vansittart). *Times Literary Supplement,* February 15, 1980 (Ian Ogg). *Books and Bookmen,* February 1980 (Jack Simmons).

A71. *Portraits and Views: Literary and Historical* (1979)
First edition. London: Macmillan, November 1979 (1,100 copies + 500 Barnes & Noble imprints). £15.

ISBN: 0 333 27241 2. viii pp + 246 pp, demy 8vo.

Contents. 38 essays: I. Jane Austen As Social Realist; Dr Johnson without Boswell: An American Interpretation; Welsh Orientalist: Sir William Jones; The Romantic Story of Charles Augustus Murray; Post-Kilvert: A Moral Tale; Kipling: A New Appreciation; A Great Writer? The Case of E. M. Forster; In Justice to Belloc; The Poetry of John Betjeman; Flannery O'Connor: A Genius of the South. II. Britannica or Americana?; Bibliography in Excelcis: The New STC; Attitudes to History; World Historical Events; Sociological versus Real History; Universities and Society; Classics of County History; Vanishing English Landscapes; Dark Ages. III. German Half-Cousins; Europe's History and Germany's; Bismarck's Responsibility; The Appalling Twentieth Century; The Great War in British Memory; Weimar and Wheeler-Bennett; German Responsibility for the War of 1914–1918; Revisionist History, 1914–1939; Hitler and British Politics; Götterdämmerung; Decline and Fall of the Liberal Party; A. J. P. Taylor on the Second German War; Lady Ottoline's Vanished World; Bertrand Russell; The Soul of King's; Disenchantment with Communism; R. H. Tawney's Influence; Priestley's England; Vanishing Britain.

First American edition. New York: Barnes & Noble Books, 1979 (500 copies). US$29.50. ISBN: 0 06 496018 8. viii pp + 246 pp, 23 cm.

Reviews. *Books and Bookmen,* June 1980 (Elizabeth Jenkins).

A72. *The Story of Britain* (1979)

First edition. London: ARTUS/Marks & Spencer, 1979. 185 pp, royal 4to. Richly illustrated, some color plates.

Contents. Nine chapters plus epilogue: 1. Island Peoples; 2. Growth of the Nation; 3. Reformation and Expansion; 4. Revolution and Reaction; 5. Social Stability and Progress; 6. The Age of Revolutions; 7. Recovery and Reform; 8. Imperialism and Liberalism; 9. The Two German Wars.

Further printings. London: Treasure Press/J. W. Books, NSW, Australia, 1979. AUS$19.95. London: Treasure Press, 1979, 1983. London: Tiger Books, 1993. London: ARTUS Books, 1993.

First American edition. The Illustrated History of Britain. New York: Crescent Books, 1979. ISBN: 0 517 28206 2. 185 pp, 31 cm. Illustrations, some in color.

Further printings. New York: British Heritage Press. Distributed by Crown in 1983 as *The Story of Britain*.

A73. *A Man of Singular Virtue* (1979)

First edition. London: The Folio Society, 1979 (48,000 copies). 128 pp, royal 8vo. 57 illustrations, 23 in full color.

Contents. Being a life of Sir Thomas More by his son-in-law William Roper and a selection of More's letters (originally published in Paris, 1626). Selected, edited, and introduced (pp 9–26) by A. L. Rowse. The 1980 presentation volume; dated 1980 on the title page.

A74. *Memories of Men and Women* (1980)

First edition. London: Eyre Methuen, October 1980. £8.50. ISBN: 0 413 47700 2. 258 pp, demy 8vo.

Contents. 10 biographical essays: My Acquaintance with Churchill; Nancy Astor; Agatha Christie; G. M. Trevelyan; Samuel Eliot Morison; André Maurois; Princess Marthe Bibesco; An Evening with Edmund Wilson; With Beaverbrook in Canada; The Poet Auden.

Further printings. Newton Abbot: Readers Union Group of Book Clubs, 1981. See also *Glimpses of the Great,* 1985 (82).

First American edition. *Memories of Men and Women American and British.* Lanham, Maryland: University Press of America, 1983. ISBN: 0 819 13582 8 (hard cover). US$14.50. ISBN 0 819 13583 6 (paperback). US$9.75. 258 pp, 8vo.

Note. Princess Marthe Bibesco and Lord Beaverbrook deleted. Admiral Chester Nimitz, T. S. Eliot, and Willa Cather added.

Reviews. *Observer*, October 26, 1980 (John Kenyon). *Sunday Times*, November 30, 1980 (Woodrow Wyatt). *The Times*, December 4, 1980 (Ian Bradley). *Sydney Morning Herald,* January 17, 1981 (R. T. Foster). *London Magazine,* January 1981 (Peter Vansittart). *Wall Street Journal,* May 22, 1984 (Edmund Fuller).

A75. *Shakespeare's Globe: His Intellectual and Moral Outlook* **(1981)**
First edition. London: Weidenfeld & Nicolson, March 12, 1981. £8.95. ISBN: 0 297 77897 8. ix pp + 210 pp, demy 8vo.

Contents. A portrait of Shakespeare's intellectual and moral equipment.

First American edition. *What Shakespeare Read, and Thought.* New York: Coward, McCann, and Geoghegan, 1981. US$12.95. ISBN: 0 698 11077 3. ix pp + 210 pp, 22 cm.

Reviews. *Publishers Weekly*, March 20, 1981 (Anon.). *Sunday Telegraph*, March 22, 1981 (Joanna Richardson). *New Republic*, April 11, 1981 (Ann Hulbert). *Times Literary Supplement*, April 17, 1981 (Stanley Wells). *Guardian Weekly*, May 10, 1981 (Anon.). *Library Journal*, June 1, 1981 (J. H. Crouch). *Christian Science Monitor*, July 15, 1981 (Gary Houston). *Choice*, July-August 1981 (Anon.). *New Yorker*, October 5, 1981 (Anon.). *New York Review of Books*, October 22, 1981 (R. M. Adams). *Études Anglaises* (France), October-December 1982 (Fernand Lagarde).

A76. *A Life: Collected Poems* **(1981)**
First edition. Edinburgh: William Blackwood, May 1981. £9.95.

ISBN: 0 85158 141 2. xvi pp + 413 pp, demy 8vo.

Contents. A. L. Rowse's inner life lay in his poetry, here covering his whole life and spanning his interests: early days, Oxford, wartime, America, and, importantly, Cornwall. In nine sections: I. Earlier Poems; II. The Thirties; III. Poems of Wartime; IV. Poems of War and Peace; V. American Poems; VI. Poems Mainly Cornish; VII. New Poems; VIII. [Untitled]; IX. Children's Verses.

Reviews. *Guardian Weekly*, December 27, 1981 (Anon.). *Times Literary Supplement*, January 8, 1982 (Anne Stevenson). *Spectator*, March 6, 1982 (Kathleen Raine). *London Magazine*, June 1986 (Robin D'Arcy). *Cornish Scene*, Autumn 1988 (Gordon Hunt).

A77. *Eminent Elizabethans* **(1983)**
First edition. London: Macmillan, March 1983 (850 copies + 2,550 University of Georgia imprints). £15. ISBN: 0 333 34515 0. x pp + 199 pp, demy 8vo. 8 plates (10 illustrations).

Contents. A Quintet of Elizabethans, eminent in their day and equally characteristic of their time: 1. Bess of Hardwick: Builder and Dynast; 2. Father Parsons, the Jesuit; 3. Edward de Vere, 17th Earl of Oxford; 4. Elizabeth I's Godson: Sir John Harington; 5. Lord Chamberlain Hunsdon.

Further printings. London: Macmillan, 1983 (500 copies + 4,500 University of Georgia imprints).

First American edition. Athens: University of Georgia Press, 1983 (2,550 copies). US$19. ISBN: 0 8 203 0649 5.

Further printings. Athens: University of Georgia Press, 1983 (4,500 copies).

Reviews. *Library Journal*, March 15, 1983 (James A. Casada). *Times Literary Supplement*, May 13, 1983 (Patrick Collinson). *Observer*, May 15, 1983

(John Kenyon). *Financial Times,* May 28, 1983 (Rosalie Mander). *Guardian Weekly,* May 29, 1983 (Anon.). *Sunday Telegraph,* May 29, 1983 (Joanna Richardson). *Choice,* September 1983 (Anon.). *Wall Street Journal,* October 10, 1983 (Edmund Fuller). *Shakespeare Quarterly,* Winter 1984 (R. J. Schoeck). *American Historical Review,* April 1984 (John R. Rilling). *Sixteenth Century Journal* (USA), Summer 1984 (D. Boyd-Rush). *Historian,* February 1986 (Robert Tittler).

A78. *Night at the Carn and Other Stories* (1984)

First edition. London: William Kimber, October 1984. £7.50. ISBN: 0 7183 0511 6. 190 pp, demy 8vo.

Contents. 22 short stories: 1. The Priest and the Pueblo; 2. Under the Toyon Berries; 3. The Persecuted Cleric; 4. Naboth's Vineyard; 5. The Pinetum; 6. After Sixty Years; 7. His Reverence; 8. The Room above the Cloisters; 9. The Paragon; 10. The Conceited Scholar; 11. Mad Miss Moll; 12. St. Carroc's Crucifix; 13. Night at the Carn; 14. The Beneficent Shoes; 15. The End of the Line; 16. The Red Bicycle; 17. The Lunatic of Landegey; 18. The Dream House; 19. The Wax Doll; 20. A Holiday by the Sea; 21. The Wise Old Serpent of King's Wood; 22. Sailor's Orchard.

A79. *Shakespeare's Characters: A Complete Guide* (1984)

First edition. London: Methuen, October 1984. £8.50. ISBN: 0 413 56710 9. viii pp + 165 pp, demy 8vo.

Contents. An A to Z that includes all of Shakespeare's characters. A convenient who's who.

Reviews. *Times Educational Supplement,* October 19, 1984 (David Self). *Times Literary Supplement,* January 11, 1985 (Terence Hawkes). *Books and Bookmen,* January 1985 (Richard Ormrod).

A80. *Prefaces to Shakespeare's Plays* (1984)

First edition. London: Orbis, November 1984. £10. ISBN: 0 85613 653 0. 256 pp, large 8vo.

Contents. Brings together all introductions to each of Shakespeare's plays, which originally appeared in *The Annotated Shakespeare,* edited by A. L. Rowse for Orbis in 1978. (See A69.)

Reviews. *Times Literary Supplement,* August 16, 1985 (Gary Taylor).

A81. *The Contemporary Shakespeare* (1984)

First edition (American). Lanham, Maryland: University Press of America, April 23, 1984. US$24.95. ISBN: 0 8191 3908 4. Hardcover edition of first volume (of 7) containing six plays.

Contents. The entire project was edited by A. L. Rowse, modern text with introduction.

Volume 1: Hamlet, The Tempest, A Midsummer Night's Dream, The Merchant of Venice, Julius Caesar, Romeo and Juliet.

Further printings. The above plays in the first volume were simultaneously published individually in paperback at US$2.95 each.

Volume 2: King Lear, Twelfth Night, King Richard II, As You Like It, Coriolanus. ISBN: 0 8191 3916 5. November 1984.

Volume 3: Macbeth, All's Well That Ends Well, Henry V, King Richard III, The Taming of the Shrew. ISBN: 0 8191 3922 X. May 1985.

Volume 4: King Henry IV, Part 1, King Henry IV, Part 2, Love's Labour's Lost, Othello, The Winter's Tale. ISBN: 0 8191 3928 9. December 1985.

Volume 5: Antony and Cleopatra, Measure for Measure, The Merry Wives of Windsor, Troilus and Cressida, The Two Gentlemen of Verona. ISBN: 0 8191 3934 3. October 1986.

Volume 6: The Comedy of Errors, Cymbeline, King Henry VIII, Much Ado about Nothing, Timon of Athens. ISBN: 0 8191 3940 8. February 1987.

Volume 7: King Henry VI, Part 1, King Henry VI, Part 3, King Henry VI, Part 2, King John, Pericles, Titus Andronicus. ISBN: 0 8191 3947 5. December 1986.

Further printings. The complete series of seven collected volumes, comprising 37 Shakespeare plays, also published individually in paperback editions from 1984 through 1987. Published by University Press of America. Distributed in Great Britain by Eurospan.

Reviews. *Time,* May 7, 1984 (Gerald Clarke). *Listener*, August 9, 1984 (Bel Mooney). *Spectator*, August 18, 1984 (Peter Levi). *Theatre Studies* 30, 1984 (Patricia B. Adams). *Times Literary Supplement*, January 11, 1985 (Terence Hawkes). *Theatre Journal* (USA), May 1985 (Roger Gross).

A82. *Glimpses of the Great* (1985)
First edition. London: Methuen, March 1985. £12.50. ISBN: 0 413 58050 4. 244 pp, demy 8vo.

Contents. 12 portraits (sequel to *Memories of Men and Women*): Bertrand Russell; J. M. Keynes; Ernest Bevin; C. R. Attlee; Lionel Curtis: "The Prophet"; John Buchan at Elsfield; Rebecca West and H. G. Wells; Elizabeth Bowen and Goronwy Rees; How Good Was Connolly?; The Infantilism of Evelyn Waugh; The Personality of C. S. Lewis; The Real Betjeman.

Further printings. *Memories and Glimpses,* London: Methuen, 1986, 515 pp. Paperback. £6.95. Combined edition of *Memories of Men and Women* and *Glimpses of the Great.*

First American edition. Lanham, Maryland: University Press of America, 1986. US$16.95. ISBN: 0 8191 5008 8.

Reviews. *The Times*, March 6, 1985 (Alan Franks). *Punch*, March 20, 1985 (Stanley Reynolds). *Observer*, March 24, 1985 (Piers Brendon). *Listener*, March 28, 1985 (Ian Hislop). *Times Literary Supplement*, May 31, 1985 (J. H. C. Leach). *Books and Bookmen,* May 1985 (Patrick Taylor-Martin). *Contemporary Review,* May 1985 (Richard Whittington-Egan). *New Statesman and Nation*, June 7, 1985 (Brian Martin). *Sunday Telegraph*, April 13, 1986 (Linda O'Callaghan). *New Statesman and Nation*, May 30, 1986 (Alan Brien).

Note. The *Sunday Telegraph* and the *New Statesman and Nation* reviews address *Memories and Glimpses*.

A83. *Shakespeare's Self-Portrait: Passages from His Work* (1985)

First edition. London: Macmillan, May 1985 (550 copies + 500 University Press of America imprints + 2,000 University Press of America imprints). £25. ISBN: 0 333 36661 1. 196 pp, demy 8vo, 8 plates (9 illustrations).

Contents. Passages from Shakespeare's work, chosen and with notes by A. L. Rowse: Shakespeare's Self-Portrait; Family; School and Schooldays; Sport; On Himself; Gentility; Theatre; Actors and Acting; Touring; The Young Patron: Southampton; The Dark Lady: Emilia Lanier; Love; The Rival Poet: Christopher Marlowe; On Poetry; On His Own Poetry; Countryman and Country Lore; Places He Knew; The Court; Elizabeth I and James I; Contemporary Persons; Tastes; The People; Some Contemporary References; Characteristic Reflections; Shakespeare's Will.

Further printings. London: Macmillan, May 1985. Paperback (850 copies). £7.95.

First American edition. Lanham, Maryland: University Press of America, 1985 (500 copies). ISBN: 0 8191 4220 4. vi pp + 187 pp, 8 plates (9 illustrations).

Further printings. Lanham, Maryland: University Press of America, 1985. Hardcover (2,000 copies).

Reviews. *Times Literary Supplement*, April 25, 1986 (Inga-Stina Ewbank).

A84. *The Little Land of Cornwall* (1986)

First edition. Gloucester: Alan Sutton, March 1986. £5.95. ISBN: 0 86299 265 6. x pp + 301 pp, crown 8vo. Paperback.

Contents. 19 essays about Cornwall: The Seven Landscapes of Cornwall; The Contribution of Cornwall and Cornishmen to Britain; Borlase's Cornwall; Richard Polwhele As Historian; The Duchy; St. Austell: Church, Town, Parish; Place, Fowey, and the Treffrys; Joseph Thomas Treffry: Industrial Leader; Nicholas Roscarrock and His Lives of the Saints; The Turbulent Career of Sir Henry Bodrugan; Henry Trecarrell of Tudor Days; The Elizabethan Plymouth Pilchard Fishery; The St. Stephens-in-Brannel Story; January Tregagle in Legend and in History; Robert Stephen Hawker of Morwenstow; Truro As Cornish Capital; The Temples; Charles Henderson, 1900–1933; Dr Johnson and Cornish Nationalism.

Further printings. Redruth, Cornwall: Dyllansow Truran, May 1992. Hardcover, 302 pp. £11.95.

A85. *Stories from Trenarren* (1986)

First edition. London: William Kimber, April 1986. £8.50. ISBN: 0 7183 0590 6. 174 pp, demy 8vo.

Contents. 26 short stories, chiefly Cornish: 1. How Dick Stephens Fought the Bear; 2. The Influence of the Planets; 3. The Lady Macbeth of Trewardreva; 4. Miss Pengrugla and Mr Roseudgeon; 5. Who Was Miss Flavell?; 6. Hotel

Bedroom in War Time; 7. Polly of Trethurgy; 8. The Fan; 9. The Rocking Horse; 10. Blue Waves; 11. The Will; 12. The Doctor's Family; 13. The Collaborator; 14. The End of the Trewinnards; 15. The House at the Cross-Roads; 16. The Bishop; 17. The Inheritor; 18. The Amateur Archaeologist; 19. How Our College Came to be Founded; 20. The Nibbled Bread; 21. Psalm 109; 22. Miss Tryphena and Miss Euphemia; 23. Captain Pollock's Fields; 24. Dereliction; 25. The Ex-Schoolmistress; 26. Sandy Trebilcock's Farm.

A86. *Reflections on the Puritan Revolution* **(1986)**
First edition. London: Methuen, 1986. £14.95. ISBN: 0 413 40880 9. 262 pp, demy 8vo.

Contents. Essays on the artistic damage wrought by the Puritan Revolution: Revolution; The Attack on the Cathedrals; Colleges, Chapels, Parish Churches; Palaces, Castles, Mansions; Works of Art; Music and Theatre; Poets and Persons; Ideology; The Ruined Age; Appendix on the Puritan Revolution.

Reviews. *Sunday Telegraph*, June 8, 1986 (Richard Ollard). *Observer*, June 22, 1986 (John Kenyon). *Spectator*, June 28, 1986 (Eric Christiansen). *Times Literary Supplement*, August 15, 1986 (Patrick Collinson). *Contemporary Review*, August 1986 (James Munson). *Punch*, September 3, 1986 (Melvyn Bragg). *History*, June 1987 (John Morrill). *English Historical Review*, April 1989 (Kevin Sharpe).

A87. *In Shakespeare's Land: A Journey through the Landscape of Elizabethan England* **(1986)**
First edition. London: Weidenfeld & Nicolson, November 13, 1986. £12.95. ISBN: 0 297 79015 3. 200 pp, royal 4to, 250 illustrations (60 in color). Photographs throughout by John Hedgecoe.

First American edition. *Shakespeare's Land*. San Francisco: Chronicle Books, 1987.

A88. *The Poet Auden: A Personal Memoir* **(1987)**
First edition. London: Methuen, April 3, 1987. £9.95. ISBN: 0 413 40390 4. 138 pp, demy 8vo.

Contents. Auden's work is viewed from the twin perspectives of England and the United States.

First American edition. New York: Weidenfeld & Nicolson, 1988. $US14.95. ISBN: 1 555 84198 8. 138 pp.

Reviews. *Spectator*, April 4, 1987 (David Sexton). *Observer*, April 12, 1987 (John Gross). *Sunday Times*, May 17, 1987 (Humphrey Carpenter). *Times Literary Supplement*, July 3, 1987 (Nicholas Jenkins). *Weekend Australian*, September 19–20, 1987 (Geoffrey Dutton). *Publishers Weekly*, February 12, 1988 (Anon.). *Library Journal*, March 1, 1988 (Michael Hennessy). *American Spectator*, September 1988 (James W. Tuttleton). *New York Review of Books*, December 21, 1989 (A. Hecht).

A89. *Court and Country: Studies in Tudor Social History* **(1987)**
First edition. Brighton: Harvester Press, July 1987. £15.95.
 ISBN: 0 7108 1147 0. x pp + 310 pp, demy 8vo.
 Contents. A series of eight portraits—poets and adventurers, courtiers and politicians, lovers and losers: Honor Grenville, Lady Lisle, and Her Circle; Edward Courtenay, Last Earl of Devon of the Elder Line; Sir Peter Carew, Soldier of Fortune; The Diary of William Carnsew, Country Gentleman; The Truth about Topcliffe; The Tragic Career of Henry Cuffe; Richard Carew, Antiquary; Sir Richard Hawkins, Last of a Dynasty.
 First American edition. Athens: University of Georgia Press, 1987. $US24.95. ISBN: 0 8203 0975 3. x pp + 310 pp, demy 8vo.
 Reviews. *Observer*, July 26, 1987 (John Kenyon). *Guardian Weekly*, August 30, 1987 (Peter Vansittart). *Library Journal*, September 15, 1987 (James A. Casada). *Times Literary Supplement*, September 18–24, 1987 (Christopher Haig). *Sixteenth Century Journal* (USA), Winter 1988 (James McGoldrick). *History Today*, March 1988 (Jenny Wormald). *Virginia Quarterly Review*, Spring 1988 (Anon.). *Albion* (USA), Summer 1988 (Arthur J. Slavin). *History*, October 1988 (Simon Adams). *Historian*, February 1989 (Allen Horstman). *American Historical Review*, April 1989 (Buchanan Sharp). *English Historical Review*, July 1990 (P. H. Ramsey).

A90. *Froude the Historian: Victorian Man of Letters* **(1987)**
First edition. Gloucester: Alan Sutton, October 1987. £9.95. ISBN: 0 86299 384 9. 127 pp, demy 8vo.
 Contents. A portrait of the famous Victorian historian who in his time was the only one to compare with Macaulay in achievement, force, and style as a writer.

A91. *Froude's Spanish Story of the Armada* **(1988)**
First edition. Gloucester: Alan Sutton, May 26, 1988. £5.95. ISBN: 0 86299 500 0. 262 pp, 8vo. Paperback.
 Contents. Froude's originally published essays from 1892. Edited and with an introduction by A. L. Rowse.
 Reviews. *History*, June 1991 (Simon Adams).

A92. *Quiller Couch: A Portrait of "Q"* **(1988)**
First edition. London: Methuen, April 1988. £14.95. ISBN: 0 413 17940 0. ix pp + 229 pp, 8vo.
 Contents. A biography of A. L. Rowse's early Cornish mentor, the writer known as "Q."
 Reviews. *Times Higher Educational Supplement*, April 1, 1988 (Donald Hawes). *Times Literary Supplement*, April 1–7, 1988 (Charles Causley). *Sunday Telegraph*, April 10, 1988 (Kingsley Amis). *Punch*, April 15, 1988 (James Wood). *Financial Times*, April 16, 1988 (Anthony Curtis). *Observer*, April 17, 1988 (John Gross). *London Magazine*, April-May 1988 (Gavin Ewart). *Spec-*

tator, June 4, 1988 (Frances Partridge). *Times Educational Supplement*, June 17, 1988 (Bernard O'Keefe). *Encounter,* July-August, 1988 (R.M. [Richard Mayne]).

A93. *A. L. Rowse's Cornwall: A Journey through Cornwall's Past and Present* (1988)

First edition. London: Weidenfeld & Nicolson, June 16, 1988. £12.95. ISBN: 0 297 79230 X. 192 pp, royal 8vo. Profusely illustrated, five maps.

Contents. Photographed throughout by John Hedgecoe. Text by A. L. Rowse.

Reviews. *Sunday Times*, July 24, 1988 (Simon Jenkins).

A94. *Friends and Contemporaries* (1989)

First edition. London: Methuen, April 1989. £14.99. ISBN: 0 413 18140 5. 297 pp, demy 8vo.

Contents. Third volume of biographical essays: Lord David Cecil; Lord Berners; Sir Maurice Bowra; Sir Arthur Bryant; Hensley Henson: Controversial Bishop; Archbishop Lang of the Abdication; Two Foreign Secretaries: Simon and Halifax; Sir Harold Acton: Citizen of the World; Graham Greene: Perverse Genius; Daphne du Maurier: Fortune and Romance; A Buried Love: Flecker and Beazley.

Reviews. *Times Educational Supplement*, March 31, 1989 (Michael De-La-Noy). *Sunday Telegraph*, April 9, 1989 (Noel Malcolm). *Spectator*, April 22, 1989 (Raymond Carr). *Times Literary Supplement*, May 12, 1989 (Gerard Irvine). *London Magazine,* August-September 1989 (Peter Vansittart). *Contemporary Review,* November 1989 (Anon.).

A95. *Transatlantic: Later Poems* (1989)

First edition. Padstow, Cornwall: Tabb House, April 1989 (only one print run). £5.95. ISBN: 0 907018 70 X. 77 pp, 8vo. Paperback.

Contents. Eighth volume of poetry; 71 poems.

Reviews. *Times Literary Supplement*, May 12, 1989 (Gerard Irvine). *Cornish Scene,* Summer 1989 (Gordon Hunt).

A96. *The Controversial Colensos* (1989)

First edition. Redruth, Cornwall: Dyllansow Truran, July 1989. £9.95. ISBN: 1 85022 047 6. 153 pp, demy 8vo.

Contents. Dual biography of two famous Cornishmen: Bishop Colenso of Natal and his cousin William Colenso, first of New Zealand naturalists.

Reviews. *Times Literary Supplement*, February 2, 1990 (Gregory Palmer). *Contemporary Review,* February 1990 (Richard Mullen).

A97. *Discovering Shakespeare: A Chapter in Literary History* (1989)

First edition. London: Weidenfeld & Nicolson, September 7, 1989. £13.50. ISBN: 0 297 79633 X. xiii pp + 177 pp, 8vo.

Contents. An autobiographical story of A. L. Rowse's quest for the solutions to the mysteries of Shakespeare's life and work, coupled with the controversial story of the "Shakespeare establishment," whose opinions have largely been made irrelevant by A. L. Rowse's contributions to Shakespearean scholarship.

Reviews. *Sunday Times*, September 3, 1989 (Stanley Wells). *The Times*, September 9, 1989 (Laurence Kitchin). *Times Literary Supplement*, October 6, 1989 (S. Schoenbaum). *Economist*, December 2, 1989 (Anon.). *Sydney Morning Herald*, March 17, 1990 (A. P. Riemer).

A98. *Selected Poems* (1990)
First edition. Penzance, Cornwall: Alison Hodge, October 1990. £6.95. ISBN: 0 906720 22 2. vii pp + 71 pp, 8vo. Paperback.

Contents. Preface and 45 poems. Ninth volume of poetry.

A99. *Prompting the Age: Poems Early and Late* (1991)
First edition. Redruth, Cornwall: Dyllansow Truran, February 1, 1991 (1990 in book). £5.95. ISBN: 185 022 056 5. vi pp + 51 pp, 8vo. Paperback.

Contents. Preface and 75 poems. Tenth and final volume of poetry.

A100. *The Sayings of Shakespeare* (1993)
First edition. London: Duckworth, 1993 (5,000 copies; includes a second impression). £4.95. ISBN: 0 7156 2458 X. 64 pp, crown 8vo. Paperback.

Contents. Quotations of Shakespeare. Selected and edited, with an introduction by A. L. Rowse.

Reviews. *An Baner Kernewek* (The Cornish Banner), August 1993 (Donald R. Rawe).

A101. *Four Caroline Portraits* (1993)
First edition. London: Duckworth, April 1993 (2,050 copies). £14.99. ISBN: 0 7156 2460 1. 184 pp, 8vo.

Contents. Four portraits illuminating the civil war of the 17th century: Thomas Hobbes; Henry Marten; Hugh Peters; John Selden.

Reviews. *The Times*, April 29, 1993 (Daniel Johnson). *Sunday Telegraph*, May 16, 1993 (Noel Malcolm). *Tablet*, May 29, 1993 (Richard Ollard). *Evening Standard*, July 1, 1993 (Anthony Quinton). *An Baner Kernewek* (The Cornish Banner), August 1993 (James Whetter). *History Today*, July 1994 (John Morrill).

A102. *All Souls in My Time* (1993)
First edition. London: Duckworth, September 1993 (2,500 copies; includes a second impression). £14.99. ISBN: 0 7156 2474 1. 214 pp, 8vo. 8 plates (22 illustrations).

Contents. An insider's intimate views of events and personalities within the walls of Oxford's most unique college, All Souls.

Reviews. *Daily Telegraph*, October 16, 1993 (Roy Jenkins). *Spectator*, October 26, 1993 (Raymond Carr). *The Times*, November 18, 1993 (Matthew d'Ancona). *Spectator*, November 20, 1993 (Bevis Hillier). *Tablet*, November 20, 1993 (Denys Forrest). *An Baner Kernewek* (The Cornish Banner), November 1993 (James Whetter). *Times Literary Supplement*, December 24, 1993 (Michael Howard). *Contemporary Review,* April 1994 (Richard Mullen). *Oxford,* May 1994 (Julian Bullard).

A103. *The Regicides: And the Puritan Revolution* (1994)
First edition. London: Duckworth, September 1994 (1,600 copies). £16.99. ISBN: 0 7156 2607 8. 183 pp, 8vo. 8 plates (14 illustrations).

Contents. A probing into the character and their social background of the regicides—a revolutionary minority of a minority.

Reviews. *Sunday Telegraph*, August 28, 1994 (John Adamson). *Spectator,* September 17, 1994 (Hugh Trevor-Roper). *New Statesman and Nation*, November 4, 1994 (Diarmaid MacCulloch). *An Baner Kernewek* (The Cornish Banner), November 1994 (James Whetter). *The Times*, February 9, 1995 (John Morrill). *Times Literary Supplement*, February 10, 1995 (A.J.F.).

A104. *Historians I Have Known* (1995)
First edition. London: Duckworth, September 21, 1995 (2,875 copies; includes a second impression). £18.95. ISBN: 0 7156 2649 3. ix pp + 208 pp, 8vo.

Contents. A. L. Rowse's penultimate book. Twenty-seven portraits of historians A. L. Rowse knew in his long life: G. M. Trevelyan; Sir Charles Firth; Sir George Clark; Sir Keith Feiling; Sir Arthur Bryant; H. A. L. Fisher; Sir Charles Oman; A. H. M. Jones; Sir Maurice Powicke; K. B. McFarlane; A. F. Pollard; Sir John Neale; Garret Mattingly; R. H. Tawney; H. R. Trevor-Roper; Christopher Hill; C. V. Wedgwood; Sir Lewis Namier; A. J. P. Taylor; Richard Pares; Samuel Eliot Morison; Allan Nevins; Sir Reginald Coupland; Sir Keith Hancock; Sir Michael Howard; Denis Mack Smith; Barbara Tuchman.

Note. A. L. Rowse in a letter to Sydney Cauveren, dated September 2, 1995: "A Book Club has taken 1,000 copies pre-publication."

Reviews. *Sunday Telegraph*, September 24, 1995 (Andrew Roberts). *The Times*, September 28, 1995 (Jonathan Clark). *Times Literary Supplement*, September 29, 1995 (Paul Johnson). *Spectator*, October 14, 1995 (Raymond Carr). *Country Life,* November 30, 1995 (Richard Ollard). *Contemporary Review,* April 1996 (Richard Mullen).

A105. *My View of Shakespeare: The Shakespeare Revolution* (1996)
First edition. London: Duckworth, September 1996 (1,250 copies). £16.99. ISBN: 0 7156 2746 5. 151 pp, 8vo.

Contents. A. L. Rowse's last book, dedicated to "HRH the Prince of Wales in our common devotion to William Shakespeare." And adding, "The monarchy and Shakespeare are the two greatest assets this country has in the world."

Reviews. *Times Literary Supplement*, November 22, 1996 (D.S.). *Sunday Telegraph*, December 15, 1996 (Jonathan Bate).

Note. Several posthumous publications can be expected. A. L. Rowse in a letter to Sydney Cauveren, dated December 1, 1990: "I have nearly finished My Books: A Testament, forty or fifty chapters about the Books, intention, reception. Also my Note Books, following in the footsteps of Samuel Butler's. There remain all the unpublished Diaries, Journals and Pocket Books, mostly in type now. Enough to keep a Rowse industry a la Boswell or Horace Walpole going next century."

B

A. L. Rowse Contributions to Books and Anthologies, and Books Edited by A. L. Rowse

B1. *Public School Verse, 1919–1920*
Poems. Edited by Martin Gilkes, Richard Hughes, and P. H. B. Lyon. Introduction by John Masefield (1921).
　　Note. *History Today,* volume 29, November 1979, in its foreword states that A. L. Rowse's first published verse appeared in *Public School Verse* in 1921. (See also *A Cornish Childhood,* A10, pp. 216–218.)

B2. *Oxford Poetry, 1923*
Poem: "Night and the Shadows," p. 51. Edited by David Cleghorn Thomson and F. W. Bateson. Oxford: Basil Blackwell, November 9, 1923 (1,500 copies).

B3. *Oxford Poetry, 1924*
Poem: "The Shadows on the Glass," p. 49. Edited by Harold Acton and Peter Quennell. Oxford: Basil Blackwell, October 22, 1924 (1,250 copies).
　　Note. First published in *Oxford Outlook,* June 1924. (See "A Cornishman at Oxford," p. 143.) Reprinted in *Poems of a Decade* (1941); *A Life: Collected Poems* (1981).

B4. *Oxford Poetry, 1925*
Poems: "Into a Quiet, Lonely Place," p. 46; "The Village," p. 47. Edited by P. Monkhouse and C. Plumb. Oxford: Basil Blackwell, 1925.

B5. *Where Stands Socialism Today?*
Essay: "Industry in the Transition to Socialism," pp. 87–129. Lectures by various authors delivered to the Fabian Society, autumn 1932. London: Rich and Cowan, 1933.

B6. *Some Makers of the Modern Spirit: A Symposium*
Essay: "Karl Marx, 1818–1883," pp. 166–178. Edited by John MacMurray. London: Methuen, 1933. One of twelve talks broadcast by the BBC in the spring of 1933.

B7. *Essays in Cornish History*
Coeditor. Charles G. Henderson. Oxford: Clarendon, 1935; Truro: D. Bradford Barton, 1963. Edited by A. L. Rowse and M. I. Henderson.

B8. *Walking in Cornwall*
Foreword. J. R. A. Hockin. London: Alexander Maclehose & Co., 1936, pp. vii–ix.

B9. *Elizabethan Studies and Other Essays in Honor of George F. Reynolds*
Essay: "The Royal Fletcher and the Loyal Heywood," pp. 192–194. Edited by Charles Frederick Tucker Brooke. University of Colorado Studies, Series B, Studies in the Humanities, vol. 2, no. 4. Boulder: University of Colorado Press, 1945.

B10. *Kilvert's Diary, 1870–1879*
Special introduction. Edited and with an introduction by William Plomer. Selections from the diary of the Reverend Francis Kilvert. New York: Macmillan, 1947.

B11. *John Buchan by His Wife and Friends*
Essay: "John Buchan at Elsfield," pp. 174–187. Susan Tweedsmuir with preface by George Trevelyan, O.M. London: Hodder & Stoughton, 1947.
   Note. Reprinted and revised in *The English Past* (1951); *Times, Persons, Places: Essays in Literature* (1965); *Glimpses of the Great* (1985).

B12. *Human Nature in Politics*
Foreword. Graham Wallas. London: Constable, 1948. Reprinted 1962, pp. 1–4, dated 1947.

B13. *In the Green Tree*
Preface. Alun Lewis. London: George Allen & Unwin, 1948, pp. 7–14.
   Note. The above volume includes *Letters from India, 1946,* in which this preface was first printed. Reprinted in *The English Past* (1951) as "Alun Lewis: A Foreword."

B14. *The County Books: Cornwall*
Foreword. Claude Berry. London: Robert Hale, 1949, pp. v–vii, from "Polmear Mine, St. Austell."

B15. *Sir Francis Drake and British Enterprise*
Text. A catalogue for an exhibition of historical relics of Sir Frances Drake. London, July 1952.

B16. *Royal Homes*
Introduction. London: Odhams, 1953.

B17. *A Cornish Waif's Story*
Foreword. An Autobiography by Emma Smith. London: Odhams, 1954, pp. 7–9.

B18. *Talking of Shakespeare*
Essay: "Elizabethan Drama and Society: An Historian's View," pp. 173–186.
Edited by John Garrett. London: Hodder & Stoughton/Max Reinhardt, 1954.
A selection of lectures delivered at the annual course for teachers at Stratford, 1948–1953.

B19. *Studies in Social History: A Tribute to G. M. Trevelyan*
Essay: "Nicholas Roscarrock and His Lives of the Saints," pp. 3–31. Edited by J. H. Plumb. London: Longmans, Green, 1955.
   Note. Reprinted in *The Little Land of Cornwall* (1986).

B20. *Churchill by His Contemporaries*
Essay: "The Summing-Up: Churchill's Place in History," chapter 39, pp. 336–349. Edited by Charles Eade. London: Hutchinson & Co./The Reprint Society, 1955. Tributes to the great wartime leader.

B21. *A True Discourse of the Present State of Virginia*
Introduction. Ralph Hamor, The Virginia State Library (USA), 1957. Reprinted from the London edition, 1615. Pages xi–xviii, dated St. Austell, Cornwall, October 1956.
   Note. A. L. Rowse is also referred to in the prefatory note by R.B.H. (Richard B. Harwell), director of publications at the Virginia State Library, pp. vii–x.

B22. *Naked to Mine Enemies: The Life of Cardinal Wolsey*
Introduction. Charles W. Ferguson, Time Reading Program Edition, 1958.

B23. *Elizabeth the Great*
Introduction. Elizabeth Jenkins, Time Reading Program Edition, c. 1958.

B24. *Essays and Studies, 1959*
Essay: "Robert Stephen Hawker of Morwenstow: A Belated Medieval," pp. 106–132. Volume 12 of the new series of essays and studies collected for the English Association by Dorothy Margaret Stuart. London: John Murray, 1959.
   Note. Reprinted in *The Little Land of Cornwall,* 1986.

B25. *Mightier Than the Sword: The P. E. N. Hermon Ould Memorial Lectures, 1953–1961*
Essay: "The Role of the Intellectuals in Society," pp. 77–98 [the 1958 lecture].
P. E. N. English Centre. London: Macmillan, 1964 (2,000 copies).
   Note. Reprinted in *Time and Tide,* November 1, 8, 1958.

B26. *The Chamberlain Letters*
Preface. A selection of the letters of John Chamberlain concerning life in England from 1597 to 1626, edited by Elizabeth Thomson. New York: Putnam, 1965; England: John Murray, 1966.

B27. *The Generall Historie of Virginia, New–England and the Summer Isles . . . 1624*
Introduction. Capt. J. Smith. Facsimile edition. World Publishing Company, 1966, full vellum, gilt, solander box. Introduction on separate booklet with this edition.

B28. *The World Encompassed* **(Sir Francis Drake, 1628);** *The Relation of a Wonderfull Voiage* **(William Cornelison Schouten, 1619)**
Introductions. World Publishing Company, 1966.

B29. *The Discoverie of Guiana* **(Sir Walter Ralegh, 1596);** *The Discoveries of the World* **(Antonio Galvao, 1601)**
Introductions. World Publishing Company, 1966.

B30. *Fair Liberty Was All His Cry: A Tercentenary Tribute to Jonathan Swift, 1667–1745*
Essay: "Swift As Poet," pp. 98–106. Edited by A. Norman Jeffares. London: Macmillan/New York, St. Martin's, 1967.
Note. Reprinted in *Swift: Modern Judgements.* Edited by A. Norman Jeffares. London: Macmillan, 1969; Nashville: Aurora, 1970. Originally printed as "Jonathan Swift" in *The English Spirit* (1944); revised edition 1966.

B31. *Essays in American Colonial History*
Essay: "The Transition from Medieval to Modern History," part 1 ("Tudor Expansion"), pp. 3–11. Edited by Paul Goodman. New York: Holt, Rinehart and Winston, 1967. Essays collated from scholarly journals about America's colonial past.
Note. First printed in *William and Mary Quarterly,* 3d series, 14 (1957): 309–316.

B32. *Dictionary of British Sculptors, 1660–1851*
Blurb (inner front flap of dust jacket). Rupert Gunnis. Rev. ed. London: Abbey Library, 1968.

B33. *Catherine the Queen*
Blurb (inner back flap of dust jacket). Mary M. Luke. London: F. Muller, 1968.

B34. *The Two Chiefs of Dunboy*
Editor and foreword (pp. 7–12). A story of eighteenth-century Ireland. J. A. Froude. London: Chatto & Windus, 1969 (2,750 copies ordered August 1969).

B35. *The History of Truro Grammar and Cathedral School*
Foreword. R. E. Davidson, M. A. Mevagissey, Cornwall: Kingston, 1970.

B36. *The Professor and the Public: The Role of the Scholar in the Modern World*
Essay: "The Scholar and Responsibility to the Public," pp. 43–72. The Franklin Memorial Lectures, vol. 20. Compiled by Goldwin Smith, Wayne State University Press, Detroit, Michigan, 1972.

B37. *A Handbook of Cornish Surnames*
Foreword. Compiled by G. Pawley White, Dyllansow Truran, 1972. 2d ed., 1981.

B38. *The Oxford Book of Twentieth-Century English Verse*
Poem: "The White Cat of Trenarren," pp. 351–352. Chosen by Philip Larkin. Oxford: Clarendon, 1973.
    Note. Reprinted in *The Poetry of Cats.* Edited by Samuel Carr. London: B. T. Batsford, 1974, pp. 86–87; *Peter: The White Cat of Trenarren,* 1974; *Three Cornish Cats,* 1979; *A Life: Collected Poems,* 1981; *A Quartet of Cornish Cats,* 1986.

B39. *Canon's Folly*
Foreword, pp. 8–10. Martin Andrews. London: Michael Joseph, 1974.

B40. *The Private Lives of the Tudor Monarchs*
Foreword. Selected and edited by Christopher Falkus. London: Folio Society, 1974.
    Note. Reprinted in *Discoveries and Reviews,* 1975.

B41. *The Genius of Thomas Hardy*
Essay: "Hardy and Cornwall," pp. 119–138. Edited by Margaret Drabble. London: Weidenfeld & Nicolson/New York: Alfred A. Knopf, 1976.

B42. *Jane Austen Society: Report for the Year 1975*
Essay: "The England of Jane Austen," pp. 17, 19–22, 24–31. Alton: Jane Austen Society, 1976.
    Note 1. The address given by A. L. Rowse at the annual meeting of the Jane Austen Society on July 19, 1975. (See also "Villagers of Chawton Fete: Its Dearest Daughter," F79).
    Note 2. Reprinted in *Portraits and Views* (1979) as "Jane Austen As Social Realist."

B43. *Gulliver's Travels*
Introduction and notes. Jonathan Swift. London: Pan Classics, 1977. 299 pp.

B44. *The History of Cornwall*
Foreword. Richard Polwhele. 1st ed., 1803–1808. Dorking: Kohler & Coombes, 1978. 6½ pp.
    Note. Reprinted in *The Little Land of Cornwall* (1986) as "Richard Polwhele As Historian."

B45. *The Story of Truro High School*
Foreword, pp. xi–xii. A. K. Clarke, with a memoir of its first Headmistress, Amy Key. Truro: Benson Foundation/Oscar Blackford, Royal Printeries, 1979.

B46. *Ritual Murder: Essays on Liturgical Reform*
Essay: "Shakespeare and the Prayer Book," pp. 47–56. Edited by Brian Morris. Manchester: Carcanet, 1980.

B47. *Pieces of Hate*
Essay: "Diminishing Returns," discussing the filth in Patrick White's book *The Twyborn Affair*, pp. 64–66. Edited by Brian Redhead and Kenneth McLeish. London: Hodder & Stoughton, 1982.

B48. *Oxford and Oxfordshire in Verse*
Poem: "Iffley," pp. 32–33. Edited and with an introduction by Antonia Fraser, with the collaboration of Flora Powell-Jones. Illustrations by Rebecca Fraser. London: Secker & Warburg, 1982.
    Note. Printed in *The Listener,* May 13, 1943; *Poems Chiefly Cornish* (1944); *A Life: Collected Poems* (1981).

B49. *Trollope Centenary Essays*
Essay: "Trollope's Autobiography," pp. 134–145. Edited by John Halperin. New York: St. Martin's, 1982.

B50. *The Ship of Stars*
Foreword. Sir Arthur Quiller-Couch ("Q"). *The Cornish Library*, no. 10. London: Anthony Mott, 1983. 287 pp.

B51. *Oxford, China, and Italy: Writings in Honour of Sir Harold Acton on His Eightieth Birthday*
Essay: "The Good-Natured Man," pp. 63–65. Edited by Edward Chaney and Neil Ritchie. London: Thames & Hudson, 1984.

B52. *Four Hundred Years of Virginia: An Anthology*
Foreword. Dora Jean Ashe. Lanham, Md.: University Press of America, 1985. 221 pp.

B53. *Tregrehan Mills, St. Austell, Cornwall*
Foreword. A record of its development and history. A village portrait, Valerie Brokenshire, Cannis Road, St. Austell, 1985.
    Dated "Trenarren, June 1985."

B54. *1936 As Recorded by "The Spectator"*
Essays: "The Encroaching Nightmare," pp. 27–35; "What Should We Fight For?" pp. 167–169. Introduced and edited by Charles Moore and Christopher Hawtree. London: Michael Joseph, 1986.
    Note. "What Should We Fight For" first printed in *The Spectator,* July 31, 1936.

B55. *For Veronica Wedgwood These: Studies in Seventeenth-Century History*
Essay: "Bishop Thornborough: A Clerical Careerist," pp. 89–108. Edited by Richard Ollard and Pamela Tudor-Craig. London: Collins, 1986.

B56. *The First Colonists: Hakluyt's Voyages in North America*
Introduction. A modern version by The Folio Society, 1986.

B57. *The Life and Work of Barbara Pym*
Essay: "Miss Pym and Miss Austen," pp. 64–71. Edited by Dale Salwak. London: Macmillan, 1987.

B58. *The Makers of English History*
Essay: "William Shakespeare, 1564–1616," pp. 80–84. General editor Norman Stone. Foreword by Asa Briggs. London: Weidenfeld & Nicolson, 1987.

B58a. *A Maryland Anthology, 1608–1986*
Foreword. Dora Jean Ashe. Lanham, Md.: University Press of America, 1987.

B59. *Thomas Dekker, the Wonderful Year 1603*
Introduction. London: The Folio Society, 1989 (1,250 copies printed).

B60. *Contemporary Poets*
Commentary: "A. L. Rowse comments . . . " [on his poetry], p. 832. London: St. James, 1991. 5th ed. with prefaces by C. Day Lewis and Diane Wakoski. Edited by Tracy Chevalier. Entry on A. L. Rowse, the poet. Also includes an extensive bibliographic listing of most of his books, pp. 830–833.

B61. *John Anstis: Garter King of Arms*
Essay. Sir Anthony Wagner. London: H.M.S.O., 1992.

B62. *A Parish Portrait St. Blazey*
Foreword, p. 2. A record of its development and history. Valerie Brokenshire, Cannis Road, St. Austell, 1993.

B63. *From Cornwall with Love*
Poem: "Trenarren: Autumn 1941," p. 43. Photographed by Bob Croxford. Introduction by Robert Hunt. Cornwall: Atmosphere, 1993.

　　　Note. Printed in *Poems Chiefly Cornish* (1944); *A Life: Collected Poems* (1981).

B64. *Far from the Valleys*
Foreword. Graham F. Thomas. Book Guild, 1996.

B65. *St. Austell: The Archive Photographs Series*
Photographs. Compiled by Valerie Brokenshire. Chalford Publishing, 1997. (Dedicated to Dr. A. L. Rowse, C.H.)

　　1.　The St. Austell County School, Tewington House in 1919, p. 39

2. A bill heading from Richard Rowse (father of A. L.), grocer and tea dealer, p. 101
3. A. L. Rowse as a young boy (c. 1913) at Tregonissey with his grandparents and Neddy the donkey, p. 126
4. Dr. A. L. Rowse, C.H., the most renowned St. Austellian scholar of this century, ranking among the literary giants of Oxford and Cambridge, p. 127

B66–116. *Teach Yourself History Library*
Note. Satellite titles in the Teach Yourself History Library, of which *The Use of History* (1946; see entry, A15) is the key and introductory volume. A. L. Rowse is general editor for the complete series and also provides a general introduction to each title. The following titles were published by the English Universities Press, London. In the 1960s the series was reissued as Men and Their Times, with some earlier books discontinued and some new ones added.

B66. *Bolivar and the Independence of Spanish America,* **J. B. Trend, 1946**

B67. *Botha, Smuts, and South Africa,* **Basil Williams, 1946**

B68. *Chatham and the British Empire,* **Sir Charles Grant Robertson, 1946**

B69. *Clemenceau and the Third Republic,* **J. Hampden Jackson, 1946**

B70. *Cook and the Opening of the Pacific,* **James A. Williamson, 1946**

B71. *Louis XIV and the Greatness of France,* **Maurice Ashley, 1946**

B72. *Milton and the English Mind,* **F. E. Hutchinson, 1946**

B73. *Alexander the Great and the Hellenistic Empire,* **A. R. Burn, August 1947**

B74. *Catherine the Great and the Expansion of Russia,* **Gladys Scott Thomson, June 1947**

B75. *Warren Hastings and British India,* **Penderel Moon, 1947**

B76. *Henry V and the Invasion of France,* **E. F. Jacob, 1947**

B77. *Lenin and the Russian Revolution,* **Christopher Hill, 1947**

B78. *Pushkin and Russian Literature,* **Janko Lavrin, 1947**

B79. *Raleigh and the British Empire,* **D. B. Quinn, October 1947**

B80. *Woodrow Wilson and American Liberalism,* **E. M. Hugh-Jones, July 1947**

B81. *Constantine and the Conversion of Europe,* **A. H. M. Jones, 1948**

B82. *Thomas Jefferson and American Democracy,* **Max Beloff, 1948**

B83. *Joan of Arc and the Recovery of France,* Alice Buchan, 1948

B84. *Abraham Lincoln and the United States,* K. C. Wheare, 1948

B85. *Pericles and Athens,* A. R. Burn, 1948

B86. *Erasmus and the Northern Renaissance,* Margaret Mann Phillips, 1949

B87. *Richelieu and the French Monarchy,* C. V. Wedgwood, 1949

B88. *Peter the Great and the Emergence of Russia,* B. H. Sumner, 1950

B89. *Cranmer and the English Reformation,* F. E. Hutchinson, 1951

B90. *Gladstone and Liberalism,* J. L. Hammond and M. R. D. Foot, 1952

B91. *Robespierre and the French Revolution,* J. M. Thompson, 1952.

B92. *John Wycliffe and the Beginnings of English Non-Conformity,* K. B. McFarlane, 1952

B93. *Agricola and Roman Britain,* A. R. Burn, 1953

B94. *Napoleon and the Awakening of Europe,* F. M. H. Markham, 1954

B95. *Lorenzo Dei Medici and the Italian Renaissance,* C. M. Ady, 1955

B96. *Livingstone and Africa,* Jack Simmons, 1955

B97. *Whitgift and the English Church,* V. J. K. Brook, 1957

B98. *Marx, Proudhon, and European Socialism,* J. Hampden Jackson, 1957

B99. *Washington and the American Revolution,* Esmond Wright, 1957

B100. *Oliver Cromwell and the Puritan Revolution,* Maurice Ashley, 1958

B101. *Alexander II and the Modernization of Russia,* W. E. Mosse, 1958

B102. *Thomas Cromwell and the English Reformation,* A. G. Dickens, 1959

B103. *Roosevelt and Modern America,* John A. Woods, 1959

B104. *Elizabeth I and the Unity of England,* Joel Hurstfield, 1960

B105. *Machiavelli and Renaissance Italy,* John R. Hale, 1961

B106. *Napoleon III and the Second Empire,* J. P. T. Bury, 1964

B107. *Ivan III and the Unification of Russia,* Ian Grey, 1964

B108. *Frederick the Great and the Rise of Prussia,* D. B. Horn, 1964

B109. *William I and the Norman Conquest,* Frank Barlow, 1965

B110. *Bismarck and Modern Germany,* W. N. Medlicott, 1965

B111. *Benjamin Franklin and American Independence,* **Esmond Wright, 1966**

B112. *Julius Caesar and Rome,* **J. P. V. D. Balsdon, 1967**

B113. *Martin Luther and the Reformation,* **A. G. Dickens, 1967**

B114. *Gandhi and Modern India,* **Penderel Moon, 1968**

B115. *Maria Theresa and the House of Austria,* **C. A. Macartney, 1969**

B116. *Gustavus Adolphus and the Rise of Sweden,* **Michael Roberts, 1973**

C

Translations of Books by A. L. Rowse

CZECHOSLOVAK

The National Library at Prague in a letter dated October 8, 1996, states that there are no translations of A. L. Rowse in the National Library. However, in a letter to Sydney Cauveren, A. L. Rowse states on May 15, 1996: "a Czech publisher is offering a large advance for a translation." No further details are known.

DANISH

C1. *Aanden i Englands historie* **(1946)**
Copenhagen: Fremad, 1946. A translation by Flemming Madsen of *The Spirit of English History.*

DUTCH

C2. *De Beteekenis der Engelsche Geschiedenis* **(1944)**
London: Longman's, 1944. A translation by A. J. Staal of *The Spirit of English History.*

C3. *Drie Katten* **(1981)**
Amsterdam: De Arbeiderspers, 1981. A translation by P. M. Vermeer of *Three Cornish Cats.*

C4. *Homosexuelen in de Geschiedenis: Over ambivalentie in maatschappy, literatuur en beeldende kunst* **(1984)**
Amsterdam: De Arbeiderspers, 1984. A translation by Mea Flothuis of *Homosexuals in History: Ambivalence in Society, Literature, and the Arts.*

FRENCH

C5. *L'esprit de l'histoire de l'Angleterre* **(1951)**
Avec une préface de André Siegfried. London: Longmans, Green, 1951. A translation by R. Julliard of *The Spirit of English History.*

C6. *William Shakespeare* **(1964)**
Paris: Plon, 1964. A translation by Henri Nolp and Pierre Tirruon with the cooperation of Jeanine Delpech of *William Shakespeare: A Biography.*

C7. *Les homosexuels célèbres: Dans l'histoire, la littérature et les arts* **(1979)**
Paris: Editeur, 1979. A translation by A. Michel of *Homosexuals in History: Ambivalence in Society, Literature, and the Arts.*

GERMAN

C8. *The Spirit of English History* **(1952)**
Stuttgart: Klett, 1952. A translation by Heinrich Eden of *The Spirit of English History.* Second edition, 1955. Third edition, 1957.

NORWEGIAN

C9. *Hovedlinjen i engelsk historie* **(1945)**
London: Longmans, 1945. A translation by Aagot Thorstad of *The Spirit of English History.*

POLISH

C10. *Duch dziejów Anglii* **(1946)**
London: Longmans, Green, 1946. A translation by Stanislaw Balinski of *The Spirit of English History.*

C11. *Anglia w epoce elzbietanskiej* **(1976)**
Volume 1: Struktura spoleczenstwa; volume 2: Ekspansja. Warszawa: Panstwowe Wydawnictwo Naukowe, 1976. Translations by Stefan Amsterdamski of *The Elizabethan Age.* Volume 1: *The England Of Elizabeth: The Structure of Society*; volume 2: *The Expansion of Elizabethan England.*

RUSSIAN

C12. *Kómnata s Prizrakom* **(Room with a ghost) (1993)**
Moscow: Nizhny Novgorod, Dekam, IMA Press, 1993. A translation by A. Kuznetzov of *All Soul's Night (Halloween)*—first published in *West-Country Stories,* 1945 (see A14). Collection of short stories, pp. 392–403.

SPANISH

C13. *Homosexuales en la historia: Estudio de la ambivalencia en la sociedad, la literatura y las artes* **(1981)**
Barcelona: Planeta, 1981. A translation by Elena Liaras Muls of *Homosexuals in History: Ambivalence in Society, Literature, and the Arts.*

SWEDISH

C14. *Englands historia i sammandrag* **(1945)**
Stockholm: Ljus, 1945. A translation by Maj Lorents of *The Spirit of English History.*
    Note. Reviews: 1. *Svenska Dagbladet* (Gosta Attorps) 2. *Ny Tid* (Ragnar Hedèn) 3. *Arboga Tidning* (Erik Brännman).

C15. *Engelskt väsen* **(1947)**
Stockholm: Ljus, 1947. A translation by Karin Granstedt of *The English Spirit.*

D

Articles by A. L. Rowse

For contributions before 1927, references are given in *A Cornishman at Oxford* to the following publications: *Oxford Outlook*; *New Oxford; Oxford Broom*; *Oxford Magazine* (the don's paper), and *The Local Leader* (a small Labour paper). Possible contributions could also be in *The Cardinal's Hat* (Christ Church College magazine, 1922–1925).

D1. *Criterion*, December 1927, pp. 542–545
Letter: About the review of Laski's communism.

D2. *Criterion*, March 1928, pp. 260–263
Letter: Reply to John G. Fletcher's letter on Laski's communism (January 1928 issue).

D3. *Literary Digest* (USA), May 12, 1928, p. 30
Poem: "The Shadows on the Glass." Reprinted in *Poems of a Decade (1941)*; *A Life: Collected Poems* (1981). (See also following entry.)

D4. *Forum* (USA), May 1928, pp. 641–645
Six poems with portrait illustration from a drawing by Johan Bull: "Night and Shadow," "The Shadows on the Glass," "Sonnet in Illness," "Before Spring," "Replication," "Knowledge."

D5. *Criterion*, September 1928, pp. 159–161
Review (untitled) of *History and Historical Research* by C. G. Crump.

D6. *Criterion*, December 1928, pp. 201–205
Review (untitled) of *Intelligent Woman's Guide* by George Bernard Shaw.

D6a. *St. Austell Hospital Handbook* (1928)
Article: "Three Great Travellers on St. Austell." Reprinted in *West-Country Stories* (1945).

D7. *New Statesman and Nation,* **March 16, 1929, pp. 733–734.**
Review entitled "Swift As Poet" of *Swift's Verse: An Essay* by F. Elrington Ball.

D8. *Criterion,* **April 1929, pp. 422–436**
Article: "The Literature of Communism: Its Origin and Theory."
    Note. "Mr. Barnes and Mr. Rowse." Response from T. S. Eliot, editor of *Criterion,* to articles by these two authors on *The Literature of Communism* (July 1929 issue).

D9. *Criterion,* **October 1929, pp. 84–88**
Article: "Marxism: A Reply."

D10. *Criterion,* **October 1929, pp. 150–155**
Review (untitled) of *The Next Ten Years in British Social and Economic Policy* by G. D. H. Cole; *Portrait of the Labour Party* by Egon Wertheimer; *A Survey of Socialism* by F. J. C. Hearnshaw.

D11. *Criterion,* **January 1930, pp. 330–333**
Review (untitled) of *Walter Rathenau: His Life and Work* by Count Harry Kessler.

D12. *Criterion,* **January 1930, pp. 353–356**
Review (untitled) of *Wolsey* by A. F. Pollard.

D13. *New Statesman and Nation,* **April 12, 1930, p. 14**
Poem: "The Field." Reprinted in *Poems of a Decade* (1941); *A Life: Collected Poems,* (1981).

D14. *Criterion,* **April 1930, pp. 451–469**
Article: "The Theory and Practice of Communism."

D15. *Economic Journal,* **September 1930, pp. 472–475**
Review of *The Economic Aspects of Sovereignty* by R. G. Hawtrey.

D16. *Criterion,* **October 1930, pp. 179–181**
Review (untitled) of *The Essentials of Democracy* by A. D. Lindsay.

D17. *The Times,* **January 1, 1931, p. 8, cols. d, e**
Letter, "Electoral Systems: The Virtue of Simplicity," offering more comments on changes in the electoral system initiated by Professor Barker and Sir John Fischer Williams.

D18. *The Times,* **January 8, 1931, p. 8, col. c**
Letter, "Electoral Systems: Simplicity and Good Government," concerning Sir John Fischer Williams's question on electoral system amendments. Rowse suggests that "the most important is the abolition of all plural voting."

D19. *Criterion,* **January 1931, pp. 222–232**
Article: "G. N. Clark's Conception of History."

D20. *Criterion,* **January 1931, pp. 366–369**
Review (untitled) of *Cromwell and Communism* by Edward Bernstein.

D21. *Economic Journal,* **March 1931, pp. 133–135**
Review of *The Protestant Ethic and the Spirit of Capitalism* by Max Weber. Translated by Talcott Parsons with foreword by R. H. Tawney.

D22. *Forum* **(USA), March 1931, p. 141**
Poem: "The Fallen Tree." Reprinted in *Poems of a Decade* (1941); *A Life: Collected Poems* (1981).

D23. *Economic Journal,* **June 1931, pp. 250–253**
Review of *Equality* by R. H. Tawney. Reprinted in *Criterion,* July 1931, pp. 731–733. (See also entry D31 below.)

D24. *Economic Journal,* **June 1931, pp. 310–312**
Review of *Marx–Engels Gesamtausgabe,* edited by D. Ryazanov.

D25. *This Quarter* **(Paris), July–September 1931, p. 97**
Poem: "Neck of Land."

D26. *This Quarter* **(Paris), July–September 1931, p. 98**
Poem: "The Dream." Reprinted in *Poems of a Decade* (1941); *A Life: Collected Poems* (1981).

D27. *New Statesman and Nation* **(new series), August 8, 1931, p. 169**
Poem: "Grown-Up to Child: Ten Commandments." Reprinted in *Poems of a Decade* (1941); *A Life: Collected Poems* (1981).

D28. *Economic History,* **January 1932, pp. 461–472**
Article: "The Dispute concerning the Plymouth Pilchard Fishery, 1584–1591." Reprinted in *The Little Land of Cornwall* (1986) as "The Elizabethan Plymouth Pilchard Fishery."

D29. *New Statesman and Nation,* **new series, February 27, 1932, pp. 253–254**
Article: "The Labour Party and the Future." A reply to Mr. Elton.

D30. *This Quarter* **(Paris), March 1932, pp. 540–541**
Poem: "The Apes." Reprinted in *Poems of a Decade* (1941); *A Life: Collected Poems* (1981).

D31. *Political Quarterly,* **April–June 1932, pp. 305–306**
Review (untitled) of *Equality* by R. H. Tawney. Revised, cheaper edition. (See also D23 above.)

D32. *New Clarion,* **June 25, 1932, pp. 61, 65**
Political article: "It's Their Funeral, A Post-War Man Says."

D33. *This Quarter* **(Paris), June 1932, pp. 630–631**
Short story: "Sunday Afternoon Walk to the Hospital."

D34. *This Quarter* **(Paris), June 1932, pp. 632–633.**
Short story: "Agnus Dei."

D35. *New Clarion,* **July 16, 1932, pp. 1, 122**
Political article: "The Old Gang Must Go! Goose-step days are here again."

D36. *Criterion,* **July 1932, pp. 735–739**
Review (untitled) of *War and Peace in Europe, 1815–1870,* and other essays by E. L. Woodward.

D37. *Political Quarterly,* **July–September 1932, pp. 409–415**
Political article: "Mr. Keynes on Socialism: A Reply."

D38. *New Clarion,* **August 6, 1932, pp. 204, 212**
Political article: "Liberalism No Remedy: Liberals Are Trying to Make Bricks without Straw. You cannot base world-peace on good intentions."

D39. *New Clarion,* **August 20, 1932, pp. 253, 255**
Political article: "The German Menace: Re-enter the 1914 Gang."

D40. *New Clarion,* **September 17, 1932, p. 348**
Political article: "Will Democracy Survive? A. L. Rowse believes that the future of the working-class Movement in Europe depends on the issue of the present struggle in Germany more than on any other single factor."

D41. *New Clarion,* **September 17, 1932, p. 358**
Letter: "European Militarism."

D42. *Nineteenth Century,* **September 1932, pp. 327–342**
Article: "Socialism and Mr. Keynes."

D43. *New Clarion,* **October 8, 1932, p. 413**
Article: "Thanks To MacDonald—A Year of Reaction: A. L. Rowse, a representative of Young Labour, reviews the Prime Minister's anniversary statement, published in the National Labour Fortnightly, in the light of the Government's achievement."

D44. *New Clarion,* **October 15, 1932, p. 438**
Article: "What Socialism Is Not: A. L. Rowse continues his analysis of Mr. MacDonald's anniversary article published in a recent issue of the organ of the National Labour Group."

D45. *History,* **October 1932, pp. 284–285**
Review (untitled) of *Cornish Seafarers* by A. K. Hamilton Jenkin.

D46. *New Clarion,* **November 19, 1932, p. 566**
Article: "Leisure Must Be Shared: The reduction of working hours is a matter

for International negotiation, and you can only rely on the Trade Unions to formulate agreements to this end—A. L. Rowse: Summary of a Lecture given under the auspices of the Fabian Society at the Kingsway Hall on November 10."

D47. *Cornish Labour News,* **November 1932, p. 1, cols. a–c**
Article entitled "False Economy: A Message to Cornish Parents and Teachers" concerning proposals put forward by the National Government to increase the costs of a secondary school education and to restrict the number of free places for children of poorer parents.

Note. A. L. Rowse was cofounder of the *Cornish Labour News,* the official monthly organ of the Cornwall Labour Federation. The Cornish Studies Library at Redruth holds only the above issue of this very rare publication.

D48. *New Clarion,* **December 17, 1932, pp. 31–32**
Article: "Will Capitalism Survive the Crisis?—Bringing order out of chaos—A.L. Rowse says NO (in reply to Lord Melchett, who says YES)."

D49. *New Clarion,* **December 31, 1932, p. 64**
Article: "A. L. Rowse Says: The Watchword for Youth Is: Keep your Eye on the Enemy!"

D50. *This Quarter* **(Paris), December 1932, pp. 275–276**
Poem: "Auguste Nept: 1877." Reprinted in *Poems of a Decade* (1941); *A Life: Collected Poems* (1981).

Note. The model for Rodin's *L'age d'Airain* was named Auguste Nept.

D51. *New Clarion,* **March 11, 1933, p. 271**
Article: "We Must Meet the Fascist Challenge!—The whole future of Socialism is at stake there, and not that only, but the future peace of Europe and the world."

D52. *New Clarion,* **April 15, 1933, p. 365**
Article: "Betraying the German Workers—We must dedicate ourselves never to rest as long as this infamy lasts in Germany."

D53. *Criterion,* **April 1933, pp. 371–389**
Article: "An Epic of Revolution: Reflections on Trotsky's History."

D54. *Spectator,* **May 12, 1933, pp. 676–677**
Article: "The Old Music School at Oxford." Reprinted in *The English Spirit* (1944; 1966).

D55. *New Clarion,* **May 27, 1933, p. 490**
Article: "The One Way to a United Front—We must build unity on the main mass-movement of the workers in this country—that mass-movement is the Labour Party."

D56. *Nineteenth Century,* **June 1933, pp. 641–652**
Article: "The National Government in Decline: A Socialist View."

D57. *Criterion,* **July 1933, pp. 674–676**
Review (untitled) of *Essays in Biography* by J. M. Keynes.

D58. *Political Quarterly,* **July–September 1933, pp. 385–402**
Article: "The House of Lords and Legislation: A Historical Survey."

D59. *New Clarion,* **August 5, 1933, p. 143**
Article: "The Graveyard of Capitalism—World Economic Conference—Why the Nations Failed to Co-operate to Save Their Own System."

D60. *New Clarion,* **September 9, 1933, p. 220**
Article: "The Banks for the Nation—What Labour Has Planned, 1."

D61. *The Times,* **October 2, 1933, p. 16, col. b**
Obituary for Mr. Charles Henderson. Tribute.

D62. *Criterion,* **October 1933, pp. 154–156**
Review (untitled) of *The Celtic Peoples and Renaissance Europe* by David Mathew.

D63. *New Clarion,* **November 4, 1933, p. 356**
Article: A. L. Rowse asks: "Are We Playing Germany's Game?"

D64. *New Clarion,* **December 16, 1933, p. 22**
Article: "We Are Not to Blame! says A. L. Rowse, who agrees that a final attempt be made to secure Germany's acceptance of a Plan of Disarmament—A Reply to Critics."

D65. *Nineteenth Century,* **December 1933, pp. 641–652**
Article: "The Labour Party from Within."

D66. *The Times,* **January 26, 1934, p. 8, col. c**
Letter: "Labour and the Press-Policy of the Party." "Concerning the misrepresentations of Labour policy in the Press . . . at the hands of a Press which is governed by their opponents."

D67. *Listener,* **April 11, 1934, pp. 607–609**
Essay: "Queen Elizabeth's Subjects (Broadcast 1), William Cecil, Lord Burghley." "Mr. A. L. Rowse, Fellow of All Souls College, Oxford, will alternate with Dr. G. B. Harrison, Reader in English Literature at the University of London, in a series of talks presenting the Elizabethan Age, through the personalities of some of its outstanding figures—politicians, courtiers, writers, adventurers, ecclesiastics and actors." (See also *Queen Elizabeth and Her Subjects,* A5.)

D68. *Listener,* **April 25, 1934, pp. 698–700**
Essay: "Queen Elizabeth's Subjects (Broadcast 3), The Earl of Essex." (See also *Queen Elizabeth and Her Subjects,* A5.)

D69. *Criterion,* **April 1934, pp. 518–520**
Review (untitled) of *Characters and Commentaries* by Lytton Strachey.

D70. *Listener,* **May 9, 1934, pp. 794–796**
Essay: "Queen Elizabeth's Subjects (Broadcast 5), Sir Walter Raleigh." (See also *Queen Elizabeth and Her Subjects*, A5.)

D71. *Listener,* **May 23, 1934, pp. 869–871**
Essay: "Queen Elizabeth's Subjects (Broadcast 7), Cardinal Allen." (See also *Queen Elizabeth and Her Subjects*, A5.)

D72. *Spectator,* **September 28, 1934, p. 450**
Review, entitled "Two Mr. Browns," of *I Was a Tramp* by John Brown and *Round the Corner* by Percy Brown.

D73. *Criterion,* **October 1934, pp. 137–141**
Review (untitled) of *Sir Thomas More and His Friends* by E. M. G. Routh and *The Reformation and the Contemplative Life* by David Mathew and Gervase Mathew.

D74. *New Statesman and Nation,* **new series, November 3, 1934, p. 622**
Poem: "The Stricken Grove." Reprinted in *Poems of a Decade* (1941); *A Life: Collected Poems* (1981).

D75. *Spectator,* **literature supplement, November 23, 1934, pp. 8, 10**
Review, entitled "The Renaissance European," of *Erasmus: Lectures and Wayfaring Sketches* by P. S. Allen and *Erasmus* by Stefan Zweig. Translated by Eden and Cedar Paul.

D76. *Nineteenth Century,* **November 1934, pp. 478–485**
Article: "Parties in Conference, II, Labour at Southport."

D77. *Spectator,* **January 25, 1935, pp. 129–130.**
Review, entitled "Blessed Thomas More," of *Sir Thomas More* by Christopher Hollis.

D78. *Criterion,* **January 1935, pp. 322–323**
Review (untitled) of *Christopher Marlowe in London* by Mark Eccles.

D79. *Spectator,* **March 22, 1935, pp. 486, 488.**
Review, entitled "Humane Politics," of *Social Judgment* by Graham Wallas.

D80. *Spectator,* **May 24, 1935, p. 884.**
Review, entitled "A Citizen of the World," of *Fifty Years of International Socialism* by M. Beer.

D81. *Spectator,* **August 2, 1935, p. 198**
Review, entitled "The Parson of St. Hilary," of *Twenty Years at St. Hilary* by Bernard Walke.

D82. *Spectator,* **August 16, 1935, pp. 269–270**
Review, entitled "An Elizabethan Courtier-Poet," of *At the Court of Queen Elizabeth: The Life and Lyrics of Sir Edward Dyer* by R. M. Sargent.

D83. *New Statesman and Nation,* **new series, October 12, 1935, p. 483**
Poem: "The Snake." Reprinted in *Poems of a Decade* (1941); *A Life: Collected Poems* (1981)

D84. *Spectator,* **October 18, 1935, p. 618**
Review, entitled "Mary Stuart and Mary Tudor," of *The Queen of Scots* by Stefan Zweig and *Mary Tudor* by Beatrice White.

D85. *Criterion,* **October 1935, pp. 107–109**
Review (untitled) of *The Nature of Capitalist Crisis* by John Strachey.

D86. *Spectator,* **literary supplement, November 22, 1935, p. 14**
Review, entitled "Queen Elizabeth as Letter-Writer," of *The Letters of Queen Elizabeth,* edited by G. B. Harrison.

D86a. *New Oxford Outlook,* **November 1935, pp. 204–231**
Long political article: "War and the Psychological Argument." E. W. F. Tomlin calls it, in *Scrutiny,* September 1936, "an extremely forceful piece of work."
   Note. See also A3, *Extempore Memorial (for C.H.),* pp. 264–266.

D87. *Listener,* **January 15, 1936, pp. 99–101**
Broadcast essay: "The Cornish Seamen and Pirates: An Elizabethan Castaway." The first of a series of talks from the West Regional Station tells the extraordinary story of Peter Carder of Veryan.

D88. *Listener,* **January 30, 1936, pp. 216–219**
Broadcast essay: "Cornish Seamen and Pirates: Piracy As a School of Seamanship."

D89. *Spectator,* **January 31, 1936, pp. 180–181**
Review, entitled "A Forgotten Elizabethan," of *Helena: Marchioness of Northampton* by C. A. Bradford.

D90. *Nineteenth Century,* **January 1936, pp. 69–79**
Article: "The Future and Prospects of the Labour Party."

D91. *Listener,* **February 12, 1936, pp. 299–302**
Broadcast essay: "Cornish Seamen and Pirates: Peter Mundy, the Traveller."

D92. *Listener,* **February 19, 1936, pp. 334–337**
Broadcast essay: "Cornish Seamen and Pirates: Bligh of the Bounty."

D93. *Spectator,* **March 13, 1936, p. 478**
Review, entitled "Dr. Coulton and Monastic Economy," of *Five Centuries of Religion,* vol. 3, *Getting and Spending,* by G. G. Coulton.

D94. *New Statesman and Nation,* **new series, March 14, 1936, p. 392**
Poem: "Homo Dicitur Rationalis."
   Reprinted in *Poems of a Decade* (1941); *A Life: Collected Poems* (1981) (as Homo Rationalis).

D95. *Spectator,* **April 10, 1936, p. 672**
Review, entitled "The Catholic Minority," of *Catholicism in England, 1535–1935* by David Mathew.

D96. *Criterion,* **April 1936, pp. 502–506**
Review (untitled) of *Soviet Communism: A New Civilisation?* by Sidney Webb and Beatrice Webb.

D97. *Spectator,* **May 15, 1936, p. 889**
Review, entitled "The Modernity of Medievalism," of *The Cambridge Medieval History,* vol. 8, *The Close of the Middle Ages,* edited by C. W. Previté-Orton and Z. N. Brooke.

D98. *Spectator,* **June 12, 1936, p. 1088**
Review, entitled "The Reign of Elizabeth," of *The Reign of Elizabeth* by J. B. Black.

D99. *New Statesman and Nation,* **new series, June 13, 1936, p. 930**
Poem: "Vox Clamantis in Deserto."

D100. *Spectator,* **June 19, 1936, pp. 1141–1142**
Review, entitled "Mr. Smith and the Babington Plot," of *The Babington Plot* by Alan Gordon Smith.

D101. *Listener,* **July 8, 1936, pp. 49–52**
Broadcast essay: "Erasmus, First of Europeans." The quartercentenary of the death of Erasmus, which falls on Saturday next, was anticipated in a broadcast programme last Sunday, giving a study of his personality as revealed in letters to and from his friends.

D102. *Spectator,* **July 10, 1936, p. 63**
Article: "Erasmus in England." Reprinted in *The English Spirit* (1944; 1966).

D103. *The Times,* **July 17, 1936, p. 10, col. c**
Letter: "Future of British Policy: An Argument from the Past." Concerning "the threat of the domination of one Power upon the Continent of Europe, which is ultimately a threat to our own security as it is to that of others."

D104. *Spectator,* **July 17, 1936, pp. 106, 108**
Review, entitled "The Father of English Musick," of *William Byrd* by E. H. Fellowes.

D105. *Spectator,* **July 31, 1936, p. 192**
Article: "What Should We Fight For? II." Second of a series of articles on the conditions under which military action by this country would be justified.

D106. *Spectator,* **July 31, 1936, pp. 208–209**
Review, entitled "The Elizabethan Mind," of *The Enchanted Glass: The Elizabethan Mind in Literature* by Hardin Craig.

D107. *Political Quarterly,* **July–September 1936, pp. 368–384**
Article: "The Dilemma of Church and State." Reprinted in *The End of an Epoch* (1947).

D108. *Political Quarterly,* **July–September 1936, pp. 441–445**
Review (untitled) of *Randall Davidson: Archbishop of Canterbury* by G. K. A. Bell.

D109. *Fortnightly* **(UK), September 1936, pp. 328–335**
Article: "A British Popular Front?"

D110. *Nineteenth Century,* **September 1936, pp. 320–332**
Article: "Mr. Keynes and the Labour Movement."

D111. *Spectator,* **October 2, 1936, p. 554**
Review, entitled "Reformation Figures," of *Characters of the Reformation* by Hilaire Belloc.

D112. *Listener,* **October 21, 1936, pp. 775–777**
Article: "Q and Cornwall." On September 24, Sir Arthur Quiller-Couch received the Freedom of the Borough of Bodmin, the town in which he was born.

D113. *Spectator,* **October 23, 1936, pp. 692, 694**
Review, entitled "Tudors and Stuarts," of *The Tudors: Personalities and Practical Politics in Sixteenth-Century England* by Conyers Read and *The Scotland of Queen Mary and the Religious Wars, 1513–1638* by Agnes Mure Mackenzie.

D114. *Spectator,* **December 11, 1936, p. 1054**
Review, entitled "A Conventional Elizabethan," of *Sir Henry Lee* by Sir E. K. Chambers.

D115. *Spectator,* **December 25, 1936, p. 1131**
Review, entitled "The Protestant Pope" of *The Right to Heresy* by Stefan Zweig and *Calvin and the Reformation* by James Mackinnon.

D116. *Criterion,* **January 1937, pp. 322–326**
Review (untitled) of *From Hegel to Marx* by Sidney Hook.

D117. *English Historical Review,* **January 1937, pp. 124–125**
Review of *The Original Writings and Correspondence of the Two Richard Hakluyts.* With an introduction and notes by Eva G. R. Taylor. 2 vols.

D118. *Nineteenth Century,* **January 1937, pp. 43–56**
Article: "The Duchy of Cornwall." Reprinted in *West-Country Stories* (1945).

D119. *Spectator,* **February 12, 1937, pp. 278, 280**
Review, entitled "The Fall of the Monasteries," of *English Monks and the Suppression of the Monasteries* by Geoffrey Baskerville.

D120. *Spectator,* **February 19, 1937, pp. 324, 326**
Review, entitled "The Spoilt Aristocrat," of *The Life and Death of Robert Devereux, Earl of Essex,* by G. B. Harrison.

D121. *Economic Journal,* **March 1937, pp. 154–156**
Review of *Karl Marx: Man and Fighter* by B. Nicolaievsky and O. Maenchen-Helfen.

D122. *The Times,* **June 4, 1937, pp. 17–18**
Article: "The Grenville Epic/A Retelling: New Light from Old Records." The first of two articles retelling in the light of recent discoveries in English and Spanish archives the epic story of Sir Richard Grenville's life and death.

D123. *The Times,* **June 5, 1937, pp. 15–16**
Article: "The Grenville Epic/At Flores in the Azores: Through Spanish Eyes." The second article on Sir Richard Grenville compares Ralegh's account of the last fight of the *Revenge* with a contemporary Spanish relation from a collection of documents in Madrid.

D124. *Spectator,* **July 2, 1937, p. 23**
Review, entitled "The Renaissance Warfare," of *A History of the Art of War in the Sixteenth Century* by Sir Charles Oman.

D125. *Criterion,* **July 1937, pp. 758–759**
Review (untitled) of *The School of Night* by M. C. Bradbrook.

D126. *Listener,* **August 4, 1937, pp. 250–252**
Article: "Robert Blake: Admiral of the Commonwealth."

D127. *Spectator,* **August 6, 1937, p. 236**
Article: "The Spanish College at Bologna." Reprinted in *The English Spirit* (1944; 1966).

D128. *New Statesman and Nation,* **new series, August 21, 1937, pp. 284–285**
Review, entitled "Protestant Martyr," of *William Tyndale* by J. F. Mozley.

D129. *The Times,* **August 23, 1937, p. 15, cols. a–b**
Letter: "British Foreign Policy/A Labour View." Concerning "the correspon-

dence in your columns on the subject of mutual toleration between democracies and dictatorships, as a principle of conduct in our foreign relations. I am sure that in this country, where the free expression of all currents of opinion is happily allowed, you will welcome a statement of Labour opinion, which so far has not been heard in the discussion."

D130. *The Times*, September 3, 1937, p. 8, col. a
Letter: "British Foreign Policy/Mr. Rowse's Reply." Concerning Rowse's "reply to some of the points to which Lord Lothian and Dr. Bevan have kindly devoted their attention."

   Note. For full correspondence from both sides, refer to *The End of an Epoch* (chap. 2, "British Foreign Policy: A Times Correspondence (1937), pp. 24–38, A17.

D131. *Spectator*, September 24, 1937, pp. 510, 512
Review, entitled "Elizabethan Tourist," of *Thomas Platter's Travels in England.* Translated and with an introduction by Clare Williams.

D132. *Nineteenth Century*, September 1937, pp. 290–303
Article: "The Position and Prospects of the Labour Party."

D133. *Criterion*, October 1937, pp. 164–168
Review (untitled) of *The Mind and Art of Jonathan Swift* by Ricardo Quintana.

D134. *Political Quarterly*, October–December 1937, pp. 610–613
Review (untitled) of *Ideology and Utopia* by Karl Mannheim.

D135. *Nineteenth Century*, November 1937, pp. 596–605
Article: "British Labour in Conference."

D136. *Spectator*, December 10, 1937, pp. 1066, 1068
Review, entitled "Light on Shakespeare's Circle," of *I, William Shakespeare, do Appoint Thomas Russell, Esquire . . .* by Leslie Hotson; *In Shakespeare's Warwickshire* by Oliver Baker.

D137. *Spectator*, December 31, 1937, p. 1188
Review, entitled "Dr. John Bull," of *Dr. John Bull* by Leigh Henry.

D138. *Criterion*, January 1938, pp. 305–311
Review (untitled) of *The Poems of Jonathan Swift,* edited by Harold Williams.

D139. *Political Quarterly*, January–March 1938, pp. 13–30
Article: "The Present and Immediate Future of the Labour Party." Reprinted in *The End of an Epoch* (1947) as *The Prospects of the Labour Party.*

D140. *Political Quarterly*, January–March 1938, pp. 141–143
Reviews (untitled) of *The Papacy and Fascism* by F. A. Ridley; *Towards the Christian Revolution* edited by R. B. Y. Scott and G. Vlastos; *Christianity, Communism, and the Ideal Society* by James Feibleman.

D141. *Spectator,* **February 11, 1938, pp. 234, 236**
Review, entitled "Stuart Political Thought," of *English Political Thought, 1603 to 1660,* vol. 1, *1603–1644,* by J. W. Allen.

D142. *The Times,* **March 16, 1938, p. 10, col. b**
Letter: "The Spanish War/A Plea for Intervention." Concerning "the very gravity of the situation with which we are confronted upon the Continent may serve to bring all sections of opinion together, as so often before in our history, to face the common danger."

D143. *Political Quarterly,* **April–June 1938, pp. 297–299**
Review (untitled) of *Michael Bakunin* by E. H. Carr.

D144. *Spectator,* **May 6, 1938, pp. 816, 818**
Review, entitled "L'Inglese Italianato," of *John Tiptoft: An Italianate Englishman, 1427–1470,* by R. J. Mitchell.

D145. *Spectator,* **June 24, 1938, pp. 1156–1157**
Review, entitled "Parliamentarian General," of *The Lord General: A Life of Thomas Fairfax* by M. A. Gibb.

D146. *Spectator,* **July 8, 1938, p. 70**
Review, entitled "A Marxist History," of *A People's History of England* by A. L. Morton.

D147. *Spectator*, **July 22, 1938, p. 155**
Review, entitled "St. Helena," of *St. Helena, 1502–1938* by Philip Gosse.

D148. *Political Quarterly,* **July–September 1938, pp. 334–350**
Article: "Reflections on the European Situation." Reprinted in *The End of an Epoch* (1947).

D149. *Spectator,* **August 5, 1938, p. 238**
Review, entitled "Tory History," of *The Second Tory Party, 1714–1832* by Keith Grahame Feiling.

D150. *Spectator,* **August 19, 1938, p. 307**
Review, entitled "The Use of History," of *The Modern Historian* by C. H. Williams.

D151. *Spectator,* **September 30, 1938, p. 524**
Review, entitled "An Oxford Figure," of *Dr. Routh* by R. D. Middleton.

D152. *Spectator,* **October 7, 1938, p. 572**
Review, entitled "Historical Scepticism," of *Aspects of History* by E. E. Kellett.

D153. *Spectator*, **October 28, 1938, p. 720**
Review, entitled "The Thirty Years' War," of *The Thirty Years' War* by C. V. Wedgwood.

D154. *Spectator,* **November 11, 1938, p. 815**
Article: "The Public Records: A National Heritage." Reprinted in *The English Spirit* (1944).

D155. *Spectator,* **December 9, 1938, p. 1012**
Review, entitled "What Is Wrong with the Germans," of *I Married a German* by Madeleine Kent.

D156. *Spectator,* **December 16, 1938, pp. 1055–1056**
Review, entitled "Eminent Henrician," of *Cuthbert Tunstal* by Charles Sturge.

D157. *New Statesman and Nation,* **new series, February 18, 1939, p. 257**
Review, entitled "A Tudor Classic," of *The Mirror for Magistrates,* edited by Lily B. Campbell.

D158. *Spectator,* **April 7, 1939, p. 599**
Review, entitled "The German Mind," of *Doctrinaires de la Revolution Allemande, 1918–1938* by Edmond Vermeil. Reprinted in *The Living Age* (USA), June 1939, pp. 394–395.

D159. *Times Literary Supplement,* **April 15, 1939, p. 217, col. c**
Letter: "Mirror for Magistrates." "*The Mirror for Magistrates* is a work of such importance in the development of Tudor literature, and the group of men who wrote it so interesting in themselves and so representative of their time, that perhaps I may be pardoned for giving some new information about the least known member of it. . . . Humphrey Cavell was a Cornishman and it is only natural that a Cornishman would have an especial interest in the great Cornish Rebellion of 1497. The Cavells were an old Cornish family seated at Trehaverock in St. Kew, but with branches elsewhere."

D160. *Spectator,* **April 28, 1939, p. 714**
Review, entitled "Pageant of London," of *The Great Chronicle of London,* edited by A. H. Thomas and I. D. Thornley.

D161. *Political Quarterly,* **April–June 1939, pp. 295–298**
Review (untitled) of *Power: A New Social Analysis* by Bertrand Russell.

D162. *Listener,* **June 1, 1939, pp. 1166–1168**
Article: "The House and the Man: John Opie and Harmony Cot."

D163. *The Times,* **June 8, 1939, p. 12, col. c**
Letter (untitled). Concerning "in view of Sir Lynden Macassey's apparent anxiety to attach the name of Oxford to the followers of Dr. Buchman, that Sir Lynden himself is not an Oxford man, but belongs to Trinity College Dublin, and London University."

D164. *Spectator,* **August 18, 1939, p. 262**
Review, entitled "The Dilemma of Our Time," of *An Autobiography* by R. G. Collingwood.

D165. *Political Quarterly,* **October–December 1939, pp. 489–501**
Article: "The Tradition of British Policy." Reprinted in *The End of an Epoch* (1947).

D166. *Political Quarterly,* **October–December 1939, pp. 614–617**
Review (untitled) of *The Economic Basis of Class Conflict and Other Essays in Political Economy* by Lionel Robbins.

D167. *The Times,* **November 11, 1939, p. 7, col. g, and p. 8, cols. a–b**
Article: "History on the Hoe/Plymouth in the Golden Age/A Galaxy of Great Names." On the 500th anniversary of the Charter of Plymouth.

D168. *Spectator,* **November 24, 1939, pp. 752, 754**
Review, entitled "A Great European," of *The Emperor Charles V* by Karl Brandi. Translated by C. V. Wedgwood.

D169. *Listener,* **December 21, 1939, pp. 1232–1233**
Article: "The Hoods and Our Naval Tradition."

D170. *Spectator,* **January 5, 1940, p. 22**
Review, entitled "Historical Marginalia," of *Pages from the Past* by H. A. L. Fisher and *In the Margin of History* by L. B. Namier.

D171. *The Times,* **January 27, 1940, p. 4, col. a**
Letter: "The Allied Cause/Germany and the Nazis." Commencing, "I should like, as a Labour candidate and a supporter of the Opposition to pay tribute to the magnificent and unanswerable statement of the Allies' cause and their aims in the speech of Lord Halifax at Leeds. No Foreign Secretary of late years has so penetrated to the heart of historic British policy, or from the historian's point of view put it more soundly, or stated the justice of the case more judicially."

D172. *Political Quarterly,* **January–March 1940, pp. 16–29**
Article: "What Is Wrong with the Germans?" Reprinted in *The End of an Epoch* (1947).

D173. *Political Quarterly,* **January–March 1940, pp. 127–130**
Review (untitled) of *Karl Marx* by I. Berlin.

D174. *The Times,* **February 17, 1940, p. 9, col. e**
Obituary: Lord Tweedsmuir. One of three contributors. Commencing, "I should not like John Buchan to pass from among us, amid so many tributes to his memory, without one word from the other side in politics. Convinced and admirable Conservative as he was, he was totally without any party acrimony or narrow partisanship."

D175. *Spectator,* **February 23, 1940, pp. 258–259**
Review, entitled "Tudor Translations," of *Tudor Translations: An Anthology.* Selected by Judge Clements.

D176. *Spectator,* **March 8, 1940, p. 328**
Review, entitled "Stage and Screen/The Theatre," of theater production *The Long Mirror* by J. B. Priestley at the Playhouse, Oxford.

D177. *New Statesman and Nation,* **new series, March 9, 1940, pp. 318–320**
Review, entitled "The Puritan Revolution," of *Archbishop Laud, 1573–1645* by H. R. Trevor-Roper; *John Pym, 1583–1643* by S. Reed Brett.

D178. *Spectator,* **March 15, 1940, pp. 374–376**
Review, entitled "Mrs. Boscawen and her Admiral," of *Admiral's Wife: The Life and Letters of Mrs. Boscawen from 1719 to 1761* by Cecil Aspinall-Oglander.

D179. *Spectator,* **March 22, 1940, pp. 419–420**
Review, entitled "The English Faust," of *Christopher Marlowe: A Biographical and Critical Study* by F. S. Boas.

D180. *Spectator,* **April 26, 1940, p. 599**
Review, entitled "Totalitarian Aggression," of *The Totalitarian Enemy* by F. Borkenau and *Germany the Aggressor* by F. J. C. Hearnshaw.

D181. *New Statesman and Nation,* **April 27, 1940, pp. 566–567**
Review, entitled "The Case of Charles II," of *The Last Rally: A Study of Charles II* by Hilaire Belloc.

D182. *The Times,* **May 9, 1940, p. 7, col. e**
Letter: "The Attitude of Labour/Industrial Leaders/A Broader Alternative Government" signed as "Labour candidate for Penryn and Falmouth." Commencing, "I should like as a Labour candidate, to express agreement with your Parliamentary correspondent's comments on the importance of our having one or two of the ablest representatives of the industrial Labour movement in Parliament at the present juncture. In particular Mr. Ernest Bevin he is the biggest man in the Labour Movement. It is absurd, as it has been a loss to the nation that he has not been in Parliament these last 10 years."

D183. *New Statesman and Nation,* **May 25, 1940, p. 676**
Review, entitled "Steenie," of *George Villiers, First Duke of Buckingham* by Hugh Ross Williamson.

D184. *Spectator,* **June 14, 1940, p. 813**
Review, entitled "Hitler and Strasser," of *Hitler et Moi* by Otto Strasser.

D185. *Economic Journal,* **June–September 1940, pp. 317–320**
Review of *The Economic Causes of War* by L. Robbins.

D186. *Spectator,* **July 5, 1940, p. 16**
Review, entitled "Books of the Day/Devonshire House in Regency Days," of *Hary-O: The Letters of Lady Harriet Cavendish, 1796–1809,* edited by Sir George Leveson-Gower and Iris Palmer.

D187. *New Statesman and Nation,* **July 20, 1940, pp. 68–70**
Review, entitled "An Episcopal Sycophant," of *Nathaniel, Lord Crewe, Bishop of Durham (1674–1721) and His Diocese* by C. E. Whiting.

D188. *Spectator,* **July 26, 1940, p. 91**
Article: "Drake's Way." Reprinted in *The English Spirit* (1944).

D189. *Spectator,* **July 26, 1940, p. 96**
Review, entitled "The Problem of the Germans," of *Germany: Jekyll and Hyde* by Sebastian Haffner and *The Canker of Germany* by Ernst G. Preuss.

189a. *Country Life,* **July 27, 1940, pp. 70–72**
Article: "Thomas Hardy and North Cornwall."

D190. *Political Quarterly,* **July–September 1940, pp. 248–260**
Article: "The End of an Epoch." Reprinted in *The End of an Epoch* (1947).

D191. *Political Quarterly,* **July–September 1940, pp. 303–305**
Review (untitled) of *Man and Society in an Age of Reconstruction* by Karl Mannheim.

D191a. *Country Life,* **August 24, 1940, p. 172**
Article: "The English Spirit." Reprinted in *The English Spirit* (1944).

D192. *Spectator,* **October 4, 1940, p. 342**
Review, entitled "Books of the Day/Britain's Economic Achievement," of *English Economic History: Mainly since 1700* by C. R. Fay.

D193. *Spectator,* **October 18, 1940, p. 398**
Review, entitled "Mary Tudor Again," of *Spanish Tudor: The Life of Bloody Mary* by H. F. M. Prescott.

D194. *Spectator,* **October 25, 1940, pp. 422, 424**
Review, entitled "Justice for Jeffreys," of *Judge Jeffreys* by H. Montgomery Hyde.

D195. *Spectator,* **November 1, 1940, p. 450**
Review, entitled "The Human Middle Ages," of *Europe's Apprenticeship* by G. G. Coulton.

D196. *Spectator,* **November 15, 1940, p. 499**
Poem: "Cornish Acres." Reprinted in *Poems of a Decade* (1941); *A Life: Collected Poems* (1981).

D197. *Spectator,* **November 22, 1940, pp. 544, 546**
Review, entitled "Parish Pride," of *The Book of Hartland* by R. Pearse Chope.

D198. *Spectator,* **December 6, 1940, p. 607**
Poem: "Duporth Camp; September 1940." Reprinted in *Poems of a Decade* (1941); *A Life: Collected Poems* (1981).

D199. *Spectator,* **December 13, 1940, p. 635**
Poem: "How Many Miles to Mylor." Reprinted in *Poems of a Decade* (1941); *A Life: Collected Poems* (1981).

D200. *Spectator,* **January 17, 1941, p. 68**
Review, entitled "The Diggers," of *Left-Wing Democracy in the English Civil War* by D. W. Petegorsky.

D201. *Spectator,* **January 17, 1941, pp. 55–56**
Article: "The Diary of William Carnsew: Part I."

D202. *Spectator,* **January 24, 1941, p. 86**
Article: "The Diary of William Carnsew: Part II."

D203. *Horizon,* **February 1941, pp. 150–152**
Review, entitled "Selected Notices," of *The Long Week-End* by Robert Graves and Alan Hodge.

D204. *Spectator,* **March 7, 1941, p. 251**
Poem: "Days of Waiting." Reprinted in *Poems of a Decade* (1941); *A Life: Collected Poems* (1981).

D205. *Listener,* **April 10, 1941, pp. 529–530**
Short story: "How Dick Stephens Fought the Bear." Reprinted in *West-Country Stories* (1945); *Cornish Stories* (1967).

D206. *Economic Journal,* **April 1941, pp. 92–95**
Review, entitled "Reviews/Economic History," of *The Twenty Years' Crisis, 1919–1939,* by E. H. Carr.

D207. *Political Quarterly,* **April–June 1941, pp. 223–225**
Review (untitled) of *The Development of Modern France, 1870–1939,* by D. W. Brogan.

D208. *Listener,* **May 22, 1941, p. 734**
Poem: "Cornish Landscape." Reprinted in *A Life: Collected Poems* (1981).

D209. *Horizon,* **May 1941, pp. 305–306**
Poem: "Epithalamium." Reprinted in *Poems of a Decade* (1941); *A Life: Collected Poems* (1981).

D210. *Spectator,* **June 20, 1941, pp. 658, 660**
Review, entitled "The Early English Humanists," of *Humanism in England during the Fifteenth Century* by R. Weiss.

D211. *Horizon,* **June 1941, pp. 384–393**
Article: "Democracy and Democratic Leadership." Reprinted in *The End of an Epoch* (1947).

D212. *Spectator,* **July 11, 1941, pp. 40, 42**
Review, entitled "The English Reformation," of *The Reformation in England* by F. M. Powicke.

D213. *Listener,* **July 17, 1941, p. 98**
Poem: "Summer Warning." Reprinted in *Poems of a Decade* (1941).

D214. *Political Quarterly,* **July–September 1941, pp. 305–317**
Article: "Reflections on Lord Baldwin." Reprinted in *The End of an Epoch* (1947).

D215. *New Statesman and Nation,* **August 2, 1941, p. 114**
Review, entitled "The Enemies of Civilisation," of *The Roots of National Socialism* by Rohan D'O. Butler; *Germany Possessed* by H. G. Baynes.

D216. *New Statesman and Nation,* **August 9, 1941, p. 133**
Article: "Matthew Arnold As Cornishman."

D217. *Spectator,* **August 29, 1941, p. 216**
Review, entitled "Cornwall a Generation Ago," of *Cornish Tales* by Charles Lee. With an introduction by "Q."

D218. *Listener,* **September 4, 1941, p. 334**
Poem: "All Souls."

D219. *New Statesman and Nation,* **September 6, 1941, p. 227**
Poem: "Visit to the Dentist." Reprinted in *Poems of a Decade* (1941).

D220. *Country Life,* **September 26, 1941, pp. 582–585**
Article: "Rialton, Near Newquay: A Cornish Monastic Manor." Reprinted in *West-Country Stories* (1945).

D221. *New Statesman and Nation,* **September 27, 1941, pp. 311–312**
Review, entitled "Jersey Oxonian," of *A Jerseyman at Oxford* by R. R. Marett.

D222. *New Statesman and Nation,* **October 18, 1941, pp. 365–366**
Review, entitled "Mr. A. E. W. Mason's Drake," of *The Life of Francis Drake* by A. E. W. Mason.

D223. *New Statesman and Nation,* **November 8, 1941, p. 412**
Review, entitled "A Topographical Elizabethan," of *The Works of Michael Drayton,* edited by J. W. Hebel. Vol. 5, Introductions, Notes, etc., edited by K. Tillotson and B. H. Newdigate; *Michael Drayton and His Circle* by B. H. Newdigate.

D224. *Harper's Magazine,* **November 1941, pp. 584–585**
Poem: "Remembrance Sunday: Coombe Church, 1940." Reprinted in *Poems of a Decade* (1941); *A Life: Collected Poems* (1981).

D225. *Times Literary Supplement,* **December 6, 1941, p. 600, col. c**
Poem: "Charlestown Harbour/(To Christopher Away at the War)." Reprinted in
Poems Chiefly Cornish (1944); *A Life: Collected Poems* (1981).

D226. *New Statesman and Nation,* **December 13, 1941, p. 494**
Article: "Books in General."

D227. *Times Literary Supplement,* **December 20, 1941, pp. 644–646**
Short story: "The Stone That Liked Company." With drawings by Bip Pares.
Reprinted in *West-Country Stories* (1945).

D227a. *Country Life,* **February 6, 1942, pp. 252–255**
Article: "The Caroline Country Parson: George Herbert's Ideal." Reprinted in
The English Spirit (1945; rev. ed., 1966).

D228. *Listener,* **February 26, 1942, p. 278**
Poem: "Moon, Snow, Winter Afternoon."

D229. *The Times,* **February 27, 1942, p. 5, col. f**
Letter: "The Future of Education/The Day School System." Commencing,
"There is a point of view as to the future of our educational system which is
of the utmost importance in the present discussions, and yet is hardly repre-
sented in them or sufficiently taken account of: that of people who pass through
elementary and secondary schools, the vast majority of the nation. It is they
who should have the largest say as to the future of education in this country."

D230. *The Times,* **March 5, 1942, p. 5, col. e**
Letter: "Character and Brains/The Test of Events/England and Her Resources."
Commencing, "It would be possible to discuss the respective merits of character and brains *in vacuo* indefinitely. But in the present situation the argument
may be clinched, for events have given us a decisive answer. And it is vitally
important that we should learn from it for the future reshaping of our educational system."
　　Note. Followed in the same column by two letters in response to A.L.R.'s
letter (D229 above) from W. W. Varney and Thomas Lowinsky.

D230a. *Observer,* **March 15, 1942, p. 3**
Review, entitled "Spanish Queen," of *Catherine of Aragon* by Garrett Mattingly.

D231. *Times Literary Supplement,* **April 11, 1942, p. 190, col. b**
Poem: "Man and Bee: An Allegory."

D231a. *Observer,* **April 12, 1942, p. 3**
Review, entitled "Nietzsche: Nazi Idol," of *Nietzsche* by Crane Brinton.

D232. *Listener,* **April 16, 1942, p. 507**
Review, entitled "Prospects in Education," of *Science and Education* by S. R.
Humby and E. J. F. James; *The Future in Education* by Sir Richard Livingstone.

D233. *Political Quarterly,* **April–June 1942, pp. 216–219**
Review (untitled) of *To the Finland Station: A Study in the Writing and Acting of History* by Edmund Wilson.

D234. *Political Quarterly,* **April–June 1942, pp. 225–228**
Review (untitled) of *Church and State in Fascist Italy* by D. A. Binchy.

D234a. *Observer,* **May 3, 1942, p. 3**
Review, entitled "Dorothy Wordsworth," of *Journals of Dorothy Wordsworth,* edited by E. de Selincourt.

D234b. *Observer,* **May 17, 1942, p. 3**
Review, entitled "Hawthorne on England," of *The English Notebooks* by Nathaniel Hawthorne, edited by Randall Stewart.

D234c. *Observer,* **May 24, 1942, p. 3**
Review, entitled "Romantic Egoist," of Savage Landor by Malcolm Elwin.

D234d. *Observer,* **June 28, 1942, p. 3**
Review, entitled "Family History," of *Bowen's Court* by Elizabeth Bowen.

D235. *Times Literary Supplement,* **August 8, 1942, p. 394, col. b**
Poem: "The Leddra at Trenarren."

D235a. *Observer,* **August 16, 1942, p. 3**
Review, entitled "The Genius Of Wordsworth," of *The Mind of a Poet* by R. D. Havens.

D235b. *Observer,* **October 11, 1942, p. 3**
Review, entitled "The English Revolution," of *Harrington's Interpretation of His Age* by R. H. Tawney.

D236. *New Statesman and Nation,* **October 17, 1942, p. 260**
Review, entitled "Novelist's History," of *King James the Last* by Jane Lane.

D237. *Listener,* **October 22, 1942, p. 535**
Letter: "What Shall We Do With The Germans?"
  Note. Responded to by G. M. Young, October 29 issue, p. 567.

D238. *Listener,* **November 5, 1942, p. 595**
Letter (untitled) in response to G. M. Young.
  Note. Responded to by J. C. Lynch, November 19 issue, p. 662.

D239. *Political Quarterly,* **October–December 1942, pp. 455–457**
Review (untitled) of *Darwin, Marx, Wagner* by Jaques Barzun.
  Note. A. L. Rowse made his first appearance on the editorial board of *Political Quarterly* in October–December 1942 and his last in April–June 1946.

D240. *New Statesman and Nation,* **November 7, 1942, p. 303**
Poem: "Trenarren: Autumn 1941." Reprinted in *Poems Chiefly Cornish* (1944); *A Life: Collected Poems* (1981).

D240a. *Observer,* **December 27, 1942, p. 3**
Review, entitled "Nelson and Drake," of *The Nelson Touch: An Anthology of Lord Nelson's Letters.* Compiled by Clemence Dane; *Founded upon the Seas* by Walter Oakeshott.

D241. *Times Literary Supplement,* **January 16, 1943, p. 32, col. a**
Poem: "Duporth Hill." Reprinted in *Poems Chiefly Cornish* (1944); *A Life: Collected Poems* (1981).

D241a. *Observer,* **January 24, 1943, p. 3**
Review, entitled "The Discoverer of America," of *Christopher Columbus: Admiral of the Ocean Sea* by Samuel Eliot Morison.

D242. *The Times,* **March 12, 1943, p. 5, col. e**
Letter: "Security in Europe/Russia and Her Neighbours/Guarantees of Peace." Commencing, "Those of us among the public who have observed the trends of British policy in recent years in terms of its historic needs and demands will welcome your analysis of them with deep agreement and satisfaction." Discusses Russia/Treaty of Versailles and Foreign policy.

D243. *New Statesman and Nation,* **March 20, 1943, p. 191**
Article: "Books in General."

D244. *Times Literary Supplement,* **March 27, 1943, p. 152, col. b**
Poem: "Call-Up." Reprinted in *Poems Chiefly Cornish* (1944); *A Life: Collected Poems* (1981).

D244a. *Observer,* **April 18, 1943, p. 3**
Review, entitled "Swiss Thinker," of *Reflections on History* by Jakob Burckhardt. Translated by M. D. Hottinger.

D244b. *Observer,* **April 25, 1943, p. 3**
Review, entitled "Two Soldiers of France," of *The Two Marshals: Bazaine and Pétain* by Philip Guedalla.

D245. *Economic Journal,* **April 1943, pp. 88–91**
Review of *The Speeches of Adolf Hitler (April 1922–August 1939): An English Translation of Representative Passages,* edited by Norman H. Baynes.

D246. *Listener,* **May 13, 1943, p. 566**
Poem: "Iffley." Reprinted in *Poems Chiefly Cornish* (1944); *A Life: Collected Poems* (1981); *Oxford and Oxfordshire in Verse* (1982), edited by Antonia Fraser.

D246a. *Observer,* **May 16, 1943, p. 3**
Review, entitled "Elizabethan Prospect," of *The Elizabethan World Picture* by E. M. W. Tillyard.

D247. *Times Literary Supplement,* **May 22, 1943, p. 244, col. b**
Poem: "Bus-Ride." Reprinted in *Poems Chiefly Cornish* (1944); *A Life: Collected Poems* (1981).

D248. *New Statesman and Nation,* **June 5, 1943, p. 370**
Article: "Books in General."

D248a. *Observer,* **June 13, 1943, p. 3**
Review, entitled "Voices of France," of *Political Thought in France from Sleyès to Sorel* by J. P. Mayer.

D248b. *Observer,* **July 4, 1943, p. 3**
Review, entitled "The Quality of 'Q'," of *Cambridge Lectures* by Sir Arthur Quiller-Couch.

D249. *New Statesman and Nation,* **September 11, 1943, p. 171**
Article: "Books in General."

D249a. *Observer,* **September 19, 1943, p. 3**
Review, entitled "German View," of *Order of the Day: Political Essays and Speeches* by Thomas Mann.

D250. *New Statesman and Nation,* **September 25, 1943, pp. 199–200**
Article: "Falkland." (Lucius Cary, Viscount Falkland, died in battle at Newbury, September 20, 1643.)

D250a. *Observer,* **October 17, 1943, p. 3**
Review, entitled "Every Inch a Queen," of *Queen Elizabeth* by Theodore Maynard; *The Age of Catherine De Medici* by J. E. Neale.

D251. *Listener,* **October 21, 1943, p. 462**
Poem: "The Gribbin." Reprinted in *Poems Chiefly Cornish* (1944); *A Life: Collected Poems* (1981).

D251a. *Observer,* **October 31, 1943, p. 3**
Review, entitled "Duchess," of *Letters of a Grandmother, 1732–1735,* edited by G. Scott Thomson.

D252. *New Statesman and Nation,* **November 13, 1943, pp. 320–321**
Review, entitled "Trinity," of *Trinity College: An Historical Sketch* by G. M. Trevelyan.

D252a. *Observer,* **November 14, 1943, p. 3**
Review, entitled "Passionate Puritan," of *Born under Saturn: A Biography of William Hazlitt* by C. M. Maclean.

D253. *Times Literary Supplement,* **November 27, 1943, pp. 570, 572**
Short story: "The Wicked Vicar of Lansillian." Reprinted in *West-Country Stories* (1945).

D254. *New Statesman and Nation,* **December 4, 1943, p. 371**
Article: "Books in General."

D254a. *Time and Tide,* **December 11, 1943, p. 1017**
Poem: "Gear." Reprinted in *Poems Chiefly Cornish* (1944); *A Life: Collected Poems* (1981).

D254b. *Observer,* **December 12, 1943, p. 3**
Review, entitled "Periwigs," of *Carteret and Newcastle: A Contrast in Contemporaries* by Basil Williams.

D255. *Times Literary Supplement,* **December 18, 1943, p. 609, col. b**
Poem: "Answer to a Young Poet." Reprinted in *Poems Chiefly Cornish* (1944); *A Life: Collected Poems* (1981).

D255a. *Observer,* **January 23, 1944, p. 3**
Review, entitled "Transatlantic," of *God's Englishman* by Leland Dewitt Baldwin.

D256. *The Times,* **February 1, 1944, p. 5, col. d**
Letter (untitled). On the elections in France and correcting a correspondent's misstatement in that France did use "proportional representation—P.R.—from 1919 to 1928 and dropped it because it was a failure."

D257. *New Statesman and Nation,* **February 12, 1944, p. 111**
Article: "Books in General."

D258. *The Times,* **March 3, 1944, p. 5, col. e**
Letter: "Policies for Europe/The Future of Germany/A Balanced Federation." On postwar settlement in Europe. Commencing, "Most historical opinion would, I think, be in agreement with the emphasis of your leading article against dismembering Germany, in spite of all her crimes. We should be against destroying her, since that would only give legitimate ground for a new outburst of fanatical nationalism in the post-war period. On the other hand, it is very important that Germany should become a federal state after the war."

D258a. *Time and Tide,* **March 25, 1944, pp. 266–267**
Reviews, entitled "Men & Books"/"The Old Poetry and the New," of *Letters to Malaya, III and IV* by Martyn Skinner; and *The Cruel Solstice* by Sidney Keyes.

D259. *History,* **March 1944, pp. 17–26**
Article: "The Turbulent Career of Sir Henry Bodrugan." Reprinted in *The Little Land of Cornwall* (1986).

D260. *Times Literary Supplement,* **April 29, 1944, p. 212, col. b**
Poem: "Before the Invasion." Reprinted in *Poems of Deliverance* (1946); *A Life: Collected Poems* (1981) as "Before D-Day."

D260a. *Observer,* **April 30, 1944, p. 3**
Review, entitled "Dutchman," of *William the Silent* by C. V. Wedgwood.

D261. *Spectator,* **May 19, 1944, pp. 448–449**
Article: "Q As Cornishman." A literary tribute.

D262. *Listener,* **June 1, 1944, p. 604**
Poem: "English Landscape, Spring 1944." Reprinted in *Poems of Deliverance* (1946) as "Spring 1944."

D262a. *Observer,* **June 4, 1944, p. 3**
Review, entitled "Hearts of Oak," of *The English Yeoman under Elizabeth and the Early Stuarts* by Mildred Campbell.

D262b. *Observer,* **July 2, 1944, p. 3**
Review, entitled "Poet's Portrait," of *A Study of Wordsworth* by J. C. Smith.

D262c. *Time and Tide,* **July 8, 1944, pp. 587–588**
Review, entitled "Mr. Churchill As War Orator," of *Onwards to Victory: War Speeches by the Rt. Hon. Winston S. Churchill* (1943).

D263. *Listener,* **July 13, 1944, pp. 45–46.**
Article: "Poets of Today."

D263a. *Observer,* **August 13, 1944, p. 3**
Review, entitled "This English Fabric," of *English Social History: A Survey of Six Centuries—Chaucer to Queen Victoria* by G. M. Trevelyan, O.M.

D263b. *Time and Tide,* **September 9, 1944, p. 790**
Article: "Cornish Conversation Piece." Reprinted in *West-Country Stories* (1945).

D263c. *Observer,* **September 10, 1944, p. 3**
Review, entitled "Behind the Dykes," of *The Dutch Nation: An Historical Study* by G. J. Renier.

D264. *New Statesman and Nation,* **October 7, 1944, p. 234**
Poem: "Autumn Is Here." Reprinted in *Poems Chiefly Cornish* (1944); *A Life: Collected Poems* (1981).

D264a. *Observer,* **October 22, 1944, p. 3**
Review, entitled "Pageant," of *The Englishman and His History* by H. Butterfield; *Historical Scholarship and Historical Thought* by G. N. Clark.

D264b. *Time and Tide,* **November 4, 1944, p. 964**
Article: "Notes on the Way."

D265. *The Times,* **December 13, 1944, p. 5, col. e**
Letter: "The Building Heritage/English Towns/An Appeal to the Big Firms."

On spoliation of town amenities by large firms. Commencing, "It is surely a good sign when an undergraduate society at Oxford protests against the destruction of a good old building and is concerned at what will take its place. After all it is a matter that affects them more than those of us who are getting older. We can be nothing but ashamed of what the last three generations, including our own, have done to disfigure the beauty of Oxford."

D265a. *Time and Tide,* **January 13, 1945, pp. 25–26**
Article: "Nottingham: A Midlands Capital."

D266. *The Times,* **February 1, 1945, p. 5, col. e**
Letter: "Hitler's Speech/The German View of the World/Britain and the Small Nations." On German policy of force. Commencing, "Hitler's speech—it may well have the importance of being his last anniversary speech—serves the purpose of defining very clearly what it is that divides German standards from those for which we stand."

D267. *The Times,* **March 21, 1945, p. 5, col. e**
Letter: "Bodmin Moor/Cornish Prehistoric Sites/Archaeology and the Bomb." On Bodmin Moor as proposed bombing range. Commencing, "No West-countryman would wish anything other than to help the Royal Navy in its work: we feel that we have a special share in its tradition and all that it means to the country. But we would ask the Admiralty to consider whether Bodmin Moor is absolutely indispensible to its work."

D268. *Welsh Review,* **March 1945, pp. 39–49**
Article: "Matthew Arnold As Cornishman."

D269. *Saturday Review of Literature (USA),* **October 27, 1945, p. 39**
Poem: "On a Dead President." First printed in *Time and Tide,* April 28, 1945. Reprinted in *Poems of Deliverance* (1946) as "On the Dead President." In *Poems of Cornwall and America* (1967) as "On the Dead President." In *A Life: Collected Poems* (1981) as "On the Dead President."

D270. *Foreign Affairs* **(USA), July 1945, pp. 658–667**
Article: "The British Labor Party: Prospects and Portents."

D271. *The Times,* **August 7, 1945, p. 5, col. f**
Letter: "University Students." On the demobilization of university students. Commencing, "Everyone at the Universities will be glad to hear of the official decision to release a certain number of arts students from the Forces to equip themselves at the university for work in the various professions where there are such serious urgent shortages."

D271a. *Time and Tide,* **August 18, 1945, p. 692**
Review, entitled "Men and Books"/"Victorian Schooldays," of *A Distant Prospect* by Lord Berners.

D272. *New Statesman and Nation,* **September 1, 1945, p. 144**
Poem: "The Owl." Reprinted in *Poems of Deliverance* (1946); *A Life: Collected Poems* (1981).

D272a. *Time and Tide,* **October 20, 1945, pp. 879–880**
Review, entitled "Men and Books"/"Kipling the Celt," of *Rudyard Kipling: A New Appreciation* by Hilton Brown.

D273. *The Saturday Book, Fifth Year,* **October 1945, pp. 49–58**
Article: "All Souls." Reprinted in *The English Past* (1951).

D273a. *Observer,* **April 28, 1946, p. 3**
Review, entitled "Soldiers of the Queen," of *Elizabeth's Army* by C. G. Cruickshank.

D274. *Listener,* **May 16, 1946, pp. 642–644**
Article: "If You Had Lived in Elizabethan England."

D275. *The Times,* **May 18, 1946, p. 5, col. g**
Letter: "Coventry Cathedral." Commencing, "The scheme for what is virtually a new cathedral at Coventry has been launched, I feel, without sufficient consideration being given to the other side of the case. There are many people I know, who are opposed to this idea of not reconstructing the church as it was, but transmogrifying it into something new and different and monstrous."

D275a. *Time and Tide,* **July 20, 1946, pp. 679–680**
Article: "Notes on the Way"/"The Intellectuals and Their Role in Society—I."

D275b. *Time and Tide,* **July 27, 1946, pp. 701–702**
Article: "Notes on the Way"/"The Intellectuals and Their Role in Society—II." These articles generated considerable correspondence to *Time and Tide.*
Note. August 3, pp. 727–728, letters from Rose Macaulay, Stephen Spender, and Geoffrey Grigson. August 10, p. 754, from L. J. Filewood, George Richards, and J. K. Popham.

D275c. *Time and Tide,* **August 24, 1946, p. 803**
Letter to the editor: "A. L. Rowse's 'Notes on the Way.'"

D275d. *Time and Tide,* **September 21, 1946, p. 893**
Article: "More about the Intellectuals."

D275e. *Time and Tide,* **September 28, 1946, pp. 917–918**
Article: "More about the Intellectuals"/"The Intellectuals: Conclusions and Prospects—1."

D275f. *Time and Tide,* **October 5, 1946, pp. 942–943**
Article: "More about the Intellectuals"/"The Intellectuals: Conclusions and Prospects—2."

D276. *Spectator,* **October 18, 1946, p. 396**
Review, entitled "Books of the Day/Servant of the State," of *Wellington* by Richard Aldington.

D276a. *Time and Tide,* **December 7, 1946, p. 1182**
Poem: "On Richard Wilson's 'Lake of Narni.'" Reprinted in *Poems of Deliverance* (1946); *A Life: Collected Poems* (1981).

D277. *The West Country Magazine,* **Winter 1946, p. 152**
Poem: "Tregonissey."

D278. *The West Country Magazine,* **Winter 1946, pp. 163–165**
Article: "Fighting an Election."

D279. *Cornish Review,* **Spring 1947, series 1, pp. 24–25**
Poem: "Cornish Poem/Charlestown Harbour by Moonlight." Reprinted in *Poems Partly American* (1959); *A Life: Collected Poems* (1981).

D280. *Britain Today,* **August 1947, pp. 12–15**
Article: "History and the Modern World."

D281. *Listener,* **October 9, 1947, p. 644**
Review, entitled "A Lovable Writer," of *Arthur Quiller-Couch: A Biographical Study of "Q"* by F. Brittain.

D282. *The Saturday Book,* **November 1947, pp. 217–231**
Article: "Hillesden." Reprinted in *The English Past* (1951).

D283. *The Times,* **December 27, 1947, p. 7, col. e**
Letter: "Obituary/Dr. F. E. Hutchinson." Commencing, "Because of his innate modesty I fear that Dr. Hutchinson's personality and achievement may not be recognized at the full value. He did indeed work manfully and hard all his life at teaching, pastoral work, and in adult education. But in addition to all this he made himself a distinguished scholar, sensitive, meticulous, exact."

D284. *New Statesman and Nation,* **April 3, 1948, p. 276**
Letter: "Death to Civilisation?"

D285. *The Times,* **September 8, 1948, p. 5, col. e**
Letter: "The Gospel of Work/Telling the People." On production. Commencing, "Mr. Alfred Edwards's letter and your own leading article on Sir Stafford Cripps's campaign for more production are pointers to what is now the crucial problem of the nation—if it is to survive as it has been. The underlying fact of the situation is that we are now a people of 50 millions and can feed from our own resources about 30 millions."

D285a. *Time and Tide,* **September 11, 1948, pp. 927–928**
Article: "Notes on the Way."

D286. *National Review* **(UK), November 1948, pp. 403–412**
Review, entitled "England in Peace and War," of *Mr. Churchill's Memoirs.* This review is also an extensive article.

D286a. *Time and Tide,* **December 4, 1948, pp. 1242–1243**
Review, entitled " 'Q' As Man of Letters," of *"Q" Anthology,* compiled by F. Brittain.

D286b. *Time and Tide,* **April 9, 1949, p. 355**
Review, entitled "A Poet of Perfection," of *The Day's Alarm* by Paul Dehn.

D286c. *Time and Tide,* **April 23, 1949, p. 405**
Review, entitled "Men and Books"/"Shakespearian Essays," of *Essays on Shakespeare and Other Elizabethans* by Tucker Brooke.

D287. *The Times,* **August 16, 1949, p. 9, col. c**
Letter: "High Expenditure on Education/Lowered Standards." Commencing, "When a country is heading for bankruptcy, it is a duty of a citizen to point out where saving may be effected."

D288. *The Times,* **September 6, 1949, p. 5, col. e**
Letter: "Expenditure on Education/The Possibilities of Economy." Commencing, "I note that the Vice-Chancellor of Leeds University completely corroborates my case. He says 'certainly after the recent expansion in the universities in England a relatively large proportion, perhaps 15 per cent, are making heavy weather of their studies.' That is not likely to be an overestimate, so far as the new universities are concerned. Those of us at the universities know what the facts are: we do not need to be told by vague benevolent theorists of a continental kind who entertain illusions about the equal educability of everyone."

D289. *The Times,* **September 16, 1949, p. 2, col. g**
Letter: "Expenditure on Education/Economy and Students' Numbers." Commencing, "Lord Lindsay puts to me three points and then proceeds to answer them for me. I prefer answering them for myself."

D290. *The Saturday Book, Ninth Year,* **October 1949, pp. 121–122**
Article: "Personal Confessions." Nine contributors.

D291. *The National Review* **(UK) November 1949, pp. 452–463**
Review, entitled "Books New and Old/Secondary Education for All/Fit or Unfit," of *Secondary Education for All* by H. C. Dent. Combination review and extensive article.

D292. *National Review* **(UK), February 1950, pp. 148–150**
Review, entitled "Eminent Edwardians," of *The Dictionary of National Biography, 1931–1940,* edited by L. G. Wickham Legg.

D293. *National Review,* **March 1950, pp. 232–235**

Review, entitled "Disillusioned Communists," of *The God That Failed.* Six studies in communism. Introduction by Richard Crossman. Reprinted in *Portraits and Views,* 1979, as *Disenchantment with Communism.*

D293a. *Time and Tide,* July 8, 1950, p. 678
Review, entitled "Men and Books"/"Trelawny and the Cornish Temperament," of *Trelawny* by R. Glyn Grylls.

D294. *National and English Review,* August 1950, pp. 220–223
Review, entitled "Churchill on the Grand Alliance," of Winston S. Churchill, *The Second World War,* vol. 3, *The Grand Alliance.*

D295. *Times Literary Supplement,* September 8, 1950, p. 565, col. d
Letter: "The *Revenge.*" Commencing, "In the interests of accuracy it may be as well to correct your 'correction' of M. Braudel last week: 'for example, the *Revenge* was not captured but sunk.' In fact, she was surrendered, not sunk. While being taken along with the Spanish fleet to Spain, she foundered off Terceira in the great storm after the engagement at Flores."

D296. *National and English Review,* October 1950, pp. 378–380
Review, entitled "The Elizabethan Conquest of Ireland," of *Elizabeth's Irish Wars* by Cyril Falls.

D296a. *Time and Tide,* November 25, 1950, pp. 1182–1183
Review, entitled "Men and Books"/"Regency Panorama," of *The Age of Elegance, 1812–1822* by Arthur Bryant.

D297. *National and English Review*, December 1950, pp. 503–506
Review, entitled "Matthew Arnold and English Education," of *The Educational Thought and Influence of Matthew Arnold* by W. F. Connell.

D298. *The Times,* September 1, 1951, p. 5, col. e
Letter: "Rebuilding of a Cathedral/War Damage for Coventry." Commencing, "All of us who are interested in the historic past of the country or its present good looks are concerned about the problem of Coventry Cathedral. But, of course, there should be no problem if only the cathedral authorities there would adopt the simple and obvious solution—and the one that is right on historic and aesthetic grounds no less than economic ones. The country in its present circumstances cannot, and ought not to, afford one million pounds on a brand new cathedral on that site."

D299. *National and English Review,* September 1951, pp. 154–157
Article: "Impressions of America."

D300. *The Times,* November 5, 1951, p. 5, col. e
Letter: "The Graduate Vote." Commencing, "In the daunting difficulties that face all Governments nowadays, no responsible person can be anything but sympathetic to the Government, of either party, which have to carry the bur-

den of responsibility. And this is what I feel, without being a Conservative, in regard to Mr. Churchill's Government. Things really are too difficult and dangerous for us to feel very partisan. With this spirit in mind, I am all the more sure it would make a most unfortunate impression, and be very unwise, if the Government were to restore a special representation to the universities. I have always thought university representation in the Commons on its present basis strictly indefensible."

D301. *National and English Review,* **January 1952, pp. 41–42**
Review, entitled "The Saint in Politics," of *George Lansbury* by Raymond Postgate.

D301a. *Time and Tide,* **April 5, 1952, pp. 338, 340**
Review, entitled "Men and Books"/"The Illusions of Mr. Bevan," of *In Place of Fear* by Aneurin Bevan.

D301b. *Time and Tide,* **April 19, 1952, pp. 388–389**
Review, entitled "Arthur and the Modern World," of *Merlin, or the Return of Arthur: A Satiric Epic* by Martyn Skinner.

D302. *English Historical Review,* **April 1952, pp. 267–268**
Review (untitled) of *Further English Voyages to Spanish America, 1583–1594.* Translated and edited by Irene A. Wright.

D302a. *Time and Tide,* **May 10, 1952, p. 475**
Poem: "Lazarus." Reprinted in *Poems Partly American* (1959); *A Life: Collected Poems* (1981), as "Lazarus in New College Chapel."

D303. *National and English Review,* **June 1952, pp. 341–345**
Article: "An Historian's View of Spain."

D304. *Times Literary Supplement,* **July 18, 1952, p. 469, col. c.**
Letter: "Haud Credo: A Shakespearian Pun." Commencing, "Though I am not a Shakespearian scholar I have a small suggestion to make that may help to make clear the meaning of the well known passage about the deer at the beginning of Act IV, Scene 2 of 'Love's Labours Lost.'"

D305. *National and English Review,* **August 1952, pp. 95–99**
Article: "The Intellectuals and the B.B.C."

D306. *Cornish Review,* **Summer 1952, series 1, p. 14**
Poem: "Spring Afternoon at Charlestown." Reprinted in *Poems Partly American* (1959). *A Life: Collected Poems* (1981).

D307. *The Times,* **September 6, 1952, p. 5, col. e**
Letter: "Science and Humanity." Commencing, "Just as this country has been living on the last decades on the accumulated capital of Victorian industry, so we continue to assume conditions of Victorian prosperity in our thinking and live off late Victorian luxury ideas."

D308. *The Times,* **September 15, 1952, p. 7, col. e**
Letter: "Science and Humanity." A brief biting paragraph: "I welcome Mr. Leonard Woolf's exposure of himself; it is so revealing of the bankruptcy of the Left intellectual. No consideration of the facts of our economic situation, dangerously poised on a razor-edge; merely a personal taunt. The complete reply to him on that level is that my books sell in America: I earn dollars for the country."

D309. *The Times,* **October 3, 1952, p. 8, col. e**
Letter: "Obituary/Lord Astor/Devotion to Plymouth." Commencing, "With a public figure who touched English life at so many points as Waldorf Astor did, there are bound to be many tributes; but among them a West Country voice should be heard. For, indeed, he loved Plymouth with that quiet, selfless devotion which was characteristic of him, where his wife served—and still serves—Plymouth with an ardent passionate devotion that is no less characteristic of her."

D310. *English Historical Review,* **October 1952, pp. 579–580**
Review (untitled) of *Tres embajadores de Felipe II en Inglaterra* by Manuel Fernandez.

D311. *History* **(UK), October 1952, p. 284**
Letter: "Collingwood's Idea of History."

D312. *Listener,* **December 4, 1952, p. 953**
Review, entitled "Tudor England," of *The Early Tudors, 1485–1558* by J. D. Mackie.

D312a. *Time and Tide,* **December 6, 1952, pp. 1460–1461**
Review, entitled "Elizabethan Woman," of *The Elizabethan Woman* by Carroll Camden; and *Hand Book of English Medieval Costume* by C. W. Cunnington and Phyllis Cunnington.

D312b. *Time and Tide,* **December 20, 1952, p. 1532**
Review, entitled "Elizabethan Doctor," of *Hamey the Stranger* by John Keevil.

D313. *Current History* **(USA), December 1952, pp. 344–349**
Article: "The Early Empire/The Elizabethans Stake Their Claims."

D313a. *Time and Tide,* **January 3, 1953, p. 14**
Letter to the editor, entitled "Elizabethan Doctor." Correcting "two historical inaccuracies which were the result of 'editing' my review."

D314. *History,* **February 1953, p. 96**
Letter: "Collingwood's Idea of History."

D315. *National and English Review,* **February 1953, pp. 111–112**
Review, entitled "The Decline of Personal Monarchy," of *George III and the Politicians* by Richard Pares.

D316. *American Mercury,* **March 1953, pp. 50–54**
Article: "Agenda for the Second Elizabethan Age."

D316a. *Time and Tide,* **May 2, 1953, p. 590**
Review, entitled "Stuart Physician," of *The Stranger's Son* by John J. Keevil.

D317. *Spectator,* **May 15, 1953, special supplement pages i–xxxii/1828–1953/ 125th anniversary number, pp. viii–ix**
Article: "Through Eight Reigns—1878."

D317a. *Time and Tide,* **May 30, 1953, p. 728**
Review, entitled "Elizabethan Recusants," of *Vaux of Harrowden: A Recusant Family* by Godfrey Anstruther.

D318. *History Today,* **May 1953, pp. 301–310**
Article: "The Coronation of Queen Elizabeth I."

D319. *English Historical Review,* **July 1953, pp. 474–475**
Review (untitled) of *The First Part of Yorkshire Archaeological Society Record Series,* vol. 116; *Miscellanea,* vol. 5, edited by F. W. Brooks.

D320. *The Times,* **August 26, 1953, p. 7, cols. f–g**
Letter: "Elizabethan Portraits." Commencing, "I welcome your Art Critic's sympathetic rehabilitation of Elizabethan portraiture in your issue of August 24. But it seems a pity to give repeated currency to Lytton Strachey's line about the strangeness, the incomprehensibility, of the Elizabethans. They may have been strange and incomprehensible to him, but so were the Victorians and, before them the Romantics."

D321. *History Today,* **September 1953, pp. 630–641**
Article: "Queen Elizabeth and the Historians." Reprinted in *The English Spirit* (1966).

D322. *National and English Review,* **December 1953, pp. 375–376**
Review (untitled) of *The Letters of Elizabeth, Queen of Bohemia.* Compiled by L. M. Barker. Introduction by C. V. Wedgwood.

D323. *Times Literary Supplement,* **January 15, 1954, p. 41, col. c**
Letter: "Literary Outlook." Commencing, "Reading your perceptive and, on the whole, discriminating article on Mr. Connolly, I was surprised by your comparing him to Paul Valery and positively shocked by your roundly declaring Mr. Connolly 'a great writer.'"

D323a. *Time and Tide,* **May 22, 1954, p. 693**
Review, entitled "Parish Lore," of *Freedom of the Parish* by Geoffrey Grigson.

D324. *United Empire,* **May–June 1954, pp. 89ff.**
Article: "The Elizabethan Age."

D325. *National and English Review,* **June 1954, pp. 374–376**
Review, entitled "Peninsular War," of *Wellington and His Army* by Godfrey Davies; *Letters from the Peninsula* by Norman Scarfe.

D325a. *Time and Tide,* **July 17, 1954, p. 964**
Poem: "The Transparent Room." Reprinted in *Poems Partly American* (1959); *A Life: Collected Poems* (1981).

D326. *Current History* **(USA), December 1954, pp. 329–336**
Article: "Burghley: Elizabethan England."

D326a. *Time and Tide,* **January 8, 1955, pp. 49–50**
Review, entitled "Men and Books"/"The Threshold of the Civil War," of *The King's Peace, 1637–1641* by C. V. Wedgwood.

D326b. *Sunday Times,* **January 16, 1955**
Review, entitled "Skelton to Donne," of *English Literature in the Sixteenth Century—Excluding Drama* by C. S. Lewis.

D327. *English Historical Review,* **January 1955, pp. 123–125**
Review (untitled) of *Tudor Artists* by Erna Auerbach.

D327a. *Time and Tide,* **February 19, 1955, p. 228**
Poem: "T.E.L." Reprinted in *Poems Partly American* (1959) as "Number 2, Polstead Road" and in *A Life: Collected Poems* (1981) as "T. E. Lawrence."

D327b. *Time and Tide,* **March 26, 1955, pp. 408–409**
Review, entitled "A Cornishwoman Tramps Down the Rhone," of *Down the Rhone on Foot* by C. C. Vyvyan.

D327c. *Time and Tide,* **April 2, 1955, p. 435**
Review, entitled "Men and Books"/"Cornwall in the Middle Ages," of *Mediaeval Cornwall* by L. E. Elliott-Binns; *The Legend of the Rood.* Translated with introduction by F. E. Halliday.

D328. *English Historical Review, April 1955,* **pp. 324–325**
Review (untitled) of *Political Thought in England, Tyndale to Hooker* by Christopher Morris.

D328a. *Time and Tide,* **May 28, 1955, p. 710**
Review, entitled "Men and Books"/"The Don Who Was a Genius," of *Thomas Gray: A Biography* by R. W. Ketton-Cremer.

D329. *Listener,* **July 7, 1955, pp. 17–18**
Article: "Sir Walter Ralegh: Last of the Elizabethans."

D329a. *Time and Tide,* **September 3, 1955, p. 1144**
Review, entitled "The Architect of St Martin-in-the-Fields," of *The Life and Work of James Gibbs, 1682–1754* by Bryan Little.

D329b. *Time and Tide,* **September 24, 1955, pp. 1231–1232**
Review, entitled "A Modern Arthuriad," of *The Return of Arthur: A Poem of the Future* by Martyn Skinner.

D330. *Times Literary Supplement,* **October 7, 1955, p. 583, col. c**
Poem: "La Figlia Che Piange."

D330a. *Time and Tide,* **October 8, 1955, pp. 1293–1294**
Review, entitled "Men and Books"/"Cambridge through Oxford Eyes," of *Catalogue of Cambridge Portraits,* vol. 1, *The University Collection* by J. W. Goodison.

D330b. *Time and Tide,* **March 17, 1956, p. 292**
Review, entitled "Men and Books"/"John Evelyn, Caroline Victorian," of *The Diary of John Evelyn,* edited by E. S. de Beer. *John Evelyn and His Family Circle* by W. G. Hiscock.

D330c. *Time and Tide,* **April 7, 1956, pp. 379–380**
Article: "Notes on the Way"/"In the South."

D330d. *Time and Tide,* **April 14, 1956, pp. 411–412**
Article: "Notes on the Way"/"In the South—II."

D330e. *Time and Tide,* **May 5, 1956, pp. 518–519**
Review, entitled "An English Chartres," of *Tudor and Stuart Lincoln* by J. W. F. Hill.

D330f. *Time and Tide,* **August 25, 1956, pp. 1022–1023**
Review, entitled "Men and Books"/"Church Militant," of *The Protestant Bishop* by Edward Carpenter.

D331. *Times Literary Supplement,* **September 14, 1956, p. 539, col. b**
Letter: "The Eccentric Idealist." Commencing, "Your middle-page article on George Orwell struck me as admirably balanced and judicious. It is obvious that some people lose all sense of proportion where Orwell is concerned. What was there so wonderful about a middle-class Etonian "going to" the people? I should have thought there was more to be said for someone of the people going to Eton. I realize that to say that, in circumstances of contemporary cant, is shocking; nevertheless, I am prepared to defend the proposition."

D332. *The Times,* **September 25, 1956, p. 11, col. e**
Letter: "Christ Church Meadow/Solving Oxford's Road Problem." Commencing, "I have expressed no opinion in all the controversy about Oxford's roads, and I do not mean to do so now. I wish to confine myself to a constructive suggestion. Could the long narrow meadow lying immediately north of Magdalen Bridge, between Cherwell and another stream, be brought into the scheme."

D332a. *Time and Tide,* **November 24, 1956, p. 1430**
Review, entitled "Men and Books"/"West Country Rebellion," of *The Monmouth Episode* by Bryan Little.

D333. *Current History* **(USA) December 1956, pp. 333–337**
Article: "Our Anglo-Saxon Legacy: A British View."

D333a. *Time and Tide,* **January 19, 1957, pp. 73–74**
Review, entitled "Men and Books"/"Pope in his Letters," of *The Correspondence of Alexander Pope,* edited by George Sherburn.

D334. *English Historical Review,* **January 1957, pp. 115–117**
Review (untitled) of *The Roanoke Voyages, 1584–1590.* Two volumes, edited by D. B. Quinn.

D334a. *Time and Tide,* **February 16, 1957, pp. 189–190**
Review, entitled "Men and Books"/"Elizabeth I's Parliaments," of *Elizabeth I and Her Parliaments, 1584–1601* by J. E. Neale.

D335. *Proceedings of the British Academy,* **1957, pp. 79–95**
Raleigh Lecture on History: "Sir Richard Grenville's Place in English History." Read March 13, 1957.
    Note. Published by the British Academy in booklet form (1957), priced at six shillings.

D336. *William and Mary Quarterly* **(USA), 3d series, July 1957, pp. 309–316**
A paper entitled "Tudor Expansion: The Transition from Medieval to Modern History" read at the annual meeting of the American Historical Association at Washington in January 1956.

D336a. *Time and Tide,* **October 5, 1957, pp. 1219–1220**
Article: "Notes on the Way"/"Summer Journeyings."

D337. *Saturday Review* **(USA), November 2, 1957, pp. 11–13, 37**
Article: "Bibliographical Portrait/Elizabeth II's Tribute to Elizabeth I."

D337a. *Time and Tide,* **December 7, 1957, pp. 1551–1553**
Review, entitled "Norfolk Figures," of *Norfolk Assembly* by R. W. Ketton-Cremer.

D337b. *Time and Tide,* **January 25, 1958, pp. 95–96**
Article: "Don in Horseless Carriage."

D337c. *Time and Tide,* **March 29, 1958, pp. 399–400**
Article: "Cornish Place-Names."

D338. *Times Literary Supplement,* **June 6, 1958, p. 313, col. c**
Letter concerning Sir Richard Grenville. Commencing, "We have reason to be

grateful to Dr. Leslie Hotson for the contributions he makes to literary scholarship, for his special mixture of detection, enthusiasm and pertinacity."

D339. *Saturday Review* **(USA), June 7, 1958, pp. 9–11, 34–35**
Article: "Europe's First Glimpse of the Russians/Elizabeth I and Ivan the Terrible: A Study in Diplomacy."

D340. *Times Literary Supplement,* **June 27, 1958, p. 364, col. b**
Poem: "Hallane: Sunday, 24 July, 1955." Reprinted in *Poems Partly American* (1959); *A Life: Collected Poems* (1981).

D341. *Harpers Magazine,* **August 1958, p. 75**
Poem: "Søren Kierkegaard." Reprinted in *Poems Partly American* (1959); *A Life: Collected Poems* (1981).

D342. *Current History* **(USA), September 1958, pp. 160–164**
Article: "English Education: A Reflection of English Society."

D343. *Prairie Schooner* **(USA), September 1958, p. 206**
Short story: "Fall in Nebraska."

D344. *Listener,* **October 2, 1958, pp. 524–527**
Review, entitled "Tudor People," of *The Last Tudor King: A Study of Edward VI* by W. Chapman; *Star Chamber Stories* by G. R. Elton.

D344a. *Time and Tide,* **November 1, 1958, pp. 1310, 1312**
Extracts from P. E. N. Hermon Ould Memorial Lecture. Entitled "The Role of the Intellectuals in Society."

D344b. *Time and Tide,* **November 8, 1958, p. 1336**
Further extracts from P. E. N. Hermon Ould Memorial Lecture.

D345. *Listener,* **November 20, 1958, p. 843**
Review (untitled) of *The New Cambridge Modern History,* vol. 2, *The Reformation, 1520–1559,* edited by G. R. Elton.

D346. *Times Literary Supplement,* **November 21, 1958, p. 677, col. c**
Poem: "November in Blenheim Park." Reprinted in *Poems Partly American* (1959); *A Life: Collected Poems* (1981).

D347. *Listener,* **December 4, 1958, pp. 941–943**
Review, entitled "When the Centre Gives Way," of *The King's War, 1641–1647* by C. V. Wedgwood.

D347a. *New Republic,* **April 20, 1959, pp. 3, 24**
Letter: "A Communication." Commencing, "I was glad to see Gerald Johnson's generous appraisal (*NR*, April 6) of Harold Macmillan's efforts and achievements to date in the diplomatic struggle with Khrushchev over Berlin. All the more because Mr. Johnson confesses candidly that the "Limey's" ability comes

to him and the majority of his fellow-Americans as a surprise. Though you may not agree with this, I think that your English contemporary, *The New Statesman,* does a great dis-service and shows little sense of responsibility denigrating the Prime Minister. . . . It is with the aim of giving a fairer picture of this man that I write you, since I have the honor of knowing something of him personally (there is some advantage in having the Prime Minister as one's publisher). . . . " A lengthy and detailed letter.

D348. *American Heritage,* **April 1959, pp. 4–15**
The first article, "The Elizabethans and America: Part I," of five by A. L. Rowse based on the book.

D349. *American Heritage,* **June 1959, pp. 4–19**
Article: "The Elizabethans and America, Part II, Of Raleigh and the First Plantation."

D350. *English Historical Review,* **July 1959, pp. 503–505**
Review (untitled) of *The Queen's Wards: Wardship and Marriage under Elizabeth I* by Joel Hurstfield.

D351. *Listener,* **August 13, 1959, p. 255**
Review, entitled "Listener's Book Chronicle," of *Lollards and Protestants in the Diocese of York, 1509–1558* by A. G. Dickens.

D352. *American Heritage,* **August 1959, pp. 22–29**
Article: "The Elizabethans and America, Part III, New England in the Earliest Days."

D353. *American Heritage,* **October 1959, pp. 48–53**
Article: "The Elizabethans and America, Part IV, Pilgrims and Puritans."

D354. *Listener,* **November 26, 1959, p. 945**
Review (untitled) of *The English Channel* by J. A. Williamson.

D355. *American Heritage,* **December 1959, pp. 46–59**
Article: "The Elizabethans and America, Part V, The Delicious Land."

D356. *Listener,* **January 7, 1960, p. 12**
Poem: "On the Sea Front at Hornsea: My Fifty-fifth Birthday." Reprinted in *Poems of Cornwall and America* (1967); *A Life: Collected Poems* (1981).

D356a. *Time and Tide,* **January 23, 1960, pp. 87–88**
Review, entitled "A Vanished World," of *Dashbury Park: A Victorian Story* by Susan Tweedsmuir. Dedicated by the author to A. L. Rowse and a fellow historian.

D357. *English Historical Review,* **January 1960, pp. 54–76**
Article: "Alltyrynys and the Cecils."

D358. *Journal of the Royal Commonwealth Society* (**formerly** *United Empire*), **March–April 1960, pp. 45ff.**
Article: "The Elizabethans and America."

D359. *Listener,* **April 21, 1960, p. 717**
Review (untitled) of *Fort Jesus and the Portuguese in Mombasa* by C. R. Boxer and Carlos de Azevedo.

D360. *Times Literary Supplement,* **May 27, 1960, p. 337, col. d**
Letter: "St. Austell Church." In full: "I think I should add to your notice of my forthcoming book (to be published by Warne's at St. Austell in the autumn) that it was undertaken to help the restoration of the church; and that though this year sees the 700th anniversary of its dedication, most of the church is of the fifteenth century, including the exterior sculpture which is so remarkable."

D361. *The Times,* **June 15, 1960, p. 15, col. a**
Letter: "Obituary/Dr. Charles Singer." Commencing, "To your account of Charles Singer's scholarly career may I add a word on the personal side? He settled in Cornwall in the 1930s for his health: such was the salubriousness of our climate that it gave him a quarter of a century of productive activity."

D362. *Listener,* **September 1, 1960, p. 354**
Review (untitled) of *The Spanish Armada* by Michael Lewis.

D363. *New York Times Book Review,* **October 23, 1960, pp. 26ff.**
Article: "New and Kind Light on George III." Two hundred years after his reign began, the record reveals that the "tyrant" against whom the colonies rebelled was a much maligned man.

D364. *Times Literary Supplement,* **November 25, 1960, p. 759, col. c**
Letter: "St. Austell." In full: "I am obliged to your reviewer for his warm and sympathetic review of my book *St. Austell: Church, Town, Parish.* But when he describes the church tower as "famous" for its splendid medieval sculpture, I should say that the whole point of the book is that it is not famous—though it ought to be. Very few people know it. The sculpture on this very ornate tower and all round the exterior of the church has never been properly studied by an expert—I wish one would; nor has the sculpture ever been recorded photographically in worthy form until this book, with the photographs by Charles Woolf, the National Trust's architectural photographer in Cornwall."

D365. *New York Times Book Review,* **January 22, 1961, pp. 20ff.**
Article: "Bacon: All Knowledge Was His Province." The many-sidedness of Sir Francis Bacon still has men of learning in his debt today.

D366. *New Yorker,* **February 11, 1961, p. 114**
Poem: "Saturday Afternoon in Madison, Wisconsin." Reprinted in *Poems of Cornwall and America* (1967); *A Life: Collected Poems* (1981).

D367. *The Times,* **March 22, 1961, p. 13, col. e**
Letter: "Morality and the Law/Justice Must Rest on Agreement." Commencing, "In this elevated debate among lawyers and philosophers as to changes in the climate of opinion and the law, perhaps an historian's comment may have a useful bearing? . . . it is impossible to administer justice on a law as to which there is a fundamental disagreement among educated opinion."

D368. *Times Literary Supplement,* **April 28, 1961, p. 263, col. c**
Letter: "All Souls and Appeasement." In full: "I write to correct a misapprehension on the part of your reviewer (April 21). Vansittart was not a hero of mine: it was just that my views of the Germans, based on my own experience and reading of German history and politics, largely coincided with his. And I may take the opportunity to record that the concept of 'Vansittartism,' invented and spread by the Leftwing weeklies, was a characteristic device to confuse counsel and prevent people from thinking straight about Germany's record in modern history, her policy and mentality, and German characteristics. It did almost as much damage as the other idiocy of demanding collective security, without any arms to support it."

D369. *English Historical Review,* **April 1961, pp. 362–363**
Review (untitled) of *English Privateering Voyages to the West Indies, 1588–1595,* edited by K. R. Andrews. *Seventeenth-Century America: Essays in Colonial History,* edited by James Morton Smith.

D370. *Times Literary Supplement,* **May 26, 1961, p. 325, col. b**
Letter: "Origins of the Second World War." Commencing, "Dr. David Thomson is not alone in observing the utter failure of your reviewer to diagnose what is the case with Mr. A. J. P. Taylor's astonishing and deplorable reconstruction of the events leading to the war, and the presentation of it as history. It is, indeed, a serious matter for the good name of English historical writing as well as for its effects upon the public."

D371. *Saturday Review* **(USA), May 27, 1961, p. 18**
Review, entitled "Speculation Plague in London," of *The South Sea Bubble* by John Carswell; *The Great Swindle: The Story of the South Sea Bubble* by Virginia Cowles.

D372. *New York Times Book Review,* **January 7, 1962, p. 6**
Review, entitled "Beneath the Whitewash the Same Old Hitler" of *The Origins of the Second World War* by A. J. P. Taylor. Reprinted in *Portraits and Views* (1979) as "A. J. P. Taylor on the Second German War."

D373. *History Today,* **January 1962, pp. 3–12**
Article: "Sir Nicholas Throckmorton, Part I."

D374. *History Today,* **February 1962, pp. 125–131**
Article: "Sir Nicholas Throckmorton, Part II."

D375. *The Times,* **March 30, 1962, p. 15 col. f, p. 17 col. c**
Article: "Revealing Diary of Elizabethan Era." "Dr. A. L. Rowse, who is in America, has sent *The Times* the account given below of an important recent discovery. He has made this hitherto unknown diary the setting for his: *Ralegh and the Throckmortons* which will be published by Macmillan on Thursday next, April 5."

Note. Letter to the editor, April 2, from Anthony R. Wagner, Garter King of Arms, suggesting the spelling of Ralegh's hitherto unknown son Damerei, could be a miswriting or misreading for Damerel?

D376. *The Times,* **April 6, 1962, p. 15, col. d**
Letter: "Ralegh's Eldest Son." In full: "I am grateful to Sir Anthony Wagner (April 2) for his suggestion as to the possible provenance of the name of Ralegh's hitherto unknown eldest son. It would be delightful if it were indeed the well-known West Country name of Damerel. But undoubtedly in the Throckmorton Diary it is written Damerei, as the photograph of the excerpt shows in any book. But this is Arthur Throckmorton's spelling: we need not exclude the possibility of a mistake on his part."

Note. Letter to the editor, April 10, from Lord Elibank suggesting "both A. L. Rowse and Sir Anthony Wagner may be right in the spelling of Damerei and Damerel, as in the sixteenth century there was no correct spelling in the sense in which it came to be accepted in after days." Letter to the Editor, April 12, from Eric J. Bartholomew concerning the surname, Ralegh, asking: "What has Dr. A. L. Rowse done with the "i"?"

D377. *The Times,* **April 14, 1962, p. 9, col. g**
Letter: "Ralegh's Eldest Son." Commencing, "Quite a lot of people seem to be bothered by the spelling of Ralegh. . . . But as it happens, Sir Walter Ralegh usually spelt his name without an 'i.'"

D378. *The Times,* **May 3, 1962, p. 15, col. e**
Letter: "Ralegh's Eldest Son." Commencing, "I am happy to say that an answer to the question where the name of Ralegh's eldest son, Damerei, came from has been found."

D379. *Times Literary Supplement,* **May 11, 1962, p. 346, col. a**
Letter: "Ralegh and the Throckmortons." Commencing, "I have to correct half a dozen mistakes in your review of my book: *Ralegh and the Throckmortons* (April 20). It may seem ungenerous of me when the review itself was positively glowing and enthusiastic, but accuracy and good standards of scholarship are more important." A. L. Rowse then proceeds to correct seven errors. Followed by a brief paragraph, our reviewer writes: "I am very sorry indeed that I should have made the mistakes, and I hope Dr. Rowse will accept my apology."

D380. *Huntington Library Quarterly,* **May 1962, pp. 165–179**
An address, "Sir Winston Churchill As a Historian," delivered on Founder's Day, February 26, 1962, at the Henry E. Huntington Library and Art Gallery, San Marino, California. Reprinted in *The English Spirit* (1966).

D381. *Saturday Review* **(USA), June 2, 1962, pp. 11–13**
Article: "Is Our Age Unique?"

D382. *The Times,* **July 31, 1962, p. 11, col. e**
Letter on "Pulse of Britain" articles. Commencing, "We have heard quite enough in the troubles of our country, from party politicians with their rival appeals to popular humbug, and economists with their mutually conflicting nostrums. Perhaps a historian may tell them what the situation of our country looks like in a slightly longer term perspective. I am not dismayed by the thought that no one will relish the diagnosis: they did not in the 1930s when they were consistently warned against the idiotic policy of appeasement on which they were so sold. But one was not wrong."

D383. *The Times,* **August 30, 1962, p. 13, col. a**
Article: "Pleasure in Reading/Widening Horizons."

D384. *The Times,* **September 7, 1962, p. 17, col. d**
Letter: "Obituary/Countess of St. Germans." Commencing, "The death of Nellie St. Germans leaves a sad gap in the hearts of those who knew her—especially in Cornwall where for the past three decades she made Port Eliot a centre of welcoming hospitality and lit that somewhat sombre great house with her charm."

D385. *Listener,* **October 25, 1962, pp. 652–655**
Article: "Kipling's Enduring Reputation."

D386. *Time and Tide,* **November 29–December 6, 1962, pp. 5–6**
Article: "The Three Courages of Sir Winston Churchill." To commemorate the eighty-eighth birthday of Sir Winston.

D387. *American Heritage,* **December 1962, pp. 81–84**
Excerpts, entitled "Sir Winston Churchill As a Historian," from an address. (See also D380).

D388. *Proceedings of the British Academy,* **1962, pp. 345–356.**
An obituary tribute: "Richard Pares, 1902–1958."

D389. *English Historical Review,* **April 1963, pp. 326–327**
Review (untitled) of *The Protestant Mind of the English Reformation, 1570–1640* by C. H. and K. George. Reprinted in *Discoveries and Reviews* (1975), as "The Protestant Mind."

D390. *The Times,* **June 18, 1963, p. 13, col. e**
Letter: "Cornwall Moorland." Signed by a group, including A. L. Rowse. Commencing, "We understand that the Admiralty is at present applying for planning permission to use approximately 355 acres of moorland, at Zennor in Cornwall, for troop training in connexion with helicopters. . . . we sincerely hope that the Admiralty will withdraw their application and look elsewhere."

D391. *The Times,* **September 17, 1963, p. 13, col. e**
Article: "Historian Answers Questions about Shakespeare—I/Only the Dark Lady Is Still a Mystery." The first of four articles by A. L. Rowse, based on his *William Shakespeare: A Biography.*

D392. *The Times,* **September 18, 1963, p. 13, col. e**
Article: "Historian Answers Questions about Shakespeare—II/Long Shadow of Marlowe in Life and Death."

D393. *The Times,* **September 19, 1963, p. 13, col. e**
Article: "Historian Answers Questions about Shakespeare—III/Identity Made Clear of the 'Onlie Begetter.'"

D394. *The Times,* **September 20, 1963, p. 13, col. e and p. 14, col. d**
Article: "Historian Answers Questions about Shakespeare—IV/Midsummer Night's Dream for Whose Marriage?"

D395. *Times Literary Supplement,* **January 16, 1964, p. 47, cols. b–d**
Letter (from USA): "Shadow and Substance in Shakespeare." Commencing, "In deference to *Times Literary Supplement* I am breaking my rule not to reply to individual reviewers of my book. For *Times Literary Supplement* with its anonymous reviewing should be all the more careful to avoid envenomed partiality and obvious disingenuousness in simply making a case against a book or more personally, against an author. I leave it to the intelligence of your readers to draw their own conclusions about a review of my book of some 500 pages, which says: 'he has to say something, but he has nothing to say.' This is an obvious and flagrant untruth. It entirely omits, for example, two subjects, among many others, which receive extended treatment, Shakespeare's view of the English past and his view of politics and society: both subjects on which an historian should have something special to contribute. Some people might more reasonably think, as some have said, that I have only too much to say."
   Note: The reviewer replies: "Will Dr. Rowse, when he quotes me, please quote me correctly?"

D396. *The Times,* **January 17, 1964, p. 11 col. f, and p. 12 col. g**
Article: "The Reception of My Shakespeare."

D397. *Times Literary Supplement,* **January 30, 1964, p. 87, col. b**
Letter (from USA): "Shadow and Substance in Shakespeare." Commencing,

"The intelligence of your readers will be able to estimate your reviewer's trifling reply at its true worth, and they will observe that he disingenuously still does not tell us what he thinks as to the main issue—the dating of the Sonnets. They will be forced to conclude that he cannot fault my dating, and that he really agrees with it. I have made my point about the churlishness of the review—described as 'disgraceful' by a leading woman writer to me, who now qualifies the reply as 'odious, and beneath the dignity of a scholar, or of what *Times Literary Supplement* used to be.' So, simply for the record and for the credit of *Times Literary Supplement*, I proceed to correct some of your reviewer's inaccuracies. Five points are corrected in detail." Then, in conclusion: "I should in fairness warn him (the anonymous reviewer[1]) that I am collecting not only misprints but misrepresentations and mistakes, the malevolent nonsense of reviewers, for a book I propose to write on: The Reception of my Shakespeare.[2] It will make a discreditable chapter in recent literary history, but it may not be without some salutary value as an exposure of the English literary scene, in the contemporary decline of standards."

Note. The reviewer replies: "Dr. Rowse is right and I was wrong about Erasmian/Erastian. I made a stupid error and he has my apologies."

1. The anonymous reviewer was one "John Crow."
2. *Discovering Shakespeare: A Chapter in Literary History* (1989). (See A97.)

D398. *Times Literary Supplement,* February 13, 1964, p. 127, col. d

Letter (from USA): "Shadow and Substance in Shakespeare." In full: "I accept your reviewer's apology for his mistakes. But I cannot acquit him of malevolence and coarseness. He says that he sees: 'no relevance in the fact that Pembroke was a roaring heterosexual,' and asks whether that is obtuse to him. Yes—exceedingly, stupidly, obtuse. For the whole point is that the young man of the Sonnets was ambivalent—as Shakespeare describes him, and as we know Shakespeare's patron, Southampton, was. Pembroke, always a roaring heterosexual, could therefore not possibly have been the young man of the Sonnets. That gives us the answer we have all been waiting for. I knew your third-rate reviewer would fall into the trap before he had ended."

Note. The reviewer replies, in full: "Let the matter there rest with Dr. Rowse holding his view of me as reviewer, while I hold my view of Dr. Rowse as biographer of Shakespeare. A word of apology though, to Dr. Leslie Hotson if a loosely phrased sentence of mine led anyone to suppose that I was prejudging his forthcoming Mr. W.H."

D399. *New York Times Magazine,* February 16, 1964, pp. 15, 44, 46, 48

Article: "It is a Marlowe Year Also—The works of Shakespeare are the glory of Elizabethan drama, but it was Christopher Marlowe—born just two months before him, in 1564—who originated it."

D400. *Show,* **February 1964, pp. 60, 63–64, 103–104**
Article: "The Real Shakespeare."

D401. *New York Times Book Review,* **March 15, 1964, p. 36**
Letter: "Shakespeare's Sonnets." In full: "An article by Stephen Spender has led my friend J. Donald Adams (Speaking of Books, Feb. 9) into a mistake of fact. For the record it should be corrected. Mr. Spender had said that Shakespeare's sonnets: 'were not published until after his death.' They were, in fact, published seven years before his death—in 1609, while Shakespeare died in 1616."

D401a. *Sunday Times,* **May 3, 1964, p. 35**
Article: "Dr. Rowse and Mr. W. H." with extensive sub-heading: "In this, his first published pronouncement since the appearance of Dr. Leslie Hotson's "Mr. W. H.," Dr. A. L. Rowse does not even entertain the notion that Shakespeare's Sonnets might be dedicated to William Hatcliff, but crystallises his own argument for William Harvey in six powerful points. These he will expand in a lecture to be given at 7.30 tonight in the surprising setting of the Royal Opera House, Covent Garden."

He concludes under subheading "Revised Scoreboard" that "the summing up of my views in the paragraph of last Sunday's Insight Scoreboard . . . about the Rival Poet is inaccurate. The correct statement of my views on this should run thus: Marlowe was the Rival Poet of the Sonnets in the last months of his life. Sonnet 86, which is, exceptionally, in the past tense, is the one that is valedictory, written after Marlowe's death: The Rival Poet is not mentioned again, the rivalry over. Marlowe left unfinished his poem Hero and Leander written in competition with Shakespeare's Venus and Adonis for Southampton's favor." (see also F53.)

D402. *The Times,* **May 6, 1964, p. 16, col. b**
Letter: "Obituary/Nancy Viscountess Astor/Love of the West Country." Commencing, "Among the many tributes to Nancy Astor, there should be one from the West Country, if only to express our gratitude for all that she did for us."

D403. *Huntington Library Quarterly,* **May 1964, pp. 193–209**
Text of an address: "The Personality of Shakespeare." Delivered on Founder's Day, February 24, 1964, at the Henry E. Huntington Library, San Marino, California.

D404. *Mademoiselle* **(USA), May 1964, pp. 124ff.**
Article: "Cornishman Looks at California."

D405. *Spectator,* **July 10, 1964, pp. 52–53**
Review, entitled "Across the Tamar," of *Cornwall: A Shell Guide* by John Betjeman.

D406. *English Historical Review,* **July 1964, pp. 606–607**
Review (untitled) of *Puritans and Yankees: The Winthrop Dynasty of New England, 1630–1717* by R. S. Dunn.

D407. *Huntington Library Quarterly,* **February 1965, pp. 105–129**
Article: "Thomas Wriothesley, First Earl of Southampton."

D408. *Vogue* **(USA), March 1, 1965, pp. 120–121**
Article: "Sir Winston Churchill: Excerpts from a Tribute."

D409. *The Times,* **May 8, 1965, p. 10, col. g**
Letter: "Obituary/Mr. Howard Spring." Commencing, "Two points may perhaps be added to your excellent account of Howard Spring. Though an extremely hard-working man, he freely gave of his time in a public-spirited way to the life of Falmouth when he came to reside there."

D410. *History Today,* **June 1965, pp. 382–390**
Article: "Thomas Wriothesley First Earl of Southampton: Eminent Henrician, Part I."

D411. *History Today,* **July 1965, pp. 468–474**
Article: "Thomas Wriothesley First Earl of Southampton. Eminent Henrician: Part II."

D411a. *Sunday Telegraph,* **September 19, 1965, p. 16**
Review, entitled "Lucky in Everything," of *John Buchan* by Janet Adam Smith.

D411b. *Sunday Telegraph,* **October 24, 1965, p. 20**
Review, entitled "One Man's Verdict," of *English History, 1914–45* by A. J. P. Taylor.

D412. *Listener,* **November 4, 1965, pp. 705–707**
Article: "The Cornish in America."

D412a. *Sunday Telegraph,* **December 19, 1965, p. 14**
Article: "Blowing Kipling's Trumpet."

D413. *History Today,* **December 1965, pp. 828–834**
Article: "Jan Tregagle: In Legend and in History." Reprinted in *The Little Land of Cornwall* (1986).

D413a. *Sunday Telegraph,* **January 2, 1966, p. 18**
Article: "My Book of the Year." Paragraph commencing, "The book of the year that gave me the greatest pleasure was Janet Adam Smith's *John Buchan.*"

D414. *English Historical Review,* **January 1966, pp. 160–161, 163**
Review (untitled) of *Sir Thomas Smith: A Tudor Intellectual in Office* by Mary Dewar; *The Catholic Laity in Elizabethan England, 1558–1603,* by W. R. Trimble.

D415. *Encounter,* **January 1966, pp. 45–50**
Article: "Churchill Considered Historically."

D416. *New York Times Book Review,* **April 10, 1966, p. 24**
Letter: "Southampton." Commencing, "I write to correct two mistakes Bernard Grebanier has made in his review of: *Shakespeare's Southampton* (March 6), lest your readers may be misled by a reviewer who evidently does not know very well what he is talking about."
   Note. The reviewer replies on the same page.

D416a. *Sunday Telegraph,* **May 29, 1966, p. 8**
Review, entitled "Solitary Survivor," of *The Kerensky Memoirs* by Alexander Kerensky.

D417. *Listener,* **June 9, 1966, p. 845**
Poem: "West Country Folksong." Reprinted in *Poems of Cornwall and America* (1967); *A Life: Collected Poems* (1981).

D418. *Listener,* **June 23, 1966, pp. 912–913**
Short Story: "The Choirmaster of Carluddon." Reprinted in *Cornish Stories* (1967).

D418a. *Sunday Telegraph,* **June 26, 1966, p. 14**
Review, entitled, "This Way to the Tombs," of *A House of Kings,* edited by Edward Carpenter.

D418b. *Sunday Telegraph,* **July 3, 1966, p. 10**
Review, entitled "Spaniards in the Works," of *Spain, 1803–1939* by Raymond Carr.

D418c. *Sunday Telegraph,* **no. 285, July 24, 1966, p. 14**
Review, entitled "Gorgeous Palaces," of *Robert Smythson and the Architecture of the Elizabethan Era* by Mark Girouard.

D419. *The Times,* **August 2, 1966, p. 12, col. g**
Letter: "Obituary/Lord Clifden." Commencing, "Perhaps a word may be added to your account of the late Lord Clifden's life of public service, both on the score of his quite exceptional Cornish patriotism and his immense private charm. His motto could well have been 'Nihil Cornubjense alienum a me puto.'"

D419a. *Sunday Telegraph,* **August 7, 1966, p. 15**
Review, entitled "Emperor without Illusions," of *Marcus Aurelius* by Anthony Birley.

D420. *Poetry Review* **(USA), Autumn 1966, pp. 131ff.**
Poetry: "Nine American Poems."

D420a. *Sunday Telegraph,* **September 11, 1966, p. 10**
Review, entitled "Artists with the Pen," of *They Looked Like This.* Compiled by Grant Uden.

D421. *History Today,* **September 1966, pp. 601–609**
Article: "The Reign of Henry IV, Part I." (An extract from *Bosworth Field and the Wars of the Roses.*)

D422. *History Today,* **October 1966, pp. 704–711**
Article: "Henry IV, Part II." (An extract from *Bosworth Field and the Wars of the Roses.*)

D423. *English Historical Review,* **October 1966, p. 828**
Review (untitled) of *The English Works of Giles Fletcher, the Elder,* edited by L. E. Berry.

D424. *History Today,* **October 1966, p. 721**
Review, entitled "Pictorial Education," of *A Visual History of Education* by Malcolm Seaborne.

D425. *History Today,* **December 1966, pp. 825–831**
Article: "The Slate Figures of Cornwall."

D426. *English Historical Review,* **January 1967, pp. 160–162**
Review (untitled) of *English Books and Readers, 1558 to 1603* by H. S. Bennett; *The Elizabethans' America,* vol. 2, edited by Dr. L. B. Wright; *The Principall Navigations, Voiages and Discoveries of the English Nation by Richard Hakluyt.* Introduction by D. B. Quinn and R. A. Skelton.

D427. *Manuscripts* **(USA), Summer 1967, pp. 6–9**
Article: "Experiences with Manuscripts."

D427a. *Sunday Telegraph,* **July 2, 1967, p. 8**
Review, entitled "Mac: The Complicated Celt," of *Macmillan: A Study in Ambiguity* by Anthony Sampson.

D428. *History Today,* **July 1967, pp. 483–486**
Article: "The Cornish China-Clay Industry."

D429. *History Today,* **July 1967, p. 491**
Review, entitled "Elizabethan Militia," of *The Elizabethan Militia, 1558–1638* by Lindsay Boynton.

D430. *The Times,* **August 12, 1967, p. 11, col. c**
Letter: "Voice for De Gaulle." Commencing, *"S*ince it is clear that no one is going to speak up for de Gaulle, perhaps an historian may—it would be a pretty poor show if there were no one in this country to understand his point of view. . . . De Gaulle is the most historically minded of statesmen, along with Churchill, and he has an historian's memory."

D431. *The Times,* **August 22, 1967, p. 9, col. c**
Letter: "Voice for De Gaulle." Commencing, "I have been astonished to find that of the many letters I have received all of them, with only one partial exception, have been in agreement and voiced their admiration for de Gaulle."

D432. *History Today,* **August 1967, p. 545**
Letter: "The Cornish China-Clay Industry." Regarding two corrections to his article (See D428).
    Note. Letter from Bernard Beringer in September 1967, p. 637, concerning the above.

D433. *History Today,* **August 1967, pp. 563–565**
Review, entitled "Cornish Tin Mining," of *A History of Tin Mining and Smelting in Cornwall* by D. B. Barton.

D433a. *Sunday Telegraph,* **September 10, 1967, p. 7**
Review, entitled "Macmillan's War Story," of *The Blast Of War, 1939–45* by Harold Macmillan.

D434. **Spectator, October 27, 1967, pp. 499–500**
Review, entitled "Elegiac Poet," of *Sidney Keyes: A Biographical Inquiry* by John Guenther.

D434a. *Sunday Telegraph,* **November 19, 1967, p. 13**
Review, entitled "State Servant," of *Slave of the Lamp* by Arthur Salter.

D434b. *Sunday Telegraph,* **December 10, 1967, p. 11**
Article: "My Book of the Year." Paragraph commencing, "I think the book I most enjoyed reading out of this year's crop was the second volume of Harold Macmillan's memoirs, *The Blast of War, 1939–45* (Macmillan, 60s.). They really are the best war-memoirs after Churchill's."

D435. *English Historical Review,* **January 1968, pp. 167–170**
Review (untitled) of *Books to Build an Empire: A Bibliographical History of English Overseas Interests to 1620* by John Parker; *John Penry and the Marprelate Controversy* by D. J. McGinn; *William Strachey, 1572–1621* by S. G. Culliford.

D436. *English Historical Review,* **July 1968, pp. 600–603**
Review (untitled) of *A Calendar of the Shrewsbury and Talbot Papers,* vol. 1, by Catherine Jamison. Revised and indexed by E. G. W. Bill. *Northern Catholics: The Catholic Recusants of the North Riding of Yorkshire, 1558–1790* by Hugh Aveling; *The Puritan Earl* by Claire Cross.

D437. *History Today,* **July 1968, pp. 504–505**
Article: "Heralds of the College of Arms."

D437a. *Sunday Telegraph,* **August 25, 1968, p. 8**
Review, entitled "Poet of Paradise," of *Milton* by W. R. Parker.

D438. *History Today,* **August 1968, pp. 585–587.**
Review, entitled "Henry VIII's Reign," of *Henry VIII* by J. J. Scarisbrick. Reprinted in *Discoveries and Reviews* (1975).

D439. *Poetry Review* **(USA), Autumn 1968, pp. 150ff.**
Poetry: "Two Californian Poems."

D440. *History Today,* **September 1968, p. 660**
Review, entitled "The South-West in Domesday," of *The Domesday Geography of South-West England,* edited by H. C. Darby and R. Weldon Finn.

D441. *English Historical Review,* **October 1968, pp. 833–834**
Review (untitled) of *The Elizabethan Puritan Movement* by Patrick Collinson.

D442. History Today, October 1968, pp. 732–733
Review, entitled "Wealden Glass," of *The Glass Industry of the Weald* by G. H. Kenyon.

D443. *English Historical Review,* **January 1969, pp. 171–172, 175–176, 189–190**
Review (untitled) of T*he Suppression of the Religious Foundations of Devon and Cornwall* by L. S. Snell; *Poor Relief in Elizabethan Ipswich,* edited by John Webb. *Burghley: Tudor Statesman, 1520–1598* by B. W. Beckingsale; *Beyond the Blaze: A Biography of Davies Gilbert* by A. C. Todd.

D444. *The Times,* **February 15, 1969, p. 9, col. f**
Letter (from USA): "Mr. W. H." Commencing, "I have only just seen your obituary of January 17 of Dr. Dover Wilson, with its reference to the Mr. W. H., to whom the publisher dedicated Shakespeare's Sonnets given in such a form as to suggest that Dover Wilson's view was the right one. Whereas it is absolutely not. One would think that responsible scholars would care for the truth of the matter: it is a duty that the public, so long confused, should get it right."
    Note. Letter from H. R. Trevor-Roper on February 18, 1969, with negative opinions.

D444a. *Sunday Telegraph,* **February 16, 1969, p. 11**
Review, entitled "Earls and Eccentrics," of *The Stanhopes of Chevening* by A. Newman.

D445. *The Times,* **February 25, 1969, p. 11, col. f.**
Letter (from USA): "Mr. W.H." Commencing, "I am sorry to have to catch Professor Trevor-Roper out in an elementary howler and to convict him of a mis-statement (February 18). Nowhere have I said, let alone 'confidently stated,' that Sir William Harvey was a Virginia Adventurer. That is purely Professor Trevor-Roper's rash imagination."

D446. *Journal of American History,* **March 1969, pp. 863ff.**
Review (untitled) of *Americans from Wales* by Hartmann.

D447. *The Times,* **April 26, 1969, p. 9, col. e**
Article: "The 'Mr. W. H.' of Shakespeare's Sonnets—and his Tomb."
    Note. Letters from Dennis Peck; Susan Corbett; Professor S. Schoenbaum and Michael Gilmour expressing various views on A. L. Rowse's latest Shakespeare controversy. April 29, 1969, p. 11.

D447a. *Sunday Telegraph,* **May 4, 1969, p. 10**
Review, entitled "Greatest Cynic of Them All?" of *Machiavelli: A Dissection* by Sydney Anglo.

D448. *The Times,* **May 5, 1969, p. 9, col. f**
Letter: "Mr. W. H." Commencing, "It was kind of Professor Schoenbaum, if superfluous, to direct my attention (April 29) to Mr. Cook's article on 'William Hervey, and Shakespeare's Sonnets': indeed I was already familiar with it, the author having generously sent me two copies."

D448a. *Sunday Telegraph,* **May 18, 1969, p. 13**
Review, entitled "Exit Queen," of *Mary Queen of Scots* by Antonia Fraser.

D449. *Spectator,* **May 30, 1969, pp. 724–725**
Review, entitled "Scilly Season," of *Augustus Smith of Scilly* by Elisabeth Inglis-Jones and *Island Treasure* by Roland Morris.

D450. *Times Literary Supplement,* **July 24, 1969, p. 819, col. c**
Letter: "The Cornish in America." Commencing, "Your review of this book (July 10) gives me the opportunity to correct a misprint which creates a rather important mistake: I hope that those of your readers who are interested in the subject may be glad of the correction. In the appendix on Cornish Surnames, page 427, the number of people in Cornwall with specifically Cornish Celtic names is given as 7,700: it should, of course, read 77,000. Since there are some 750 such names in use, that gives an average of roughly 100 people to an old Celtic name. I confess I had been waiting for some such reviewer to write just that sort of casual review, creating a false impression of faults that don't exist, and then missing the one mistake that matters to a scrupulous scholar."
    Note. The reviewer replies.

D451. *Times Literary Supplement,* **August 7, 1969, p. 883, col. d**
Letter: "The Cornish in America." Commencing, "Your reviewer of my book: *The Cornish in America*, has taken a great deal more trouble over his reply (July 24) and at far greater length—than he did with his casual review (July 10). He does not succeed in justifying himself. To be concise, where he is incapable of getting to the point. . . . His denigration of a pioneering work is much to be regretted by scholars who care for the subject."
    Note. Letter from R. A. Johnson, August 21, 1969, p. 931, criticizing A. L. Rowse's explanations of Cornish surnames in the book, for example, Trehane as "homestead of John."

D452. *The Times,* **August 9, 1969, p. 7, col. e**
Letter: "Dilemma over Russia." Commencing, "Mr. Graham Greene, C.H., proposes an embargo on the publication of his and his fellow-novelists' novels in Soviet Russia, on account of the Kuznetsov affair."
    Note: Letter from Graham Greene, C.H., in response, August 15, 1969, p. 7.

D452a. *Sunday Telegraph,* **August 10, 1969, p. 8**
Review, entitled "Outsize Public Face," of *Charles James Fox: A Man for the People* by Loren Reid.

D453. *The Times,* **August 20, 1969, p. 9, col. d**
Letter: "Published in Russia." Commencing, "I am sorry that my simple question (August 9) should have nettled Mr. Graham Greene (August 15) to provoke such unnecessary rudeness."

D454. *History Today,* **August 1969, pp. 584–585**
Review, entitled "Two English Republicans," of *Two English Republican Tracts,* edited by Caroline Robbins.

D455. *Spectator,* **September 6, 1969, p. 306**
Review, entitled "Walk of Life," of *Milestones on the Dover Road* by J. Dover Wilson.

D456. *Times Literary Supplement,* **September 25, 1969, p. 1080, col. e**
Letter: "The Cornish in America." Commencing, "I am grateful to your correspondent with the un-Cornish name of Johnson for suggesting an alternative meaning of the surname Trehane (August 21). I should like to adopt it, but it was another authority who suggested the meaning, 'homestead of John.'"

D457. *English Historical Review,* **October 1969, pp. 843–844**
Review (untitled) of *Shakespeare and the Earl of Southampton* by G. P. V. Akrigg.

D458. *History Today,* **October 1969, pp. 730–731**
Review, entitled "Mapping the World," of *Mercator* by A. S. Osley.

D459. *The Times,* **December 23, 1969, p. 7, col. c**
Letter: "Canonizing the 40 English Martyrs: Faith and Politics." Commencing, "It is a pity that the case of Elizabeth I's Government should go by default, and some of your readers may welcome a statement of what the historical situation was. The fact is that by its Bull of 1570, Regnans in Exelsis, the Papacy declared war on Elizabeth I, not only excommunicating her, but deposing her, releasing her subjects from their allegiance and enjoining upon Catholics the duty of opposing her by every means. This was one of the gravest mistakes the Papacy ever made."

D459a. *Sunday Telegraph,* **December 28, 1969, p. 18**
Article: "My Book of the Year." Paragraph commencing, "The book that gave me most pleasure this year (apart from Montherlant's *Les Garcons* a brilliant work by the greatest living French writer) was Lovat Dickson's *H. G. Wells: His Turbulent Life and Times* (Macmillan 75s.)."

D460. *History Today,* **December 1969, pp. 869–871**
Review, entitled "Tudor and Jacobean Portraits," of *Tudor and Jacobean Portraits* by Roy Strong. Volume 1 includes text and volume 2, plates.
    Note. Editorial point on the above review, February 1970, p. 145.

D460a. *Sunday Telegraph,* **January 11, 1970, p. 19**
Review, entitled "Guilty Queen," of *The First Trial of Mary Queen of Scots* by Gordon Donaldson; *Mary Queen of Scots* by Madeleine Bingham.

D461. *English Historical Review,* **January 1970, pp. 122–124**
Review (untitled) of *Sir Walter Ralegh ecrivain l'oeuvre et les idées* by Pierre Lefranc; *Manuscripts of the Marquess of Bath at Longleat,* vol. 4, *Seymour Papers, 1532–1686,* edited by Marjorie Blatcher. *Abstracts of Abbotside Wills, 1552–1688,* edited by H. Thwaite. *In Enterprise and Empire: Merchant and Gentry Investment in the Expansion of England, 1575–1630* by Theodore K. Rabb. Lefranc review reprinted in *Discoveries and Reviews* (1975), as "Ralegh As Writer." Rabb review reprinted in *Discoveries and Reviews* (1975), as "Computer's History."

D461a. *Sunday Telegraph,* **February 22, 1970, p. 12**
Review, entitled "Plymouth Fathers," of *The Hawkins Dynasty* by Michael Lewis.

D462. *History Today,* **February 1970, pp. 138–139**
Review, entitled "Elizabethan Composer," of *Thomas Weelkes: A Biographical and Critical Study* by David Brown.

D462a. *Sunday Telegraph,* **April 5, 1970, p. 12**
Review, entitled "Troubled Time," of *1919: Red Mirage* by David Mitchell; *The Russian Revolution* by Marcel Liebman.

D463. *English Historical Review,* **April 1970, pp. 414–415**
Review (untitled) of *The Marvellous Chance: Thomas Howard, Fourth Duke of Norfolk and the Ridolphi Plot, 1570–1572* by Father Francis Edwards, S.J.

D464. *The Times,* **May 19, 1970, p. 9, col. d**
Letter: "University Expansion." Commencing, "Since *The Times*'s common-sense views on university education have been attacked by a junior Minister (report, May 16) perhaps one who is qualified to speak may say a word in evidence. I have spent all my life in a university."

D464a. *Sunday Telegraph,* **June 7, 1970, p. 12**
Review, entitled "Pretenders and Poets," of *The Royal House of Scotland* by Eric Linklater.

D465. *Poetry Review,* **Summer 1970, pp. 138–139**
Poem: "Strange Encounter." Reprinted in *Strange Encounter* (1972); *A Life: Collected Poems* (1981).

D466. *History Today,* **July 1970, p. 515**
Review, entitled "Henry VIII and Parliament," of *The Reformation Parliament, 1529–1536* by S. E. Lehmberg.

D467. *The Times,* **August 8, 1970, p. 13, col. e**
Article: "John Felton—Was He Martyr or Traitor?" Commencing, "Four

hundred years ago today, August 8, 1570, John Felton was hanged in St. Paul's churchyard, the place where he had fixed the Papal Bull excommunicating and deposing Queen Elizabeth, on the Bishop of London's gate a couple of months before."

D468. *The Times,* **August 21, 1970, p. 9, col. d**
Letter: "John Felton." Commenting on a letter from Father Edwards, S.J., published August 15.

D469. *History Today,* **August 1970, pp. 586–589**
Review, entitled "Transport in History," of *Transport Museums in Britain and Western Europe* by Jack Simmons.

D469a. *Listener,* **September 10, 1970, pp. 342–344**
Important autobiographical essay: "Transition and Triumph."

D470. *The Times,* **September 18, 1970, p. 9, col. e**
Letter: "Popular Opinion." Commencing, "May I dare, at the risk of being thought illiberal, to dissent from your opinion about this German ex-student leader?"

D470a. *Sunday Telegraph,* **September 20, 1970, p. 12**
Review, entitled "Inconsequential Queen," of *Anne of Denmark* by Ethel Carleton Wiliams.

D471. *Spectator,* **September 26, 1970, pp. 337–340**
Article: "Shakespeare and the Elizabethan Historian."

D471a. *Sunday Telegraph,* **November 29, 1970, p. 19**
Review, entitled "Bluff Hal's Men," of *The Courtiers of Henry VIII* by David Mathew.

D472. *Contemporary Review,* **November 1970, pp. 231–235**
Article: "Lord Burghley: The Relevance of a Great Elizabethan Today."

D473. *Spectator,* **December 5, 1970, p. 724**
Article: "As I Saw It: Once More on the Campus Trek."

D473a. *Sunday Telegraph,* **December 20, 1970, p. 14**
Article: "My Book of the Year." Paragraph commencing, *"The Letters of Sir William Jones* edited by Garland Cannon (2 vols., Oxford, £12.10s) was a real discovery for me and gave me the greatest pleasure."

D474. *Daily Telegraph,* **January 9, 1971, p. 10, cols. c–e**
Article: "A Lesson from the Past." A. L. Rowse looks at the problems of teaching history in schools and universities.

D474a. *New York Times Book Review,* **January 17, 1971, pp. 2, 24, 26, 28**
Article: "London Letters Falling Down."

D475. *English Historical Review,* **January 1971, p. 169**
Review (untitled) of *The Last Days of the Lancashire Monasteries and the Pilgrimage of Grace* by Christopher Haigh.

D476. *History Today,* **January 1971, pp. 57–64**
Article: "Welsh Orientalist: Sir William Jones." Reprinted in *Portraits and Views* (1979).

D477. *The Times,* **February 13, 1971, p. 10, col. a.**
Article: "Elizabethan Trouble-Shooter." On the 400th anniversary of the death of Sir Nicholas Throckmorton.

D477a. *Sunday Telegraph,* **February 28, 1971, p. 8**
Review, entitled "Great European," of *Erasmus of Christendom* by R. H. Bainton; *Erasmus of Rotterdam* by George Faludy. First review reprinted in *Discoveries and Reviews* (1975), as "Erasmus: Great European."

D478. *History Today,* **February 1971, pp. 145–146**
Review, entitled "The Second Essex," of *Essex: Parliamentarian General* by V. F. Snow.

D478a. *New York Times Book Review,* **April 18, 1971, pp. 27–28, 30**
Article: Review, entitled "Elizabethan Heterodox," of *The Traces of Thomas Hariot* by Muriel Rukeyser. Reprinted in *Discoveries and Reviews* (1975), as "Thomas Hariot: Elizabethan Scientist."

D479. *The Times,* **April 24, 1971, p. 12, col. a**
Article: "Shakespeare, the Sexiest Writer in the Language/A. L. Rowse Discusses Sexuality in Elizabethan Literature."
   Note. Letters to the above article from the Reverend Francis Edwards; Professor S. Schoenbaum; Mrs. M. Lesage; Mrs. J. V. Twigg. April 27, 1971, p. 17. Letter from Mr. James Reeves. April 30, 1971, p. 15.

D479a. *Sunday Telegraph,* **April 25, 1971, p. 13**
Review, entitled "Spoiled Gallant" of *Robert, Earl of Essex* by Robert Lacey; *The Great Seamen of Elizabeth I* by Bryan Bevan.

D480. *English Historical Review,* **April 1971, pp. 404–405**
Review (untitled) of *The Royal Supremacy in the Elizabethan Church* by Claire Cross.

D481. *English Historical Review,* **April 1971, pp. 410–411**
Review (untitled) of *The Jamestown Voyages under the First Charter, 1606–1609.* 2 vol, edited by Philip L. Barbour.

D482. *History Today,* **April 1971, pp. 291–293**
Review, entitled "Medieval Duchy," of *Rural Economy and Society in the Duchy of Cornwall, 1300–1500* by John Hatcher.

D482a. *Sunday Telegraph,* **May 23, 1971, p. 10**
Review, entitled "England and Sir George," of *English History: A Survey* by Sir George Clark.

D482b. *Sunday Telegraph*, **July 18, 1971, p. 10**
Review, entitled "Palm, Pine, and Profits," of *The European Discovery of America: The Northern Voyages, AD 500–1600* by S. E. Morison; *Trade and Dominion: The European Overseas Empires in the Eighteenth Century* by J. H. Parry.

D483. *The Times,* **July 24, 1971, p. 12, col. d**
Article: "Oxford's Relic of the English Romeo/A. L. Rowse on the Man Who Founded the Botanical Gardens."

D484. *History Today,* **July 1971, pp. 523–524**
Review, entitled "Henry VIII and Tournai," of *The English Occupation of Tournai, 1513–1519* by C. G. Cruickshank.

D485. *History Today,* **August 1971, pp. 595–596**
Review, entitled "Paston Letters," of *Paston Letters and Papers of the Fifteenth Century,* edited by Norman Davis.

D486. *Contemporary Review,* **August 1971, pp. 93–99**
Article: "Holywell Cemetery: Victorian Oxford."

D487. *Contemporary Review,* **September 1971, pp. 153–154**
Poem: "Summer Siesta." Reprinted in *Strange Encounter* (1972); *A Life: Collected Poems* (1981).

D488. *The Times,* **October 28, 1971, p. 17, col. d**
Letter: "New Zealand Cornishman." Commencing, "It is agreeable to read your tributes to Professor Beaglehole (October 13; 19; 21); but they omit to notice what he wrote to me himself, that he was a Cornishman by descent, his name coming from the St. Ives district."

D488a. *Sunday Telegraph,* **October 31, 1971, p. 16**
Review, entitled "History for Fun," of *The English Experience* by John Bowle.

D489. *History Today,* **November 1971, pp. 819–821**
Review, entitled "Dictionary of National Biography 1951–1960," of *Dictionary of National Biography, 1951–1960.*

D489a. *Sunday Telegraph,* **December 19, 1971, p. 16**
Article: "My Book of the Year." Paragraph commencing, "The book that gave me most pleasure is also the one from which I learned the most: Baldwin Smith's *Henry VIII* (Cape, £2.95)."

D490. *Spectator,* **December 25, 1971, pp. 933–935**
Short story: "Ailourophilia—Chalky Jenkins: Little Cat Lost."

D491. *London and Middlesex Archaeological Society,* **1971, pp. 15–18**
Commemoration Address: "John Stow As an Historian." Reprinted in *Discoveries and Reviews* (1975).

D491a. *Sunday Telegraph,* **February 6, 1972, p. 14**
Review, entitled "Hold That Tiger!" of *Richelieu and His Age,* vol. 3 by Carl J. Burckhardt.

D491b. *Sunday Telegraph,* **February 27, 1972, p. 14**
Review, entitled "Two Cheers for Bloody Mary," of *The Lady Mary* by Milton Waldman.

D492. *Books and Bookmen,* **February 1972, p. 38**
Review, entitled "The Appalling 20th Century," of *The Twentieth Century,* edited by Alan Bullock. Reprinted in *Portraits and Views,* 1979.

D492a. *Sunday Telegraph,* **March 26, 1972, p. 16**
Review, entitled "Mater v. Pater," of *Matthew Arnold* by Douglas Bush; *Clough: The Critical Heritage,* edited by Michael Thorpe.

D493. *Books and Bookmen,* **March 1972, p. 45**
Review, entitled "The Shakespeare Industry," of *Shakespeare Survey 24* by Kenneth Muir; *Full Circle: Shakespeare and Moral Development* by Alan Hobson; *The Age of Shakespeare* by Nathaniel Harris. Reprinted in *Discoveries and Reviews* (1975).

D493a. *Sunday Telegraph,* **April 30, 1972, p. 14**
Review, entitled "Royal Pecker Up," of *The Life and Times of Charles II* by Christopher Falkus.

D494. *Books and Bookmen,* **April 1972, p. 27**
Review, entitled "The Iron Century," of *The Iron Century: Social Change in Europe, 1550–1660* by H. Kamen. Reprinted in *Discoveries and Reviews* (1975).

D495. *English Historical Review,* **April 1972, pp. 405–409**
Review (untitled) of *The Churchwardens' Accounts of Ashburton, 1479–1580,* edited and introduced by A. Hanham. *The Radical Arts* by Dr. J. A. van Dorsten; *English Books and Readers, 1603–1640* by H. S. Bennett.

D496. *The Times,* **May 30, 1972, p. 13, col. d**
Letter: "The Nobel Prize." Commencing, "It is surprising that no one dares to say that there is something to be said for the Russian point of view with regard to Solzenitsyn's Nobel Prize. . . . Nobel prizes for literature are slanted in the direction of left liberalism. . . . This is the point about Solzenitsyn. Anyone with real literary standards should know that, as a writer, he is a whole class below Montherlant, probably the greatest living writer. But the Nobel people would never dream of nominating Montherlant because he is a man of the right and does not suit the requirements of the left liberal orthodoxy."

D497. *Old Cornwall,* **Spring 1972, pp. 437–444**
Address: "Henry Trecarrell: A Commemoration Address." Commencing, "Henry Trecarrell must have been well known in the Cornwall of his time— getting on for 500 years ago—but little is known of him today. However, he did great things for his neighbourhood, for Linkinhorne church and Launceston parish church in particular, besides leaving the finest medieval house in Cornwall, though unfinished—except for Cotehele." Reprinted in *The Little Land of Cornwall* (1986) as "Henry Trecarrell of Tudor Days."

D498. *Books and Bookmen,* **May 1972, pp. 38–39**
Review, entitled "Flannery O'Connor: Genius of the South," of *Mystery and Manners: Occasional Prose by Flannery O'Connor.* Reprinted in *Portraits and Views* (1979).

D499. *History Today,* **May 1972, p. 375**
Review, entitled "Henry VIII's Court," of *Henry VIII and His Court* by Neville Williams.

D499a. *Sunday Telegraph,* **June 25, 1972, p. 16**
Review, entitled "Levellers' Nonsense," of *The World Turned Upside Down: Radical Ideas during the English Revolution* by Christopher Hill. Reprinted in *Discoveries and Reviews* (1975).

D500. *Books and Bookmen,* **June 1972, p. 47**
Review, entitled "McFarlane the Master," of *Lancastrian Kings and Lollard Knights* by K. B. McFarlane. Reprinted in *Discoveries and Reviews* (1975), as "Part I: McFarlane on the Fifteenth Century."

D501. *History Today,* **June 1972, p. 445**
Review, entitled "Elizabethan Song-Writer," of *John Dowland* by Diana Poulton. Reprinted in *Discoveries and Reviews* (1975).

D502. *History Today,* **June 1972, pp. 447–448**
Review, entitled "Elizabethan Magus," of *John Dee: The World of an Elizabethan Magus* by P. J. French. Reprinted in *Discoveries and Reviews* (1975).

D503. *Books and Bookmen,* **July 1972, pp. 40–41**
Review, entitled "McFarlane on Memling," of *Hans Memling* by K. B. McFarlane. Reprinted in *Discoveries and Reviews* (1975), as "Part II: McFarlane on the Fifteenth Century."

D504. *History Today,* **July 1972, p. 519**
Review, entitled "Putting the Reformation Across," of *Policy and Police: The Enforcement of the Reformation in the Age of Thomas Cromwell* by G. R. Elton.

D505. *History Today,* **August 1972, p. 598**
Review, entitled "The Enigma of Young," of *The Correspondence of Edward Young, 1683–1765,* edited by Henry Pettit.

D505a. *Sunday Telegraph,* **September 10, 1972, p. 12**
Review, entitled "What the Island Race Needs," of *The Offshore Islanders* by Paul Johnson.

D505b. *Sunday Telegraph,* **September 17, 1972, p. 17**
Review, entitled "Royal Bogeyman," of *King George III* by John Brooke.

D506. *The Times,* **September 28, 1972, p. 18, col. g**
Letter, "Obituary/Henry de Montherlant." Commencing, "A greater writer than Gide, less great than Proust, Montherlant was at the time of his death the world's foremost and best writer. One would hardly realize that from the obituaries, or from the notice given."

D507. *Books and Bookmen,* **September 1972, p. 63**
Review, entitled "The Fifth Monarchy Men," of *The Fifth Monarchy Men* by B. S. Capp. Reprinted in *Discoveries and Reviews* (1975).

D508. *English Historical Review,* **October 1972, pp. 867–868**
Review (untitled) of *English Enterprise in Newfoundland, 1577–1660* by G. T. Cell.

D509. *History Today,* **October 1972, p. 746**
Review, entitled "County Life: Seventeenth-Century Record," of *The Diary of Thomas Isham of Lamport, 1671–1673.* Translated by N. Marlow. Introduction and notes by Sir Gyles Isham. Reprinted in *Discoveries and Reviews* (1975), as "Country Life in Restoration Northamptonshire."

D510. *The Times,* **November 11, 1972, p. 12, col. a**
Article: "Saturday Review Column/A. L. Rowse/Enjoying Today in the Past." Commencing, "Why is history so excessively popular today? Almost too much so; for I do not think it altogether a good sign for contemporary society—rather a reflection on it."

D511. *Contemporary Review,* **November 1972, pp. 234–238**
Article: "Charles Kingsley at Eversley: Part I."

D511a. *Sunday Telegraph,* **December 10, 1972, p. 16**
Article: "My Book of the Year." Paragraph commencing, "Leon Edel's life of Henry James is the greatest literary biography of our time, and the last volume this year: *Henry James: The Master, 1901–1916* (Hart-Davis, £6.95) gave me immense pleasure."

D511b. *Sunday Telegraph,* **December 24, 1972, p. 8**
Review, entitled "Unfair to Hanover!" of *The Life and Times of George III* by John Clarke; *The Life and Times of George IV* by Alan Palmer; *Wicked Uncles in Love* by Morris Marples.

D512. *Contemporary Review,* **December 1972, pp. 322–326**
Article: "Kingsley at Eversley, Part II."

D513. *London and Middlesex Archaeological Society,* **1972, pp. 209–213**
Paper read at St. Olave's Church, Hart Street, London, June 14, 1972: "Pepys and His Oxford Friends." Reprinted in *Discoveries and Reviews* (1975).

D514. *Books and Bookmen,* **January 1973, pp. 58–59**
Review, entitled "Walpole's Bauble," of *The History of the Order of the Bath and Its Insignia* by James C. Risk.

D515. *Contemporary Review,* **January 1973, pp. 7–12**
Article: "Kingsley at Eversley, Part III."

D516. *English Historical Review,* **January 1973, pp. 182–183**
Review (untitled) of *The Trade of Elizabethan Chester* by D. M. Woodward; *Elizabethan Recusancy in Cheshire* by K. R. Wark; *The History of the Most Renowned and Victorious Princess Elizabeth Late Queen of England* by William Camden, edited and with an introduction by W. T. MacCaffrey.

D517. *History Today,* **January 1973, p. 67**
Review, entitled "The First Tudor," of *Henry VII* by S. B. Chrimes.

D518. *The Times,* **January 20, 1973, p. 15, col. g**
Letter: "The President and Opinion Leaders." Commencing, "Perhaps I could help Mr. James Reston (article, January 11) to explain what President Nixon means in his justifiable complaint against the so-called opinion leaders—and not only this President but his Democratic predecessor. They do not ask for unconditional support—no one would expect that."

D519. *The Times,* **January 29, 1973, p. 12, col. a**
Article: "Revealed at Last, Shakespeare's Dark Lady/Historian Dr. A. L. Rowse Says He Has Solved the Centuries-Old Mystery of the Sonnets." Triggered an avalanche of correspondence to *The Times.*
   Note. February 1, p. 17, letters from Sir James Fergusson of Kilkerran, Mr. John Chaplin, and Mr. Colin MacInnes. February 2, p. 15, from the Reverend Francis Edwards, S.J., and Dr. Henry Kamen. February 3, p. 15, from Dame Agatha Christie. February 6, p. 15, from Rev. S. John Forrest, Mrs. Margaret Smith, and Mrs. Pauline Phillips. February 14, p. 15, from Mr. Richard Buckle. February 15, p. 19, from Mr. Chaim Raphael. February 17, p. 15, from Mr. Ian Spink and Sir Anthony Wagner.

D520. *The Times,* **February 20, 1973, p. 15, col. g**
Letter: "The Dark Lady: Nature of Historical Proof." Commencing, "I am delighted by your correspondents giving us more information about the prolific Bassano and Lanier families—on whom I am no authority and am glad to learn more. But I think Mr. Spink (February 17) is right in thinking that there were two Emilia Laniers."
   Note. February 22, p. 17, letter from Mr. A. N. Wells and Mrs. Verna Kendall; February 23, p. 17, letter from Professor J. P. Kenyon and Mr. F. Bloom.

D521. *Books and Bookmen,* **March 1973, pp. 52–53**
Review, entitled "Civil War without Settlement," of *The Interregnum: The Quest for Settlement, 1646–1660,* edited by G. E. Aylmer. Reprinted in *Discoveries and Reviews* (1975) as "What Did the Civil War Settle?"

D522. *History Today,* **March 1973, pp. 211–213**
Review, entitled "Elizabeth I's Court," of *All the Queen's Men: Elizabeth I and Her Courtiers* by Neville Williams.

D523. *Spectator,* **April 21, 1973, pp. 486–487**
Article: "The True Story of Mary Fitton." Reprinted in *Discoveries and Reviews* (1975).

D524. *The Times,* **April 23, 1973, p. 6, col. c**
Article: "Secrets of Shakespeare's Landlady/The Historian Who Discovered the Dark Lady Reveals New Information on Shakespeare the Lodger." Commencing, "Any factual information that illuminates Shakespeare's background is of value, revealing him as an Elizabethan among other Elizabethans—as opposed to the useless conjectures about him in many volumes and many languages, which have created only confusion and can now go on the scrap-heap."

D525. *Books and Bookmen,* **April 1973, p. 4**
Letter (untitled): Commencing, "The historian's proof convinces historians, where some Eng Lit people fail to see the decisive necessity of correct dating and its importance, along with the complete concatenation of circumstances, the chain of evidence which cannot be disputed at any point, let alone disproved."

D526. *Books and Bookmen,* **April 1973, pp. 12–13**
Review, entitled "Shakespeare at Work," of *The Profession of Dramatist in Shakespeare's Time* by G. E. Bentley; *Shakespeare the Professional* by K. Muir. Illustrated with photo by Thomas, Photos Oxford, with caption: "Rowse at work." Text only reprinted in *Discoveries and Reviews* (1975).

D527. *English Historical Review,* **April 1973, pp. 437–439**
Review (untitled) of *The Life of Fulke Greville* by R. A. Rebholz. Reprinted in *Discoveries and Reviews* (1975), as "Fulke Greville."

D528. *English Historical Review,* **April 1973, p. 439**
Review (untitled) of *The Last Voyage of Drake and Hawkins,* edited by K. R. Andrews.

D529. *History Today,* **April 1973, pp. 293–294**
Review, entitled "Religion at War," of *The Massacre of St. Bartholomew and the European Conflict, 1559–1572* by N. M. Sutherland.

D530. *The Times,* **May 5, 1973, p. 13, col. e**
Letter: "Watergate and the Credit of the U.S." Commencing, "Any student of

American history knows the American habit of making things excessively difficult for their government. It has been like it since 1776—and before."

D531. *Listener,* May 10, 1973, p. 619, col. b
Letter: "Shakespeare's Dark Lady." Commencing, "I am more open-minded than my critics think—or perhaps than they are—and I am quite willing to accept Dr. Wells and John Carey's reading (*Listener,* May 3) of Forman's word as 'brave.' (In any case I always modernise archaic spelling: no point in ye olde Tudor tea-schoppe spelling). But what difference does it make? A little, but very little. What is clear is that the Lord Chamberlain had a mistress who was half-Italian, and a. musical as in the Sonnets, b. discarded and married to a musician called Will, as is the husband in the Sonnets, c. pinpointed to the year 1593 when those sonnets were written, who was, d. of a bad reputation, with all the characteristics Forman observed in her in complete agreement with the character of the woman in the Sonnets. "
   Note. May 10 letter from Mary Edmond; May 17 letter from Jack Westrup.

D532. *Times Literary Supplement,* May 11, 1973, p. 528, col. b
Letter: "The Dark Lady." Commencing, "How unexpected that so much space should be devoted to my modest little book (*Shakespeare the Man*—reviewed April 27 issue), which is only a by-product of my wider researches into Simon Forman. And how excessively generous to pay such tribute to my 'unflagging' energy, which only stops short of equating energy with genius."
   Note. May 11 letters from Stanley Wells and G. Wilson Knight.

D533. *Times Literary Supplement,* May 18, 1973, p. 556, col. a
Letter: "The Dark Lady." One paragraph: "Professor Wilson Knight has still not noticed the simple and obvious fact that 'Mr. W.H.' is the publisher Thomas Thorp's dedicatee and not Shakespeare's young man at all. It is impossible to dispute that he is Thorp's 'Mr. W.H.' That is all."
   Note. Letters dated May 18 from William Empson and Ivor R. W. Cook; letter dated May 25 from G. Wilson Knight.

D534. *Listener,* May 17, 1973, p. 655, col. a
Letter: "The Dark Lady." Commencing, "1. I agree with Dr. Wells that Forman's word can be read as 'brave,' but not 'barane' as Miss Edmond suggests (letters May 10). That contains too many strokes for Forman's word. 2. It is obvious that the word 'Willia' cannot be read as Millia for Emilia: for William's age is given as 24, and Emilia's as 27. 3. So it is William whom Forman immediately after refers to as Emilia's husband. 4. I think that the answer to Miss Edmond's problem is that there are two Emilias."
   Note. May 31 letter from Mary Edmond.

D535. *Books and Bookmen,* May 1973, pp. 71–72
Review, entitled "McFarlane's Nobles," of *The Nobility of Later Medieval England* by K. B. McFarlane. Reprinted in *Discoveries and Reviews* (1975) as "McFarlane on the Fifteenth Century."

D536. *Spectator,* **June 2, 1973, pp. 681–683**
Article: "Shakespearian Controversies: The Consolations of Being Right."

D537. *Spectator,* **June 9, 1973, p. 729**
Letter: "Rowse on Shakespeare."
   Note. Letter of June 9, from Mary Edmond and R. W. Dyson and of June 16, from Noel Fermor and Mary Edmond (who states she was misquoted as saying the Dark Lady was "stone deaf," when she actually said "tone deaf").

D537a. *Sunday Telegraph,* **June 10, 1973, p. 12**
Review, entitled "The Protector Large As Life," of *Cromwell, Our Chief of Men* by Antonia Fraser; *Oliver Cromwell* by C. V. Wedgwood. First review reprinted in *Discoveries and Reviews* (1975), as "Oliver Cromwell."

D538. *Books and Bookmen,* **June 1973, pp. 53–54**
Review, entitled "With Strings Attached," of *Founders' Kin: Privilege and Pedigree* by George D. Squibb.

D539. *The Times,* **July 2, 1973, p. 14, col. c**
Article: "The Dark Lady, from a Woman's Point of View/Professor A. L. Rowse Continues His Examination of Shakespeare's Affairs." Commencing, "Everybody has looked at Shakespeare's affair with his dark lady from the man's point of view. Isn't it time that we looked at it from the woman's?"

D540. *The Times,* **July 3, 1973, p. 16, col. c**
Article: "The Dark Lady's Conversion and Fight against Poverty." (Second and concluding part on Shakespeare's Dark Lady.)

D541. *Books and Bookmen,* **July 1973, pp. 40–41**
Review, entitled "The Young Macaulay," of *Thomas Babington Macaulay: The Shaping of the Historian* by John Clive.

D542. *Books and Bookmen,* **July 1973, p. 89**
Review, entitled "Somerset Conflict," of *Somerset in the Civil War and Interregnum* by David Underdown. Reprinted in *Discoveries and Reviews* (1975).

D543. *History Today,* **July 1973, p. 513**
Review, entitled "Thomas Cromwell As Reformer," of *Reform and Renewal: Thomas Cromwell and the Commonweal* by G. R. Elton. Reprinted in *Discoveries and Reviews* (1975).

D544. *History Today,* **July 1973, pp. 518–520**
Review, entitled "Whig Interpretations of the Civil War," of *The Origins of the English Civil War,* edited by Conrad Russell.

D545. *Spectator,* **August 25, 1973, pp. 241–245**
Article: "Swift and Stella at Moor Park."

D545a. *Sunday Telegraph,* **August 26, 1973, p. 14**
Review, entitled "Enid's Ego Trouble," of *Enid Starkie* by Joanna Richardson.

D546. *Books and Bookmen,* August 1973, pp. 26–27
Review, entitled "Victorian Ethics and Aesthetics," of *The Victorian Treasure House* by Peter Conrad.

D547. *Books and Bookmen,* September 1973, pp. 14–15
Review, entitled "The Charm of Gibbon," of *The English Essays of Edward Gibbon,* edited by Patricia B. Craddock.

D548. *Books and Bookmen,* September 1973, pp. 61–62
Review, entitled "The Soul of King's," of *The Autobiography of G. Lowes Dickinson,* edited by Dennis Proctor. Reprinted in *Portraits and Views* (1979).

D549. *The Times,* October 12, 1973, p. 20, col. a
Article: "Debt We Owe to Shakespeare's Southampton." Commencing, "Four hundred years ago, on October 6, 1573, Shakespeare's Southampton—his patron and friend to be—was born at Cowdray House in Sussex, his mother's home. His own home was Titchfield in Hampshire where one can see him as a boy on the splendid pile of the family tomb."

D550. *Spectator,* October 20, 1973, pp. 515–516
Review, entitled "All in the Family," of *The Cecils of Hatfield House* by David Cecil.

D551. *Books and Bookmen,* October 1973, pp. 12–14
Review, entitled "Priestley's England," of *The English* by J. B. Priestley. Reprinted in *Portraits and Views* (1979).

D552. *Books and Bookmen,* October 1973, pp. 78–79
Review, entitled "Cardinal Newman: The Last Phase," of *The Letters and Diaries of John Henry Newman,* edited by C. S. Dessain and T. Gornall.

D552a. *Sunday Telegraph,* November 18, 1973, p. 16
Review, entitled "Sharp Eyes at George II's Court," of *Lord Hervey* by Robert Halsband; *George II* by C. C. Trench; *The Life and Times of George I* by Joyce Marlow.

D553. *Books and Bookmen,* November 1973, pp. 18–20.
Review, entitled "Classics of County History," of *The History and Topographical Survey of the County of Kent* by Edward Hasted with introduction by Alan Everitt; *The History and Antiquities of the County Palatine of Durham* by Robert Surtees with introduction by E. Birley; *The History and Antiquities of the County of Rutland* by James Wright with introduction by Jack Simmons. Reprinted in *Portraits and Views* (1979).

D554. *Books and Bookmen,* November 1973, pp. 20–22
Review, entitled "Vanishing English Landscape," of *English Landscapes* by W. G. Hoskins; *The Suffolk Landscape* by Norman Scarfe; *The Lake District: A Landscape History* by W. H. Pearsall and Winifred Pennington. Reprinted in *Portraits and Views* (1979).

D555. *Spectator,* **December 8, 1973, pp. 747–748**
Review, entitled "Renaissance Spectacle," of *Splendour at Court: Renaissance Spectacle and Illusion* by Roy Strong.

D555a. *Sunday Telegraph,* **December 9, 1973, p. 13**
Article: "My Book of the Year." Paragraph: "The book that gave me the purest pleasure this past year was *The English Essays of Edward Gibbon,* edited by P. B. Craddock (Oxford, £10.50). I adore reading about the Eighteenth Century, such a relief from today: then everything was in accord with the human scale, architecture, arts and science, writing. There is a charm in reading Gibbon—he was so pleased with himself, as he had every reason to be. Then, too, everything he wrote is alive, with his own personal stamp upon it."

D556. *Books and Bookmen,* **December 1973, pp. 50–51**
Review, entitled "Marlowe in Full," of *The Complete Works of Christopher Marlowe,* edited by Fredson Bowers. Reprinted in *Discoveries and Reviews* (1975).

D557. *Books and Bookmen,* **December 1973, pp. 58–59**
Review, entitled "Jupiter Carlyle," of *Anecdotes and Characters of the Times* by Alexander Carlyle, edited by J. Kinsley.

D558. *History Today,* **December 1973, pp. 879–883**
Review, entitled "Borlase's Cornwall," of *W. Borlase: Antiquities Historical and Monumental of the County of Cornwall.* New introduction by P. A. S. Pool and Charles Thomas. Reprinted in *The Little Land of Cornwall* (1986).

D559. *Spectator,* **January 12, 1974, p. 44**
Review, entitled "Amateur History," of *Queen Katherine Parr* by Anthony Martienssen. Reprinted in *Discoveries and Reviews* (1975), as *Katherine Parr: an American View.*

D560. *Books and Bookmen,* **January 1974, pp. 27–28**
Review, entitled "Mediterranean Epic," of *The Mediterranean . . . in the Age of Philip II,* vol. 2, by F. Braudel. Reprinted in *Discoveries and Reviews* (1975).

D560a. *Sunday Telegraph,* **February 24, 1974, p. 14**
Review, entitled "King Hal's Greatest Love," of *Anne Boleyn* by Hester W. Chapman. Reprinted in *Discoveries and Reviews (1975)* as "Anne Boleyn."

D561. *Books and Bookmen,* **February 1974, pp. 18–20**
Review, entitled "Civil War Facts and Fantasies," of *Politics, Religion, and the English Civil War,* edited by B. Manning; *Memoirs of the Life of Colonel Hutchinson,* edited by J. Sutherland. Reprinted in *Discoveries and Reviews* (1975).

D562. *History Today,* **February 1974, pp. 136–137**
Review, entitled "Medieval Tin," of *English Tin Production and Trade before 1550* by John Hatcher.

D563. *The Times,* **March 5, 1974, p. 15, col. d**
Letter on the general election. Commencing, "The sinister dialectic of party-government has brought us to where a historian could see all along that it would: confusion and chaos, and economic disaster."

D564. *Books and Bookmen,* **March 1974, p. 21**
Review, entitled "Utopia v. Realism," of *The Vision of Politics on the Eve of the Reformation: More, Machiavelli, and Seyssel* by J. H. Hexter. Reprinted in *Discoveries and Reviews* (1975)

D565. *History Today,* **March 1974, pp. 211–212**
Review, entitled "Urban History," of *Perspectives in English Urban History,* edited by Alan Everitt.

D566. *Spectator,* **April 13, 1974, p. 454**
Review, entitled "Under the Dome," of *That Noble Cabinet: A History of the British Museum* by Edward Miller.

D567. *The Times,* **April 13, 1974, p. 12, col. a**
Article: "The Extraordinary Life Story of Byron's Cornish Grand-mother/ Professor A. L. Rowse on a Little Known Aspect of the Great Poet Who Died 150 Years Ago This Month." Commencing, "Many people will know beautiful and romantically situated Caerhay's Castle in Cornwall, not far from St. Austell, its Nash tower and turrets rising above that lovely valley to look down on the beach below. A very appropriate setting for the poet's Cornish ancestry."

D568. *Listener,* **April 18, 1974, pp. 494–496**
Article: "Simon Forman and the Dark Lady." Reprinted in *Discoveries and Reviews* (1975).

D569. *The Times,* **April 23, 1974, p. 16, col. c**
Article: "Popular Misconceptions about William Shakespeare." Commencing, "Much of the nonsense written about Shakespeare comes from people who know nothing of the Elizabethan Age in which he lived." Reprinted in *Discoveries and Reviews* (1975).

D570. *Times Literary Supplement,* **April 26, 1974, p. 447, col. b**
Letter: "Shakespeare and Emilia." Commencing, "An American correspondent, Dr. Joseph T. Freeman of Philadelphia, has thrown a little new light on young John Lane's slander against Shakespeare's daughter, Susanna Hall, and permits me to quote him."

D571. *Spectator,* **April 27, 1974, pp. 518–519**
Review, entitled "A Virtuous Historian," of *Studies in Tudor and Stuart Politics and Government: Papers and Reviews, 1946–1972.* Two volumes by G. R. Elton. Reprinted in *Discoveries and Reviews* (1975) as "Tudor Politics."

D572. *Books and Bookmen,* **April 1974, pp. 26–27**
Review, entitled "Puritan Administrators," of *The State's Servants: The Civil*

Service of the English Republic, 1649–1660 by G. E. Aylmer. Reprinted in
Discoveries and Reviews (1975).

D573. *English Historical Review,* April 1974, pp. 430–431
Reviews (untitled) of *The Memoirs of Robert Carey,* edited by F. H. Mares.
Shakespeare and the Bawdy Court of Stratford by Dr. E. R. C. Brinkworth. *The
New Found Land of Stephen Parmenius,* edited and translated with commentaries by D. B. Quinn and N. M. Cheshire.

D574. *The Times,* May 27, 1974, p. 6, col. a
Article: "Passion and Misery in the Strange Affair of Medora/A. L. Rowse
Further Explores the Remarkable History of Lord Byron's Cornish Relatives."
Commencing, "One day some years ago, in the dining-room of an hotel along
the Great North Road, I looked up to see the self-same Medusa-like head that
had looked down upon the fatal marriage of Byron to Annabella Milbanke on
that snowy New Year's day, 1815."

D575. *Books and Bookmen,* May 1974, pp. 57–58
Review, entitled "Question of Origin," of *Our German Cousins: Anglo-German
Relations in the Nineteenth and Twentieth Centuries* by John Mander. Reprinted
in *Portraits and Views* (1979) as "German Half-Cousins."

D576. *History Today,* May 1974, pp. 361–362
Review, entitled "The Rump," of *The Rump Parliament, 1648–1653* by B.
Worden. Reprinted in *Discoveries and Reviews* (1975).

D577. *Daily Telegraph,* June 11, 1974, p. 15, cols. a–c
Article: "Students to Get Rid Of/Universities to Close/A working-man's View
of the Waste (and the Wreckers) in Education."

D578. *Spectator,* June 15, 1974, pp. 738–739
Review, entitled "The Affairs of Lord Byron," of *Lord Byron: Accounts Rendered* by Doris Langley Moore; *Byron's Daughter* by Catherine Turney; *The
Byron Women* by Margot Strickland.

D579. *Books and Bookmen,* June 1974, pp. 15–18
Review, entitled "The Shakespeare Trade Union," of *The Riverside Shakespeare,*
edited by G. Blakemore Evans. Reprinted in *Discoveries and Reviews* (1975).

D580. *Daily Telegraph,* July 4, 1974, p. 14, cols. a–c
Article: "Cut the Humbug!/Get Back to Education." Last month we published
Dr. Rowse's "working man's view" of students at the new universities. It stirred
up considerable interest. Here he returns to the attack.

D581. *Spectator,* July 13, 1974, p. 52
Review, entitled "America Found," of *England and the Discovery of America,
1481–1620* by D. B. Quinn.

D582. *Spectator,* July 20, 1974, p. 71
Article: "A Spectator's Notebook" (guest contributor to the *Notebook*).

D583. *Spectator,* **July 27, 1974, p. 103**
Article: "A Spectator's Notebook" (guest contributor to the *Notebook*).

D584. *Books and Bookmen,* **July 1974, pp. 32–34**
Review, entitled "Shakespeare Trade Unionists and Others," of *Dream in Shakespeare: From Metaphor to Metamorphosis* by Marjorie B. Garber; *Shakespeare's Comedy of Love* by Alexander Leggatt; *The Dramatic Use of Bawdy in Shakespeare* by E. A. M. Colman; *Shakespeare: The Critical Heritage,* vol. 1, *1623–1692* by Brian Vickers; *The Labyrinth of Shakespeare's Sonnets* by Martin Green. Reprinted in *Discoveries and Reviews* (1975).

D585. *Books and Bookmen,* **July 1974, pp. 70–72**
Review, entitled "Britannica or Americana?" of *Encyclopaedia Britannica,* 30 vols. Reprinted in *Portraits and Views* (1979).

D586. *Books and Bookmen,* **July 1974, pp. 78–79**
Review, entitled "A Taste for Life," of *Selected Letters of Horace Walpole,* edited by W. S. Lewis.

D587. *History Today,* **July 1974, p. 509**
Review, entitled "The Gentry at War," of *Cheshire, 1630–1660* by J. S. Morrill. Reprinted in *Discoveries and Reviews* (1975) as "Civil War Cheshire."

D588. *Cornish Review,* **Summer 1974, series 2, pp. 11–13**
Poem: "The Devil from Linkinhorne." Reprinted in *The Road to Oxford* (1978); *A Life: Collected Poems* (1981).

D588a. *Sunday Telegraph,* **August 25, 1974, p. 12**
Review, entitled "Socialist Sense and Nonsense," of *R. H. Tawney and His Times: Socialism As Fellowship* by Ross Terrill. Reprinted in *Portraits and Views* (1979) as "R. H. Tawney's Influence."

D589. *Books and Bookmen,* **August 1974, pp. 28–29**
Review, entitled "Edifice Completed," of *Oxfordshire* by J. Sherwood and N. Pevsner; *Staffordshire* by N. Pevsner; *The History of Oxford University* by V. H. H. Green.

D590. *Books and Bookmen,* **August 1974, pp. 48–49**
Review, entitled "Elizabethiana," of *Elizabeth I: A Study in Power and Intellect* by Paul Johnson; *Gloriana: The Years of Elizabeth I* by Mary M. Luke; *Elizabethan Adventurer: Captain Christopher Carleill* by Rachel Lloyd; *Elizabethan Life: Morals and the Church Courts* by F. G. Emmison; *A Place in History* by Paul Johnson. Reprinted in *Discoveries and Reviews* (1975).

D591. *Books and Bookmen,* **August 1974, pp. 94–95**
Review, entitled "Wise after the Event," of *This Solemn Mockery* by John Whitehead.

D592. *History Today,* **August 1974, p. 579**
Review, entitled "Norden's Maps," of John Norden's *Manuscript Maps of Cornwall and Its Nine Hundreds.* Introduction by W. Ravenhill.

D592a. *Sunday Telegraph,* **September 8, 1974, p. 15**
Review, entitled "England As She Is Seen," of *Britain through American Eyes,* edited by H. S. Commager.

D593. *Spectator,* **September 14, 1974, p. 336**
Review, entitled "A. L. Rowse on Pepys/The Complete Gentleman," of *Pepys: A Biography* by Richard Ollard. Reprinted in *Discoveries and Reviews* (1975) as "Pepys in History."

D594. *Spectator,* **September 28, 1974, Children's Book Show Supplement, p. xxiii**
Poem: "A Directory: How to Pronounce Cornish Names."

D595. *Books and Bookmen,* **September 1974, pp. 73–74**
Review, entitled "Big Whig," of *The Letters of Thomas Babington Macaulay,* vol. 1, *1807–February 1831*; vol. 2, *March 1831–December 1833*, edited by Thomas Pinney.

D596. *History Today,* **September 1974, pp. 657–658**
Review, entitled "Penzance," of *The History of the Town and Borough of Penzance* by P. A. S. Pool.

D597. *Daily Telegraph,* **October 3, 1974, p. 15, cols. f–h**
Article: "Oxbridge: The Humbug and Waste." A. L. Rowse continues his attack on "liberal" educationalists.

D597a. *Sunday Telegraph,* **October 6, 1974, p. 14**
Review, entitled "That Dangerous Greasy Pole," of *The Prime Ministers,* vol. 1, *Sir Robert Walpole to Sir Robert Peel,* edited by Herbert Van Thal.

D598. *Spectator,* **October 26, 1974, pp. 538–539**
Review, entitled "Eupeptic Van," of *Masks and Facades: Sir John Vanbrugh* by Madeleine Bingham.

D599. *Books and Bookmen,* **October 1974, p. 27**
Review, entitled "Delights of Bibliography," of *The New Cambridge Bibliography of English Literature,* vol. 1, *600–1660,* edited by G. Watson.

D600. *English Historical Review,* **October 1974, p. 892**
Review (untitled) of *Ralph Fitch: Elizabethan in the Indies* by Michael Edwardes; *The Spanish Company* by Pauline Croft.

D601. *History Today,* **October 1974, pp. 730–731**
Review, entitled "Durham in Transition," of *Family, Lineage, and Civil*

Society. . . in the Durham Region, 1500–1640 by Mervyn James. Reprinted in *Discoveries and Reviews* (1975).

D602. *Times Literary Supplement,* November 22, 1974, p. 1305, col. a
Review, entitled "Celtic Highlights," of *The Cornish Language and Its Literature* by P. Berresford Ellis; *The Hard-Rock Men: Cornish Immigrants and the North American Mining Frontier* by John Rowe.

D603. *The Times,* November 30, 1974, p. 14, col. a
Article: "Remembering the Man behind the Churchill Legend/On the 100th Anniversary of the Birth of Sir Winston Churchill, A. L. Rowse Recalls a Day Spent at Chartwell." Commencing, "Quite the most wonderful day I have spent in my life was the whole day I spent alone with Churchill at Chartwell, on Monday, July 11, 1955."

D604. *Books and Bookmen,* November 1974, pp. 22–24
Review, entitled "Delights of Destruction," of *Sir Harry Vane: His Life and Times, 1613–1662* by J. H. Adamson and H. F. Folland; *The English Civil War, 1642–1651* by Brigadier Peter Young and Richard Holmes; *The Reformation of Images: Destruction of Art in England, 1535–1660* by John Phillips.

D605. *Encounter,* November 1974, pp. 89–92
Article: "Discussion/Robbins to Sloman to Annan/Mushroom Universities."

D606. *History Today,* November 1974, p. 811
Review, entitled "Cornish Clerics, 1673–1735," of *Calendar of Cornish Glebe Terriers, 1673–1735,* edited by Richard Potts.

D607. *Daily Telegraph,* December 5, 1974, p. 15, cols. e–h
Article: "The Pride of a Cornishman." "The rise of Cornish feeling is a healthy reaction against the sameness of mass-civilisation."

D608. *Spectator,* December 7, 1974, pp. 735, 738–739
Review, entitled "Children's Books: Fairy Gold," of *The Classic Fairy Tales* by Iona and Peter Opie; *Cap O'Rushes and Other Folk Tales* by Winifred Finlay; *In a Certain Kingdom: Twelve Russian Fairy Tales* by Thomas P. Whitney; *Fairy Tales from Many Lands* illustrated by Arthur Rackham.

D608a. *Sunday Telegraph,* December 15, 1974, p. 17
Review, entitled "Commander with the Winning Ways," of *Marlborough* by Correlli Barnett; *Blenheim* by David Green.

D608b. *Sunday Telegraph,* December 29, 1974, p. 10
Review, entitled "In the Wake of Columbus," of *The European Discovery of America: The Southern Voyages, 1492–1616* by S. E. Morison; *Columbus and the Conquest of the Impossible* by F. Fernandez-Armesto; *The Exploration of North America* by D. B. Quinn, W. P. Cumming, S. E. Hillier and G. Williams.

D609. *London Topographical Record,* **1974, pp. 91–96**
Address: "Wenceslas Hollar in Perspective." (Given at unveiling of a new memorial tablet to Wenceslas Hollar [1607–1677] in the Church of St. Margaret, Westminster, on June 28, 1972.) Reprinted in *Discoveries and Reviews* (1975).

D610. *Books and Bookmen,* **January 1975, pp. 34–35**
Review, entitled "Nottinghamshire Lad," of *The Pleasant Years, 1947–1972* by Cecil Roberts.

D611. *History Today,* **January 1975, pp. 61–65**
Review, entitled "Leicester's Millennium," of *Leicester, Past and Present,* vol. 1, *Ancient Borough to 1860*; vol. 2, *Modern City, 1860–1974* by Jack Simmons.

D612. *History Today,* **January 1975, pp. 69–71**
Review, entitled "The Eastern Association," of *The Eastern Association in the English Civil War* by Clive Holmes.

D613. *Daily Telegraph,* **February 3, 1975, p. 9, cols. f–h**
Article: "Cornwall . . . For Better or Worse." A. L. Rowse on the fascination of the Cornish landscape.

D614. *Spectator,* **February 8, 1975, pp. 156–157**
Review, entitled "Ancient Conflicts," of *Cases of Conscience: Alternatives Open to Recusants and Puritans under Elizabeth I and James I* by Elliot Rose.

D614a. *Sunday Telegraph,* **February 9, 1975, p. 18**
Review, entitled "Mad Goings-on at the Palace," of *Queen Charlotte* by Olwen Hedley; *George III at Home* by Nesta Pain.

D615. *Books and Bookmen,* **February 1975, pp. 29–30.**
Review, entitled "Europe's History and Germany's," of *The Shape of European History* by W. H. McNeill; *The Germans,* edited by R. Kimber and R. Kimber. Reprinted in *Portraits and Views* (1979).

D616. *History Today,* **February 1975, pp. 141–142**
Review, entitled "Puritan Cambridgeshire," of *Contrasting Communities: English Villagers in the Sixteenth and Seventeenth Centuries* by M. Spufford.

D617. *Books and Bookmen,* **March 1975, pp. 20–21**
Review, entitled "Spanish Counter-Reformation," of *The Counter Reformation, 1559–1610* by Marvin R. O'Connell; *King of Two Worlds: Philip II of Spain* by Edward Grierson; *The Spanish Terror: Spanish Imperialism in the Sixteenth Century* by M. Rowdon.

D618. *Encounter,* **March 1975, pp. 25–32**
Article: "Byron's Friends, Bankes: A Portrait."

D619. *History Today,* **March 1975, p. 217**
Review, entitled "The British Pewter Industry," of *A History of British Pewter* by John Hatcher and T. C. Barker.

D620. *Spectator,* **April 19, 1975, pp. 467–468**
Article: "Shakespeare and Stratford: Answering the Sceptical."

D621. *Books and Bookmen,* **April 1975, pp. 40–41**
Review, entitled "Puritan and Cavaliers," of *The Improbable Puritan: A Life of Bulstrode Whitelocke, 1605–1675* by Ruth Spalding; *The Cavalier Army* by Peter Young and W. Emberton; *King Charles, Prince Rupert and the Civil War,* edited by Charles Petrie.

D622. *Books and Bookmen,* **May 1975, pp. 24–27**
Review, entitled "Shakespeare in the Documents," of *William Shakespeare: A Documentary Life* by Samuel Schoenbaum.

D623. *Books and Bookmen,* **June 1975, pp. 47–49**
Review, entitled "Shakespeare and the Critics," of *The Critical Heritage,* vol. 2, *1693–1733*; vol. 3, *1733–1752,* edited by Brian Vickers; *Shakespeare's Last Plays: A New Approach* by Frances A. Yates.

D624. *Spectator,* **June 28, 1975, pp. 779–780**
Review, entitled "German Guilt," of *War of Illusions: German Policies from 1911 to 1914* by Fritz Fischer. Reprinted in *Portraits and Views* (1979) as "German Responsibility for the War of 1914–1918."

D625. *Books and Bookmen,* **July 1975, pp. 46–48**
Review, entitled "Weimar and Wheeler-Bennett," of *Knaves, Fools, and Heroes in Europe between the Wars* by John Wheeler-Bennett; *Weimar: A Cultural History, 1918–1933* by Walter Laqueur. Reprinted in *Portraits and Views* (1979).

D626. *History Today,* **July 1975, pp. 507–508**
Review, entitled "Reformation Lancashire," of *Reformation and Resistance in Tudor Lancashire* by Christopher Haigh.

D627. *Spectator,* **August 23, 1975, p. 250**
Review, entitled "Men of Power," of *The Cardinal and the Secretary* by Neville Williams and *Henry V: The Cautious Conqueror* by M. W. Labarge.

D628. *History Today,* **August 1975, pp. 584–585**
Review, entitled "London and Antwerp," of *The City of London, in International Politics at the Accession of Elizabeth Tudor* by G. D. Ramsay.

D629. *Books and Bookmen,* **September 1975, pp. 20–22**
Review, entitled "Literary Treasure Trove," of Horace Walpole's *Correspondence,* vols. 37–39, edited by W. S. Lewis; *The Treasure of Auchinleck: The Story of the Boswell Papers* by David Buchanan.

D630. *History Today,* **September 1975, p. 649**
Review, entitled "Universities and Society," of *The University in Society* by Lawrence Stone. Reprinted in *Portraits and Views* (1979).

D631. *English Historical Review,* **October 1975, pp. 892–893**
Review (untitled) of *Statesman and Schemer: William, First Lord Paget* by S. R. Gammon.

D631a. *Sunday Telegraph,* **November 23, 1975, p. 14**
Review, entitled "How Bony Cared for His Own," of *The Bonapartes* by Felix Markham.

D632. *Books and Bookmen,* **November 1975, pp. 21–22**
Review, entitled "Seeking Historical Truth," of *The King's Parliament of England* by G. O. Sayles; *Francis Bacon: Discovery and the Art of Discourse* by Lisa Jardine.

D633. *Journal of the Royal Society of Arts,* **November 1975, pp. 763–769**
Text ("Windsor Castle in the History of the Nation") of a talk given to the Society on Wednesday March 5, 1975, with the Right Reverend Robin Woods, KCVO, Bishop of Worcester, and formerly Dean of Windsor, as chair.

D634. *Books and Bookmen,* **December 1975, pp. 38–39**
Review, entitled "Genius and Folly," of *The Life of Bertrand Russell* by Ronald W. Clark. Reprinted in *Portraits and Views* (1979) as "Part 1: Bertrand Russell."

D635. *Daily Telegraph,* **December 6, 1975, p. 14, cols. c–e**
Article: "Buchan, The Modest Romantic." A. L. Rowse on a beloved writer's centenary.

D636. *History Today,* **December 1975, pp. 861–863**
Review, entitled "Guide to Hakluyt," of *The Hakluyt Handbook,* edited by D. B. Quinn.

D637. *Books and Bookmen,* **January 1976, pp. 48–50**
Review, entitled "God's Variety," of *Golden Lads: A Study of Anthony Bacon, Francis, and Their Friends* by Daphne Du Maurier; *John Donne and His World* by Derek Parker; *Prayers and Meditations* by Samuel Johnson.

D638. *English Historical Review,* **January 1976, pp. 193–196**
Review (untitled) of *County and Court: Government and Politics in Norfolk, 1558–1603* by A. Hassell Smith; *George Owen of Henllys: A Welsh Elizabethan* by B. G. Charles.

D639. *History Today,* **January 1976, p. 61**
Review, entitled "Hitler and British Politics," of *The Impact of Hitler: British Politics and British Policy, 1933–1940* by M. Cowling. Reprinted in *Portraits and Views* (1979).

D639a. *Sunday Telegraph,* **February 15, 1976, p. 16**
Article: "Striding through English History." "A. L. Rowse honours the late G. M. Trevelyan who was born 100 years ago tomorrow." Commencing, "G. M. Trevelyan, Regius Professor of Modern History at Cambridge and later Master of Trinity College, was not only an eminent historian but a great man. He had that quality of crashing integrity which I have observed in others of the truly great: Robert Bridges the poet, Winston Churchill, and Samuel Eliot Morison, the American historian. They share this quality of uncompromising straightness, with which they can knock one out—and then prove themselves warm-hearted and encouraging."

D640. *Books and Bookmen,* **March 1976, pp. 20–21**
Review, entitled "Moral Backbone," of *John Calvin* by T. H. L. Parker; *Cromwell and the New Model Foreign Policy* by C. P. Korr; *James Boswell and His World* by D. Daiches.

D641. *History Today,* **April 1976, pp. 269–271**
Review, entitled "The Great War in British Memory," of *The Great War and Modern Memory* by Paul Fussell. Reprinted in *Portraits and Views* (1979).

D642. *Spectator,* **May 15, 1976, p. 24**
Review, entitled "Forlorn Hope," of *The Protestant Duke: A Life of Monmouth* by Violet Wyndham.

D642a. *Sunday Telegraph,* **May 16, 1976, p. 9**
Review, entitled "Genius That Was Lawrence," of *A Prince of Our Disorder: The Life of T. E. Lawrence* by J. E. Mack.

D643. *Books and Bookmen,* **May 1976, pp. 46–48**
Review, entitled "Attitudes to History," of *Style in History* by Peter Gay; *A Short History of the World,* vol. 2, edited by A. Z. Mander; *The Medieval Universities* by A. B. Cobban; *Suitors to the Queen* by Josephine Ross. Reprinted in *Portraits and Views* (1979).

D644. *History Today,* **May 1976, pp. 338–339**
Review, entitled "Bishop Gardiner, Machiavellian," of *A Machiavellian Treatise,* edited by Stephen Gardiner. Translated by P. S. Donaldson.

D645. *History Today,* **May 1976, pp. 340–342**
Review, entitled "Elizabethan Social Life in Sussex," of *Calendar of Assize Records: Sussex Indictments, Elizabeth I,* edited by J. S. Cockburn.

D646. *Books and Bookmen,* **June 1976, pp. 40–42**
Review, entitled "Portrait of Society in 1976." of *Who's Who 1976: An Annual Biographical Dictionary.*

D647. *History Today,* **June 1976, pp. 402–407**
Article: "The Godolphin-Marlborough Duumvirate." On the prime minister and the chief commander in the field during the long war of Queen Anne's reign.

Note. Letter in November 1976 issue from W. Calvin Dickinson in reference to the above.

D648. *Books and Bookmen,* **July 1976, pp. 20–22**
Review, entitled "A Vanished World," of *Ottoline: The Life of Lady Ottoline Morrell* by Sandra Jobson Darroch. Reprinted in *Portraits and Views* (1979) as "Lady Ottoline's Vanished World."

D649. *History Today,* **July 1976, p. 478**
Review, entitled "The English Revolution, 1640–1649," of *The English People and the English Revolution, 1640–1649* by Brian Manning.
Note. Letter in July 1976 issue from G. T. Buckley referring to A. L. Rowse's first-rate reviews.

D650. *Spectator,* **August 21, 1976, p. 9**
Review, entitled "Oxford Remembered," of *Grey Ghosts and Voices* by May Wedderburn Cannan.

D651. *Books and Bookmen,* **August 1976, pp. 41–42**
Review, entitled "World Historical Events," of *Chronology of World History from 3000 BC to AD 1973,* edited by G. S. P. Freeman-Grenville. Reprinted in *Portraits and Views* (1979).

D652. *Wall Street Journal,* **September 3, 1976, p. 6, col. f**
Article: "The Bicentennial: An English View." Commencing, "All Souls College, Oxford, is known to many Americans for its special distinction of having no students and also as the model Abraham Flexner had in mind in founding the Institute for Advanced Studies at Princeton. It is still more familiar to the growing number of Visiting Fellows who come to us every year from America. This summer All Souls has been celebrating the Bicentennial of 1776 with a fascinating exhibition of some of the rare Americana in its Library. The splendid Codrington Library, familiar to so many Americans, is itself a bequest to Oxford from the New World."

D653. *Books and Bookmen,* **September 1976, pp. 14–15**
Review, entitled "In Stuart Times," of *Lives of the Stuart Age, 1603–1714,* edited by Edwin Ridell; *Warrior Prince: The Life of Prince Rupert of the Rhine* by George Malcolm Thompson.

D654. *History Today,* **September 1976, pp. 619–620**
Review, entitled "Sir John Davies in Literature and History," of *The Poems of Sir John Davies,* edited by R. Krueger.

D655. *Books and Bookmen,* **October 1976, pp. 48–49**
Review, entitled "Tudor Portraits," of *The House of Tudor* by Alison Plowden; *Peace, Print, and Protestantism, 1450–1558* by C. S. L. Davies; *Elizabeth Tudor: Portrait of a Queen* by Lacey Baldwin.

D656. *History Today,* **October 1976, pp. 689–690**
Review, entitled "Decline and Fall of the Liberal Party" of *A Short History of*

the Liberal Party, 1900–1976 by Chris Cook. Reprinted in *Portraits and Views* (1979).

D657. *Books and Bookmen,* November 1976, pp. 28–29
Review, entitled "Macaulay in His Letters," of *The Letters of T. B. Macaulay,* vol. 3, *January 1834–August 1841,* edited by Thomas Pinney.

D658. *Books and Bookmen,* December 1976, pp. 20–22
Review, entitled "Bibliography in Excelsis: The New STC," of *A Short Title Catalogue of Books Printed in England, Scotland, and Ireland, and of English Books Printed Abroad, 1475–1640,* vol. 2, *L–Z* (2d ed. revised and enlarged by W. A. Jackson, F. S. Ferguson, and Katherine F. Pantzer) by A. W. Pollard and G. R. Redgrave. Reprinted in *Portraits and Views* (1979).

D659. *History Today,* December 1976, pp. 826–829
Review, entitled "The Coastguard Service," of *Coastguard: An Official History of H. M. Coastguard* by William Webb.

D660. *Books and Bookmen,* January 1977, pp. 34–35
Review, entitled "King and Commons," of *This War without an Enemy* by Richard Ollard; *A Life of John Hampden* by John Adair; *Cromwell: Portrait of a Soldier* by John Gillingham.

D661. *English Historical Review,* January 1977, pp. 199–200
Review (untitled) of *Cornwall in the 17th Century: An Economic History of Kernow* by James Whetter.

D662. *History Today,* January 1977, pp. 62–63
Review, entitled "Civil-War Sussex," of *A County Community in Peace and War, Sussex 1600–1660* by Anthony Fletcher.

D663. *Saturday Evening Post* (USA), January 1977, pp. 29ff.
Article: "Adventures of the Mind: The Idea of a University."

D664. *Books and Bookmen,* February 1977, pp. 31–33
Review, entitled "Dark Ages," of *Northumbria in the Days of Bede* by P. Hunter Blair; *The Framework of Anglo-Saxon History* by Kenneth Harrison; *The Celts* by Gerhard Herm. Reprinted in *Portraits and Views* (1979).

D665. *History Today,* February 1977, p. 133
Review, entitled "Great Elizabethan Household," of *John Petre* by A. C. Edwards.

D666. *Sunday Telegraph,* March 20, 1977
Review, entitled "A Model Secretary," of *Servant of the Cecils: The Life of Sir Michael Hickes, 1543–1612* by A. G. R. Smith.

D667. *Books and Bookmen,* March 1977, pp. 16–18
Review, entitled "Bloomsbury Queen," of *Lady Ottoline's Album.* Introduced by Lord David Cecil, edited by Carolyn G. Heilbrun.

D668. *History Today,* **March 1977, pp. 198–199**
Review, entitled "Caroline Philosopher," of *The Life of Edward, First Lord Herbert of Cherbury,* edited by J. M. Shuttleworth.

D669. *Books and Bookmen,* **April 1977, pp. 21–22**
Review, entitled "An Oxford Oddity," of *Spooner: A Biography* by William Hayter.

D670. *English Historical Review,* **April 1977, pp. 430–431**
Review (untitled) of *A Spaniard in Elizabethan England: The Correspondence of Antonio Perez's Exile,* vol. 1, by Gustav Ungerer.

D671. *Books and Bookmen,* **May 1977, pp. 20–21**
Review, entitled "The Play's the Thing," of *Shakespeare: The Man and His Achievement* by Robert Speaight.

D671a. *Sunday Telegraph,* **June 12, 1977, p. 14**
Review, entitled "Petticoat-Power," of *Bess of Hardwick: Portrait of an Elizabethan Dynast* by D. N. Durant; *Mary of Guise* by Rosalind K. Marshall.

D672. *Books and Bookmen,* **June 1977, pp. 48–50**
Review, entitled "Royalist Wit and Wisdom," of *The English Revolution: Oxford Royalist Notebooks,* 4 vols.; *General Monck* by Maurice Ashley.

D673. *History Today,* **June 1977, pp. 406–407**
Review, entitled "Restoration Politician," of *The Diaries and Papers of Sir Edward Dering, 2nd Bart., 1644–1684,* edited by M. F. Bond.

D674. *Books and Bookmen,* **July 1977, pp. 27–29**
Review, entitled "Sentiment and Reason in History," of *The Age of Plunder* by W. G. Hoskins; *Beaulieu: King John's Abbey* by Dom Frederick Hockey; *Nicholas Bacon: The Making of a Tudor Statesman* by Robert Tittler.

D675. *History Today,* **July 1977, pp. 476–478**
Review, entitled "The Elizabethans and Ireland," of *The Elizabethan Conquest of Ireland: A Pattern Established, 1565–1576* by Nicholas Canny.

D675a. *Sunday Telegraph,* **August 14, 1977, p. 11**
Review, entitled "Games Elizabeth Played," of *Marriage with My Kingdom: The Courtships of Elizabeth I* by Alison Plowden.

D676. *Books and Bookmen,* **August 1977, pp. 40–41**
Review, entitled "Vanishing Britain," of *Vanishing Britain* by Roy Christian; *Landscapes of Britain* by Roy Millward and Adrian Robinson; *Devon and Cornwall* by Denis Kay-Robinson; *Minehead: A New History* by Hilary Binding and Douglas Stevens; *Harbour Village: Yesterday in Cornwall* by Leo Tregenza. Reprinted in *Portraits and Views* (1979).

D677. *History Today,* **August 1977, pp. 539–542**
Article: "Truro As Cornish Capital." "The centre of administrative life in

Cornwall enjoyed a varied history from Plantagenet to modern times." Reprinted in *The Little Land of Cornwall* (1986).

D678. *History Today,* **August 1977, pp. 547–548**
Review, entitled "Elizabethan Chaplain at Sea," of *An Elizabethan in 1582: The Diary of Richard Madox, Fellow of All Souls,* edited by E. S. Donno.

D679. *History Today,* **August 1977, pp. 548–549**
Review, entitled "Medieval Education in the West Country," of *Education in the West of England, 1066–1548* by Nicholas Orme.

D679a. *Sunday Telegraph,* **September 18, 1977, p. 14**
Review, entitled "Almost a Goddess," of *The Cult of Elizabeth* by Roy Strong.

D680. *Books and Bookmen,* **September 1977, pp. 34–35**
Review, entitled "Goetterdaemmerung," of *The History of German Resistance, 1933–1945* by Peter Hoffmann. Reprinted in *Portraits and Views* (1979).

D681. *Punch,* **October 19, 1977, pp. 732–734**
Review, entitled "Austen Mini?" of *Excellent Women* and *A Glass of Blessings* by Barbara Pym.

D682. *Books and Bookmen,* **October 1977, pp. 14–15**
Review, entitled "Tudor Parliaments," of *The Later Parliaments of Henry VIII* by S. E. Lehmberg.

D683. *History Today,* **October 1977, pp. 681–682**
Review, entitled "Gibbon Analysed," of *Gibbon et Rome à la lumière de l'historiographie moderne.*

D684. *Books and Bookmen,* **November 1977, pp. 21–22**
Review, entitled "An Age Brought Alive," of *The Henslowe Papers,* edited by A. Foakes.

D685. *History Today,* **November 1977, pp. 747–749**
Review, entitled "Revisionist History, 1914–1939," of *The British Revolution: British Politics, 1880–1939,* vol. 2, *From Asquith to Chamberlain, 1914–1939* by Robert Rhodes James. Reprinted in *Portraits and Views* (1979).

D685a. *Sunday Telegraph,* **December 4, 1977, p. 14**
Review, entitled "Brothers in Arms," of *Prince Eugene of Savoy* by Derek McKay.

D686. *Wall Street Journal,* **December 29, 1977, p. 8, col. d**
Article: "The 'Fortunate Captain's' Remarkable Voyage." Commencing, "This month marks the beginning of the celebration of what was, all things considered, probably the greatest voyage in the world's history—Sir Francis Drake's voyage round the world from 1577–1580."

D687. *Books and Bookmen,* **December 1977, pp. 10–11**
Review, entitled "Lucky Jim," of *Prophesying Peace* by James Lees-Milne.

D688. *History Today,* **December 1977, pp. 823–824**
Review, entitled "Vae Victis!" of *The Vision of the Vanquished: The Spanish Conquest of Peru through Indian Eyes, 1530–1570* by Nathan Wachtel.

D689. *Books and Bookmen,* **January 1978, pp. 7–8**
Review, entitled "An Upright Bore," of *The Diary of Ralph Josselin, 1616–1683,* edited by Alan McFarlane.

D690. *English Historical Review,* **January 1978, p. 187**
Review (untitled) of *The Diary of John Manningham of the Middle Temple, 1602–1603* by R. P. Sorlien.

D691. *History Today,* **January 1978, p. 62**
Review, entitled "Elizabethan Controversy," of *Religious Controversies of the Elizabethan Age* by Peter Milward.

D692. *Blackwood's Magazine,* **February 1978, pp. 100–106**
Article: "The Poetry of John Betjeman." Reprinted in *Portraits and Views* (1979).

D693. *Books and Bookmen,* **February 1978, pp. 20–22**
Review, entitled "Sociological v. Real History," of *The Family, Sex, and Marriage in England, 1500–1800* by L. Stone. Reprinted in *Portraits and Views* (1979).

D694. *History Today,* **February 1978, pp. 133–134**
Review, entitled "An Elizabethan on Parliament," of *Parliament in Elizabethan England: John Hooker's Order and Usage,* edited by Vernon F. Snow.

D695. *Books and Bookmen,* **March 1978, pp. 31–32**
Review, entitled "Shakespeare Scholasticism," of *Shakespeare Survey,* edited by K. Muir; *Shakespeare: The Critical Heritage,* vol. 4, *1753–1765,* edited by B. Vickers.

D696. *History Today,* **March 1978, p. 202**
Review, entitled "Star Chamber," of *The Cardinal's Court: The Impact of Thomas Wolsey in Star Chamber* by J. A. Guy.

D697. *The Times,* **April 22, 1978, p. 14, col. g**
Article: "Shakespeare's Passionate Lady Blames It All on the Men." Commencing, "In 1609 Thomas Thorp got hold of Shakespeare's Sonnets and published them with his own dedication to Mr. W.H., and not Shakespeare's young Lord of years before when the Sonnets were written (1592–1595) the obvious person, his patron, young Southampton. We will not repeat here what is already known, but concentrate on what is new."

D698. *Blackwood's Magazine,* **April 1978, pp. 318–322**
Article: "Modesty."

D699. *Books and Bookmen,* **April 1978, pp. 12–14**
Review, entitled "Somnambulist in History," of *Cromwell* by Roger Howell.

D700. *English Historical Review,* **April 1978, p. 441**
Review (untitled) of *A Spaniard in Elizabethan England: The Correspondence of Antonio Perez's Exile,* vol. 2, by Gustav Ungerer.

D701. *Books and Bookmen,* **May 1978, pp. 33–34**
Review, entitled "Rebels, Rogues, Bureaucrats," of *Monmouth's Rebels* by Peter Earle; *The Elizabethan Underworld* by Gamini Salgado; *English Historical Facts, 1485–1603* by Ken Powell and Chris Cook.

D702. *History Today,* **May 1978, pp. 345–347**
Review, entitled "A Commonwealth Doctrinaire," of *The Political Works of James Harrington,* edited with an introduction by J. G. A. Pocock.

D703. *History Today,* **May 1978, p. 347**
Letter: "Elizabethan Controversy."

D703a. *Sunday Telegraph,* **June 4, 1978, p. 13**
Review, entitled "War, War," of *War and the Liberal Conscience* by Michael Howard.

D704. *Blackwood's Magazine,* **June 1978, pp. 468–474**
Article: "Kipling: A New Appreciation." Reprinted in *Portraits and Views* (1979).

D705. *Books and Bookmen,* **June 1978, pp. 16–18**
Review, entitled "Invective and Humbug," of *The Letters of Junius,* edited by John Cannon.

D706. *History Today,* **June 1978, pp. 414–416**
Review, entitled "Jacobean Potentate," of *Law and Politics in Jacobean England: The Tracts of Lord Chancellor Ellesmere* by L. A. Knafla.

D707. *The Times,* **July 11, 1978, p. 15, col. f**
Letter (untitled) commenting on remarks made by the Prince of Wales on doctrinal arguments. Commencing, "May I express the view of the great bulk of people today who no longer believe doctrine or dogma. Namely: those who will believe nonsense must expect awkward consequences."

D708. *Blackwood's Magazine,* **July 1978, pp. 43–47**
Short story: "The Lunatic of Landegey." Reprinted in *Night at the Carn* (1984).

D709. *History Today,* **July 1978, pp. 482–483**
Review, entitled "Elizabethan Catholics," of *The Catholic Subjects of Elizabeth I* by Adrian Morey.

D710. *History Today,* **July 1978, pp. 484–485**
Review, entitled "Elizabethan London's Rulers," of *The Politics of Stability: A Portrait of the Rulers in Elizabethan London* by F. F. Foster.

D711. *The Times,* **August 25, 1978, p. 10, col. a**
Article: "What's Good for California Is Good for Cornwall." Commencing, "A feature of the twentieth century has been the resurgence of the Celtic peoples, now that the unifying influence of the old governing class has broken down."

D712. *Blackwood's Magazine,* **August 1978, pp. 100–109**
Article: "A Great Writer?—The Case of E. M. Forster." Reprinted in *Portraits and Views* (1979).

D713. *Books and Bookmen,* **August 1978, p. 4**
Letter (untitled): Commencing, "It is very good of 'books and bookmen,' if a trifle superfluous, to allow Lady Mosley the free expression of her pro-Nazi opinions (June 1978) and so to expose the political idiocy of the Mitfords, of which this country has had more than enough. Their line would have ended in subjugating this country to Germany's Nazi thugs—of whose charm and truth–telling qualities she tells us a pretty tale."

Note. Letter in Response, August 1978, from Diana Mosley. Commencing, "It is very good of 'books and bookmen,' if a trifle superfluous, to allow Mr. Rowse yet another go at the 'intolerable Mitfords' as he called us in your December issue."

D714. *Books and Bookmen,* **September 1978, pp. 12–13**
Review, entitled "Shell Guides and Others," of *Staffordshire: A Shell Guide* by Henry Thorold; *East Sussex: A Shell Guide* by W. S. Mitchell; *A History of York Minster*, edited by G. E. Aylmer and Reginald Cant.

D715. *The Times,* **October 6, 1978, p. 18, col. c**
Poem: "Le Pape Est Mort." Reprinted in *A Life: Collected Poems* (1981).

D716. *Blackwood's Magazine,* **October 1978, pp. 296–303**
Review, entitled "Dr. Johnson without Boswell: An American Interpretation," of *Samuel Johnson* by W. Jackson Bate. Reprinted in *Portraits and Views* (1979).

D717. *Books and Bookmen,* **October 1978, pp. 10–11**
Review, entitled "Politicians Are Only Human," of *The War Diaries of Oliver Harvey, 1941–1945* by John Harvey.

D718. *Blackwood's Magazine,* **November 1978, pp. 408–420**
Article: "In Justice to Belloc." Reprinted in *Portraits and Views* (1979).

D719. *Books and Bookmen,* **November 1978, pp. 12–14**
Review, entitled "Two Splendid Sailors," of *Bligh* by Gavin Kennedy; *Cochrane* by Donald Thomas.

D720. *Blackwood's Magazine,* **December 1978, pp. 484–489**
Short story: "Hotel Bedroom in Wartime." Reprinted in *Stories from Trenarren* (1986).

D721. *Books and Bookmen,* **December 1978, pp. 16–18**
Review, entitled "Literary Squalor," of *Scott and Ernest: The Fitzgerald–Hemingway Relationship* by Matthew J. Bruccoli; *London and the Life of Literature in Late Victorian England: The Diary of George Gissing, Novelist* by Pierre Coustillas.

D722. *Blackwood's Magazine,* **January 1979, pp. 52–53**
Poem: "Roseland Year: A Children's Calendar." Reprinted in *A Life: Collected Poems* (1981).

D723. *Books and Bookmen,* **January 1979, pp. 21–24**
Review, entitled "Apotheosis of Hill," of *Puritans and Revolutionaries,* edited by D. Pennington and K. Thomas; *Stuart England* by J. P. Kenyon; *Bloody Mary* by Carolly Erickson.

D724. *History Today,* **January 1979, pp. 3–12**
Article: "The Duchy of Cornwall." Edward III created the Duchy of Cornwall as an estate for the Black Prince; it has been held ever since by the sovereign's heir or lain dormant in the Crown. Reprinted in *The Little Land of Cornwall* (1986) as "The Duchy."

D725. *Books and Bookmen,* **February 1979, pp. 14–15**
Review, entitled "A Crazy Pitt," of *The Half-Mad Lord* by Nikolai Tolstoy.

D726. *History Today,* **February 1979, p. 124**
Review, entitled "Ancestor of the Foxes," of *Public Finance and Private Wealth: The Career of Sir Stephen Fox, 1627–1716* by Christopher Clay.

D727. *History Today,* **February 1979, pp. 127–128**
Review, entitled "Vansittart and Policy," of *Vansittart: Study of a Diplomat* by Norman Rose.

D728. *Blackwood's Magazine,* **March 1979, pp. 215–221**
Review, entitled "Post-Kilvert: A Moral Tale," of *After Kilvert* by A. L. Le Quesne. Reprinted in *Portraits and Views* (1979).

D729. *Books and Bookmen,* **March 1979, pp. 18–19**
Review, entitled "Elizabethan Ireland," of *The Twilight Lords* by Richard Berleth.

D730. *History Today,* **March 1979, p. 200**
Review, entitled "Law and Society," of *The Court of King's Bench, 1450–1550* by M. Blatcher.

D731. *Daily Telegraph,* **April 21, 1979, p. 18, col. c**
Article: "Southampton and the Dark Lady." "As Shakespeare's 415th birthday anniversary approaches, A. L. Rowse discusses the poet's sexual ambivalence."

D731a. *Sunday Telegraph,* **April 29, 1979, p. 12**
Review, entitled "Old South Bank," of *A London Life in Brazen Age: Francis Langley, 1548–1602* by William Ingram.

D732. *Blackwood's Magazine,* **April 1979, pp. 323–330**
Article: "The Romantic Story of Charles Augustus Murray." Reprinted in *Portraits and Views* (1979).

D733. *Books and Bookmen,* **April 1979, pp. 15–17**
Review, entitled "Writing for the Comrades," of *English Provincial Society from the Reformation to the Revolution* by Peter Clark; *The English Civil War: Conservatism and Revolution, 1603–1649* by Robert Ashton; *Rebels and Their Causes,* edited by M. Cornforth.

D734. *History Today,* **April 1979, p. 269**
Review, entitled "Jacobean Religious Controversy," of *Religious Controversies of the Jacobean Age: A Survey of Printed Sources,* by Peter Milward, S.J.

D735. *History Today,* **May 1979, p. 336.**
Review, entitled "County Historians," of *English County Historians* by Jack Simmons.

D735a. *Sunday Telegraph,* **June 17, 1979, p. 12**
Review, entitled "Giving James His Due," of *James VI of Scotland* by Caroline Bingham.

D736. *Books and Bookmen,* **June 1979, pp. 15–16**
Review, entitled "Lord George Germain," of *The Coward of Minden: The Affair of Lord George Sackville* by P. Mackesy.

D737. *Books and Bookmen,* **July 1979, pp. 12–13**
Review, entitled "From Liberalism to Socialism," of *Liberals and Social Democrats* by Peter Clarke.

D738. *English Historical Review,* **July 1979, pp. 635–636**
Review (untitled) of *The Queen's Two Bodies: Drama and the Elizabethan Succession* by Marie Axton.

D739. *History Today,* **July 1979, p. 479**
Review, entitled "Anthology of Places" of *A Selective Guide to England by Jack Simmons.*

D739a. *Sunday Telegraph,* **August 12, 1979, p. 12**
Review, entitled "Society of Friends," of *Barclay Fox's Journal,* edited by R. L. Brett.

D740. *Books and Bookmen,* **August 1979, pp. 10–12**
Review, entitled "Fashionable History," of *The Territory of the Historian* by E. R. L. Ladurie. Translated by B. Reynolds and S. Reynolds.

D740a. *Sunday Telegraph,* **September 2, 1979, p. 14**
Review, entitled "The Rhyming Duke," of *Portrait of a Cavalier: William Cavendish, First Duke of Newcastle* by Geoffrey Trease.

D741. *Books and Bookmen,* **September 1979, p. 20**
Review, entitled "Almanachs," of *Astrology and the Popular Press: English Almanacs, 1500–1800* by Bernard Capp.

D742. *History Today,* **September 1979, pp. 619–620**
Review, entitled "The Red Fox," of *Sir Richard Grenville of the Civil War* by Amos C. Miller.

D743. *Books and Bookmen,* **October 1979, pp. 18–19**
Review, entitled "Homo Homini Lupus," of *Victims of Piracy: The Admiralty Court, 1575–1678* by Evelyn Berckman; *Captain-General and Rebel Chief: The Life of James, Duke of Monmouth* by J. P. N. Watson.

D744. *Books and Bookmen,* **November 1979, pp. 19–20**
Review, entitled "The Webbs: Personal Notes," of *A Victorian Courtship* by Jeanne Mackenzie.

D745. *History Today,* **November 1979, pp. 701–705**
Article: "A Tribute to P. Q. and A. H." A personal tribute to Peter Quennell and Alan Hodge, joint editors of *History Today* for record period 1951–1979.

D746. *Books and Bookmen,* **December 1979, pp. 24–25**
Review, entitled "The Centuries Roll On," of *Catholic Loyalism in Elizabethan England* by Arnold Pritchard; *The City and the Court, 1603–1643* by Robert Ashton; *Pepys and the Revolution* by Arthur Bryant; *History of His Own Time* by Gilbert Burnet; *A Gentleman Volunteer: The Letters of George Hennell from the Peninsular War 1812–1813,* edited by Michael Glover.

D747. *History Today,* **December 1979, pp. 848–849**
Review, entitled "Old College, Oxford" of *New College, Oxford, 1379–1979,* edited by J. Buxton and P. Williams.

D748. *Yale Literary Magazine,* **December 1979, p. 13**
Poem: "Te Lucis Ante Terminum." Reprinted in *Blackwood's Magazine,* January 1980, p. 26; *A Life: Collected Poems* (1981).

D749. *Books and Bookmen,* **January 1980, pp. 17–18**
Review, entitled "Housman the Genius," of *A. E. Housman: The Scholar-Poet* by Richard Perceval Graves.

D750. *English Historical Review,* **January 1980, p. 206**
Review (untitled) of *The Registers of St. Paul's School, 1509–1748* by Sir Michael McDonnell.

D751. *Daily Telegraph,* **February 5, 1980, p. 16**
Article: "Our Century of Humbug." A. L. Rowse looks back on—and abominates—our century of humbug.

D752. *Books and Bookmen,* **February 1980, pp. 14–16**
Review, entitled "Two Literary Cats," of *The Nabokov-Wilson Letters,* edited by S. Karlinsky.

D753. *Blackwood's Magazine,* **March 1980, pp. 164–173**
Article: "The Voice of Australia: Judith Wright."

D754. *Books and Bookmen,* **March 1980, pp. 14–15**
Review, entitled "A Good German," of *Canaris* by Heinz Hohne. Translated by J. M. Brownjohn.

D755. *Times Literary Supplement,* **April 18, 1980, p. 441, col. a**
Letter: "W. H. Auden." Commencing, "As an old friend of Auden from his undergraduate days, may I say that it is important not to get Charles Osborne's biography of him out of proportion (Letters, April 4). The fundamental question is whether he has got the portrait of Wystan right; I think he has to a remarkable degree, both sympathetic and true, and also affectionate."

D756. *The Times,* **April 23, 1980, p. 16, col. g**
Article: "Shakespeare and the Tell-Tale Sonnet." On the 416th anniversary of his birth, A. L. Rowse writes on the latest Bardic research. Commencing, "It ought not to surprise us—and it is rather a consoling thought—that we are able in our time to make new discoveries about the Elizabethan age."
  Note. Letter from Professor Muriel Bradbrook, *The Times,* April 29, 1980.

D757. *Books and Bookmen,* **April 1980, pp. 26–27**
Review, entitled "Great Victorian Architect," of *John Loughborough Pearson* by Anthony Quiney.

D758. *English Historical Review,* **April 1980, pp. 438–439**
Review (untitled) of *Cornish Immigrants to South Africa* by Graham B. Dickason.

D759. *History Today,* **April 1980, p. 55**
Review, entitled "After Marx," of *Marxism after Marx* by David McLellan.

D759a. *Sunday Telegraph,* **May 4, 1980, p. 12**
Review, entitled "Keeping His Cool," of *The Wanton Chase: An Autobiography from 1939* by Peter Quennell.

D760. *Daily Telegraph,* **May 5, 1980, p. 12, cols. c–e**
Article: "When the English were Individual." A. L. Rowse recalls the glorious age of eccentricity.

D761. *The Times,* **May 13, 1980, p. 17, col. g**
Letter: "The Tell-Tale Sonnet." Commencing, "I am afraid that, owing to absence in America, I missed the letter of the ex-Mistress of Girton (April 29) about that sonnet published in *The Passionate Pilgrim* by Jaggard, along with other pieces by Shakespeare."
  Note. Letter from Professor Muriel Bradbrook, *The Times,* May 20, 1980.

D762. *Times Literary Supplement,* **May 23, 1980, p. 584, col. d**
Letter: "Shakespeare's Sonnets." In full: "May I ask simply for a piece of information? The reviewer of yet more books on Shakespeare's Sonnets (May 9) refers to his having been 'godfather to one of Jonson's children.' What is the evidence for this? I am amused by the reference to 'those who identify' the Dark Lady with Emilia Lanier—in the plural; since only one person identified her, though others now follow."

Note. Letter from Katherine Duncan-Jones, *Times Literary Supplement,* June 6, 1980, replying to the question.

D763. *Books and Bookmen,* **May 1980, pp. 30–31**
Review, entitled "History by the Hundredweight," of *A History of Europe* by John Bowle; *The Reign of Mary Tudor* by D. M. Loades; *Robert Harley and the Press* by J. A. Downie; *On Historians* by J. H. Hexter.

D764. *History Today,* **May 1980, p. 55**
Review, entitled "Isaiah Berlin's Thinkers," of *Against the Current: Essays in the History of Ideas* by Isaiah Berlin.

D764a. *Sunday Telegraph,* **June 8, 1980, p. 12**
Review, entitled "Brave Nancy," of *Nancy Astor: Portrait of a Pioneer* by John Grigg.

D764b. *Sunday Telegraph,* **June 15, 1980, p. 12**
Review, entitled "Pleasures of the Past," of *Georgian Delights* by J. H. Plumb.

D765. *Times Literary Supplement,* **June 20, 1980, p. 705, col. c**
Letter: "Shakespeare and Ben Jonson." Commencing, "I am most grateful to Katherine Duncan-Jones (Letters June 6) for giving us Sir Nicholas L'Estrange as the source of the tradition that Shakespeare stood godfather to one of Ben Jonson's children. It is inherently not improbable, and I am delighted to learn it. But, of course, we must distinguish between what is only an unsupported tradition and the identification of Emilia Bassano, Mrs. Lanier, which rests on the concurrence of all the evidence from all sources, circumstances, characteristics, made definite by dating."

D766. *Blackwood's Magazine,* **June 1980, p. 442**
Poem "Intimations of Mortality." Reprinted in *A Life: Collected Poems* (1981).

D767. *Books and Bookmen,* **June 1980, pp. 10–11**
Review, entitled "Spenser's Mentor," of *Gabriel Harvey: His Life, Marginalia, and Library* by V. F. Stern.

D768. *History Today,* **June 1980, pp. 24–27**
Article: "Sir Richard Hawkins: Last of a Dynasty." The epic voyage of this Elizabethan adventurer to Peru and his subsequent capture by its Spanish masters inspired Charles Kingsley's "Westward Ho!"

D769. *History Today,* **June 1980, p. 52**
Review, entitled "Disgraced Archbishop," of *Archbishop Grindal, 1519–1583* by P. Collinson.

D769a. *Sunday Telegraph,* **July 20, 1980, p. 14**
Review, entitled "Married Muse," of *Mrs. Browning: The Story of Elizabeth Barrett* by Rosalie Mander.

D770. *Books and Bookmen,* **July 1980, pp. 14–15**
Review, entitled "The Insufferable Baxter," of *Richard Baxter and the Millennium* by William M. Lamont.

D770a. *Sunday Telegraph,* **August 10, 1980, p. 11**
Review, entitled "While Rome Churned," of *Power and Imagination: City-States in Renaissance Italy* by Lauro Martines.

D771. *Blackwood's Magazine,* **August 1980, pp. 84–98**
Article: "On the Track of Willa Cather in Nebraska, Part I."

D772. *Blackwood's Magazine,* **September 1980, pp. 164–171**
Article: "On the Track of Willa Cather in Nebraska, Part II."

D773. *The Times,* **September 26, 1980, p. 16, col. a**
Article: "Drake's Astonishing Voyage into History." The enormous advantages that Britain gained in diplomacy, geography, and botany were even more important than the booty, worth 50 million pounds at present values, that packed the decks of the *Golden Hind* as it sailed into Plymouth 400 years ago today. Commencing, "Today we celebrate—in California as well as the West Country—Sir Francis Drake's return from the most remarkable voyage in history."

D774. *Literary Review* **(UK), October 17–30, 1980, pp. 24–26**
Review, entitled "Renaissance Jewelry," of *Renaissance Jewelry* by Yvonne Hackenbroch.

D775. *Times Literary Supplement,* **November 7, 1980, p. 1261, col. c**
Letter: "Lord Halifax." Commencing, "I write to correct a simple misstatement: It was not Neville Chamberlain whom I stated to have not read *Mein Kampf,* but Halifax."

D776. *Daily Telegraph,* **November 28, 1980, p. 18, cols. c–e**
Article: "The Illusionist Who Produced a Conscience out of Socialism." A. L. Rowse on the flaws in R. H. Tawney.

D776a. *Sunday Telegraph,* **November 30, 1980, p. 16**
Review, entitled "What Price Revolution?" of *Some Intellectual Consequences of the English Revolution* by Christopher Hill.

D777. *Blackwood's Magazine,* **November 1980, p. 354**
Poem: "Summer's End." Reprinted in *A Life: Collected Poems* (1981).

D778. *Listener,* **December 11, 1980, p. 794**
Letter (untitled) correcting author Richard Hoggart on his article about George Orwell in issue dated November 27, 1980.

D779. *Blackwood's Magazine,* **December 1980, p. 447**
Poem: "St. Endellion." Reprinted in *A Life: Collected Poems* (1981).

D780. *History Today,* **December 1980, p. 62**
Letter: "Country Houses Values." Defending country houses and the journal *Country Life*: "It exemplifies excellent standards, both artistic and scholarly, in a society of vulgar glossies and the squalid standards of suburbia."

D781. *Jahrbuch Deutsche Shakespeare-Gesellschaft West* **(Heidelberg, Germany), 1980, pp. 59–72**
Article: "Shakespeare's Universal Appeal."

D782. *The Times,* **January 21, 1981, p. 11, col. e**
Article: "Fallen Idol: Thomas Carlyle." Commencing, "On February 4, 1881, died Thomas Carlyle, whom Sir Leslie Stephen describes as 'the acknowledged head of English literature' in his time. I think that was generally agreed to be so, but it is very difficult for us to understand why today."

D783. *English Historical Review,* **January 1981, pp. 141–143**
Review (untitled) of *List and Analysis of State Papers, Foreign Series Elizabeth I,* vol. 3, *June 1591–April 1592,* edited by R. B. Wernham.

D784. *Listener,* **January 22, 1981, p. 114**
Letter: "Orwell's Origins." Response to letter from Nicolas Walter, January 8, 1981.

D785. *Listener,* **February 12, 1981, p. 214**
Letter: "Orwells Origins." Noting the "imperceptiveness" of correspondent Bernard Crick, January 29, 1981.
  Note. Letter from D. E. A. Rash, February 19, 1981, questioning the word "imperceptiveness" in Rowse's letter.

D786. *Yale Literary Magazine,* **February 1981, pp. 52–61**
Article: "An Evening with Edmund Wilson." Reprinted in *Memories of Men and Women* (1980).

D787. *The Times,* **March 7, 1981, p. 14, col. g**
Article: "Bevin, Born with an Instinct to Rule." Commencing, "Ernest Bevin was an indubitably great man. Clem Attlee, most unenthusiastic of men, called him the greatest trade unionist of his time and one of the outstanding Englishmen of that generation, well worthy to stand historically alongside Churchill."

D788. *Contemporary Review,* **March 1981, pp. 131–136**
Article: "The Oxford of 1887 and Today."

D789. *New Standard* (UK) April 24, 1981, p. 17
Article: "My Weekend/Struggles in the Wilderness." Now 77, historian and biographer, Dr. A. L. Rowse's latest book: *Shakespeare's Globe,* was published in March. Commencing, "A working class boy, I had nobody to tell me how to conduct my life or answer the questions I so much wanted to know—so I learned something valuable from what I read somewhere. I think it was Robert Louis Stevenson who said that a real writer must make his writing the condition of his life: it must come first and everything else must fit in. That is what I learned very early, and I have followed the rule ever since. As I sometimes tell people when provoked, I don't write in order to live, I live in order to write."

D790. *Daily Telegraph,* April 25, 1981, p. 16, cols. c–e
Article: "How Nixon Sees the Kremlin's Cross." A. L. Rowse heard the ex–President's thoughts on Russia's mounting problems.

D791. *Spectator,* May 2, 1981, pp. 22–23
Review, entitled "Politics in the Bedchamber," of *Sweet Robin: Robert Dudley, Earl of Leicester, 1533–1588* by Derek Wilson.

D792. *Sunday Times,* May 17, 1981, p. 19, col. f
Letter: "Shakespeare, the Secretary and Sonneteer." Commencing, "Absence in America has prevented me from commenting on the Earl of Southampton's letter and your article on it (page 3, April 19). I am no handwriting expert, and I agree with Mr. Croft that it is very uncertain to base too much on a script which is fairly common in Elizabethan handwriting. On the other hand, I can say as an historian that there is nothing whatever against Mr. Sams's conjecture that Shakespeare might have written the letter on behalf of the young patron he served."

D793. *Times Literary Supplement,* May 22, 1981, p. 573, col. a
Theatrical review, entitled "Commentary/Cats and Dogs," on *Cats,* New London Theatre. Commencing, "I am afraid I am the last man to be a theatre critic: I sit there ingenuous and enthralled, like a visitor to fairyland or Walt Disney land, a perfect stooge for theatre people, producers, actors, all of them. Perhaps that is not a bad frame of mind in which to enter the world of children and animals, and to appreciate such works as Ravel and Colette's 'L'enfant et les sortileges,' with its climactic 'Miaow!' above the orchestra."

D794. *Times Literary Supplement,* May 29, 1981, p. 605, col. a
Letter: "Droeshout's Engraving." Commencing, "My friend John Bayley refers to my 'one-man enthusiasm' for the Droeshout engraving of Shakespeare (May 1). No one is enthusiastic about it artistically. But fancy being so imperceptive and lacking in imagination—so like a critic—as not to appreciate its importance as an authentic representation of Shakespeare and not to notice the quite exceptional high forehead and immense cranium it reveals."

D795. *Yale Literary Magazine,* **May 1981, pp. 70–90**
Article: "A Portrait of Dublin: Pages from 1929."

D795a. *Sunday Telegraph,* **July 5, 1981, p. 12**
Review, entitled "Sides of Bacon," of *Sir Francis Bacon* by Jean Overton Fuller.

D796. *Spectator,* **July 18, 1981, pp. 18–19**
Review, entitled "News from the Sixteenth Century," of *The Lisle Letters,* edited by M. St. Clare Byrne.

D797. *Spectator,* **September 5, 1981, pp. 22–23**
Review, entitled "In the Family," of *The Rebecca Notebook and Other Memories* by Daphne du Maurier.

D798. *Spectator,* **September 26, 1981, pp. 19–20**
Review, entitled "Philanthropic," of *A Devon Family: The Story of the Aclands* by Anne Acland.

D799. *English Historical Review,* **October 1981, pp. 905–906**
Review (untitled) of *Tide of Empires,* vol. 1, *1481–1654* by Peter Padfield.

D800. *Spectator,* **December 5, 1981, p. 17**
Rowse contributes a paragraph to "Christmas Books II/Books of the Year" in which he lists as his selection *The Lisle Letters*, Charles Thomas's *Christianity in Roman Britain to AD 500,* and Susan Chitty's *Gwen John.*

D801. *Spectator,* **December 19, 1981, pp. 28–29**
Review, entitled "To Us Who Know," of *The Golden Age Restored: The Culture of the Stuart Court, 1603–1642* by Graham Parry.

D802. *Yale Literary Magazine,* **December 1981, pp. 67–73**
Article: "T. S. Eliot Fifty Years After."

D803. *History Today,* **January 1982, pp. 58–59**
Review, entitled "Elizabethan England," of *Who's Who in Shakespeare's England* by A. Palmer and V. Palmer.

D804. *Spectator,* **February 13, 1982, p. 27**
Review, entitled "The Man Luther," of *Luther: A Life* by J. M. Todd.

D805. *History Today,* **February 1982, pp. 59–60**
Review, entitled "Elizabethan England," of *The Diary of Baron Waldstein.* Translated and annotated by G. W. Groos.

D806. *Yale Literary Magazine,* **February 1982, pp. 80–90**
Short Story: "The Persecuted Cleric." Reprinted in *Night at the Carn* (1984).

D807. *Spectator,* **March 6, 1982, pp. 24–25**
Review, entitled "Pan-Germanism," of *Evangelist of Race: The Germanic Vision of Houston Stewart Chamberlain* by G. G. Field.

D808. *Wall Street Journal,* **March 12, 1982, p. 23, col. a**
Article: "Would'st Thou "Prevent" Modernizing Shakespeare?" Commencing, "I have a revolutionary proposal regarding Shakespeare; but like most revolutions—especially the American Revolution—it is both far-going and conservative. The language of Shakespeare's plays is 500 years old, and naturally some of it, obsolete words and grammatical forms, stands in the way of our appreciating and sometimes even understanding him. . . . We need the whole enormous text of Shakespeare—almost as large as the Bible, which we now have in modern versions—rid of obsolete words and forms, while at the same time retaining every line, giving the modern equivalent and not changing anything more than necessary."

D809. *Spectator,* **April 10, 1982, pp. 23–24**
Article: "A Book in My Life." About George Santayana.

D810. *Books and Bookmen,* **April 1982, pp. 34–35**
Review, entitled "Candid Historian," of *Practicing History: Selected Essays* by Barbara W. Tuchman.

D811. *English Historical Review,* **April 1982, pp. 416–417, 431–432**
Review (untitled) of *Epistolae Academicae, 1508–1596,* edited by W. T. Mitchell. *Studies in Eighteenth-Century Culture,* vol. 9, edited by Roseann Runte.

D812. *Financial Times,* **June 12, 1982, p. 12, col. a**
Review, entitled "Aubrey Observes," of John Aubrey's *Monumenta Britannica: A Miscellany of British Antiquities,* edited by John Fowles and Rodney Legg.

D813. *Financial Times,* **July 3, 1982, p. 8, col. d**
Review, entitled "Bread-Fruit Bligh," of *The Mutiny of the Bounty* by Sir John Barrow, edited by Gavin Kennedy.

D814. *Spectator,* **July 3, 1982, pp. 21–22**
Review, entitled "Back to Polonius," of *Hamlet,* by William Shakespeare, edited by Harold Jenkins.

D815. *English Historical Review,* **July 1982, pp. 677–678**
Review (untitled) of *Montague Rhodes James* by R. W. Pfaff.

D816. *Financial Times,* **August 7, 1982, p. 10, col. d**
Review, entitled "Royal Lines," of *Royal Highness: Ancestry of the Royal Child* by Sir Iain Moncreiffe.

D817. *Financial Times,* **August 28, 1982, p. 10, col. a**
Review, entitled "Pam's Staying Power," of *Palmerston: The Early Years, 1784–1841* by Kenneth Bourne.

D818. *Books and Bookmen,* **August 1982, p. 30**
Review, entitled "Elizabethan Parliament," of *The History of Parliament: The House of Commons, 1558–1603,* 3 vols, edited by P. W. Hasler.

D819. *Spectator,* **September 4, 1982, p. 18**
Review, entitled "A Publisher on Shakespeare," of *The Book Known As Q: A Consideration of Shakespeare's Sonnets* by R. Giroux.

D820. *Financial Times,* **October 2, 1982, p. 10, col. e**
Review, entitled "Real Alice," of *Beyond the Looking Glass* by Colin Gordon.

D821. *Financial Times,* **October 30, 1982, p. 12, col. a**
Review, entitled "Busy Dizzy," of *Disraeli* by Sarah Bradford.

D822. *Books and Bookmen,* **October 1982, pp. 11–12**
Review, entitled "Wolsey and More in Contrast," of *The Statesman and the Fanatic* by Jasper Ridley.

D823. *Contemporary Review,* **October 1982, pp. 186–194**
Article: "The Contradictions of George Orwell."

D824. *New York Times,* **November 28, 1982, sec. 10, pp. 14, 16**
Article: "Following the Footsteps of the Bard." Commencing, "The chief pleasure of living in an old country—as against the discouragements of the brave new social order—is that it is feet deep in associations, historical, literary and visual, for those that have eyes to see. And actually there is much more in existence of the England that William Shakespeare knew than people realize."

D825. *Books and Bookmen,* **November 1982, p. 14**
Review, entitled "Mrs. Sidney Webb," of *The Diary of Beatrice Webb,* vol. 1, *1873–1982,* edited by N. MacKenzie and J. MacKenzie.

D826. *Spectator,* **December 11, 1982, pp. 22, 24**
Review, entitled "A Plague on Both Your Houses," of *The Royalist War Effort, 1642–1646* by R. Hutton.

D827. *Financial Times,* **December 18, 1982, p. 8, col. a**
Review, entitled "Bulging Gladstone Bag," of *Gladstone,* vol. 1, *1809–1865* by Richard Shannon.

D828. *Spectator,* **December 18, 1982, p. 45**
Paragraph in "Books of the Year." A. L. Rowse cites his favorite books through 1982, including *Attlee* by Kenneth Harris; *An English Education* by Richard Ollard; Betjeman's *Uncollected Verse;* and Barbara Pym's *A Few Green Leaves.*

D829. *Blackwood's Magazine,* **December 1982, pp. 489–495 (final issue)**
Short Story: "The Priest and the Pueblo." Reprinted in *Night at the Carn* (1984).

D830. *Books and Bookmen,* **December 1982, pp. 16–17**
Review, entitled "Scribbling Dick," of *Richard Baxter: Puritan Man of Letters* by N. H. Keeble.

D831. *Spectator,* **January 22, 1983, pp. 21–22**
Review, entitled "A Life Apart," of *Montherlant Sans Masque: Tome I, 1895–1932* by Pierre Sipriot.

D832. *Financial Times,* **January 29, 1983, p. 18, col. a**
Review, entitled "Noble Family Story," of *The Dukes of Norfolk* by J. M. Robinson.

D833. *Books and Bookmen,* **January 1983, p. 12**
Review, entitled "Ladurie in Proportion," of *The Territory of the Historian* by E. Le Roy Ladurie; *Love, Death, and Money in the Pays d'Oc* by E. Le Roy Ladurie.

D834. *History Today,* **January 1983, p. 52**
Review, entitled "Contemporary Cameos," of *Customs and Characters* by Peter Quennell.

D835. *Daily Telegraph,* **February 7, 1983, p. 14, cols. c–e**
Article: "The Folly of Youth Is to Listen to Elders Who Don't Know Better." A. L. Rowse, a don at Oxford when the Union held its "King and Country" debate 50 years ago, considers this week's re-staging of that famous vote.

D836. *Spectator,* **February 26, 1983, pp. 21–22**
Review, entitled "Post-War England," of *Caves of Ice* by James Lees-Milne.

D837. *Books and Bookmen,* **February 1983, pp. 18–20**
Review, entitled "Civil War Radicals," of *Biographical Dictionary of British Radicals in the Seventeenth Century,* vol. 1, *A–F,* edited by R. L. Greaves and R. Zaller.

D838. *New York Times,* **March 6, 1983, sec. 10, p. 9**
Article: "Historic Devonshire." The West Country offers a mild climate, two coasts, and memories of Raleigh. Commencing, "Devon is heaven—though it hardly becomes a Cornishman to say so, for there is a certain rivalry between these two westernmost counties of Britain. But Devon, three times the size of Cornwall, is one of the largest of English counties, with a historic cathedral city, Exeter, thrown in."

D839. *Daily Telegraph,* **March 7, 1983, p. 14, cols. c–e**
Article: "False Prophet of the Proletariat." A. L. Rowse on the centenary of Karl Marx's death . . . why Communism failed. Commencing, "I suppose that Karl Marx has done more damage in the modern world than any other writer that one can think of—except his disciples Lenin and Stalin, though they were practical politicians rather than writers."

D840. *The Times,* **March 17, 1983, p. 11, col. g**
Review, entitled "Kinquering Congs," of *King Edward III* by Michael Packe, edited by L. C. B. Seaman; *Richard III: England's Black Legend* by Desmond Seward.

D841. *Spectator,* **March 19, 1983, pp. 12–14**
Article: "What Is Left of Marxism?"

D842. *Financial Times,* **March 19, 1983, p. 12, col. a**
Review, entitled "Past Masters," of *The History Men* by John Kenyon.

D843. *Spectator,* **March 26, 1983, pp. 24–26**
Review, entitled "Tout Ca Change," of *Fortune and Men's Eyes: The Career of J. P. Collier* by Dewey Ganzel.

D844. *Books and Bookmen,* **March 1983, pp. 11–12**
Review, entitled "Macaulay in His Letters," of *Selected Letters of T. B. Macaulay,* edited by T. Pinney.

D845. *Spectator,* **April 23, 1983, pp. 21–23**
Review, entitled "The Anachronistic Approach to Shakespeare," of *Henry V* by William Shakespeare, edited by G. Taylor, and *Troilus and Cressida* by William Shakespeare, edited by K. Muir.

D846. *Books and Bookmen,* **April 1983, pp. 14–15**
Review, entitled "Fertile Foolery," of *The World of the Muggletonians* by Christopher Hill and others.

D847. *English Historical Review,* **April 1983, pp. 368–370, 409–410**
Review (untitled) of *The Lisle Letters.* 6 vols, edited by M. St. C. Byrne. *The Cornish Ordinalia: A Critical Study* by Jane A. Bakere.

D848. *Books and Bookmen,* **May 1983, pp. 17–18**
Review, entitled "Poor Richard III," of *Richard III: England's Black Legend* by Desmond Seward.

D849. *Books and Bookmen,* **June 1983, p. 12**
Review, entitled "Rumours of Wars," of *The Causes of the Wars* by Michael Howard.

D850. *Spectator,* **July 16, 1983, p. 26**
Article: "New Light on Shakespeare."

D851. *Spectator,* **August 13, 1983, p. 26**
Review, entitled "Libertarian Humbug," of *Absolute Liberty: Articles and Papers of Caroline Robbins,* edited by Barbara Taft.

D852. *Financial Times,* **August 20, 1983, p. 8, col. a**
Review, entitled "Sailor King," of *King George V* by Kenneth Rose; *George and Elizabeth: A Royal Marriage* by David Duff.

D853. *Books and Bookmen,* **August 1983, pp. 14–15**
Review, entitled "The Jacobean Church," of *The Religion of Protestants* by P. Collinson; *Charles I* by C. Carlton.

D854. *New York Times,* **September 3, 1983, sec. 1, p. 23, col. b**
Article: "Assessing Elizabeth I on Her 450th Birthday." Commencing, "Next Wednesday will mark the 450th anniversary of the birth of Elizabeth I, great-

est of English rulers, certainly the one who has imposed herself longest upon that living memory of peoples that is history."

D855. *Spectator,* **September 3, 1983, pp. 21–22**
Review, entitled "Queen of Scots," of *All The Queen's Men: Power and Politics in Mary Stuart's Scotland* by Gordon Donaldson.

D856. *Financial Times,* **September 17, 1983, p. 22, col. a**
Review, entitled "Brilliant Bunch," of *The House of Commons, 1660–1690,* 3 vols., edited by Basil Duke Henning.

D857. *Financial Times,* **September 24, 1983, p. 12, col. f**
Review, entitled "Browsers' Oasis," of *Blackwell's, 1879–1979: The History of a Family Firm* by A. L. P. Norrington.

D858. *Spectator,* **October 22, 1983, p. 24**
Poem: "Jumbo Jet." Reprinted in *Transatlantic: Later Poems* (1989).

D859. *Books and Bookmen,* **October 1983, pp. 12–14**
Review, entitled "Nazis and Germans," of *Popular Opinion and Political Dissent in the Third Reich: Bavaria, 1933–45* by Ian Kershaw.

D860. *Books and Bookmen,* **November 1983, pp. 14–15**
Review, entitled "Ranters' Nonsense," of *Ranter Writings from the Seventeenth Century,* edited by N. Smith.

D861. *Contemporary Review,* **November 1983, pp. 261–265**
Article: "Oxford—Then and Now."

D862. *Weekend Australian,* **December 3–4, 1983, Magazine Color Supplement, pp. 15ff.**
Article: "The Guardian Angel Who Saved Dorset's Ancient Dream World." Emeritus Fellow of All Souls College, Oxford, A. L. Rowse, author of many books on British history, including several on Shakespeare and the Elizabethan period, pays tribute to pastoral Dorset, with its castles, churches, historic towns and fascinating places to explore. Commencing, "If I were not so irredeemably rooted in Cornwall, I should choose to live in Dorset. Climatically, the best part of Britain is the south-west peninsula—the five counties, Wiltshire, Somerset, Dorset, Devon and Cornwall. Of these, Cornwall is for the spring. Dorset for the autumn or even early winter, the climate is so mild. To my mind, Dorset is historically the most full of interest—castles, towns, country mansions with their parks and gardens, churches, prehistoric forts and Roman ruins. Even the coast, though much less than Cornwall's, is spectacular."

D863. *Financial Times,* **December 10, 1983, p. 10, col. a**
Paragraph: "My Book of the Year." Our Reviewers Choose the Books Published This Year They Have Most Enjoyed Reading. In full: "I do not expect to be alone in making my book of the year Kenneth Rose's *King George V*

(Weidenfeld & Nicolson). Rarely has there been such a chorus of praise for an historical biography and a royal biography is such a tricky subject too."

D864. *Financial Times,* December 31, 1983, p. 17, col. e
Review, entitled "Sack of Cadiz," of *The Counter-Armada, 1596: The Journal of the "Mary Rose"* by Stephen and Elizabeth Usherwood.

D865. *Books and Bookmen,* January 1984, p. 18
Review, entitled "Life and Death Under Henry VIII," of *The Lisle Letters,* edited by M. St. Clare Byrne. Selected and arranged by Bridget Boland.

D866. *English Historical Review,* January 1984, pp. 174–175
Review (untitled) of *Martin Marprelate, Gentleman: Master Job Throckmorton Laid Open in His True Colors* by L. H. Carlson.

D867. *Financial Times,* February 25, 1984, p. 12, col. f
Review, entitled "Elizabethan Scientist," of *Thomas Harriot: A Biography* by J. W. Shirley.

D868. *Books and Bookmen,* February 1984, pp. 16–17
Review, entitled "Seventeenth-Century Amenities," of *Clarendon and the English Revolution* by R. W. Harris.

D869. *Financial Times,* March 17, 1984, p. 14, col. f
Review, entitled "Godly Wreckers," of *The Puritan Gentry* by J. T. Cliffe.

D870. *New York Times,* March 18, 1984, sec. 5, pp. 40ff.
Article: "The Avon: A Journey." The Looping Bending River Runs Deep with Historic and Literary Associations. Commencing, "The word Avon does not occur in the *Oxford English Dictionary,* for it is a Celtic word, meaning river, going back before the Anglo-Saxons arrived from North Germany to drive us ancient Britons into the western fastnesses of our land."

D871. *Books and Bookmen,* March 1984, pp. 15–16
Review, entitled "Bishop Stapeldon of Exeter," of *Politics, Finance and the Church in the Reign of Edward II, Walter Stapeldon, Treasurer of England* by M. Buck.

D872. *Wall Street Journal,* April 23, 1984, p. 28, col. a
Article: "History's Verdict on Will and George." Commencing, "Orwell or Shakespeare: Which of the two has more to offer us? George Orwell has a somewhat adventitious importance today, partly because of the title of his most famous book, *1984.* Good critics are agreed that his best book is *Animal Farm.*"

D873. *English Historical Review,* April 1984, p. 434
Review (untitled) of *Studies in Eighteenth-Century Culture,* vol. 10, edited by Harry C. Payne.

D874. *Financial Times,* **May 5, 1984, p. 12, col. a**
Review, entitled "Second Sex," of *The Weaker Vessel: Woman's Lot in Seventeenth Century England* by Antonia Fraser; *Family Life in the Seventeenth Century: The Verneys of Claydon House* by Miriam Slater.

D875. *New York Times,* **May 20, 1984, sec. 10, pp. 9ff.**
Article: "An Old Oxonian's Oxford: A Grand Tapestry of Spires and Battlements, Traceried Windows, and a Splendid Central Dome." Commencing, "Everyone knows that Oxford is not only one of the most historic but also, in large part, one of the most beautiful cities in Europe, a treasured possession of the English speaking world. There is something in it for everybody—history and architecture, ancient colleges and gardens, picture galleries and museums, science and music—to say nothing of its magical situation between two rivers."

D876. *Books and Bookmen,* **May 1984, p. 21**
Review, entitled "World Economies in History," of *The Perspective of the World: Civilisation and Capitalism in the Fifteenth to Eighteenth Century,* vol. 3, by Fernand Braudel.

D877. *Contemporary Review,* **May 1984, pp. 249–256**
Article: "Shakespeare As Autobiographer."

D878. *Books and Bookmen,* **July 1984, pp. 21–22**
Review, entitled "Democratic Standards," of *The Slumber of Apollo* by John Holloway.

D879. *Financial Times,* **August 11, 1984, p. 10**
Review, entitled "Alma Mater," of *The Early Oxford Schools*, vol. 1 of *The History of the University of Oxford,* edited by J. I. Catto. General Editor T. H. Aston.

D880. *Financial Times,* **August 25, 1984, p. 10, col. a**
Review, entitled "The Heritage of Christianity," of *Christian England,* vol. 1 (paperback) by D. L. Edwards.

D881. *Books and Bookmen,* **August 1984, p. 17**
Review, entitled "The War against Spain," of *After the Armada: Elizabethan England and the Struggle for Western Europe, 1588–1595* by R. B. Wernham.

D882. *Spectator,* **September 15, 1984, p. 26**
Letter: "Leading Authority." In reference to Peter Levi's review of *The Contemporary Shakespeare.*

D883. *New York Times,* **October 21, 1984, sec. 10, pp. 15ff.**
Article: "A Somerset Ramble: Visiting a Historic Corner of Britain, from Arthurian Glastonbury to Victorian Resorts." Commencing, "As a West Country man I am no doubt prejudiced, but I am convinced that, climatically, the peninsula that lies between the Bristol and the English Channels is much the

best region of Britain to live in. The whole of the west coast of Britain is warmed by the Gulf Stream; so that—though we are in the latitude of Labrador—we enjoy the climate of Northern California or British Columbia."

D884. *Financial Times,* **November 17, 1984, p. 20, col. a**
Review, entitled "Famous Family That Was Just 'Too Much,'" of *The House of Mitford* by Jonathan Guinness with Catherine Guinness.

D885. *Financial Times,* **December 1, 1984, p. 14**
Article: "My Book of the Year." Paragraph commencing, "Best book for me was *A Very Private Eye: Barbara Pym's Autobiography in Letters and Diaries* (Macmillan). It has every kind of appeal, biographical and autobiographical—most people don't distinguish between the two. It offers a full portrait at last of one of the nicest Oxford women of my generation."

D886. *Spectator,* **December 1, 1984, pp. 33–34**
Review, entitled "Oxon Treasures," of *Church Treasures in the Oxford District* by E. B. Ford and J. S. Haywood.

D887. *Books and Bookmen,* **December 1984, pp. 28–29**
Review, entitled "St. Beatrice of the LSE," of *The Diary of Beatrice Webb,* vol. 3, *1905–1924,* edited by N. MacKenzie and J. MacKenzie.

D888. *Spectator,* **January 12, 1985, p. 22**
Review, entitled "Best of Notts," of *Nottinghamshire: A Shell Guide* by Henry Thorold.

D889. *Financial Times,* **January 26, 1985, p. 18, col. e**
Review, entitled "Mother Tongue As She Spoke It," of *The English Language* by Robert Burchfield.

D890. *The Times,* **January 31, 1985, p. 11, col. d**
Letter: "Oxford Railway Station." Commencing, "I should like to raise a protest against the continued neglect of the public in enforcing the use of only one side of the railway station at Oxford: a much more useful subject to protest about than raising a silly fuss against the most eminent Oxford woman of the day being given, quite properly, an honorary degree."

D891. *English Historical Review,* **January 1985, pp. 179, 181–182, 186–188**
Review (untitled) of *Early European Settlement and Exploitation in Atlantic Canada, Selected Papers,* edited by G. M. Story. *Newfoundland Discovered,* edited by G. T. Cell. *The Parliamentary Survey of the Duchy of Cornwall,* pt. 1 (Austell Prior-Saltash), edited with introduction by N. J. G. Pounds. *Tide of Empires: Decisive Naval Campaigns in the Rise of the West,* vol. 2, *1654–1763* by Peter Padfield.

D892. *Times Literary Supplement,* **February 1, 1985, p. 119, col. a**
Letter: "Editing Shakespeare." Commencing, "The statement of the scholarly

editor of the Oxford Shakespeare as to his editorial policy (Letters, January 18) is of importance and of general interest. Dr. Wells suggests that we are not to suppose that any of the surviving texts of the plays, 'necessarily represents anything like a definitive state . . . the words that Shakespeare wished to be spoken. . . . The editor, of course, can only work with that stage of the script that has survived.' I should not dare to go as far as this scepticism, but keep to the ground of common sense."

Note 1. Letters from Stanley Wells and Stephen Corrin about Terence Hawkes's review of A. L. Rowse's *The Contemporary Shakespeare* in issue January 18, 1985.

Note 2. Letters from Terence Hawkes and Eric Sams about T*he Contemporary Shakespeare* in issue February 1, 1985.

D893. *Spectator,* **February 16, 1985, pp. 31–32**
Article: "Shakespeare and the Danvers-Long Feud: A New Source for Romeo and Juliet?"

D894. *Contemporary Review,* **February 1985, pp. 83–88**
Article: "An Alternative All Souls."

D895. *Contemporary Review,* **March 1985, pp. 135–141**
Article: "All Souls Stories."

D896. *Financial Times,* **April 13, 1985, p. 12, col. f**
Review, entitled "Noble Family," of *The Earls of Derby, 1485–1985* by J. J. Bagley.

D897. *New York Times,* **April 21, 1985, sec. 10, pp. 9ff.**
Article: "Tracing Willa Cather's Nebraska: Red Cloud Preserves Her Memory." Commencing, "Few Americans seem to realize what a treasure they have in Red Cloud, a veritable little ville musée. How many people know where it is, or have ever been there?*"*

D898. *English Historical Review,* **April 1985, pp. 395–397**
Review (untitled) of English Reformation literature. *The Tudor Origins of the Protestant Tradition* by John N. King; *Elizabethan England and Europe: Forty Unprinted Letters from Elizabeth I to Protestant Powers,* edited by E. I. Kouri.

D899. *The Times,* **May 4, 1985, p. 8, col. b**
Article: "A Playwright for Today." A. L. Rowse on Shakespeare's message for the twentieth century. Commencing, "We might take as our text what Ben Jonson, who knew Shakespeare well, said of him: 'He is for all time.' Perhaps Jonson spoke better than even he imagined for nothing brings home the truth of his forecast more than Shakespeare's relevance to events in the world today."

D900. *Spectator,* **May 11, 1985, p. 31**
Review, entitled "Shakespeare and Non-Historians," of *Shakespeare: The "Lost Years"* by E. A. J. Honingmann.

D901. *Books and Bookmen,* **May 1985, pp. 15–16**
Review, entitled "Saints and Martyrs," of *Thomas More: A Biography* by Richard Marius.

D902. *Notes and Queries, n.s.,* **June 1985, pp. 270–271**
Review (untitled) of *Cornish Heritage* by Keith Skues.

D903. *Financial Times,* **July 6, 1985,** *Weekend FT* **XII, col. f**
Review, entitled "History Is Fun—Discuss," of *F. W. Maitland* by G. R. Elton.

D904. *Contemporary Review,* **July 1985, p. 44**
Letter: "A Different Slant on India."

D905. *English Historical Review,* **July 1985, pp. 663–664**
Review (untitled) of *Calendar of the Patent Rolls: Elizabeth I,* vol. 7, *1575–1578,* edited in the Public Record Office.

D906. *Books and Bookmen,* **August 1985, p. 15**
Review, entitled "The Cult of the Scillies," of *Exploration of a Drowned Landscape* by Charles Thomas.

D907. *New York Times,* **September 14, 1985, p. 23, col. a**
Article: "500 Years Later, Richard III Is Still an Issue: Ricardians in England and the U.S. Still Won't Face the Facts." Commencing, "Just over 500 years ago, the battle of Bosworth was fought and King Richard III was killed. Five centuries later, there are Richard III Societies in New York and London to keep his memory green."

D908. *Spectator,* **October 12, 1985, pp. 20–21**
Article: "First-Rate Versus Third-Rate." A. L. Rowse explains why one ought to have a good conceit of oneself.

D909. *Financial Times,* **October 19, 1985,** *Weekend FT* **14, col. b.**
Review, entitled "Post-Haste," of *Royal Mail: The Post Office since 1840* by M. J. Daunton.

D910. *Contemporary Review,* **October 1985, p. 212**
Letter: "Sir Keith Joseph and the 'Better School.'"

D911. *Financial Times,* **November 30, 1985,** *Weekend FT* **18**
Paragraph: "My Book of the Year," A. L. Rowse selection. Commencing, "The book that has interested me most and given me the greatest pleasure is Marie-Claire Bancquart's Anatole France (Calmann-Levy). No English book that I read this year came anywhere near it. Anatole France is a writer who has always appealed to me—a great writer, ridiculously depreciated in the generation after his death, now coming back again."

D912. *Financial Times,* **December 7, 1985,** *Weekend FT* **14, col. a**
Review, entitled "Conqueror's Inventory," of *The Domesday Book,* edited by Thomas Hinde.

D913. *New York Times,* **December 8, 1985, sec. 4, p. 26, col. d**
Letter: "Finding Fault with the Shakespeare Find." Commencing, "I have been requested from several quarters to give my opinion on the supposed discovery of a new Shakespeare poem (front page, November 24). It is utterly improbable for the following reasons: a. It is quite unlike any poem that Shakespeare ever wrote. b. We know quite well from the early poems *A Lover's Complaint* and *Venus and Adonis* what Shakespeare's early style was; and this new poem is utterly unlike it. c. Shakespeare was so famous in his own time that people would not have overlooked anything of his. Quite the reverse."

D914. *Financial Times,* **December 21, 1985,** *Weekend FT* **10, col. a**
Review, entitled "Stern and Bracing Creed," of *International Calvinism 1541–1715,* edited by M. Prestwich.

D915. *Spectator,* **December 21–28, 1985, pp. 58–60**
Article: "A Buried Love: Flecker and Beazley."

D916. *Books and Bookmen,* **December 1985, pp. 18–19**
Review, entitled "Close Harmony," of *No Fine but a Glass of Wine: Cathedral Life at Gloucester in Stuart Times* by S. Eward.

D917. *Financial Times,* **January 18, 1986,** *Weekend FT* **12, col. g**
Review, entitled "Pioneer Sailor," of *Christopher Columbus: A Biography* by B. Granzotto, translated by S. Sartorelli.

D918. *New York Times,* **January 19, 1986, sec. 10, pp. 15ff.**
Article: "At Home with History in London: Four Houses Distinguished by Their Illustrious Former Tenants As Well As Their Design." Commencing, "One of the pleasures of living in, or visiting, an old country is the plenitude of places with historic and literary associations."

D919. *English Historical Review,* **January 1986, pp. 228–229**
Review (untitled) of *The Elizabethan Pamphleteers* by Sandra Clark.

D920. *Cornish Scene,* **February–March 1986, pp. 4–5**
Obituary/Tribute: "L. H. Tippett." An old friend from A. L. Rowse's early school days at St. Austell Grammar School, in their day known as the County School—St. ACS for short.

D921. *Financial Times,* **March 29, 1986,** *Weekend FT* **12, col. f**
Review, entitled "Lyre and Trumpet," of *Early Verse by Rudyard Kipling, 1879–1889,* edited by Andrew Rutherford.

D922. *Financial Times,* **April 12, 1986,** *Weekend FT* **16, col. a**
Review, entitled "Across the Wild Waste of Canada," of *Company of Adventurers: The Story of the Hudson's Bay Company,* vol. 1, by Peter C. Newman.

D923. *Spectator,* **April 26, 1986, pp. 39–40**
Article: "Further Light on Shakespeare."

D924. *Financial Times,* **June 14, 1986,** *Weekend FT* **14, col. c.**
Review, entitled "Godly Calling," of *The Gladstone Diaries,* vol. 9, January 1875–November 1880, edited by H. C. G. Matthew.

D925. *Contemporary Review,* **July 1986, pp. 21–26**
Article: "The Mandelstam Experience."

D926. *New York Times,* **August 10, 1986, sec. 10, pp. 15ff.**
Article: "In Venice, the Sweep of History. A Short Walk Can Lead to Byzantium." Commencing, "It has been said a thousand times before, but it must be said again. Venice is unique, the most wonderful creation among historic cities. I regard New York as the most splendid urban creation of our 20th century, but it has taken many centuries to build up the fabulous creation that Venice is, on its islands and waterways. There is nothing to equal it."

D927. *Financial Times,* **October 25, 1986,** *Weekend FT* **22, col. f**
Review, entitled "Chronicle of Colleges," of *History of the University of Oxford,* vol. 3, *The Collegiate University*; vol. 5, *The Eighteenth Century.*

D928. *Cornish Scene,* **October-November 1986, p. 18**
Poem: "Friends Gone Before." Reprinted in *Transatlantic: Later Poems* (1989).

D929. *Financial Times,* **November 29, 1986,** *Weekend FT* **18, col. d**
Article: "My Book of the Year," A. L. Rowse selection. Quoted in full: "Ambivalent as I am between literature and history, two books have given me much pleasure this year. On the literary side I greatly enjoyed Joanna Richardson's *The Brownings* (Folio Society). I learned more from it than any number of books about the Brownings, both of them. Perceptive and sympathetic, Miss Richardson is kinder to the old monster, Mr. Barrett of Wimpole Street, than I should be. But I put that down to the inexhaustible charity of women towards men.

On the historical side Charles Thomas's *Celtic Britain* (Thames & Hudson) throws a flood of light on that dark period in our history, after the departure of the Romans. He is our leading authority on the subject, and, though a devout archaeologist who can write archaeological jargon, he has written this book like a civilised man, and that pleased me."

D930. *New York Times,* **December 13, 1986, sec. 1, p. 27, col. b**
Article: "Let's Be Fair to Edward and Wallis." Commencing, "The extraordinary story of the abdication of Edward VIII in December 1936 has never lost its hold on the public. In the long history of the British monarchy, he was the only one to abdicate voluntarily. And he did it for an American, Mrs. Wallis Simpson, formerly a Mrs. Spencer, with two husbands living: that was the snag Edward and Wallis could not get over or around."

D931. *The Times,* **December 15, 1986, p. 15, col. d**
Letter: "President at Bay." "All that is wrong with President Reagan is that as constitutional monarch he needs a proper Prime Minister . . . such as we have."

D932. *Renaissance Quarterly* **(USA), Winter 1986, pp. 759–760**
Review (untitled) of *The Battle of Bosworth* by Michael Bennett.

D933. *Financial Times,* **January 3, 1987,** *Weekend FT* **12, col. f**
Review, entitled "After the Crown," of *Pretenders* by Jeremy Potter.

D934. *Contemporary Review,* **January 1987, pp. 37–40**
Article: "The Stones."

D935. *New York Times,* **February 8, 1987, sec. 10, p. 15**
Article: "The Road to Fotheringhay: In the Footsteps of Mary Queen of Scots, a Route Steeped in Intrigue, Politics, and Mystery." Commencing, "Four hundred years ago, on February 8, 1587, was enacted that last tragic scene, when Mary Stuart's head fell to the executioner, but the reverberations of the act have gone on ever since."

D936. *Spectator,* **February 14, 1987, pp. 18–19**
Article: "Some Chance for a Chancellor." A. L. Rowse surveys the history of suitable and awkward Oxford officers.

D937. *Spectator,* **April 11, 1987, pp. 42–43**
Review, entitled "Justice for Celts," of *Celtic Britain* by Charles Thomas.

D938. *Spectator,* **April 25, 1987, pp. 14, 17**
Article: "Gibbon and Cornwall." A. L. Rowse celebrates the historian's political and family ambitions.

D939. *Sunday Times,* **April 26, 1987, Magazine, pp. 60–62**
Article: "My Time of Life/80s/A. L. Rowse." Commencing, "Old age has a rather bad press in literature. 'Crabbed age and youth cannot live together, Youth is full of pleasaunce, age is full of care,' wrote William Shakespeare. And he goes on to say, 'Age, I do abhore thee; Youth I do adore thee.' I am sorry to disagree with Shakespeare, but my experience had been rather the other way round. For me youth was full of care, with a good deal of illness, anxiety and worry; I am a reformed character in old age."

Illustrated with large photo, by Evelyn Hofer, of A. L. Rowse sitting up at work in bed, with the caption: A. L. Rowse at 83 finds, "You must break the day in two and go to bed properly after lunch for an hour or so."

D940. *English Historical Review,* **April 1987, pp. 486–487, 497–498**
Review (untitled) of *List and Analysis of State Papers, Foreign Series, Elizabeth I, Preserved in the Public Record Office,* vol. 4, *May 1592–June 1593,* edited by R. B. Wernham; *The Parliamentary Survey of the Duchy of Cornwall,* pt. 2, *Isles of Scilly: West Antony and Manors in Devon,* edited by Norman J. G. Pounds.

D941. *Financial Times,* **May 23, 1987,** *Weekend FT* **16, col. e**
Review, entitled "Poet Apart," of *A Choice of Robert Bridges' Verse.* Selected with an introduction by Lord David Cecil.

D942. *Spectator,* **May 23, 1987, p. 13**
Article: "The Beastliest in the Realm." A. L. Rowse shows how the North-South divide has existed through English history.

D943. *Financial Times,* **June 20, 1987,** *Weekend FT* **22, col. e**
Review, entitled "A. L. Rowse on an Early Chancellor/Don's Vision," of *Robert Grosseteste: The Growth of an English Mind in Medieval Europe* by R. W. Southern.

D944. *Cornish Scene,* **July-August 1987, p. 16**
Poem: "At Charlestown/For David Treffry." Reprinted in *Transatlantic: Later Poems* (1989).

D945. *Contemporary Review,* **August 1987, p. 102**
Poems: "Christ Church Meadows" and "The Soul." Reprinted in *Transatlantic: Later Poems* (1989).

D946. *Financial Times,* **September 19, 1987,** *Weekend FT* **20, col. g**
Review, entitled "A. L. Rowse on a Small Land's Domestic Vision of Life/Dutch Uncles," of *The Embarrassment of Riches: An Interpretation of Dutch Culture in the Golden Age* by Simon Schama.

D947. *Spectator,* **September 26, 1987, p. 20**
Letter: "Mosley Contra Mundum." Regarding Diana Mosley and the Hitler era.

D948. *Spectator,* **September 26, 1987, pp. 38–39**
Review, entitled "A Cornish Scholar," of *William Borlase* by P. A. S. Pool.

D949. *Antaeus* **(USA), Autumn 1987, sec. 4, pp. 168–175**
Article: "Literature As Pleasure."

D950. *Financial Times,* **November 14, 1987,** *Weekend FT* **18, col. f**
Review, entitled "Legal Ways to Power," of *The Rise of the Barrister: A Social History of the English Bar, 1590–1640* by W. R. Prest.

D951. *Spectator,* **November 14, 1987, p. 59**
One paragraph: "Where I Eat Alone/Wine and Food."

D952. *Financial Times,* **November 28, 1987,** *Weekend FT* **16, col. a**
Article: "My Book of the Year." Contribution in full: "May I nominate two books that represent my ambivalent equipollent interests in both history and literature? Richard Ollard's *Clarendon and His Friends* (Collins) strikes me as the best of the year for history: such mastery of the subject, so perceptive and sympathetic and beautifully written. Ollard is one of the very few first-rate historians now writing—too many third-rate ones cluttering the field.

Victoria Glendinning has accomplished a difficult job triumphantly with her biography of Rebecca West (Weidenfeld and Nicolson). Almost impossible to get Rebecca quite right—so contradictory, inconsistent, part masculine, part feminine, Scots-Anglo-Irish, brilliantly clever and always fun. Glendinning treats her with justice and understanding."

D953. *An Baner Kernewek* (**The Cornish Banner**), **November 1987, pp. 5–6**
Article: "The Essence of Cornishry." Commencing, "What is it to be Cornish? What does it mean? It is a difficult subject to think out, isn't it? First, is there a Cornish temperament? Of course, it is generally said that there is such a thing as a Celtic temperament."

D954. *House and Garden* (**USA**), **November 1987, pp. 54, 60, 64**
Article: "All Booked Up." A bibliophile's advice on how to live with too much of a good thing.

D955. *Spectator,* **December 5, 1987, pp. 56–57**
Review, entitled "More Spencer Than Churchill," of *The Profligate Duke: Fifth Duke of Marlborough and His Duchess* by Mary Soames.

D956. *Spectator,* **December 19–26, 1987, pp. 36–38**
Article: "What Kind of Man Was Drake?" A. L. Rowse reviews the character and achievements of a West Country hero. Commencing, "Francis Drake was a folk hero down here in the West Country, where I write, and there is a good deal of folklore about him still. But, of course, dull, disillusioned historians, like myself, have to stick to the facts. We have our uses: many years ago I was able to settle the year of his birth, hitherto unknown, as 1541."

D956a. *The New Standard,* **December 31, 1987**
Article: "Who Could Forget Margaret the Brave?" As Mrs. Thatcher enters the record books again, historian A. L. Rowse argues that she alone has put the Great back into Britain.

D957. *Guardian Weekly,* **March 13, 1988, pp. 22–23**
Article: "A Famous Victory." This year sees the four hundredth anniversary of the defeat of the Spanish Armada.

D958. *Contemporary Review,* **March 1988, pp. 129–134**
Article: "Hammarskjöld's Dream."

D959. *Financial Times,* **April 23, 1988, Weekend FT 23, col. d**
Review, entitled "Rock of Ages," of *The Rock of the Gibraltarians: A History of Gibraltar* by Sir William G. F. Jackson.

D960. *Financial Times,* **April 30, 1988, Weekend FT 22, col. c**
Review, entitled "A Monumental Tale," of *Caesars of the Wilderness: Company of Adventurers,* vol. 2, by Peter C. Newman.

D961. *Spectator,* **April 30, 1988, pp. 32–33**
Review, entitled "Ambiguity of a Good German," of *A Noble Combat: The Letters of Sheila Grant Duff and Adam von Trott, 1932–1939,* edited by K. von Klemperer.

D962. *Cornish Scene,* **Summer 1988, p. 23**
Poem: "The Dying Poet." Reprinted in *Transatlantic: Later Poems* (1989).

D963. *Financial Times,* **July 23, 1988,** *Weekend FT* **16, col. d**
Review, entitled "Rivals Only to a Certain Degree," of *Oxford and Cambridge* by Christopher Brooke and Roger Highfield with photographs by Wim Swaan; *Balliol College: A History, 1263–1939* by John Jones.

D964. *Financial Times,* **July 30, 1988,** *Weekend FT* **16, col. f**
Review, entitled "Toll of the Guillotine," of *Le cout de la revolution française* by René Sédillot.

D965. *Guardian Weekly,* **July 31, 1988, p. 25**
Article: "The Sensible Revolution." A. L. Rowse argues that the events of 1688 were a victory for people's liberties and made modern Britain possible.

D966. *The Author* **(UK) Autumn 1988**
Article: "Writers Remembered: T. S. Eliot." Commencing, "I owe T. S. Eliot a great debt. He was effectively the first person to publish me and encourage my work. It is true that a first little essay "On History" had been published by that remarkable Cambridge eccentric, C. K. Ogden, of "The Meaning of Meaning" and other such works. But he, with his prosaic utilitarianism, was not at all my fancy. I was all for history and poetry. So at Cambridge my admiration was for G. M. Trevelyan. Eliot was an Oxford man, linked to All Souls, through Geoffrey Faber, our Estates Bursar."

D967. *Financial Times,* **September 3, 1988,** *Weekend FT* **18, col. g**
Review, entitled "Medici Rule OK," of *The Letters of Marsilio Ficino,* vol. 4. Translated by members of the School of Economic Science, London.

D968. *The Times,* **October 13, 1988, p. 17, col. d**
Letter: "Eliot's Letters." Commencing, "As against Michael Hasting's ungenerous view (October 5) of Valerie Eliot's scholarship we have the public evidence of her edition of the full text of *The Waste Land.* All agree that it is a remarkable example of conscientious, careful scholarship."

D969. *Financial Times,* **October 15, 1988,** *Weekend FT* **21, col. f**
Review, entitled "From Warrior Queens to the New Woman." A. L. Rowse on a colorful account of the lives of female rulers throughout the ages of *Boadicea's Chariot: The Warrior Queens* by Antonia Fraser.

D970. *Financial Times,* **October 22, 1988,** *Weekend FT* **23, col. a**
Review, entitled "The Good Old Days," of *The Pleasures of Old Age* by Robert Morley.

D971. *English Historical Review,* **October 1988, pp. 1044–1045**
Review (untitled) of *Raleigh in Exeter* (1985), edited by Joyce Youings.

D972. *Financial Times,* **November 12, 1988,** *Weekend FT* **18, col. f**
Review, entitled "When Britain Made Do without Money." A. L. Rowse reflects

on the role of cash in olden times of *Money and Its Use in Medieval Europe* by P. Spufford.

D973. *Financial Times,* **November 26, 1988,** *Weekend FT* **20, col. a**
Article: "My Book of the Year." A. L. Rowse's contribution in full: "For once I may be with the majority in having particularly enjoyed Michael Holroyd's first volume of his Shaw biography, *Bernard Shaw: The Search for Love* (Chatto & Windus). Perhaps also because I did not expect to: I thought that we knew enough about Shaw already. But this book is about the early GBS, whom none of us knew, and about his philandering with the ladies, when we suspected him of being an impotent Puritan. I knew Shaw a little and think that Holroyd has got him exactly right—conscientious, impartial, without prejudice, and thoroughly understanding. About music too."

D974. *Financial Times,* **December 17, 1988,** *Weekend FT* **15, col. a**
Review, entitled "The Quiet Revolution" of *A Kingdom without a King: The Journal of the Provisional Government in the Revolution of 1688,* edited by Robert Beddard.

D975. *Financial Times,* **January 28, 1989,** *Weekend FT* **15, col. c**
Review, entitled "Their Lordships Take a View," of *A History of the House of Lords* by Lord Longford.

D976. *Spectator,* **February 18, 1989, pp. 30–31**
Review, entitled "Truth about Marlowe," of *Christopher Marlowe and Canterbury* by William Urry.

D977. *Financial Times,* **March 18, 1989,** *Weekend FT* **10, col. e**
Review, entitled "Setting the Scene in a Mediaeval Power-Play," A. L. Rowse on a succinct examination of how Britain became the mother of parliaments, of *A History of Parliament: The Middle Ages* by Ronald Butt.

D978. *Guardian Weekly,* **March 26, 1989, p. 25**
Article: "1789—A Middle-Class Revolution That Went Wrong: Reflections on the Bicentenary Year of the French Revolution."

D979. *Financial Times,* **April 15, 1989,** *Weekend FT* **19, col. a**
Review, entitled "City of Charms," of *The Memoir of Marco Parenti* by Mark Phillips.

D979a. *Sunday Telegraph,* **April 23, 1989, p. 20**
Article: "Always True to Cornwall: A. L. Rowse remembers Daphne du Maurier who died last week." Commencing, "Daphne du Maurier was a best-seller all over the world, her books in all the airports everywhere, yet no-one has assessed her work as a whole. In re-reading her books for a study of her in my recent book, *Friends and Contemporaries,* I considered that she has been underestimated as a writer."

D980. *Financial Times,* **May 27, 1989,** *Weekend FT* **18, col. a**
Review, entitled "Before and after Indian Partition," A. L. Rowse praises a monument to "a truly great man," of *The British Conquest and Dominion of India* by Sir Penderel Moon.

D981. *Financial Times,* **July 1, 1989,** *Weekend FT* **14, col. c**
Review, entitled "Four Portraits," of Clarendon's *Four Portraits,* edited by Richard Ollard.

D982. *Observer, Colour Magazine,* **July 9, 1989, pp. 12–13.**
Article: "The Experts' Expert/Historians." Jenny Knight asks leading historians who they feel is a past master. Twelve contributors, including A. L. Rowse, who is quoted in full: "Most of the people I really admire are dead, like, perhaps the greatest of English historians, Gibbon. Everybody will laugh if I say that I have lived to be so old that I think I am really perhaps the best. But, I can't think of anybody who is better. A historian ought not to have any illusions, and be very down-to-earth and I think I am. He also ought to have a sense of the poetry of the past, and your poor old friend is also a poet. I think I really have lasted to be the best so I nominate A. L. Rowse."

D983. *Guardian Weekly,* **July 23, 1989**
Review, entitled "Populists on the American Revolution," of *Paine and Cobbett: The Transatlantic Connection* by D. A. Wilson.

D984. *Spectator,* **August 5, 1989, pp. 31–32**
Review, entitled "The Sage of the Realm," of *Robert Cecil, 1st Earl of Salisbury* by Alan Haynes.

D985. *Contemporary Review,* **September 1989, pp. 135–142**
Article: "The Eve of the War, 1939: A Notebook."

D986. *Contemporary Review,* **September 1989, p. 157**
Poem: "The Trees." Reprinted in *Prompting the Age: Poems Early and Late* (1990).

D987. *Cornish Scene,* **Autumn 1989, p. 95**
Poem: "The Spirit of the House." Reprinted in *Prompting the Age: Poems Early and Late* (1990).

D988. *Financial Times,* **October 28, 1989,** *Weekend FT* **15, col. f**
Review, entitled "A Latin Master of Poetry," of *Marullus: Soldier Poet of the Renaissance* by Carol Kidwell.

D989. *Financial Times,* **November 25, 1989,** *Weekend FT* **18, col. b**
Article: "My Book of the Year." Quoted in full: "I don't know that it was precisely pleasure, but the book that interested me the most this past year was David Irving's biography of Göring (Macmillan). I do not share Irving's eccentric point of view: for one thing he has rather an anti-British angle, and he is too favourable to the Nazi thug. After all, Göring was a murderer—he master-

minded the murders of scores of opponents and comrades alike in the Night of the Long Knives, June 30, 1934. But Irving has done a lot of research and added some facts to our knowledge of that disgraceful era.

D990. *New York Times,* **November 26, 1989, sec. 5, pp. 8–9**
Article: "England's Unheralded Gems: A Guide to the Rich Pasts of Grantham, Stamford, Sherborne, and Chichester." Commencing, "For me the charm of an old country largely consists in its historic cities, cathedrals, palaces, and mansions. But England has a large number of lesser historic towns, some of them with special associations for Americans."

D991. *Financial Times,* **December 16, 1989, Weekend FT 10, col. a**
Review, entitled "Life of a History Man," of *Marc Bloch: A Life in History* by Carole Fink.

D992. *Financial Times,* **January 13, 1990, Weekend FT 19, col. f**
Review, entitled "Hazardous Paths," of *The Medieval Traveller* by Norbert Ohler. Translated by C. Hillier.

D993. *Contemporary Review,* **January 1990, p. 22**
Poem: "Home." Reprinted in *Prompting the Age: Poems Early and Late* (1990).

D994. *Contemporary Review,* **January 1990, pp. 49–50**
Review, entitled "Hitler's No. 2 Man," of *Göring: A Biography* by David Irving.

D995. *English Historical Review,* **January 1990, pp. 200–201**
Review (untitled) of *William Borlase* by P. A. S. Pool.

D996. *English Historical Review,* **April 1990, p. 465**
Review (untitled) of *Natives and Newcomers: Canada's "Heroic Age" Reconsidered* by Bruce G. Trigger.

D997. *Financial Times,* **May 12, 1990, Weekend FT 16, col. g**
Review, entitled "Trapped by Anne Boleyn," of *The King's Cardinal* by Peter Gwyn.

D998. *Contemporary Review,* **May 1990, pp. 277–278**
Review, entitled "Hero of German Resistance?" of *A Good German* by G. MacDonogh.

D999. *New York Times,* **June 3, 1990, sec. 5, pp. 8ff.**
Article: "Memorable Gardens in England's Oxbridge: Strolling in the Leafy Spaces Clustered amid the Colleges." Commencing, "The Backs at Cambridge offer one of the most famous scenes in England and, it has been said, one of the most beautiful in the world. The name refers to the wonderful semicircle of buildings, including King's College Chapel, Gibbs's splendid Fellows' Building and Wren's Trinity College Library. What a grouping!"

D1000. *English Historical Review,* July 1990, pp. 721, 736–737
Review (untitled) of *The Duchy of Cornwall,* edited by Crispin Gill. *Fighting Joshua: A Study of the Career of Sir Jonathan Trelawny, Bart., Bishop of Bristol, Exeter, and Winchester* by M. G. Smith.

D1001. *Contemporary Review,* August 1990, pp. 99–104
Article: "Fragments from the Past: A Notebook."

D1002. *Contemporary Review,* August 1990, pp. 108–110
Review, entitled "Trollope in the Round," of *Anthony Trollope: A Victorian in His World* by Richard Mullen

D1003. *Contemporary Review,* September 1990, pp. 125–128
Article: "A Note on Brecht's "Utopianism."

D1004. *New York Times,* October 14, 1990, sec. 7, pp. 53ff.
Article: "Ah, Sweet Mystery! The Agatha I Knew." Commencing, "My interest in Agatha Christie was personal—she knew that I was not a reader of hers. I came to know her through her husband, Max Mallowan, a colleague at All Souls College, Oxford, before I had ever read any of her books. I still have not read many, and must be one of the few people left who have never seen "The Mousetrap."

D1005. *Contemporary Review,* October 1990, pp. 218–220
Review, entitled "The New Germany: What to Expect?" of *The New Germany at the Cross-Roads* by David Marsh.

D1006. *Contemporary Review,* November 1990, pp. 253–256
Article: "Arthur Symons: The Symbolist Movement in Literature."

D1007. *Financial Times,* December 1, 1990, *Weekend FT* 25, col. c
Article: "My Book of the Year." In full: I am not an addict of spy stories, and no authority on espionage. I have never spied anybody, so perhaps I am allowed to say that I found Christopher Andrew and Oleg Gordievsky's *KGB: The Inside Story* (Hodder & Stoughton) compulsive reading. I suppose that is a form of pleasure, though I read about those Cambridge spies with old-fashioned disapproval—not much pride in KGB's tribute that they were the ablest agents of the lot, damn them. I don't so much mind their activities when Russia was our ally against Hitler, or even before against Nazi Germany, but when Stalin became an enemy they were no other than enemies of their country. As for the awful Philby, he was in fact a murderer, and I'd have him hanged as such."

D1008. *Financial Times,* March 2, 1991, *Weekend FT* 14, col. e
Review, entitled "Trains of Thought," A. L. Rowse muses on the cultural, literary, and historic consequences of the great railways, of *The Victorian Railway* by Jack Simmons; *Railways: An Anthology,* compiled by Jack Simmons.

D1008a. *Evening Standard,* April 18, 1991, p. 36
Review, entitled "Blazing Trails," of *Robert Byron: Letters Home,* edited by Lucy Butler.

D1008b. *Evening Standard,* **April 25, 1991, p. 37**
Review, entitled "Eager to Appease," of *Lord Halifax: A Biography* by Andrew Roberts.

D1009. *Financial Times,* **April 27, 1991,** *Weekend FT* **18, col. d**
Review, entitled "Civil War Revisited," of *The Fall of the British Monarchies, 1637–1642* by Conrad Russell.

D1010. *Contemporary Review,* **May 1991, pp. 274–276**
Review, entitled "Victorian Rebel," of *Samuel Butler: A Biography* by Peter Raby.

D1011. *Field,* **May 1991, p. 170**
Article: "The Clay Country," illustrated with photographs by Kit Houghton with caption: Professor A. L. Rowse: his part of Cornwall is "under appreciated."

D1011a. *Evening Standard,* **June 27, 1991, p. 39**
Review, entitled "To Have and to Scold," of *The Six Wives of Henry VIII* by Alison Weir.

D1012. *Financial Times,* **June 29, 1991,** *Weekend FT* **16, col. d**
Review, entitled "Feminine View of the Virgin Queen," of *Elizabeth I* by Anne Somerset.

D1013. *Contemporary Review,* **July 1991, pp. 37–39**
Article: "Voice of New Zealand: The Poetry of Allen Curnow." Reprinted in *Verse* (USA) 8, no. 2 (1991): 31–32.

D1014. *Spectator,* **August 10, 1991, p. 6**
Review, entitled "Life of a Best-Seller," of *Daphne: A Portrait of Daphne Du Maurier* by Judith Cook.

D1015. *Contemporary Review,* **August 1991, pp. 87–90**
Article: "Sartre: Beau-Ideal of a Left Intellectual."

D1016. *Spectator,* **September 21, 1991, p. 8**
Article: "A Conundrum Solved."

D1017. *Contemporary Review,* **September 1991, pp. 157–160**
Article: "Cornwall in the History of Literature."

D1018. *The Times,* **October 21, 1991, p. 15, col. d**
Letter: "Cornwall's Dilemma over Proposals for Relief Road." Commencing, "We here in mid-Cornwall who care for its beauty and amenities are appalled at the proposal to run a new road through the park at Tregrehan and on stilts across the entrance to the lovely Luxulyan Valley. Both are as yet unspoiled."

D1019. *Contemporary Review,* **December 1991, pp. 328–329**
Review, entitled "The East India Company," of *The Honourable Company* by John Keay.

D1020. *The Times,* **February 8, 1992,** *Weekend,* **p. 13, col. f**
Column of answers to set questions, in this case, "My Perfect Weekend." People in the public eye are asked to reveal the private fantasies that would turn a weekend into 48 hours of pure magic. Rosanna Greenstreet with A. L. Rowse.

D1020a. *Evening Standard,* **March 26, 1992, p. 39**
Review, entitled "Dark Lady's Lost Lines," of *The Penguin Book of Renaissance Verse, 1509–1659,* edited by D. Norbrook and H. R. Woudhuysen.

D1021. *Financial Times,* **April 11, 1992,** *Weekend FT* **16, col. a**
Review, entitled "This Royal Throne of Myth," A. L. Rowse takes the poet laureate to task for his view of Shakespeare, of *Shakespeare and the Goddess of Complete Being* by Ted Hughes.

Note. In a copy of this item received from A. L. Rowse, he has crossed out the title "This Royal Throne of Myth" and replaced this with "A Mythical Shakespeare."

D1021a. *Evening Standard,* **May 21, 1992, p. 43**
Review, entitled "Much Ado about the Bard," of S*hakespeare: His Life, Work, and Era* by Dennis Kay.

D1022. *Financial Times,* **May 30, 1992,** *Weekend FT* **18, col. f**
Review, entitled "History in the Broad Sweep," of *From Counter Reformation to Glorious Revolution* by Hugh Trevor-Roper.

D1022a. *Evening Standard,* **June 25, 1992, p. 40**
Review, entitled "Too Many Words, Maestro," of *Rain-Charm for the Duchy and Other Laureate Poems* by Ted Hughes.

D1023. *Contemporary Review,* **June 1992, pp. 320–323**
Article: "Santayana: A Prophet of Our Time."

D1024. *Contemporary Review,* **June 1992, pp. 329–330**
Review, entitled "Tudor Matriarch," of *The King's Mother: Lady Margaret Beaufort* by M. K. Jones and M. G. Underwood.

D1025. *Financial Times,* **July 4, 1992,** *Weekend FT* **16, col. f**
Review, entitled "Demise of a Shady Genius," of *The Reckoning* by Charles Nicholl.

D1025a. *Evening Standard,* **July 9, 1992, p. 45**
Review, entitled "Avoid That Thinking Feeling," of *The Intellectuals and the Masses* by John Carey.

D1025b. *Evening Standard,* **August 13, 1992, p. 34**
Review, entitled "Peddling Leaves of Gold," of *The Two Forgers* by John Collins.

D1025c. *Evening Standard,* **August 27, 1992, p. 36**
Review, entitled "Like Wives to the Slaughter," of *The Six Wives of Henry VIII* by Antonia Fraser.

D1026. *Contemporary Review,* **August 1992, pp. 106–107**
Review, entitled "Who Are the Kurds?" of *No Friends but the Mountains: The Tragic History of the Kurds* by J. Bulloch and H. Morris.

D1027. *Contemporary Review,* **September 1992, pp. 159–160**
Review, entitled "Keynes, Pro and Con," of *Maynard Keynes: An Economist's Biography* by D. E. Moggridge.

D1027a. *Evening Standard,* **October 8, 1992, p. 42**
Review, entitled "Living Happily in the Past," of *G. M. Trevelyan: A Life in History* by David Cannadine.

D1027b. *Evening Standard,* **October 22, 1992, p. 46**
Review, entitled "Tripping Over the Stately Piles," of *People and Places: Country House Donors and the National Trust* by James Lees-Milne.

D1028. *Contemporary Review,* **November 1992, pp. 272–273**
Review, entitled "The Impeccable," of *Simon: A Political Biography of Sir John Simon* by D. Dutton.

D1029. *Cornish Banner,* **November 1992, p. 14**
Poem: "The Organ in Davidstow Church."

D1030. *Evening Standard,* **December 17, 1992, p. 45**
Review, entitled "Out of Touch but Sound of Mind," of *The Personal Rule of Charles I* by Kevin Sharpe.

D1031. *Contemporary Review,* **February 1993, pp. 106–108**
Review, entitled "Beaverbrook," of *Beaverbrook: A Life* by Anne Chisholm and Michael Davie.

D1031a. *Evening Standard,* **March 18, 1993, p. 44**
Review, entitled "Genius Buried in Ambivalence," of *Daphne du Maurier* by Margaret Forster.

D1032. *Contemporary Review,* **March 1993, pp. 162–163**
Review, entitled "What Was Wrong with Larkin?" of *Selected Letters of Philip Larkin,* edited by Anthony Thwaite.

D1033. *Cornish Banner,* **May 1993, p. 29**
Article: "Cornish Lanes." Commencing, "Thousands, if not millions, of people know our roads, but how many of them know our Cornish lanes? Yet they are far more in character and hold our secrets."
  Note. Issue also contains two poems from *A Life: Collected Poems* (1981).

D1034. *Cornish Banner,* **August 1993**
Article: "Celebrating A. L. Rowse." Special issue featuring eight new poems and articles honoring "one of Cornwall's greatest sons." Photograph on cover with caption: "Dr. A. L. Rowse, the doyen of Cornish writers, 90 this year, on a recent visit to Malpas near Truro."
Poems: "Trenarren," p. 13; "Visionary," p. 15; "The Road to Penrice," p. 17;

"O That It Might Be So," p. 19; "The Trees," p. 21; "St. Dennis," p. 23; "Trenarren Lane," p. 32; "Beauty Of Life," p. 33.

Note 1. "Parade of Cornish Heroes." p. 3, editorial introduction with photograph of A. L. Rowse by his former birthplace at Tregonissey, now a shop.

Note 2. "The Poetry of A. L. Rowse." p. 11, by Andrew C. Symons.

D1035. *Contemporary Review,* **August 1993, pp. 86–92**
Article: "Justice for Robert Bridges."

D1035a. *Evening Standard,* **September 16, 1993, p. 44**
Review, entitled "Dramatist with the Midas Touch." of *Shakespeare, the Evidence: Unlocking the Mysteries of the Man and His Work* by Ian Wilson.

D1035b. *Evening Standard,* **October 7, 1993, p. 44**
Review, entitled "Tudor Waterworks and Royal Toilets," of *The Royal Palaces of Tudor England* (Yale University).

D1036. *Spectator,* **October 26, 1993, p. 34**
Review, entitled "Perfection Cannot Endure the Insult," of *The Chatto Book of Cats,* edited by Francis Wheen.

D1036a. *Evening Standard,* **November 18, 1993, p. 44**
Review, entitled "The Serial Conqueror," of *The Conquest of Mexico* by Hugh Thomas.

D1037. *The Times,* **November 18, 1993, p. 39, col. a**
Review, entitled "The Vertiginous Elizabethan," A. L. Rowse on a new life of Raleigh: courtier, writer, sailor, and smoker. His arrogance led to his downfall, of *A Play of Passion: The Life of Sir Walter Raleigh* by Stephen Coote.

D1038. *The Times,* **December 3, 1993, p. 18, col. d**
Article: "Found: Will's Lost Years." A. L. Rowse repudiates a popular theory about Shakespeare's early life. Commencing, "To anyone properly acquainted with the Elizabethan age there is no mystery in a gap in our knowledge of any Elizabethan. Scholars of that age know that it is quite regular feature. It is more remarkable when we know as much as we do about the lives of such people as Shakespeare or Marlowe."

D1038a. *Evening Standard,* **January 20, 1994, p. 42**
Review, entitled "History and Hot Air," of *A. J. P. Taylor: A Biography* by Adam Sisman.

D1039. *Cornish Banner,* **February 1994, pp. 10–11, 25**
Article: "Then and Now." Commencing, "In the course of a long life, covering nearly the whole of this century, what are the changes that I chiefly notice? In the first place, there has been an enormous improvement in the material circumstances of the people. In the village I grew up there were no indoor sanitation, no water supply."

Poems: "The Village Revisited," p. 10; "Original Sin," p. 25.

D1040. *Contemporary Review,* **February 1994, pp. 94–97**
Article: "Shakespeare's Supposed 'Lost' Years."

D1040a. *Evening Standard,* **March 24, 1994, p. 42**
Review, entitled "Notes on Rhyme and Reason," of *Winter Pollen* by Ted Hughes.

D1041. *Contemporary Review,* **March 1994, p. 146**
Poem: "St. Dennis."

D1042. *New York Times,* **April 3, 1994, sec. 7, pp. 12–13**
Review, entitled "The Death of Christopher Marlowe Inspires a Book That's Part Conjecture, Part Detection," of *The Reckoning: The Murder of Christopher Marlowe* by Charles Nicholl.

D1042a. *Evening Standard,* **April 18, 1994, p. 25**
Review, entitled "Lifelong Idealism Italian Style," of *Mazzini* by Denis Mack Smith.

D1042b. *Evening Standard,* **April 25, 1994, p. 27**
Review, entitled "Genius with a Kind Heart," of *John Betjeman: Letters,* vol. 1, *1926 to 1951,* edited and introduced by Candida Lycett-Green.

D1043. *Contemporary Review,* **April 1994, pp. 178–182**
Article: "A. J. P. Taylor As Historian."

D1044. *Contemporary Review,* **June 1994, pp. 329–330**
Review, entitled "Europe at War, 1740–1748," of *The War of the Austrian Succession* by Reed Browning.

D1045. *English Historical Review,* **June 1994, p. 723**
Review (untitled) of *Early Stuart Mariners and Shipping: The Maritime Surveys of Devon and Cornwall, 1619–1635,* edited by Todd Gray.

D1046. *Contemporary Review,* **July 1994, pp. 45–46**
Review, entitled "Jane Austen's Clerical Background," of *Jane Austen and the Clergy* by Irene Collins.

D1047. *The Times,* **August 19, 1994, p. 16, cols. c–f**
Article: "A Sentimental History." Sir Arthur Bryant has been attacked as soft on Nazism, but A. L. Rowse says the historian had important qualities. Commencing, "By the academic world he was overlooked; by English society, particularly in London, Sir Arthur Bryant was thought to be the greatest of living historians. Now Andrew Roberts has attacked him in his book *Eminent Churchillians.* But it is difficult to strike a balance and give a just estimate of his work. He was the most popular historian of his time—and above all an emotional, even a sentimental one."

D1048. *The Times,* **August 22, 1994, p. 29, cols. a–c**
Review, entitled "Rabelaisian Regality," of *Renaissance Warrior and Patron: The Reign of Francis I* by R. J. Knecht.

D1049. *Times Literary Supplement,* **August 26, 1994, p. 15, col. d**
Letter: "Aemilia Lanyer." Commencing, "May I—to keep the scholarly record straight—correct Katherine Duncan-Jones's statement (in her review of *The Poems of Aemilia Lanyer,* August 19) that I do not seem to understand that 'Aemilia's account of her upbringing "on the bankes of Kent" does not refer to the county, but to the houshold of the Countess of Kent?' In my edition of her poems, *The Poems of Shakespeare's Dark Lady,* I specifically say that 'She had been brought up with the Countess of Kent.' On p. 22 I quote."

D1050. *Contemporary Review,* **August 1994, pp. 90–93**
Article: "Hardy's Vocabulary."

D1051. *Cornish Banner,* **August 1994, p. 26**
Article: "All Hail to Q!" Commencing, "All we who write about Cornwall regard Q as our head and Master, especially if we are Cornish ourselves. Actually Q was half-Cornish, half-Devon. But it was he, more than anybody, who put Cornwall on the literary map."

D1051a. *Evening Standard,* **October 10, 1994, p. 28**
Review, entitled "Prince of War," of *Prince Rupert: Portrait of a Soldier* by Frank Kitson.

D1051b. *Evening Standard,* **October 31, 1994, p. 28**
Review, entitled "Pleasures Really to Treasure," of *A Mingled Measure: Diaries, 1953–1972* by James Lees-Milne.

D1052. *Weekly Telegraph,* **November 9–15, 1994, p. 22**
Article: "Where There Is a Will . . ." The language of Shakespeare remains a part of everyday English. A. L. Rowse explains how the Bard still speaks for us 400 years on.
   Note. Originally published in the *Daily Telegraph,* October 22, 1994.

D1052a. *Evening Standard,* **November 21, 1994, p. 25**
Review (untitled) of *London* by John Russell.

D1053. *Times Literary Supplement,* **November 25, 1994, p. 15, col. d**
Letter: "The Second Best Bed." Commencing, "It is a pity to repeat (as Katherine Duncan-Jones does, November 18) the entirely modern misconception that Shakespeare's provision of the second best bed for his widow was in any way 'shabby.' I know of no other such provision in any Elizabethan wills. It was exceptional. A better perception would see that it showed exceptional care for the comfort of his widow—since naturally the best big double bed would be occupied by the couple, his daughter (his heir) and her husband. Mere common sense."

D1054. *Contemporary Review,* **December 1994, p. 302**
Poem: "Milton and Dante."

D1055. *Antique and New Art* **8, no. 2, 1994, p. 607**
Article: "Sins of Omission." Commencing, "God may forgive us for the sins we have committed, but who shall forgive us for the sins we have failed to commit? The relevance of this 'Sprichwort' comes into my mind every time I think of some delightful object I failed to buy. Almost always they were antiques, pictures, furniture, silver and textiles, and in practically every case a bargain."

D1056. *Daily Telegraph,* **January 21, 1995, p. 12**
Article: "An Everyday Satire on Country Folk." Distinguished scholar A. L. Rowse suggests that modern audiences need not go seeking hidden meanings in a West End production of *As You Like It.* By using an all-male cast it simply remains faithful to Elizabethan theatre.

D1057. *Contemporary Review,* **January 1995, pp. 25–28**
Article: "Scholars and Crackpots."

D1057a. *Evening Standard,* **March 3, 1995, p. 24**
Review, entitled "Life of a Not So Simple Country Boy," of *John Gay* by D. Nokes.

D1058. *Sunday Times,* **April 9, 1995, sec. 3, p. 6, cols. f–g**
Letter: "Historians' Feuds." Commencing, "I have to correct Norman Stone when he says that I hated A. J. P. Taylor. He is too young to have known the facts and may like to learn them. The truth is that I strongly disapproved of Taylor's irresponsibility. He knew that Beaverbrook lied, and yet sycophantically hailed him as a great historian."

D1059. *Contemporary Review,* **April 1995, pp. 217–218**
Review, entitled "The Tragic Twentieth Century," of *The Age of Extremes, 1914–1991* by Eric Hobsbawm.

D1060. *Contemporary Review,* **May 1995, p. 260**
Poem: "St. Mewan Church Bells." Reprinted in the *Cornish Banner,* August 1995.

D1061. *Cornish Banner,* **May 1995, pp. 12–13**
Article: "Restinnes? Restinnes?" Commencing, "It happened to me the other day—what I had often hoped for in vain before—to be lost within a few miles of my home. The Cornish have an expression for such an experience—and indeed the experience itself was in the old days well known enough: it is to be 'pisky-laden.'" Printed in *West–Country Stories* (1945).

D1062. *English Historical Review,* **June 1995, p. 816**
Review (untitled) of *The Making of Modern Cornwall: Historical Experience and the Persistence of Difference* by Philip Payton.

D1063. *Contemporary Review,* **August 1995, pp. 110–112**
Review, entitled "The Poems of the Dark Lady," of *The Poems of Aemilia Lanyer,* edited by Suzanne Woods.

D1064. *Contemporary Review,* **September 1995, p. 158**
Poem: "Premonition." Reprinted in the *Cornish Banner*, November 1995.

D1064a. *Evening Standard,* **October 2, 1995, p. 24**
Review, entitled "Sensitive Enchanter with So Many Lives," of *John Betjeman: Letters,* vol. 2, *1951 to 1984,* edited and introduced by Candida Lycett-Green.

D1065. *Contemporary Review,* **October 1995, pp. 217–218**
Review, entitled "Revisionist History," of *Churchill's Grand Alliance* by J. Charmley.

D1066. *Contemporary Review,* **November 1995, pp. 270–272**
Review, entitled "Peasant of Genius," of *Moral Desperado: A Life of Thomas Carlyle* by Simon Heffer.

D1066a. *Evening Standard,* **January 29, 1996, p. 16**
Article: "A Word for Francis Drake."

D1067. *Contemporary Review,* **January 1996, pp. 33–37**
Review, entitled "Shakespeare and the Musicians from Venice," of *The Bassanos: Venetian Musicians in England, 1531–1665* by D. Lasocki with R. Prior.

D1067a. *Evening Standard,* **February 26, 1996, p. 25**
Review, entitled "Battle of Rhetoric and Humbug," of *A Struggle for Power* by Theodore Draper.

D1068. *Cornish Banner,* **February 1996, p. 11**
Poem: "Cornish Place-Rhymes."

D1069. *Sunday Times,* **March 10, 1996, sec. 7, p. 7**
Review, entitled "On the Shelf," A. L. Rowse explains the importance of the unjustly neglected egotism in German philosophy by George Santayana, of *Egotism in German Philosophy* by George Santayana.

D1070. *Spectator,* **March 30, 1996, pp. 12–14**
Article: "Lawrence of Oxford." And others among the strange, famous, or crooked whom A. L. Rowse has been meeting for years.

D1071. *Spectator,* **April 20, 1996, pp. 18–19**
Article: "Keynes Right and Wrong." A. L. Rowse remembers his benefactor and adversary who died 50 years ago.

D1071a. *Evening Standard,* **June 17, 1996, p. 26**
Review, entitled "Burning Truth about Cranmer," of a biography of Archbishop Cranmer.

D1072. *Contemporary Review,* **June 1996, pp. 326–327**
Review, entitled "Armada Propaganda," of *Brags and Boasts: Propaganda in the Year of the Armada* by B. T. Whitehead.

D1073. *Times Literary Supplement,* **July 5, 1996, p. 17, col. d**
Letter: "Cagey Victorians." Suggesting a slight emendation of Nicholas Shrimpton's phrase (June 14 review) that Matthew Arnold's Marguerite is "as much of a mystery as the Dark Lady of Shakespeare's sonnets," to read "much more of a mystery than." For the Dark Lady is no longer a mystery at all.

Note. Possibly last letter published. A. L. Rowse suffered a stroke on July 23, 1996, which ended his writing career.

D1074. *Contemporary Review,* **July 1996, pp. 54–55**
Review, entitled "Queen Victoria's Uncommon Daughter," of *An Uncommon Woman: The Empress Frederick* by H. Pakula.

D1075. *Contemporary Review,* **August 1996, p. 104**
Review, entitled "A Great Scholar and Benefactor," of *Esmond de Beer (1895– 1990): A Personal Memoir* by Michael Strachan.

D1075a. *Evening Standard,* **September 2, 1996, p. 26**
Review, entitled "Fury, Fighting and Bad Language," of *Wellington's Welsh General: A Life of Sir Thomas Picton* by Robert Harvard.

D1076. *The Independent,* **March 11, 1997, p. 12**
Obituary tribute: "Dame Veronica Wedgwood." (Prewritten and on file.)

E

A. L. Rowse Recordings

The items listed in this section are full-length, unabridged audio books (readings on cassettes), commercially produced by Books on Tape, Inc., Newport Beach, California. Duvall Y. Hecht is president and founder. A. L. Rowse in a letter to Sydney Cauveren dated "New Year 1993" (postmarked January 6, 1993): "Many of my books are on tape in U.S. . . . . They have just sent me the whole book *A Man of the Thirties*. Fancy that! . . . D. Y. Hecht visited me here, a fine superior fellow."

TALKING BOOKS

E1. *The Churchills* (1080-A, part 1) 8 1½-hour cassettes. (1080-B, part 2) 7 1½-hour cassettes. Read by Richard Green (British).

E2. *Shakespeare the Man* (1090) 7 1½-hour cassettes. Read by Richard Green.

E3. *Jonathan Swift* (1182) 8 1-hour cassettes. Read by Erik Bauersfeld (British).

E4. *The England of Elizabeth* (1555-A, part 1) 10 1½-hour cassettes. (1555-B, part 2) 10 1½-hour cassettes. Read by Jill Masters (British).

E5. *The Elizabethans in America* (1556) 7 1½-hour cassettes. Read by Jill Masters.

E6. *The Expansion of Elizabethan England* (1557) 15 1½-hour cassettes. Read by Jill Masters.

E7. *The Use of History* (1561) 8 1-hour cassettes. Read by Stuart Courtney (British).

E8. *Appeasement: A Study in Political Decline* (1562) 5 1-hour cassettes. Read by Stuart Courtney.

E9. *A Cornishman Abroad* (1875) 10 1½-hour cassettes. Read by Stuart Courtney.

E10. *Milton the Puritan* (1921) 10 1½-hour cassettes. Read by Stuart Courtney.

E11. *A Cornishman at Oxford* (1982) 8 1½-hour cassettes. Read by Stuart Courtney.

E12. *Christopher Marlowe: His Life and Times* (2172) 7 1-hour cassettes. Read by Bill Kelsey (British).

E13. *Bosworth Field and the Wars of the Roses* (2209) 8 1½-hour cassettes. Read by Bill Kelsey.

E14. *Eminent Elizabethans* (2249) 8 1½-hour cassettes. Read by Bill Kelsey.

E15. *The Cousin Jacks: The Cornish in America* (2268) 10 1½-hour cassettes. Read by Bill Kelsey.

E16. *Memories of Men and Women* (2291) 7 1½-hour cassettes. Read by Bill Kelsey.

E17. *Glimpses of the Great* (2326) 7 1½-hour cassettes. Read by Bill Kelsey.

E18. *A Quartet of Cornish Cats* (2777) 5 1-hour cassettes. Read by Bill Kelsey.

E19. *Prefaces to Shakespeare's Plays* (2953) 7 1½-hour cassettes. Read by Bill Kelsey.

E20. *A Cornish Childhood* (2962) 9 1½-hour cassettes. Read by Bill Kelsey.

E21. *A Man of the Thirties* (3074) 6 1½-hour cassettes. Read by Bill Kelsey.

E22. *Homosexuals in History* (3738) 12 1½-hour cassettes. Read by Ian Whitcomb (British).

E23. *The Early Churchills* (4016) 11 1½-hour cassettes. Read by David Case (British).

E24. *Historians I Have Known* (14604) 6 1½-hour cassettes. Read by David Case.

E25. *My View of Shakespeare* (16063) Future recording rights received (1997).

LECTURES AND READINGS ON CASSETTE

Commercially produced by Sentinel Records—Job and Irene Morris, Paul, Penzance, Cornwall.

E26. *A Cornishman at Oxford and in America* (Senc 1048)
Recorded and produced at Trenarren, February 1981.

Side 1: How Many Miles to Mylor? 2. Cheelie 3. Leaving Home—Going to Oxford 4. Duporth Hill 5. The Old Churchyard at St. Austell 6. Tudor Cornwall 7. The Garden at Trenarren in Spring.

Side 2: All Souls Day in Wyoming 2. Mineral Point, Wisconsin, and Uncle Ab's Tavern There 3. Ardevora Veor 4. Shakespeare's Death-Bed 5. Marytavy 6. The Choice 7. Peter, the White Cat of Trenarren.

E27. Shakespeare's Sonnets and His Dark Lady with an Introduction to a Modern Shakespeare (Senc 1055)
Recorded at Trenarren House, the home of Dr. A. L. Rowse.

Side 1: Shakespeare's Sonnets and His Dark Lady.

Side 2: Shakespeare's Sonnets and His Dark Lady (conclusion); An Introduction to a Modern Shakespeare.

E28. Cornish Stories and Poems (Senc 1058)
Produced and recorded at Trenarren, August 1983.

Side 1: A Cornish Background 2. "St. Endellion" 3. St. Austell Parish Church 4. Talks with Local People 5. "Yarcombe Hill," "Native Sky," and Extracts from "Duporth."

Side 2: Literary associations with Matthew Arnold, Byron and Quiller-Couch. 2. Bus-Ride 3. Helman Tor. 4. The Wise Old Serpent of King's Wood.

E29. The Elizabethans and America (Senc 1060)
Produced and recorded at Trenarren, September 1983.

Side 1 and side 2: The full-length, informed lecture, with a wealth of detail, delivered in A. L. Rowse's customarily enthusiastic and entertaining style.

E30. Shakespeare's Self-Portrait (Senc 1064)
Recorded at Trenarren House, 1984.

Side 1 and side 2: A full-length lecture in which Dr. Rowse skillfully builds a clear portrait of William Shakespeare, the man, from the information to be found in Shakespeare's own writings.

E31. Famous People I Have Known (Senc 1065)
Recorded at Trenarren, 1984.

Side 1: Winston Churchill 2. Nancy Astor 3. Clem Attlee 4. Ernest Bevin 5. John Buchan 6. Agatha Christie.

Side 2: Agatha Christie (conclusion) 2. H. G. Wells 3. Rebecca West 4. T. S. Eliot.

Absorbing stories of famous figures of the literary and political worlds told with intriguing and personal sidelights by A. L. Rowse.

E32. Transatlantic (Senc 1078)

Recorded at Trenarren on the morning of Tuesday, February 14, 1989. It was taken with one break only, to change reels, and has been left entirely unprocessed at the request of Dr. Rowse.

Side 1 and side 2: American scenes included with those of Cornwall, West Country, Oxford, and others.

F

Reports about and Interviews with A. L. Rowse

F1. "Labourer's Son's Scholastic Successes" (*The Times*, September 23, 1922, p. 11, col. b)
Report: "The successes by A. L. Rowse, the son of a labourer of St. Austell, Cornwall, since he became a scholar at the secondary school at St. Austell, have gained him an Oxford University education, through scholarships amounting to 200 pounds per annum, tenable for four years, at Christ Church. He took the Oxford Junior Examination, second class honours in 1917; the Senior Oxford Examination, third class honours, distinction in history, in 1918; the Oxford Senior Local, first class honours with distinction in English and History, in 1919; the first division London University Matriculation in 1920; and won the Draper's Company Soley Scholarship, value 60 pounds per year, for four years, and the Oxford English Literature Scholarship, 80 pounds per annum for four years, in an examination open to all the public schools in England, for which the competition is keen." (Report quoted in full.)

F2. "All Souls Fellowship" (*The Times*, November 4, 1925, p. 14, col. g)
Report: "Mr. A. L. Rowse and Mr. R. M. Makins both of Christ Church, were elected Fellows of All Souls College yesterday. In addition to being undergraduates of the same foundation, the two new Fellows both read the Modern History School and were both placed in the first class this year. Neither is yet 22 years of age. Both have taken a prominent part in undergraduate politics . . . Mr. Rowse is a Cornishman and came to Oxford with a scholarship from the St. Austell County School."

F3. Untitled Report (*Cornwall Education Week Handbook* 1927, May 30– June 4, 1927, City Hall, Truro, p. 62)
Report: "Perhaps the highest ascent on the County Educational ladder has been attained by an elementary school boy at St. Austell, Alfred Leslie Rowse. He

185

began his climb from Carclaze Council School when he won a free place in St. Austell Secondary School. In 1921 he won a County University Scholarship and also an open scholarship at Christ Church, Oxford. Three years later he got a brilliant First in Greats and was advised to compete for an All Souls Fellowship. He was first in the competition and is now studying in Germany. He has brought real distinction to the Cornish Educational system, and given good health a brilliant future would seem to be assured to him." [Full-page photograph on p. 72.]

F4. "List of Candidates for the General Election" (*The Times*, October 10, 1931, p. 8, col. d)

Listed under English Counties—Cornwall: Penryn and Falmouth: Petherick, M. (U); + Simon, E. D. (L Nat); Rowse A. L. (Lab). (L, 1138).

F5. "Candidates for General Election Were Nominated Yesterday throughout Great Britain and Northern Ireland" (*The Times*, October 17, 1931, p. 6, col. d)

See F4.

F6. "Election Campaign" (*The Times*, October 27, 1931, p. 6, col. b)

Report: "Cornwall: The Liberals expect to hold Cornwall but . . . the contest is, perhaps even keener in the Penryn and Falmouth Division, where there is a strong Labour vote. The candidates are Mr. E. D. Simon, Parliamentary Secretary to the Ministry of Health, Liberal; Mr. Petherick, Unionist, and, Mr. Rowse, Labour."

F7. "General Election Results" (*The Times*, October 29, 1931, election supplement p. 4, col. e)

Report: "A. L. Rowse defeated, Cornwall, Penryn and Falmouth:
Electors: 50,767; Men 23,525; Women 27,242
Petherick, M. (U) 16,388
+ Simon, E. D. (L) 14,006
Rowse, A. L. (Lab) 10,098
Unionist majority 2,382"

F8. The Fabian Society Kingsway Hall Lectures, Autumn 1932 (*New Clarion*, October 1, 1932, p. 402)

Notice: "Thursday November 10, 1932—Industry in the Transition to Socialism—Chairman: Mr. St. John Ervine. Lecturer: Mr. A. L. Rowse."

F9. "Home News/Liberals and Labour" (*The Times*, August 4, 1934, p. 7, col. a)

Report from the Liberal Summer School at Oxford: "Mr. A. L. Rowse, Labour candidate for Penryn and Falmouth at the last election, said yesterday that Liberals and Labour had got to get together. He prophesised that at the next election Labour would go back as a largest single party, but still not with an independent majority. He said that if there was another minority government the real danger from Fascism would emerge."

F10. "At Thirty Fourth Annual Conference of The Labour Party at Southport" (*The Times*, October 3, 1934, p. 7, col. b)

Report: "Mr. A. L. Rowse (Penryn and Falmouth) . . . supports the Executive on the ground that the first thing to do was for the Labour Government to get its hands firmly on the levers of political power, because that was the only way by which the levers of economic control could be operated later."

F11. "General Election 1935" (*The Times*, November 16, 1935, election supplement, p. 4, col. g)

Report: "A. L. Rowse defeated, Cornwall, Penryn and Falmouth:
Electors: 52,559; Men 24,460; Women 28,099
Petherick, M. (U) 16,136
Rowse A. L. (Lab) 13,105
Allen, Sir R. W. (L) 11,537
Unionist majority 3,031"

F12. "Shakespeare Politics/A Conservative and a Sceptic" (*The Times*, September 6, 1938, p. 10, col. e)

Report: "The Shakespeare Conference at Stratford-on-Avon was continued yesterday with a lecture by Mr. A. L. Rowse on 'Shakespeare and Politics.' It was curious, he said, how little Shakespeare has been regarded from this angle."

F13. "News and Notes/The World and the Parish" (*Times Literary Supplement*, June 28, 1941, p. 1)

Report: "Mr. A. L. Rowse, whose study of Tudor Cornwall is announced on another page, urges that the time has come in our historical writing for a synthesis of local and national history. 'One may go further,' he writes, 'to see the history of one's own parish as part of the history of Europe, a moment in the movement of the human spirit.'"

F14. "News and Notes/Literary Award" (*Times Literary Supplement*, November 1941, p. 1)

Report: "The Jenner Medal, which has been awarded to Mr. A. L. Rowse for his historical work, particularly for his book Tudor Cornwall, which was reviewed in T.L.S. of September 27, was founded some years ago by the Royal Institution of Cornwall to commemorate the work in antiquarian scholarship of Henry Jenner."

F15. "Mr Churchill's Foresight/Historian as Prime Minister/Mr. Rowse on Tradition" (*The Times*, May 6, 1944, p. 2, col. e)

Report: "Mr. Rowse spoke at the Royal Institution yesterday on 'Mr. Churchill and English History.' It was, he said, a striking historical propriety that in these years when we had been fighting the closest struggle in our history for our existence, and had held the door open for the existence of others, the whole inspiration of the grand alliance against the aggressor should have been a Churchill—descendant of the great Marlborough, who did the same thing 200 years ago."

F16. "A Slighted Inheritance" (*Times Literary Supplement*, December 2, 1944, p. 583, col. b)
Report: "Mr. A. L. Rowse's new volume (reviewed on our front page), though a collection of recent articles and reviews written originally for the occasion, is fortunate for the thread of English history which runs through its parts, Mr. Rowse being primarily a historian."

F17. Untitled Report (*Times Literary Supplement*, March 17, 1945, p. 123, col. c)
Report: "In *The English Spirit,* a volume which by its good humour, its variety and its sense of historical proportion does justice to its title, Mr. A. L. Rowse has an essay on 'The Historical Tradition of British Policy.' In it he claims that what has been accounted to us, by certain foreign historians, for Machiavellian cynicism or plain greed, may be very differently explained as action required of us by historical circumstances."

F18. "Linch-Pin of World Alliance/Mr. A. L. Rowse's Tribute to Mr. Churchill" (*The Times*, May 3, 1945, p. 2, col. d)
Report: "Mr. A. L. Rowse, Fellow of All Souls, addressed [on May 2] the Oxford branch of the English-Speaking Union at its annual meeting this evening on 'Mr. Churchill in English History.' He said that Mr. Churchill, as a student of history, had always understood better than any other of our statesmen that the proper policy of Great Britain was to realize the potential common interest that existed all along between this country, Soviet Russia and the United States; in short, the century-long policy of the Grand Alliance. He had realized that it was to our great danger that we had departed from that policy in the pre-war years."

F19. Court Circular (*The Times*, February 23, 1951, p. 8, col. b)
Notice: "Mr. A. L. Rowse is leaving for the United States and will be away until the end of June."

F20. Biographical Sketch and Portrait (*Saturday Review of Literature* [USA], July 28, 1951, p. 8)

F21. "Court Circular/English Association" (*The Times*, March 21, 1952, p. 8, col. b)
Notice: "Because of Ministerial duties, Mr. Harold Macmillan, M.P., has found it necessary to resign the presidency of the English Association. Mr. A. L. Rowse has been elected to the office and will deliver the presidential address on 'A New Elizabethan Age?' at the annual meeting on May 24."

F22. "Need of Social Conservatism / Mr. Rowse on Pride in the Past" (*The Times*, May 26, 1952, p. 4, col. c)

Report: "Mr. A. L. Rowse in his presidential address to the English Association in London on Saturday took his subject "A New Elizabethan Age?". There was, he said, a similarity between our situation and that of the Elizabethans—'the consciousness of having faced and come through a great danger, all the fibres of the nation's being tested and strung up by a great ordeal, and the triumph against such odds, against overwhelming might and power.'"

F23. "Creation v. Criticism / A Misleading Antithesis" (*The Times*, May 30, 1952, p. 8, col. f)

Report (by "our music critic"): "We suffer from too much criticism, said Mr. A. L. Rowse to the English Association last week. The temper of our present age puts too much emphasis on criticism, which he added was "antithetical" but his argument implied antipathy, prejudicial even, to creation. And he specifically included the criticism of music in his strictures—'too much musical criticism for the health of music.'"

F24. "Elizabethan Ages" (*Times Literary Supplement*, September 5, 1952, p. 581, col. a)

Report: "Can the spirit of the Elizabethan poets transfer itself from the Elizabethan world to ours? Do the formidable conditions of to-day favour a profound spiritual impulse comparable with that which accompanied the perils threatening mankind four centuries ago? Mr. A. L. Rowse, impressed by external resemblances, would raise our hopes, not very high but sufficient for kindling. In his Presidential Address to the English Association he points out that our second Queen Elizabeth ascended the Throne at the same age as the first Elizabeth; that her Prime Minister is already a historic figure; and that, so we hope, the wars are over."

F25. "Portrait Gallery/An Elizabethan/A. L. Rowse" (*Sunday Times*, November 1, 1953)

Report: "This Portrait is a study in paradoxes: the eminent historian vying with the great master J. E. Neale as interpreter and discoverer of Elizabethan history, the author of *The England of Elizabeth*, *Tudor Cornwall*, and *Sir Richard Grenville* an output that some of his academic critics might well envy, were it his all." [Biographical sketch includes photograph by Douglas Glass.]

F26. "Sir Philip Sidney Exhibition/Family Treasures" (*The Times*, June 26, 1954, p. 8, col. f)

Report: "The 400th anniversary of the birth of Sir Philip Sidney falls this year, and the nearness of Tunbridge Wells to Penshurst, his birthplace, has inspired the borough corporation to arrange in their art gallery the commemorative exhibition which Mr. A. L. Rowse, the historian, opened to-day [June 25]. The material has been lent by Sir Philip Sidney's successor, Lord De L'Isle and Dudley, V.C., the Air Minister."

F27. Untitled Report signed "G.W." [possibly Gerald Alfred Wilkes] (*Southerly* [Australia], vol. 15, no. 2 [1954], pp. 132–133)
Report: "In his Presidential Address to the English Association for 1952, Dr. A. L. Rowse develops a parallel between the emergence of Britain from the recent war and the emergence of Elizabethan England from the struggle with Spain, and asks if we may now expect 'a new outburst of creativeness in the arts and sciences' to make the parallel complete."

F28. "From Oxford to Urbana" (*Newsweek* [USA], September 26, 1955, pp. 112–113)
Article: "Two years ago, Alfred Leslie Rowse, M.A., D.Litt., and fellow of All Souls College at Oxford, received an invitation from the University of Illinois to become one of its first George A. Miller Visiting Professors. Rowse declined. 'In point of fact,' the historian remarked, 'he couldn't bear to go—he was too immersed in the production of his fourteenth book.' The university undaunted, renewed the offer and last week, while the fourteenth book, *The Expansion of Elizabethan England* lay happily on the publisher's desk, Rowse was at Urbana, Illinois, much to the university's delight. It considers him probably the top living scholar of English Tudor history, and his publishers, who find him also expertly Elizabethan ('I and II of course'), concur."

F29. "Frontiers of Fact and Fiction/Mr. Forster's Aunt" (*The Times,* July 14, 1956, p. 4, col. c)
Report: "The last literary session yesterday of the international P.E.N. conference at Bedford College, Regent's Park, was concerned with history and biography and with M. André Maurios, Mr. E. M. Forster, Professor A. L. Rowse, Mr. Sholem Asch and Captain B. H. Liddell Hart on the platform to pool their experiences the occasion was bound to be exceptionally fruitful. . . . Professor Rowse proclaimed himself 'a mere plain historian,' and proceeded to attack those reviewers who forgot that history is a branch of literature and those academic historians who did not regard their work as art. He was no less strict with historians who were prepared to sacrifice facts for the sake of general intellectual constructs."

F30. "World Writers End Successful Parley" (*New York Times Book Review,* July 14, 1956, p. 3, col. a)
Report: "The International P.E.N. Club completed today what was believed to have been the largest and most successful congress of its history. . . . A. L. Rowse, one of England's most noted historians, maintained that it was 'indefensible to impose a thesis on history.'"

F31. "First G. M. Trevelyan Lectures" (*The Times,* January 17, 1958, p. 12, col. d)
Notice: "Mr. A. L. Rowse has chosen 'The Elizabethans and America' as the

subject for the first G. M. Trevelyan lectures which he is to deliver at Cambridge during the Michaelmas term."

F32. "Luncheon" (*The Times*, June 25, 1958, p. 12, col. d)

Notice: "Mr. Daniel Macmillan (chairman) and the directors of Macmillan and Company gave a luncheon party at the Dorchester Hotel yesterday in honour of Dr. A. L. Rowse . . . The guests included . . . The Duchess of Marlborough, Earl Spencer, Viscount De L'Isle, Nancy Viscountess Astor, Sir John Neale."

F33. "The Role of the Intellectual/Dr. Rowse Criticizes Some Modern Trends" (*The Times*, October 15, 1958, p. 16, col. c)

Report: " 'Whatever the world around us, whatever the fate that awaits us, we can but behave with responsibility and probity. Our comments will be of the more value, and our criticisms more worthy of respect; if they are not acceptable, that will then not be our fault. Let us always adhere to truth, and an essential sincerity, even if we are not all in a position to command candour—which may yet, in an iron age, be more valuable than politeness. Our role as intellectuals should be to clarify, not confuse counsel, to interpret, expound. For that we need to be willing to learn, for there is a great deal we do not know, before we are prepared to teach!' With this statement of purpose Dr. A. L. Rowse, delivering the Hermon Ould Memorial Lecture in London last night, set the theme for the three-day conference arranged by the English centre of international P.E.N. His lecture was entitled 'The Role of the Intellectuals in Society.' "

F34. "Dr. Rowse Rebuts 'An Injustice/Elizabethan Voyagers' Debt to Their Queen'" (*The Times*, October 18, 1958, p. 10, col. b)

Report: "It is not often that the work of an historian can safely be called gallant, but this compliment was clearly deserved by Dr. A. L. Rowse, when he began the first series of Trevelyan lectures at Cambridge last night."

F35. "U.S.S.R. Wants Cultural Relations Extended/Banning of English Books from Moscow Exhibition" (*The Times*, November 23, 1959, p. 12, col. e)

Report (under subheading "Books Withdrawn/Rather Friendly"): "Mr. A. L. Rowse, Fellow of All Souls (*The Later Churchills*) said—'I am a little surprised. I should have thought that the whole tendency of my book was rather friendly to Russia. . . . I suppose the Russians really object to just a few comments I made about Stalin, but these comments are nothing like so harsh as those made by Mr. Khruschev. . . . I think the Russians have slipped up a little on this. They have rather cashiered someone who is rather friendly to them.' "

F36. "Universities Need of Independence/Task of Assessing Society's Values" (*The Times*, May 5, 1960, p. 8, col. g)

Report: "Amongst others, Dr. A. L. Rowse, the historian, is reported as having received an honorary degree from the Exeter University."

F37. "Cutting Traffic in Historic Towns/Dr. A. L. Rowse Urges Restrictions" (*The Times,* June 20, 1960, p. 7, col. c)
Report: "A suggestion that the historic beauty of places like Oxford and Shrewsbury should be preserved by making them traffic-restricted areas was made by Dr. A. L. Rowse . . . when he presented the prizes at Shrewsbury School speech day yesterday."

F38. "Social News" (*The Times,* September 15, 1961, p. 14, col. b)
Notice: "Dr. A. L. Rowse has left for America where he will be at the Huntington Library, San Marino, California, till April. Letters will be forwarded."

F39. "Throckmorton Ms. Riddle" (*The Times,* April 9, 1962, p. 10, col. g)
Report: "The question of the whereabouts of the Throckmorton diary manuscript, raised by *The Times* review of Dr. Rowse's new book *Ralegh and the Throckmortons,* was still being debated yesterday. . . . speaking from the Queen Mary in mid-Atlantic, Dr. Rowse told *The Times*: 'It is in the possession of the Canterbury Cathedral chapter library.'"

F40. "Dr. Rowse Ends Manuscript Mystery/The Throckmorton Diary 'In My Rooms' (*The Times,* April 10, 1962, p. 12, col. e)
Report: "Doubts about the whereabouts of the Throckmorton Diary manuscript were settled yesterday by Dr. A. L. Rowse . . . Speaking from the Queen Mary before the liner docked at Southampton, Dr. Rowse said that the manuscript: 'is in my rooms at All Souls and will be returned to Canterbury as soon as I return.'"

F41. "Old Diary Sheds Light on Raleigh. Reveals Essex as Godfather of Son of Sir Walter by a Secret Marriage/Wedding Irked Queen/Journal Found in Woodshed/Work of Bride's Brother—Becomes Basis of Book" (*New York Times Book Review,* April 10, 1962, p. 45, col. h)
Report: "London, April 9—A diary begun nearly 400 years ago and still almost intact sheds new light on Sir Walter Raleigh, the versatile gallant who dreamed of empire for England in the New World. The diary was kept by Sir Arthur Throckmorton, Raleigh's brother-in-law. . . . The diary was found in a woodshed in the precincts of Canterbury Cathedral. Dr. A. L. Rowse, historian and authority on Elizabethan times, has written a book, *Ralegh and the Throckmortons,* based on the diary."

F42. "Oxford Historian "Solves" Sonnets/Shakespeare's Poems Said to be Autobiographical" (*New York Times Book Review,* September 18, 1963, p. 36, col. a)
Report (by Sydney Gruson): "London, September 17—A noted Elizabethan historian has turned literary detective and in a book to be published next month asserts that he has solved 'the greatest puzzle in the history of English literature'—the sonnets of Shakespeare. Professor A. L. Rowse, a Fellow of All Souls College at Oxford, is the historian. His book is *William Shakespeare: A Biography.*"

F43. "Oxford Historian Meets Scholars/Rowse Discusses Sonnets of Shakespeare Here" (*New York Times Book Review*, September 25, 1963, p. 40, cols. c–e)
Report (by Harry Gilroy): "A. L. Rowse, the Oxford historian, confronted an audience that he himself described as 'embattled literary scholars' at the Pierpont Morgan Library yesterday and assured them that he was 'astonished at the simplicity with which the problems connected with Shakespeare's sonnets could be worked out.' His account of his 'solutions' delivered in a style that produced rippling laughter, apparently convinced many in the audience."

F44. "Dr. Rowse Faces U.S. Scholars" (*The Times*, September 26, 1963, p. 12, col. f)
Report: "Dr. A. L. Rowse, the Oxford historian, introduced the results of his research into Shakespeare's sonnets to an American audience of what he called 'embattled literary scholars' in New York yesterday. . . . Dr. Rowse's address before an overflow audience in the Pierpont Morgan Library was heard in silence; and from comments made afterwards it is clear that his findings are regarded, as he had expected, as controversial."

F45. "A. L. Rowse Solves Sonnets" (*Publishers Weekly* [USA], September 30, 1963, p. 31)
Publisher's Weekly interview.

F46. "Historian" (*New Yorker*, October 19, 1963, pp. 43–45)
Interview/article.

F47. "Critic at Large/The Stupidity of Shakespearian Scholars Amazes A. L. Rowse, Historian" (*New York Times Book Review*, October 22, 1963, p. 34, col. b)
Article (by Brooks Atkinson): "Speaking as an authority on Elizabethan history, A. L. Rowse is amazed by the stupidity of Shakespearian scholars. A Fellow of All Souls College, Oxford, he declares with bountiful self-satisfaction that he has solved the problems of the Shakespeare sonnets."

F48. "Shakespeare in London" (*New York Times Book Review*, November 3, 1963, p. 30)
Article (by John Bowen): "Autumn is the literary harvest time in London when books that, have been long a-writing, long a-printing, suddenly burst all together from the publishers' cellars. The British have many pretty customs for such a time. One that has taken place this season is the Ritual Sacrifice of A. L. Rowse." Discusses the furore over *William Shakespeare: A Biography.*

F49. "Two Scholars Lead a Sonnet War While Colleagues Gird for 1964" (*New York Times Book Review*, December 2, 1963, p. 49, col. g)
Article (by Harry Gilroy): "News from two publishers that on January 6, books by the two eminent British scholars A. L. Rowse and J. Dover Wilson, will give opposed explanations of Shakespeare's 154 sonnets."

F50. "A. L. Rowse: A Study in Versatility" (*Saturday Review* [USA], **January 11, 1964, p. 57**)
Interview by Robert Halsband.

F51. "Shakespeare's 400th Anniversary/World Acclaims England's Towering Genius" (*Time and Tide,* **April 23, 1964, pp. 7–8**)
Report: "And 400 different authors have written 400 books on every aspect of Shakespeare's life and works. Of these, the most important has undoubtedly been Dr. Rowse's William Shakespeare."

F52. "INSIGHT-Literature: Shakespearology: The Scoreboard" (*Sunday Times,* **April 26, 1964, p. 6**)
Report including a chart presenting main issues of the "hottest of all Shakespeare controversies: the Sonnets . . . The dispute is divided into three main camps, headed by Professor J. Dover Wilson of Caius, Cambridge, Dr. A. L. Rowse of All Souls and Dr. Leslie Hotson, all of whom have produced recent books. . . . Added to these is a huge fringe with theories ranging from the possible to the absurd. A selection from these is given in *The Field.*" (See also D401a).

F53. "Identity of 'W. H.' Reaffirmed" (*The Times,* **May 4, 1964, p. 9, col. a**)
Report: "Dr. A. L. Rowse reaffirmed last night that he had solved the question of the identity of 'W. H.' the 'onlie begetter' of the dedication of Shakespeare's sonnets. He was lecturing to 200 members of the Friends of Covent Garden in the auditorium of the Opera House."

F54. "Mr. 'W. H' Cannot Be Lord Herbert/Dr. Rowse's Reasons" (*The Times,* **July 10, 1964, p. 16, col. e**)
Report: "There were two inspirers, not one, of Shakespeare's sonnets, the Dark Lady and the Young Man, said Dr. A. L. Rowse, the Elizabethan historian, giving the Giff Edmonds memorial lecture at the Royal Society of Literature in London yesterday."

F55. "Autumn Pick/Non-fiction/A Selection of Titles Scheduled to Appear between Next Month and December" (*Sunday Times,* **August 23, 1964, p. 27**)
Report including *A Cornishman at Oxford* by A. L. Rowse (Cape, January)—a long pondered sequel to *A Cornish Childhood*—and *Christopher Marlowe* by A. L. Rowse (Macmillan, September).

F56. "The Writer in Cornwall" (*John O'London's Books of the Month,* **November 1964, pp. 18-19**)
Article by John Birkett about British writers living in Cornwall and its pervasiveness. Details Daphne du Maurier, Howard Spring, Colin Wilson, and A. L. Rowse.

F57. "Dr. Rowse Returns to the Attack" (*The Times,* **April 24, 1965, p. 5, col. g)**
Report: "The reception of his solutions of some of the 'hoary problems' about Shakespeare last year was a discreditable chapter in literary history, Dr. A. L. Rowse, the historian, Fellow of All Souls, said today at the Oxford Preservation Trust's Shakespeare commemoration ceremony."

F58. "Looking Ahead" (*Sunday Times,* **August 22, 1965, p. 34)**
Report: "Slightly fewer books were published in the first six months of 1965 than in the same period of 1964. This autumn's thousands of titles, however, seems likely to redress the balance. Here is a selection of exceptionally interesting titles . . . List includes: *Shakespeare's Southampton* by A. L. Rowse (Macmillan). Literary detection, putting Southampton in perspective both as Shakespeare's patron and as a professional statesman."

F59. "Books of 1965/Sunday Times Contributors' Choice" (*Sunday Times,* **January 2, 1966, p. 35)**
Paragraph (by J. W. Lambert): "Agog, amused, amazed, outraged and ultimately all admiring, I salute the ravaged and abrasive charm of A. L. Rowse's *A Cornishman at Oxford* (Cape). I believe that with its precursor, *A Cornish Childhood,* this will turn out to be one of the most enduring of twentieth-century autobiographies."

F60. "Irving Stones Set Two Literary Prizes/Hoping to Spur Biographical and Historical Novels" (*New York Times,* **January 19, 1968, p. 45, col. a)**
Report (by Harry Gilroy): "Irving Stone, the author, and Jean Stone, his wife, editor and business manager, have set up two prizes for the work of other authors. Doubleday & Co. announced yesterday that it would administer the Stones's $1,000 annual awards for the best biographical and historical novels. Allan Nevins, the Columbia University historian, A. L. Rowse, the Oxford historian, and Budd Schulberg, the novelist, will be judges this year."

F61. "Nation's Cornish Get a Spokesman/Rowse Calls Them the Most Neglected Minority" (*New York Times Book Review,* **March 23, 1969, p. 96, col. a)**
Report (by John Leo): "What is the most neglected minority group in America? 'Why, the Cornish, of course.' said A. L. Rowse, the noted Oxford historian and Cornishman. 'Your blacks and Puerto Ricans have greater problems, but at least the rest of you have heard of them. Nobody's heard of the Cornish.' Aside from the fact that there are a million largely unnoticed Cornishmen in the United States, why has Professor Rowse, an authority on Elizabethan England, spent five years producing a history of Cornish Americans? 'My dear boy,' he said, in an interview last week in the Pan Am Buiding's Copter Club, 'after all, I am the leading Cornish writer in the world.' Professor Rowse's book is *The Cousin Jacks,* published last week by Scribner's."

F62. "The Poetry of A. L. Rowse" (*Poetry Review,* Summer 1970, pp. 140–161)

(The following article by Colin Wilson is an important, in-depth appreciation and constitutes an essential reference source to understanding A. L. Rowse the poet.)

Concluding, "this poetry is as English as the music of Delius and Elgar, and it has their qualities of beauty, nostalgia, sadness. It has remained unfashionable for the same reason that Delius and Elgar were unfashionable in the era of Walton, Hindemith and Stravinsky; its simplicity, lack of concern with technique as such, seem to place it in an earlier period. Its colours are perhaps too dark for it ever to achieve the kind of acclaim that came to Betjeman after the publication of his collected poems; but it should at least be known to all who care about English poetry. . . . Rowse's own explanation of this lack of interest is that people do not expect a historian to be a good poet. He is, after all, the only English historian, apart from Macaulay, who has also been a poet. No doubt he is right. My own feeling is that he is a poet who happens to be, by some strange chance, a good historian."

F63. "Transition and Triumph" (*Listener,* September 10, 1970, pp. 342–344)

Text from autobiographical broadcast on BBC Radio 4, "The Time of My Life."

F64. "The Times Diary/Rowse: Sex and the Elizabethans" (*The Times,* March 20, 1971, p. 12, col. d)

Report: "That well-known Elizabethan; A. L. Rowse, is likely to raise a few eyebrows on Thursday when he gives the Tredegar Memorial Lecture to the Royal Society of Literature. The subject is: 'Sex in the Elizabethan Age,' and Rowse is already concerned that the subject may prove slightly shocking to some of his friends."

F65. "In the Springtime of a Culture" (*Daily Telegraph Magazine,* October 8, 1971, pp. 33, 35)

Article "What were the Elizabethans really like? Away from the Court, how did people live? What did they eat? In a new book (*The Elizabethan Renaissance: The Life of the Society,* to be published by Macmillan on October 14) from which we print some extracts, A. L. Rowse tells us of the lesser-known aspects of a golden age."

F66. "Scourge of the Idiot People/Terry Coleman Interviews A. L. Rowse, Historian, Misogynist, Cornishman (*Guardian,* October 30, 1971, p. 9, col. a)

Article/interview (by Terry Coleman): "A. L. Rowse is a very plentiful historian. He is a poet. He is a biographer—of Shakespeare and Marlowe. He is a Cornishman. I think that any self-respecting liberal would find it essential to add that Dr. Rowse is also an intolerant man and this would be true. I never heard a man who could be intolerant on more subjects. It is an entertaining intolerance, and well reasoned. He is now 67."

F67. "Elections to the Athenaeum" (*The Times*, **April 25, 1972, p. 4, col. b)**
Report: "The committee of The Athenaeum has elected the following under the provision of Rule II of the club, which empowers the annual election by the committee of a certain number of persons of distinguished eminence in science, literature or the arts, or for their public services. . . . Dr. Alfred Leslie Rowse, fellow of All Souls College, Oxford, historian and author."

F68. "The Times Diary" (*The Times*, **June 14, 1972, p. 16, col. d)**
Report: "Dr. A. L. Rowse will be taking a rather unusual line when he gives this year's address at the memorial service for Samuel Pepys in St. Olave's Hart Street. Pepys is usually regarded as very much a Cambridge man, but Rowse, a fellow of All Souls, Oxford, will be devoting his address to Pepys's Oxford friendships—foremost among them, of course, his friendly correspondence with John Evelyn. Among Rowse's observations: via his friendship with Sir Nathaniel Lloyd, a former fellow of All Souls, Pepys managed to get Thomas Tanner (later Bishop of St. Asaph) elected to the Oxford college."

F69. "Books of the Year" (*The Times*, **November 30, 1972, Books for Christmas supplement, p. 8, col. h)**
Article (by David Williams): "The book I enjoyed most this year was volume 3 of A. L. Rowse's *The Elizabethan Renaissance*."

F70. "The Dark Lady Is Not for Cheering" (*Guardian*, **January 30, 1973, p. 26)**
Article (by John Ezard): "Dr. A. L. Rowse's claim to have solved 'the greatest mystery in world literature'—the identity of the Dark Lady of Shakespeare's Sonnets—got mixed notices from academic critics yesterday. . . . 'Comparable in magnitude to the discovery of Linear B' (Dr. Rowse, himself). 'She could have been Charlemagne's mistress for all I know or care' (A. J. P. Taylor). 'Extra-ordinarily interesting—and very likely right' (Mr. John Bayley, lecturer in English at Oxford) . . . 'If you quote me, he will never speak to me again' (Anonymous senior don)."

F71. "The Times Diary/Dark Secrets" (*The Times*, **February 6, 1973, p. 14, col. g)**
Report: "If A. L. Rowse has discovered the identity of the Dark Lady of Shakespeare's sonnets, he can thank Victorian prudery for keeping his scoop secret for so long."

F72. "Will in Over-Plus" (*Listener,* **May 3, 1973, pp. 585–586, col. c)**
Editorial: "On page 589 John Carey discusses A. L. Rowse's identification of Shakespeare's Dark Lady: Rowse believes she was Emilia Lanier, the wife of a musician, Will Lanier. On Radio 4 he claimed this explained one of the famous 'Will' sonnets."

F73. "A. L. Rowse from the portrait by Andrew Freeth R. A." (*Books and Bookmen,* May 1973, p. 1)
Full cover illustration of this watercolor painting.

F74. "The Originator of Oxford Brags" (*Daily Telegraph Magazine,* September 7, 1973, pp. 45–46, 51)
Interview/article (by Byron Rogers): "A. L. Rowse, the cheeky chappie of Oxford scholarship, is almost 70. Age cannot wither the Shakespearean scholar; custom will never stale the infinite variety of the self publicist. Death itself has been outwitted: 'Seven-eights of my writing is in the form of journals, to be published only after my death.'" [Illustrated with two photographs by John Goldblatt and Patrick Eagar.]

F75. "In Passing to Mr. A. L. R., That Eternitie Promised" (*Daily Telegraph Magazine,* September 14, 1973, pp. 17–18)
Satirical response (by Paul Jennings): "Has Paul Jennings discovered the final proof of identity of Shakespeare's Dark Lady of the Sonnets?"

F76. "Books/Portrait of a Lady" (New Yorker, March 18, 1974, pp. 142–150)
Article by George Steiner reviewing A. L. Rowse's books on, and discoveries about, Shakespeare and his Dark Lady in the Sonnets.

F77. "The Times Diary/Feline" (*The Times*, March 29, 1974, p. 18, col. e)
Report: "A. L. Rowse, the Oxford historian, is surprised that anyone should be surprised that he has written the biography of a cat. 'I think it is because they have a limited picture of me as just another academic interested in Elizabethan history, while I think of myself as a real writer and always have done.'"

F78. "Look!/Confessions of a Catty Fellow" (*Sunday Times,* April 7, 1974, pp. 44, col. f)
Interview (by Sue Read about the launch of *Peter: The White Cat of Trenarren*): "Because you are a lady I shall take off my dusty old writing jacket and put on my special visitors' jacket."

F79. "Villagers of Chawton Fete Its Dearest Daughter" (*The Times*, July 19, 1975, p. 2, col. e)
Report (on the 200th anniversary of Jane Austen's birth): "Today 600 members of the Jane Austen Society meet in a marquee at Chawton House, for tea and a talk by Professor A. L. Rowse."

F80. "Books for Christmas" (*Sunday Telegraph,* December 7, 1975, p. 13)
Report by Kenneth Rose stating that Elizabeth Jenkins has dedicated her latest book, *The Mystery of King Arthur,* to A. L. Rowse.

F81. "The Times Diary/Book Bang" (*The Times*, July 1, 1976, p. 16, col. d)
Report: "Congratulating *Books and Bookmen* on its 250th issue, and referring to A. L. Rowse's review therein of Sandra Darroch's biography of Lady Ottoline

Morrell. . . . Rowse weighs into Bertrand Russell, Lady Ottoline's lover, with evident delight."

F82. "Dr. Dee's Magic Mirror—Reflecting Two Elizabethan Worlds" (*Listener,* December 23 & 30, 1976, pp. 824–826)

Article: Transcription article of a discussion program entitled Patterns of the Past (BBC World Service) conducted by Clive Jordan who Interviewed Hugh Tait, Dr. Peter French and Dr. A. L. Rowse. "No one ever questioned that he could contact angels; the only question was: were they devils?"

F83. "Atticus/Rowstabout" (*Sunday Times,* May 1, 1977, p. 32, col. e)

Interview/article (by Anthony Holden): "A. L. Rowse is overcome, every ten minutes or so, by furious surges of choler which seem physically to possess him. The voice rises in pitch and volume, and a trembling, icy anger pours forth on London intellectuals, liberal humbug, family life, mental softness, the working-class from which he sprang ('the swine won't work'), the *New Statesman,* E. M. Forster, the Shakespeare industry, and, above all the 'envious' academics who challenge his discoveries and query his scholarship." [Article illustrated with a cartoon by Barry Fantoni.]

F84. "Dr. Rowse Looks Longingly to the Earlier Elizabethans" (*The Times,* June 9, 1977, p. 2, col. d)

Report: "An eminent historian and the Queen's most recent and best-selling biographer conspired last night to leave 50 loyal East Enders wondering exactly what they had been celebrating during the past few days. Dr. A. L. Rowse and Robert Lacey, author of *Majesty,* were talking on "The Two Elizabethan Ages" at Shoreditch Parish Church, Hackney. . . . Dr. Rowse's adulation of the first Elizabethan age turned frequently into bitter condemnation of the present one."

F85. "On the Other Hand/Taking the Biscuit" (*Times Higher Educational Supplement,* June 17, 1977, p. 5, col. a)

Anonymous column: "Now a special post-jubilee award for the most ridiculous comment uttered by student or don in Thames television's film, "City in a Dream," which purported to examine life at Oxford University and gave yet more ammunition to the lobby that wants it turned into a biscuit factory . . . Did the silliest comment come from A. L. Rowse, fellow of All Souls, who put his duodenal ulcer down to sexual repression while studying, then said: 'I have always thought of myself as parallel to D. H. Lawrence'? (Presumably he meant some other one: Dingwall Humphrey Lawrence, the repressed correspondence course fanatic.)"

F86. "Visit with A. L. Rowse" (*New York Times Book Review,* June 26, 1977, p. 3)

Interview/article (by Auberon Waugh): "A. L. Rowse, 73-year-old bachelor, eccentric, misanthropist, poet and, whatever his detractors may say, foremost Elizabethan scholar of his age, lives in a fine, stone-built Georgian manor house overlooking St. Austell bay on the South Cornish coast of England. 'Started

without a bean, look where I am now,' he says, pointing to the well-tended
lawns, the pretty 18th-century French porcelain, the delicate ivory card cases.
I have come to interview him about his new work *Homosexuals in History*; an
intriguing, immensely readable book which manages to give us the benefit of
Mr. Rowse's opinion on Russia, the early Nazis, French literature, Bloomsbury,
and the American puritan conscience as well as potted biographies of eminent
homosexuals since the Middle Ages."

Note. Reprinted in *National Times* (Australia) July 25–30, 1977, pp. 19–20.

F87. "Reporter's Notebook: Off-Off Publishing" (*New York Times Book Review,* May 31, 1978, p. 20)

Report (by Herbert Mitgang from Atlanta): "The thousands of titles placed here
by publishing houses for the benefit of the American Booksellers Association
during its annual conclave bear a resemblance to the themes and styles of
Broadway . . . Off Broadway and Off Off Broadway, book division. . . . Those
who were really lucky did not shake hands with monsters, or even with any of
the show-business personalities promoting their books, but with three of the
more erudite authors who turned up bearing only intelligent conversation: A.
L. Rowse, the Oxford don, whose three-volume *Annotated Shakespeare* is coming from Clarkson N. Potter–Crown Publishers."

F88. "Atticus Note/Rowse Rows" (*Sunday Times,* August 6, 1978, p. 32, col. d)

Report (by Russell Miller): "The makings of a wonderfully acrimonious—and
hopefully long-running—literary row may be found in this month's edition of
the magazine *Books and Bookmen.* The protagonists are gold-medallists in the
genre: on our right, in the red corner, we have Lady Diana Mosley, the third
Mitford daughter; on our left, in the blue corner, is battling A. L. Rowse, the
crusty old historian. Mr. Rowse threw the first below-the-belt punch back in
December with a few choice and gratuitous insults in a review of James Lees-
Milne's war-time diary, *Prophesying Peace.* 'In my humble opinion,' he wrote,
'these Mitfords were otiose idiots. As for Unity Mitford, with her fixation on
Hitler—fancy writing a book about the ignorant young bitch, as if she knew
anything about what was involved.'"

F89. "The Bard for a New Generation" (*Time,* November 13, 1978, pp. 100–102)

Interview/article: "When Alfred Leslie Rowse and the century were young, he
used to perch on the high stone wall surrounding a Cornish manor house. 'I'd
sit there and wonder,' recalls the owlish bachelor, 'why couldn't it be mine?
Well, I finally made it.'"

F90. "Topics/Titles, Lost and Found/Bliss vs. Folly" (*New York Times Book Review,* November 26, 1978, p. 20, col. b)

Editorial: "British historian A. L. Rowse says he has finally and absolutely
resolved the identity of the Dark Lady of Shakespeare's sonnets. She was, he

avers, Emilia Bassano, the daughter of one Italian musician at the court of Elizabeth I and the wife of another."

F91. "Cornwall's Written Images" (*Illustrated London News,* Christmas number 1978, pp. 39–42)

Article by Denys Val Baker about British writers and their fascination with Cornwall, including Dame Daphne du Maurier, John Le Carré, Charles Causley, and A. L. Rowse. Includes two photographs: of Rowse and of Trenarren House, his home on the west side of St. Austell Bay.

F92. "Shakespeare's 'Dark Lady' Peers from the Shadow" (*New York Times Book Review,* December 27, 1978, p. 24, col. a)

Report (by Herbert Mitgang): "Although A. L. Rowse, editor of the newly published *The Annotated Shakespeare,* has devoted decades to the three-volume work—and though he had done with it—he is still haunted by an Elizabethan woman. She is 'the dark lady of the sonnets,' and Professor Rowse is still pursuing research into her life as a clue to Shakespeare's personality."

F93. "A. L. Rowse—Taking His Feline Friends Seriously" (*Daily Telegraph,* March 16, 1979, p. 17)

Interview/article by Avril Groom about cats, on the occasion of the publication of *Three Cornish Cats.*

F94. "Cat-Man" (*Listener,* May 17, 1979, p. 683)

Editorial column about *Woman's Hour* (BBC Radio 4), for which A. L. Rowse was interviewed about his love for cats (broadcast May 2, 1979).

F95. Anonymous interview, *Monthly Biographical Journal* (USA) (*Current Biography,* July 1979, pp. 25-29)

F96. *Foreword (History Today,* November 1979, pp. 699–700)

Editorial tribute to A. L. Rowse as "undoubtedly their most regular contributor."

F97. "Rowse Honoured" (*The Times,* December 8, 1982, p. 12, col. a)

Report: "The Royal Society of Literature has awarded the Benson Silver Medal to Dr. A. L. Rowse, in recognition of his services to literature. It will be presented to him by Mr. C. M. Woodhouse, the chairman, at the Society's Rooms tomorrow evening."

F98. Untitled Report (*Times Literary Supplement,* December 17, 1982, p. 1404, col. e)

Report: "The Royal Society of Literature has announced that Sir Angus Wilson has accepted the invitation to become its President in succession to the late Lord Butler. The award of its twenty-seventh Benson Silver Medal (founded in 1916 by A. C. Benson) has been conferred upon Dr. A. L. Rowse and was presented by C. M. Woodhouse on December 9."

F99. "Profile: Dr. A. L. Rowse/By Chance or Changing Nature's Course Untrimm'd" (*The Times*, March 7, 1983, p. 7)
Interview/article (by Alan Hamilton): "People resent my wide span because of their union mentality. . . . I am a far better poet than most published today . . . I don't live my life among ordinary human fools."

F100. "Hitler Knocks Out the Big Guns/World 'Scoop' That Turned into a Scrap" (*Sun Herald* [Australia], May 1, 1983)
Article (by Bill Mellor about the spurious Hitler diaries): "But this time it appears Lord Dacre—family motto: 'My hope is in God'—may be on a loser. And the historians with whom he has jousted may be excused for revelling in his discomfiture. One is the eminent but eccentric Dr. A. L. Rowse, who has been on the receiving end of Lord Dacre's thrusts. In an article in the *London Daily Mail* last week, Dr. Rowse recalled how Trevor-Roper had been sceptical of his claims to have discovered the identity of the "dark lady" of Shakespeare's sonnets. Rowse wrote gleefully: "Trevor-Roper was completely wrong about that and he did rush to conclusions without going into the evidence sufficiently, if even at all. So he may be wrong about the question of these diaries, as he was certainly wrong about Shakespeare. He certainly gives the impression of being a young man in a hurry, and really, at nearly 70, he ought not to worry about reputation, as if his virginity were at stake."

F101. "The Times Diary/Fan Fare" (*The Times*, April 4, 1984, p. 12, col. a)
Report: "A. L. Rowse has added a surprising dedication to his latest Modern Edition of Shakespeare's Sonnets. . . . 'To President Ronald Reagan for his professional appreciation of William Shakespeare.'"

F102. "Shakespeare's Language Is Updated" (*New York Times Book Review*, April 23, 1984, p. 11, col. a)
Report (by Herbert Mitgang): "That formidable and controversial Shakespearian scholar, A. L. Rowse, is about to strike again: He is turning the traditional language of 37 Shakespeare plays into modern English. To coincide with Shakespeare's 420th birthday today, the first six plays in this venture are being released by the University Press of America."

F103. "New Fardels for the Bard/No Thees or Thous in a Streamlined Shakespeare" (*Time*, May 7, 1984, p. 98)
Interview/article by Gerald Clarke promoting *The Contemporary Shakespeare.*

F104. "Shakespeare Goes Hip" (*Oxford Mail*, July 23, 1984, p. 6, cols. c–h)
Interview/article (by Don Chapman): "Dr. A. L. Rowse paused at the doorway of Sir Keith Joseph's room at All Souls where he has been staying during his latest visit to Oxford. 'You can find your way out again?' the Shakespearian scholar and poet asked politely. Then waving a hand in the direction of the

stonemasons at work in the college quadrangle he added impishly: 'You will notice the place has to be touched up every 100 years. Like Shakespeare.'"

F105. "Shakespeare Canned and Served in 57 Varieties" (*Guardian,* July 25, 1984, p. 9, col. a)
Article by Hugh Herbert about TV Channel 4 in Britain, starting a nine-part series on playing Shakespeare and, the unprecedented publishing boom of the Bard's works, including A. L. Rowse's Contemporary Shakespeare Series, published by University Press of America/Eurospan.

F106. "Alas, Poor Shakespeare" (*Daily Telegraph,* August 10, 1984, p. 13, cols. a–c)
Article by David Holloway on the Contemporary Shakespeare Series.

F107. "Contemporary Error" (*Daily Telegraph,* August 13, 1984, p. 10, col. a)
Editorial column on A. L. Rowse's Contemporary Shakespeare Series.

F108. "Survivors: A Cornish Genius" (*Spectator,* March 30, 1985, pp. 13–14.
Anonymous article paying tribute to A. L. Rowse.

F109. "At Stratford, A Lively 421st Birthday" (*New York Times Book Review,* April 24, 1985, p. 8, col. b)
Report (by Dirk Johnson): "Hortensio dressed like a beatnik, and Christopher Sly reeked of Brooklynese. But the play was still the thing, and some novice theatergoers learned today that Shakespeare—despite his schoolyard reputation—can be fun." Concerning the American Shakespeare Theater's production of *The Taming of the Shrew* based on an interpretation by A. L. Rowse.

F110. "A. L. Rowse: The Poet and the Man" (Stereo Radio 2RSR, Sydney, Australia, June 12, 1985)
A broadcast written and presented by Sydney Cauveren concentrating on A. L. Rowse as a poet. Thirty minutes live, on the University of Sydney Poetry Society Programme.

F111. "PW Interviews—A. L. Rowse" (*Publishers Weekly,* August 9, 1985, pp. 78–79)
Interview/article (by Neil Baldwin): "'I am not out to supersede the Bard!' says the venerable Elizabethan scholar, discussing his works that render Shakespeare in contemporary language.'"

F112. "Londoner's Diary/Rowse Rows on Lost Labours" (*London Standard,* January 31, 1986, p. 6)
Article (anonymous): "The Cornish giant wakens. A. L. Rowse, Elizabethan scholar, poet, discoverer of the Dark Lady of the Sonnets, has been uncharacteristically silent of late on the subject of new 'Shakespeare discoveries.' A play

called *Edmund Ironside* and a love poem have recently been attributed to the Bard—but there's been silence from Dr. Rowse. Until now: from St. Austell the 82-year-old Rowse tells me that the new claims are quite wrong and that every play Shakespeare wrote was known in his own lifetime.'"

F113. "Washington Talk/Briefing/Baffling Epigraph" (*New York Times Book Review,* May 20, 1986, p. 22, col. b)

Report: "A. L. Rowse, an emeritus fellow at All Souls College, Oxford, who is the author of numerous works on British history and a leading Shakespeare scholar, dedicates his recent study of the elusive playwright, *Shakespeare's Self-Portrait,* to 'President Ronald Reagan for his historic honour to Shakespeare's profession.' The dedication left Inga-Stines Ewbank, who reviewed the book for *The Times Literary Supplement* in London a bit puzzled. 'Is he being ironic?' she asked. 'And what exactly does he mean? With Flamineo, I am in a mist.'"

F114. "Reflections on a Century: An Oxford Visit with Author A. L. Rowse" (*Advocate* [USA], May 27, 1986, pp. 40, 122)

Interview/article (by Jere Real): "In his 1984 book *Memories of Men and Women,* British historian A. L. Rowse—the eminent Elizabethan scholar, Emeritus Fellow of All Souls College, Oxford and author of dozens of books of history, biography, poetry and autobiography—tells how poet W. H. Auden tried to seduce him."

F115. "New Answers to Shakespeare Riddle" (*New York Times Book Review,* March 3, 1987, p. 13, col. a)

Report (by Herbert Mitgang): "After 378 years, one of the great literary mysteries of the English-speaking world—who is the 'W. H.' to whom Shakespeare's sonnets are dedicated?—has at last been solved. Twice. And with two utterly simple, but totally different, professorial answers. This is an American professor's solution: 'W. H.' is a typographical error. . . . Speaking from his home in Cornwall the other evening, A. L. Rowse, that unshy Elizabethan scholar from All Souls College, who is author of a three-volume *Annotated Shakespeare,* sputtered: 'Rubbish! Absolute rot! Is there no end to human foolery.'"

F116. "Scholar Who Re-Writes Shakespeare" (*Sydney Morning Herald,* February 1, 1988)

Interview/article (by Deborah Telford): "'Most people have third-rate minds,' declares Dr. A. L. Rowse with the indignation of a contradicted Victorian schoolmaster. At 84, Dr. Rowse, one of the world's most brilliant living historians, a controversial literary biographer and Shakespearian expert, refuses to let old age moderate his withering remarks or his prolific output."

F117. "Shall I Compare Thee to a Shakespeare Fake?" (*The Times*, April 22, 1988, p. 1, col. b)

Report (by Alan Hamilton): "'Isn't it extraordinary,' shouted Professor A. L. Rowse from the end of a telephone line, and his patience, at his home in Cornwall, 'that any tiny thing relating to Shakespeare sends people absolutely haywire?' Professor Rowse, onlie begetter of the Dark Lady of the Sonnets is one of the few outsiders to have set eyes on what is being claimed as a hitherto undiscovered poem by Shakespeare unearthed in a Californian library by Professor Peter Levi, holder of the chair of poetry at Oxford University."

F118. "Shall I Compare Thee to a Shakespeare Sonnet?" (*Sydney Morning Herald,* April 25, 1988)

Report: "Sceptical scholars around the world have unleashed a torrent of questions in response to a British professor's claim that a newly-found poem glued to a manuscript in an American library might have been written by Shakespeare. Professor Peter Levi of Oxford University will hold a press conference in London tomorrow to explain why he believes Shakespeare wrote the two pages of untitled verse that were discovered in the Huntington Library collection in San Marino, California. . . . Professor A. L. Rowse, who has written extensively about Shakespeare, said: 'While the verses are rather better than some previous alleged Shakespeare finds, and while Peter Levi has a good ear for poetry, the hand of Shakespeare can be no more than a remote possibility.'" [Report originally appeared in the *Los Angeles Times.*]

F119. "Much Ado about Nothing, Say the Sceptics" (*Australian,* April 27, 1988)

Report (by Nicholas Rothwell): "Nervous in pin-stripes, fingering his black cane, beleaguered Oxford Professor of Poetry Peter Levi went once more into the breach yesterday to suffer the slings and arrows of outrageous critics. Professor Levi claims to have uncovered a new Shakespeare poem. . . . But even as Professor Levi was making his case before the cameras, the doyen of Shakespeare historians, Professor A. L. Rowse, noted caustically that 'the world's greatest writer is so famous that he seems to go to people's heads, and often in the wrong way—in my view there are no further discoveries about Shakespeare to be made. We have got it all.'"

F120. "Don Insists Shakespeare Poem Genuine" (*Straits Times* [Singapore], April 27, 1988)

Report: "An Oxford poetry professor who sparked a literary controversy when he claimed to have found an unknown Shakespeare poem said he was confident the document was authentic. Professor Peter Levi said on Monday that he had made no mistake over its authorship. . . . Dr. A. L. Rowse, one of Britain's most distinguished Shakespeare scholars, said the poem was 'almost certainly not one of the Bard's works.'"

F121. "Another Year on the Shelf/Guardian Critics Discuss the Year's Best Books" (*Guardian Weekly,* December 16, 1990, p. 28)

Article (by William Golding): "Another book I've found fascinating is the reprint of Tudor England (sic Tudor Cornwall), by A. L. Rowse (Dyllansow Truran). It has altered the face of Cornwall for me. Deeply involved with Cornwall as the author must be, some perhaps unexpected flashes of compassion will out through the historian's objectivity."

F122. "Rowse to the Rescue of the Hetero Bard/The Valerie Grove Interview" (*Sunday Times,* **February 24, 1991, p. 3**)
Interview/article (by Valerie Grove): "Shakespeare in danger of being dropped from the school A-level syllabus? It was time to call on Dr. A. L. Rowse. The unmistakable high-pitched voice responds: 'My dear, come at once, I am at your disposal morning noon and night. The only thing you need to say is, Shakespeare is our greatest asset, in every country in the world he takes the first place. So we don't need any discussion about it, but I will talk for two and a half hours.'" [Illustrated with photograph of a smiling Rowse, with caption: Pot-shots at the Establishment: Rowse rails against the "Minnows and bloody idiots" who envy his popular success.]

F123. "Commentary/The Man of Letters in a Closed Shop" (*Times Literary Supplement,* **November 15, 1991, p. 15**)
Anonymous article about criticism and reviewers that A. L. Rowse brought to the attention of the bibliographer, with his note across the top: "This partly explains the obstruction all my work has encountered in the past 2 or 3 decades—from the Third Rate. A.L.R."

F124. Untitled letter by Sydney Cauveren (*Sydney Morning Herald,* **August 31, 1992**)
Letter correcting feature writer Bob Ellis, who stated in an article (*Herald,* August 24) that William Shakespeare was "a promiscuous homosexual." The writer suggests that "Mr Ellis reads that great Elizabethan historian, Dr. A. L. Rowse—his books: *Shakespeare the Man* and *Shakespeare's Sonnets,* will set him right."

F125. "Londoner's Diary/Rowse's Pals Say 'Please Sir' to PM" (*London Evening Standard,* **September 8, 1993**)
Article: "Recent literary knighthoods have included Sir Kingsley Amis and Sir Peter Quennell. However, one who has scandalously not received any recognition at all is the historian, poet, critic and self-proclaimed Cornish genius, Dr. A. L. Rowse."

F126. "Are There Sonnets Still for Tea?"—A. L. Rowse, the great Shakespearian authority, historian, and eccentric, talks about his new book on All Souls to Terry Coleman, over the scones and cream (*Guardian,* **October 30, 1993, pt. 2, p. 29**)
Interview/article (by Terry Coleman): "To Trenarren in deep Cornwall, driving from St. Austell between high hedges on tracks only wide enough for one car, to see A. L. Rowse, who, since he does not at all intend to be eccentric, will not thank me for saying that he is one of those few people who give eccentricity a good name." [Article illustrated with photograph by John Redman.]

F127. "Time to Honour the History Man" (*Evening Standard,* **November 19, 1993, p. 11**)

Article (by A. N. Wilson): "The distinguished historian and regular Evening Standard reviewer Dr. A. L. Rowse will be 90 years old on 4 December. His reviews are as sharp and well-turned as ever. . . . Rowse should be knighted to mark his 90th birthday and the Duke of Cornwall should go down to dub him. . . . It should be no ordinary knighthood, but, as befits a man who has done so much to recapture our chivalric and heroic past, Dr. Rowse should become a Knight of the Garter."

F128. "Haunted Forever by the Dark Lady" (*Weekly Telegraph,* **November 24–30, 1993, p. 3)**
Interview/article by Martyn Harris with the following caption: "A. L. Rowse's outspoken views—and claim to have discovered Shakespeare's elusive figure—have made him a controversial voice in the academic worlds of history and literature for many years. But, aged 90 next month, how does he reconcile himself to continuing hostility in his old age?"
Note. Originally published in the *Daily Telegraph,* November 17, 1993.

F129. Editorial Paragraph with Photograph (*The Times*, **December 3, 1993, p. 18, col. e)**
"Tomorrow A. L. Rowse, poet, Cornishman, fellow of All Souls and historian of Tudor England celebrates his 90th birthday."

F130. "No Shrinking Violet, He" (*Independent, Colour Magazine,* **December 4, 1993, pp. 29, 30, 32)**
Interview/article by Adam Sisman with the following caption: "A. L. Rowse is 90 years old today, and as convinced as ever that he is a genius, undervalued by third-rate minds. Adam Sisman met the cantankerous scholar in Cornwall." [Illustrated with photograph by George Wright.]

F131. "Londoner's Diary/Not Gone but Forgotten" (*Evening Standard,* **December 31, 1993, p. 8)**
Article: "That Distinguished Cornish historian, Professor A. L. Rowse, who has just turned 90, is in for a belated shock. For a forthcoming book, *Something in Linoleum* by Paul Vaughan, implies he is already dead."

F132. "Diary/Gay Bard of Avon" (*The Times*, **January 28, 1994, p. 14, col. b)**
Note: "Round two in a battle over William Shakespeare's personal life is enjoined. The combative 90-year-old historian A. L. Rowse and Martin Seymour-Smith, who famously clashed 30 years ago when the latter claimed the Bard's sonnets were written for a homosexual lover, have locked horns again."

F133. "Bligh Spirit" (*Australian Antique Collector,* **January-June 1994, pp. 57–58)**
Article by Sydney Cauveren quoting Bligh's fellow Cornishman A. L. Rowse from a review originally printed in the *Financial Times* (London), July 3, 1982.

F134. Could This Man's Mind Have Thought Up the Great Works? Some doubt whether Shakespeare, a "Warwickshire lad," was capable of writing the plays attributed to him (*Daily Telegraph,* **August 30, 1994**)
Article (by Allan Massie, who argues that all a great author really needs is a vivid imagination): "If both Ben Jonson in the 17th century and Dr. Rowse in our own have been certain that Shakespeare wrote Shakespeare, that is more than good enough for me".
Note. Reprinted in the *Weekly Telegraph,* September 7–13, 1994.

F135. "N.B." (*Times Literary Supplement,* **November 11, 1994, p. 16, cols. b–c)**
Columnist (signed "D.S.") comments on The BBC's Shakespeare season, "Bard on the Box" and refers to a "vintage performance by A. L. Rowse, writing in the *Daily Telegraph* (October 22) . . . explaining just why Shakespeare still matters, in that straightforward style so rarely met with in today's complex world."

F136. "N.B." (*Times Literary Supplement,* **December 23, 1994, p. 14, cols. c–d)**
Columnist ("D.S.") comments on an extraordinary Radio 4 interview in which "perhaps the greatest living Celt, A. L. Rowse, made an entertaining appearance on December 16, chatting to Ned Sherrin in the first programme in a new series of 'Ninety Not Out' (conversations with still living nonagenarians). Dr. Rowse was in fine form."

F137. "Warts and All, A Rude Historian of Genius" (*Sunday Times,* **April 2, 1995, p. 7, cols. a–g)**
Norman Stone, professor of modern history at Oxford, defends the flawed genius of the late A. J. P. Taylor against a fresh onslaught from an academic enemy. A defense of Taylor, against the portrait by A. L. Rowse in his memoir *Historians I Have Known.*

F138. "Londoner's Diary/Death Sentence" (*Evening Standard,* **July 10, 1995, p. 8)**
Article: "A. L. Rowse is alive and living in Cornwall. His existence is in ostentatious defiance of a book which has repeatedly suggested that he is dead. . . . *Something in Linoleum* by Paul Vaughan . . . now the paperback edition . . . publisher credits a Rowse poem to 'the estate of A. L. Rowse, and Jonathan Cape.' The inference is that Rowse is no longer on the scene."

F139. "How Historian Rowse Settles a Few Old Scores" (*Sunday Telegraph,* **August 27, 1995, p. 8)**
Article by John Gaskell about controversies in *Historians I Have Known,* published on September 21.

F140. "Londoner's Diary" (*Evening Standard,* **August 30, 1995, p. 8)**
Article: "Connoisseurs of bile have long cherished A. L. Rowse. His forthcoming *Historians I Have Known* does not disappoint."

F141. "In Bed with the History Man/Terry Coleman interviews A. L. Rowse at 91—our most colourful historian—over Cornish cream to discuss sex, the monarchy, and his new book" (*London Evening Standard*, September 21, 1995, p. 28, col. a)

Interview/article (by Terry Coleman): "A. L. Rowse, the great and notorious Cornishman, Tudor historian and discoverer of Shakespeare's dark lady of the sonnets, is now 91 and spends most of his time in bed, in a room where his window overlooks St. Austell Bay. He is a big man lying there, with a fine head. His voice is strong and his convictions implacable, and he is frisky. He told me to pull up a chair. 'We'll have some tea, dear. Come nearer, if you dare.'"

F142. "Why Does the Establishment Hate Our Best Historian?" (*Evening Standard*, January 29, 1996, p. 16)

Article (by A. N. Wilson): "The redoubtable 92-year-old Cornishman A. L. Rowse, is, beyond question, the most distinguished popular historian still alive, worthy to be spoken of in the same breath as Lord Macaulay. But he is not Lord Rowse. . . . But if you mention in Establishment circles that Rowse deserves at least a knighthood, you can be sure of being shouted down by The Great And The Good . . . Why? Considered on merit alone, Rowse seems not just deserving, but an eminently 20th-century phenomenon. . . . But what is it about Rowse that sticks in the throat of the Establishment? . . . People, especially Establishment people, are extraordinarily thin-skinned and touchy. They don't like being dismissed as third-raters. . . . When I asked a Cabinet Minister why Rowse hadn't got a knighthood, he told me that he had asked the Prime Minister the same question and been told that it had been vetoed by a small body of men who have power over such things. He told me who was responsible for the veto—a knight and an O.M. [Sir Isaiah Berlin O.M.—from an anonymous source.] The Duke of Cornwall, aka Prince Charles, is known to revere this great Shakespearian and doughty man-of-letters. The Prince should ask the Queen to overrule the stuffpots and give Leslie Rowse the knighthood he deserves."

F143. "Historian Suffers Stroke" (*Cornish Guardian* [St. Austell and District], July 27, 1996, p. 1)

Report: "Historian and author A. L. Rowse was said to be 'comfortable'" after suffering a stroke at his Trenarren home." [A. L. Rowse suffered his major stroke on Tuesday evening July 23, 1996, and was found by his housekeeper, Valerie Brokenshire, when she arrived for work on Wednesday morning.]

F144. "Doyen of Shakespearians Gets the Dramatist Just So/Great Writer: Cornishman's life of literary and historical contribution reaches next milestone" (*Western Morning News* [Plymouth], November 28, 1996, p. 15)

Article by Dr. James Whetter paying tribute to Dr. A. L. Rowse on his approaching 93rd birthday and his latest book *My View of Shakespeare*. Illustrated with fine photograph over the following caption: "Dr. A. L. Rowse: Supreme scholar of Shakespeare."

F145. "Famous Historian Celebrates 93rd Birthday" (*Cornish Guardian,* **December 7, 1996, p. 2**)
Report with small photograph of A. L. Rowse in bed, pictured with Sheila Downes.

F146. "New Year Honours/Rowse Finally Honoured at 93" (*Western Morning News,* **December 31, 1996, p. 9**)
Report: "Dr. A. L. Rowse, a charismatic and unfailingly controversial scholar affectionately known as "the greatest living Cornishman," at last appears in an honours list at the age of 93. Conspicious by his omission from these lists for decades, he has been made a Companion of Honour in recognition of his prolific and invariably colourful services to history and literature. . . . Apart from a knighthood, which he never coveted, and the even more exclusive Order of Merit, it is the highest honour available and he is believed to be the first Cornishman to be awarded it." [Illustrated with file photograph of Dr. Rowse seated at his desk in the drawing room at Trenarren.]

F147. "Prince Sends His Special Message to Poet/Dr. A. L. Rowse: Charles was 'delighted' to receive copy of book" (*Western Morning News,* **January 1, 1997, p. 5**)
Report (by James Mildren): "A telegram from Prince Charles was among many messages of congratulations that poured into Dr. A. L. Rowse's home at Trenarren, St. Austell, yesterday, from all over the country. 'I was so delighted to hear the splendid news of your honour,' wrote the Prince, 'and wanted to send you my warmest possible congratulations.'" [Illustrated with a photograph by Tony Carney.]

F148. "First Honour" (*Cornish Guardian,* **January 2, 1997, p. 2**)
Report on Dr. Rowse being made a Companion of Honour: "He is one of only 65 Companions of Honour."

F149. "Albany/No Honours Easy for A. L. Rowse" (*Weekly Telegraph,* **January 8, 1997**)
Article (by Kenneth Rose): "Behind the appointment of Dr. A. L. Rowse to be a Companion of Honour lies a protracted campaign to thwart his enemies in high places. The work of our leading Elizabethan historian could—and should—have won some recognition from the Crown at any time in the past half-century. It has been delayed until his 94th year and declining health. . . . The award nevertheless reflects well on a Prime Minister who has risen to the occasion after others had felt unable to overrule a panel of advisers on honours, themselves garlanded like Christmas trees."

F150. "Queen's Tribute to Top Cornish Scholar A. L. Rowse" (*Western Morning News,* **March 8, 1997**)
Report: "Internationally respected Dr. A. L. Rowse made more history at the age of 93 yesterday when he became the first Cornishman to be presented with

a Companion of Honour gold medal. . . . Since suffering a stroke last summer he has been confined to his home where the honour was presented to him yesterday on behalf of the Queen by Cornwall's Lord Lieutenant Lady Mary Holborow."

F151. "Love's Labour's Found—Honouring the Literary Legacy of A. L. Rowse, C.H." (*Biblio,* **August 1997, pp. 52–57**)
Article by Sydney Cauveren details the author's story of his friendship with and reasons for compiling A. L. Rowse's bibliography.

F152. "Tributes to 'Greatest Historian' Rowse/Prince One of the Last Visitors" (*Sunday Independent,* **October 5, 1997**)
Report (by Stuart Fraser): "Cornwall was last night mourning the death of the writer revered as "the greatest living Cornishman."

F153. "Historian A. L. Rowse Dies" (*Sunday Telegraph,* **October 5, 1997**)
Report (by Catherine Elsworth): "Tributes were paid yesterday to Dr. Alfred Leslie Rowse, the eminent historian, poet, academic and discoverer of Shakespeare's Dark Lady of the sonnets. He died on Friday aged 93."
Reprinted in the *Cornish Banner,* November 1997, p. 7.

F154. "Scholar with an Acid Tongue/Kenneth Rose pays tribute to a friend whose mind was razor-sharp to the end" (*Sunday Telegraph,* **October 5, 1997**)
Article (by Kenneth Rose): "The last time I saw Dr. A. L. Rowse was shortly before his 93rd birthday, when two of his proteges, William Waldegrave and myself, went to see him at his house in Cornwall."
Reprinted in the *Cornish Banner,* November 1997, p. 7.

F155. "Rowse, Finder of the Dark Lady, Dies at 93" (*Sunday Times,* **October 5, 1997, p. 12**)
Report (by Rajeev Syal): "A. L. Rowse, the combative British historian and Elizabethan scholar who claimed to have identified the elusive Dark Lady of William Shakespeare's sonnets has died, aged 93."

F156. "Cornwall Honours Giant of Literature/Special memorial service planned to mark A. L. Rowse's achievements" (*Western Morning News,* **October 6, 1997, pp. 1, 4**)
Report (by Robert Jobson): "Friends of Dr. A. L. Rowse, the greatest Cornishman of this century who has died at his home near St. Austell aged 93, are planning a fitting memorial service to mark his vast contributions to Cornwall."

F157. "Cornwall's Greatest Son Took On World and Won/China clay country boy grew up to be Duchy's most passionate scholar and ambassador" (*Western Morning News,* **October 6, 1997, p. 4**)
Article by Robert Jobson, who looks back on Dr. Rowse's distinguished life.

Article by Douglas Williams, who pays a personal tribute as he recalls travelling with Dr. Rowse to and from the annual Humphry Davy Lecture in 1983.

F158. "Obituaries: A. L. Rowse" (*The Times*, **October 6, 1997, p. 23**)
"An historian and autobiographer of rare quality, A. L. Rowse was a man whose work was too often sadly defaced by trivial absurdities. His splendid gifts and solid accomplishment were easily devalued by his rivals since he himself provided them, in abundance, with the means of doing so." [Reprinted in the *Cornish Banner*, November 1997, pp. 9, 10.]

F159. "The People's Don/ A. L. Rowse proved Parnassus could be visited by all" (*The Times*, **October 6, 1997, p. 21**)
Editorial: "Born just after the turn of the present century, A. L. Rowse has died sadly too soon to see in the turn of the next. But the historian, poet and Shakespearian scholar leaves much that can and should be built on."
Reprinted in the *Cornish Banner,* November 1997, p. 8.

F160. "Rowse Papers for University" (*Daily Telegraph,* **October 6, 1997**)
Report (by Tim King): "The library and papers of A. L. Rowse, the historian, poet and Shakespeare scholar, whose death at the age of 93 was announced at the weekend, are being deposited with Exeter University."

F161. "Obituaries: A. L. Rowse/Combative scholar of the Elizabethan Age who wrote 90 books and claimed to have solved the puzzles of Shakespeare's sonnets" (*Daily Telegraph,* **October 6, 1997, p. 23**)
Anonymous tribute: "A. L. Rowse, who has died aged 93, was one of the most controversial, prolific, and prickly scholars of the century." Reprinted in the *Weekly Telegraph,* October 15, 1997, p. 35, and in the *Cornish Banner,* November 1997, p. 13.

F162. "Wide-ranging Rowse" (*Daily Telegraph,* **October 6, 1997, p. 21**)
Editorial: "The irascible historian, poet and professional Cornishman A. L. Rowse was, as he would have been first to insist, 'sui generis.' But he was also one of the last examples of a man who tilled many furrows in the field of scholarship, and was able to present the fruits of his labours to a wide market."

F163. "Obituaries: A. L. Rowse" (*Independent,* **October 6, 1997, p. 16**)
Tribute (by Jack Simmons): "A. L. Rowse was among the outstanding personalities in Britain of his time. As historian, poet, essayist, commentator on politics and many other branches of public life, he was quick and witty, forthright, often brilliant and never afraid of the consequences of his plain speaking."
Tribute (by James Fergusson): "A. L. Rowse will, like Horace, not altogether die. 'The true sign of genius,' he rejoiced in a dictum of Goethe's, 'is posthumous productivity.' Prodigiously prolific in his lifetime, Rowse boasted that he would be even more prolific in death. He leaves behind him a vast mass of papers, an archive of unpublished work and correspondence that, he said, would make the Yale editions of Boswell and Johnson look like a minor cottage industry." [Reprinted in the *Independent International,* October 8, 1997, p. 18;

both tributes were reprinted in the *Cornish Banner,* November 1997, pp. 11–12.]

F164. "Obituaries: A. L. Rowse/New Elizabethan" (*Guardian,* **October 6, 1997, p. 13)**
Tribute (by Charles Nevin): "A. L. Rowse, who has died aged 93, was one of those rare but familiar figures in English letters whose entertaining personality, longevity and matching output rather interfered with a proper consideration of his reputation." [Reprinted anonymously in the *Sydney Morning Herald,* October 7, 1997, p. 32.]

F165. "A. L. Rowse, Masterly Shakespeare Scholar, Dies at 93/Wrote some 90 books, and said he settled the Dark Lady mystery" (*New York Times,* **October 6, 1997, p. B7)**
Tribute (by Robert McG. Thomas, Jr.): "A. L. Rowse, the brilliant authority on Shakespeare and Elizabethan England whose grandiose opinions of his scholarship were not always shared by rival historians he invariably dismissed as third-rate, died on Friday at his home in Cornwall."

F166. "Hardcastle/Ephraim" (*Daily Mail,* **October 9, 1997, p. 11)**
Paragraph: "The death at 93 of historian A. L. Rowse, Emeritus Fellow of All Souls, may herald the diaries of the century. Dr. Rowse was a waspish bachelor who knew all of the top royal, political and social figures and noted everything."

F167. "Speculation Begins on A. L. Rowse's Biography" (*West Briton,* **October 9, 1997, p. 1)**
Front page report: "The funeral service for Cornish historian and poet A. L. Rowse took place at Bodmin yesterday and speculation has already started on the likely contents of a forthcoming biography, writes Richard Shimell."

F168. "Above All Else a Cornishman/Historian and poet mellowed little with old age" (*West Briton,* **October 9, 1997, p. 5)**
Tribute (by "J. B."): "The former editor of the *West Briton* once observed of A. L. Rowse that to much of his writing on history he gave the quality of poetry and to his poetry, the quality of history. In doing so, Claude Berry at once encapsulated the substance and feeling of Dr. Rowse's work."

F169. "Dr. A. L. Rowse, 1903–1997" (*West Briton,* **October 9, 1997, p. 6)**
A collection of tributes from various persons, including Cyril Bunn and Douglas Williams.

F170. "Dr. A. L. Rowse, 1903–1997/Tributes to Proud Genius/Richard Shimell reflects upon the controversial life of an entertaining yet outrageous personality" (*West Briton,* **October 9, 1997, p. 7)**
A collection of tributes with the following subheadings: "He was only difficult in a Cornish way" and "Honoured by Queen."

F171. "Time and Tide/Obituaries/Historian defied literary critics" *(Australian,* **October 10, 1997, p. 13)**
Tribute (by Sydney Cauveren): "Tudor historian and man of letters Dr. A. L. Rowse was one of Cornwall's greatest citizens, and one of Britain's most prolific and interesting literary figures."

F172. "Obituary/ A. L. Rowse/A Modern Elizabethan" *(Economist,* **October 18, 1997, p. 108)**
Tribute (anonymous): "The Books that A. L. Rowse became famous for are a vivid recreation of Elizabethan England. They have sold in large numbers. His admirers said that, as a popular historian, he was as good as Macaulay."

F173. "Dark Theories" *(Weekly Telegraph,* **October 22, 1997, p. 26)**
Letter to the editor (by Peter Bassano): "Sadly A. L. Rowse is no longer with us to hector those who disagree with his identification of Emilia Bassano as the Dark Lady. . . . Rowse 'found' Emilia—daughter of one of the Queen's Venetian musicians and from whose uncle Anthony I am decended . . . through a description of her in the diaries of the Elizabethan astrologer Simon Forman . . . 'Titus Andronicus' has an Aemilius and a Bassianus . . . Shakespeare's two Venetian plays—'Othello' and 'The Merchant'—have an Emilia in one and a Bass(i)ano in the other."

F174. "Loyalty, Passion, and Poetry/Richard Ollard uncovers the vulnerability of Tudor historian A. L. Rowse" *(Daily Telegraph,* **November 8, 1997, p. A6)**
Feature (by Richard Ollard): "Four years ago, I was asked if I would write the biography of A. L. Rowse, then in his late eighties. I accepted on condition that nothing I wrote should appear during his lifetime and that I should have exclusive access to all his papers until he died. He gladly accepted."

F175. "Dr. A. L. Rowse" *(Cornish Banner,* **November 1997, p. 3)**
Tribute (by James Whetter): "One thinks of Dr. Rowse's place in history. Looking from the angle of Cornwall one can see that little land, as he would call it, has produced no writer of such talent and phenomenal output, in this century, ever. One thinks of Quiller-Couch, Borlase, Carew, there is no one to compare."
    Note. pp. 7-13 reprints tributes from national presses re A. L. Rowse and as recorded above.

F176. "In the Margins/Letters to the Editor and Commentary/In Memory" *(Biblio,* **December 1997, p. 8)**
Editorial tribute: "*Biblio* joins the worldwide community of bibliophiles in mourning the passing of Elizabethan and Shakespearian scholar A. L. Rowse."

F177. "Remembering A. L. Rowse" *(Shakespeare Newsletter* **[USA], Summer/Fall 1997, p. 53)**
Tribute (by Stephanie Cowell): "He was old enough to be my grandfather. He came into my life on blue airmail stationery postmarked St. Austell, Cornwall, some ten years ago. I was beginning a novel about an Elizabethan actor, and having just discovered his books, wrote him in deep admiration."

F178. "Farewell to Cornwall's Leading Man of Letters/Friends and admirers fill St. Austell church to remember Dr. A. L. Rowse" (*Western Morning News,* **December 5, 1997, p. 7)**
Report (by Robert Jobson): "Two hundred friends and admirers of Dr. A. L. Rowse, one of the greatest Cornishmen of this century, converged from all over the county yesterday to attend his memorial service in St. Austell."

F179. "Cob-walled Cottages the Colour of Clotted Cream and Saffron" (*Western Morning News,* **December 5, 1997, p. 7)**
Extract, abridged, from *A Cornish Childhood.*

F180. "A. L. Rowse: Tony Capstick Pays Tribute to the Distinguished Historian and Biographer" (*Book and Magazine Collector* **[UK], December, 1997, pp. 72–81)**
Article by Tony Capstick. Includes a potted book listing of U.K. first editions and a guide to current values.

F181. "A. L. Rowse: In Memoriam" (*Contemporary Review,* **December 1997, pp. 300–304)**
Article by Eric Glasgow.

F182. "Obituaries" (*Current Biography,* **January 1998, p. 61)**
Anonymous tribute.

F183. "Obituaries/A. L. Rowse" (*Oxford Today: The University Magazine,* **Hilary Issue 1998, p. 53)**
Anonymous tribute.

BROADCASTS

Note. In 1924 and 1925, two pioneering BBC broadcasts of poetry readings were presented by Oxford undergraduates, including A. L. Rowse, Graham Greene, Harold Acton, and P. Monkhouse. (See *A Cornishman at Oxford,* pp.138, 206; see also G41.)

1933

F201. "Makers of the Modern Spirit." Talk written and read by. BBC Radio Broadcast, March 27, 1933. Script held at BBC Written Archives Centre (WAC).

F202. "Queen Elizabeth 1533–1933." Talk written and read by. BBC Radio Broadcast, September 20, 1933. Script at BBC (WAC).

1934

F203. "Queen Elizabeth's Subjects—William Cecil, Lord Burghley." Talk written and read by. BBC Radio Broadcast, April 8, 1934. Script at BBC (WAC).

F204. "Queen Elizabeth's Subjects—The Earl of Essex." Talk written and read by. BBC Radio Broadcast, April 22, 1934. Script at BBC (WAC). See also D68.

F205. "Queen Elizabeth's Subjects—Sir Walter Raleigh." Talk written and read by. BBC Radio Broadcast, May 6, 1934. Script at BBC (WAC). See also D70.

F206. "Queen Elizabeth's Subjects—Cardinal Allen." Talk written and read by. BBC Radio Broadcast, May 20, 1934. Script at BBC (WAC). See also D71.

1937

F207. "Admirals All—Plymouth and the Hawkins Family." Talk written and read by. BBC Radio Broadcast, August 7, 1937. Script at BBC (WAC).

F208. "Admirals All—Merchants and Adventurers of Bristol." Talk written and read by. BBC Radio Broadcast, September 18, 1937. Script at BBC (WAC).

1939

F209. "Sir Richard Grenville of Stow." Talk written and read by. BBC Radio—Regional, February 23, 1939. Script held at BBC (WAC).

F210. "John Opie at Harmony Cot." Talk written and read by. BBC Radio—Regional, May 10, 1939. Script at BBC (WAC). See also D162.

F211. "The Hoods and the British Naval Tradition." Talk written and read by. BBC Radio Broadcast, December 9, 1939. Script at BBC (WAC). See also D169.

1940

F212. "This Heritage—The British Tradition." Talk written and read by. BBC Radio Broadcast, October 26, 1940. Script at BBC (WAC).

1941

F213. "Cornish Yarn—How Dick Stephens Fought the Bear." Short story written and read by. BBC Home Service, March 15, 1941. Script at BBC (WAC). See also D205.

1942

F214. "Poems of Cornwall." Poetry written and read by. BBC Home Service, August 3, 1942. Script at BBC (WAC).

F215. "We Speak to India—Some Books." E. M. Forster reviews recent books of interest to English-speaking people in India. Reviews *A Cornish Childhood* by. BBC Overseas Service-Eastern Transmission in the English Language, October 14, 1942. Script at BBC (WAC).

F216. "Passage from the Bible in Spain by George Barrow." Talk written and read by. BBC Radio Broadcast, December 11, 1942. Script at BBC (WAC).

1944

F217. "Poets of Today." Poetry written and read by. BBC Radio Broadcast, June 29, 1944. Script at BBC (WAC) See also D263.

1945

F218. "The Patterns of English Life." Talk written and read by. BBC Radio Broadcasts, April 28, July 7–8, 1945. Scripts at BBC (WAC).

F219. "Western Readings No. 6—The Story of Polrudden." Short story written and read by. BBC Home Service-West, September 16, 1945.

F220. "Western Men No. 5—Sir Arthur Quiller-Couch." Talk written and read by. BBC Home Service-West, October 5, 1945. Script at BBC (WAC).

F221. "West-Country Short Stories—The Beneficent Shoes." Short story written and read by. BBC Home Service-West, December 20, 1945. Script at BBC (WAC).

1946

F222. "Literature in the West." Talk written and read by. BBC Home Service-West, January 6, 1946.

F223. "Literature in the West—R. Carew." Talk written and read by. BBC Home Service-West, January 7, 1946. Script at BBC (WAC).

F224. "The English Way of Life." Talk written and read by. BBC Radio Broadcast, March 31, 1946. Script at BBC (WAC).

F225. "If You Had Lived Then—Life in Elizabethan England in 1600 AD." Talk written and read by. BBC Home Service, May 6, 1946. Script at BBC (WAC). See also D274.

F226. "Literature in the West—Sidney Godolphin: The Cavalier Poet." Talk written and read by. BBC Home Service-West, May 19, 1946. Script at BBC (WAC).

F227. "Do Great Men Make History?" Participated in talk. BBC Radio Broadcast, July 30, 1946. Script at BBC (WAC).

F228. "On the Map—St. Michael's Mount." Talk written and read by. BBC Home Service-West, August 1, 1946. Script at BBC (WAC).

F229. "The Brains Trust." Participated in talk. BBC Home Service, October 22, 1946.

1947

F230. "Literature in the West—James Anthony Froude." Talk written and read by. BBC Home Service-West, April 11, 1947. Script at BBC (WAC).

F231. "Writers and Places—Tennyson in Cornwall." Talk written and read by. BBC Home Service-West, June 22, 1947. Script at BBC (WAC).

F232. "Reader Takes Over." Talk written and read by. BBC North American Service, October 15–16, 1947. Script at BBC (WAC).

1948

F233. "Stories from Studio Five—The Stone That Liked Company." Short story written and read by. BBC Home Service-West, June 3, 1948. Script at BBC (WAC).

1949

F234. "The West in England's Story—The West and English History." Talk written and read by. BBC Home Service-West, February 1, 1949. Script at BBC (WAC).

F235. "The West in England's Story—Tudor Cornwall." Talk written and read by. BBC Home Service-West, March 15, 1949. Script at BBC (WAC).

F236. "The West in England's Story—The Spirit of the West." Talk written and read by. BBC Home Service-West, May 31, 1949. Script at BBC (WAC).

F237. "What Is the Future of British Education?" Participated in talk. BBC General Overseas Service, October 17, 1949. Script at BBC (WAC).

1950

F238. *For Your Book List.* Reviews *The West in English History* by. BBC Home Service-West, June 23, 1950.

F239. *The Royal Family* by Dermot Morrah. Reviewed by. BBC Home Service, December 15, 1950. Script at BBC (WAC).

1951

F240. *For Your Book List.* Reviews *The England of Elizabeth* by. BBC Home Service-West, January 16, 1951.

F241. *Elizabeth's England.* C. J. Sisson reviews *The England of Elizabeth* by. BBC Broadcast, February 27, 1951.

F242. *What Shall I Read?* Reviews *The England of Elizabeth* by. BBC Broadcast, March 12, 1951.

1952

F243. *Devonshire Studies* by W. G. Hoskins and H. P. R. Finberg, and *Tavistock Abbey* by H. P. R. Finberg, both reviewed by. BBC Broadcast, May 18, 1952. Script at BBC (WAC).

1953

F244. *Talking of Books.* Reviews *The England of Elizabeth* by. BBC Home Service, June 28, 1953.

F245. "**Midweek Talk—Reflections on Coronation Year.**" Talk written and read by. BBC General Overseas Service, December 30, 1953. Script at BBC (WAC).

1954

F246. "**Week's Good Cause—Restoration Fund of Maker Church, Cornwall.**" Talk written and read by. BBC Home Service-West, September 5, 1954.

1955

F247. "**Portraits from the Past—Sir Walter Raleigh.**" Talk written and read by. BBC Home Service, June 19, 1955. Script at BBC (WAC). See also D329.

F248. "**Writers in the West.**" E. W. Martin speaks about A. L. Rowse. BBC Home Service-West, July 5, 1955.

F249. *The Critics.* Reviews *The Expansion of Elizabethan England* by. BBC Home Service, December 26, 1955.

1956

F250. "**Signature.**" On John Betjeman. Talk written and read by. BBC Home Service-West, April 13, 1956.

F251. *Books to Read. History of the English-Speaking Peoples* by Sir Winston Churchill. Reviewed by. BBC General Overseas Service, April 25, 1956. Script at BBC (WAC).

F252. "**Buckland Abbey.**" Participated in talk. BBC Home Service-West, May 15, 1956. Script at BBC (WAC).

F253. "**Our Ways of Life—The Various Peoples Who Make Up British Stock.**" Talk written and read by. BBC General Overseas Service, May 17, 1956. Script at BBC (WAC).

F254. "**Dear To My Heart—'Seeing' the things you look at.**" Talk written and read by. BBC Home Service-West, October 15, 1956. Script at BBC (WAC).

F255. "Rowse's Ark." Talk written and read by. BBC Home Service, October 21, 1956. Script at BBC (WAC).

1957

F256. "A. L. Rowse As a Literary Man." Poetry written and read by. BBC Home Service-West, January 29, 1957.

F257. "The Britain We Know—The Cornish Coast." Talk written and read by. BBC General Overseas Service, February 28, 1957. Script at BBC (WAC).

F258. "Jamestown 1607." Talk written and read by. BBC General Overseas Service, May 13, 1957. Script at BBC (WAC).

F259. *The World of Books.* Sir Winston Churchill's third volume of his *History of the English-Speaking Peoples: The Age of Revolution.* Reviewed by. BBC Network 3,October 12, 1957. Script at BBC (WAC).

F260. *Just Published.* Interviewed by Kenneth Hudson about his book *The Churchills.* BBC Home Service-West, October 27, 1957. Script at BBC (WAC).

1958

F261. *Town Forum.* Participated in talk. BBC Broadcast, February 5, 1958.

F262. "A Portrait of 'Q.'" Talk written and read by. BBC Home Service, May 4, 1958.

F263. *The Critics.* Reviews *The Later Churchills* by. BBC Home Service, July 20, 1958.

1959

F264. "The Elizabethans and America—The Contribution of the Queen." Talk written and read by. BBC Home Service, January 28, 1959. Script at BBC (WAC).

F265. "The Elizabethans and America—Virginia and New England." Talk written and read by. BBC Home Service, January 29, 1959. Script at BBC (WAC).

F266. *Books and Authors.* Reviews *Poems Partly American* by. BBC Home Service-West, February 16, 1959.

F267. *The World of Books*. Reviews *Poems Partly American* by. BBC Network 3, April 4, 1959.

F268. *Prose and Verse Readings.* From *West-Country Stories,* "How Dick Stephens Fought the Bear." Short story written and read by. BBC Home Service, June 29, 1959. Script at BBC (WAC).

F269. "Wales through the Ages." Talk written and read by. BBC Wales, December 16, 1959.

1960

F270. *Round Up.* Interviewed about his book *St. Austell: Church, Town, Parish.* BBC Home Service-West, October 10, 1960.

1961

F271. *Round Up.* Reviews *A Cornish Childhood* by. BBC Home Service-West, June 21, 1961.

F272. *Time at Trenarren.* Interviewed by Charles Causley about his life, work and childhood in Cornwall. BBC Home Service-West, September 17, 1961. Script at BBC (WAC).

1962

F273. *The Critics.* Reviews *Ralegh and the Throckmortons* by. BBC Home Service, April 8, 1962.

F274. *Books and Authors.* Reviews *Ralegh and the Throckmortons* by. BBC Home Service-West, May 10, 1962.

1963

F275. *The Masters.* On Rudyard Kipling. Participated in talk. BBC Home Service, April 16, 1963. Script at BBC (WAC).

F276. *Woman's Hour.* Guest of the week. BBC Home Service, May 22, 1963.

F277. *Today.* Interviewed on *Who Was the Dark Lady of the Sonnets?* BBC Home Service, September 20, 1963.

F278. *Ten O'Clock News.* Interviewed on new Shakespeare biography. BBC Home Service, September 20, 1963.

F279. *The World of Books.* Reviews *William Shakespeare: A Biography* by. BBC Home Service, November 2, 1963.

F280. "The Advowson of Lambethow." Short story written and read by. BBC Home Service, December 11, 1963. Script at BBC (WAC).

1964

F281. *Voice of the North.* Interviewed in Leeds. BBC Home Service-North, May 7, 1964.

F282. *The World of Books.* Interviewed by Lionel Hale about his book *Christopher Marlowe.* BBC Home Service, September 5, 1964. Script at BBC (WAC).

1965

F283. *The Critics.* Janet Adam Smith reviews *A Cornishman at Oxford* by. BBC Home Service, January 31,1965.

F284. *The First of the Cornish Painters.* An appraisal of the life and work of Peter Lanyon. Participated in talk. BBC Home Service-West, February 26, 1965.

F285. "Prose and Verse Readings No. 8—How Dick Stephens Fought the Bear." Short story written and read by. BBC Home Service, June 28, 1965. Script at BBC (WAC).

F286. "The Interval—The Cornish in America." Talk written and read by. BBC Home Service, September 17, 1965. Script at BBC (WAC). See also D412.

1966

F287. "The Wicked Vicar of Lansillian." Short story written and read by. BBC Home Service, April 12, 1966.

F288. "The Choirmaster of Carluddon." Short story written and read by. BBC Home Service-West, May 12, 1966. See also D418.

F289. *The Masters—John Betjeman.* Participated in talk. BBC Home Service, August 25, 1966. Script at BBC (WAC).

F290. *Home This Afternoon—Looking at Books.* Reviews *A Cornishman at Oxford* by. BBC Home Service, October 10, 1966.

F291. "The Squire of Reluggas." Short story written and read by. BBC Home Service-West, November 10, 1966.

1967

F292. *Woman's Hour—Paper Backs.* Joan Yorks reviews *The Churchills* by. BBC Home Service, March 6, 1967.

F293. *The World of Books.* Alan Gibson reviews *Cornish Stories* and *Poems of Cornwall and America* by. BBC Home Service, April 11, 1967.

F294. "Night at the Carn." Short story written and read by. BBC Radio 4, October 27, 1967. Script at BBC (WAC).

1968

F295. *Scenes That Are Brightest.* A. L. Rowse speaks from "Time at Trenarren" (ex September 17, 1961). BBC Radio 4, June 23, 1968. See F272.

F296. *Today from the South and West.* Tom Salmon reviews *A Cornish Anthology* by. BBC Home Service, November 20, 1968.

F297. ***Woman's Hour.*** Review of *Bosworth Field: And the Wars of the Roses* by. BBC Radio 2, December 9, 1968.

1969

F298. ***Home This Afternoon—From My Library Van.*** Reviews *A Cornish Anthology* by. BBC Radio 4, March 24, 1969.

F299. ***Home This Afternoon—Books I Like.*** Reviews *William Shakespeare: A Biography* by. BBC Radio 4, March 31, 1969.

F300. **"Three Cornish Blacksmiths."** Short story written and read by. BBC Radio 4, April 4, 1969.

F301. **"Interval Talk—The End of the Line."** Short story written and read by. BBC Radio 4, September 24, 1969. Script at BBC (WAC).

1970

F302. ***Home This Afternoon—Books for Your Tokens.*** Reviews *The Churchills* by. BBC Radio 4, January 19, 1970.

F303. ***Scenes That Are Brightest.*** Speaks from "Time at Trenarren" (September 17, 1961). BBC Radio 4, April 10, 1970. See F272, F295.

F304. **"With Great Pleasure."** Paul Rogers reviews *A Cornish Childhood* by. BBC Radio 4, May 10, 1970.

F305. **"The Time of My Life."** Autobiographical talk written and read by. BBC Radio 4, August 15, 1970. Repeated August 20 and selected "Pick of the Week," August 21. See also D469a, F63.

1971

F306. ***P.M.*** Interviewed by Sue McGregor on source for his Elizabethan books—the Simon Forman diaries. BBC Radio 4, October 14, 1971.

1972

F307. ***Pick of the Week—Late Night Line Up.*** Interviewed by Michael Dean about contemporary humbug. BBC Radio 4, August 11, 1972.

1973

F308. ***P.M. Reports.*** Interviewed by Gordon Clough about Shakespeare's sonnets. BBC Radio 4, January 30, 1973.

F309. ***Woman's Hour.*** Interviewed by Pamela Howe about the "Dark Lady" of the Sonnets. BBC Radio 4, April 13, 1973. Repeated extract in "The Week-Woman's Hour," April 21.

F310. *As Black As Hell—As Dark As Night.* Participated in discussion on the "Dark Lady" of Shakespeare's Sonnets. BBC Radio 4, April 22, 1973. See also F72.

F311. *Kaleidoscope.* Interviewed about *Tom of Lincoln*, Thomas Heywood's newly discovered play. BBC Radio 4, October 22, 1973. Repeated October 27.

F312. *P.M. Reports.* Interviewed on his 70th birthday. BBC Radio 4, December 4, 1973.

1974

F313. *P.M. Reports.* Interviewed about his book *Windsor Castle.* BBC Radio 4, February 26, 1974.

F314. *P.M. Reports.* Interviewed by William Hardcastle about his book *Peter: The White Cat of Trenarren.* BBC Radio 4, March 28, 1974.

F315. "Simon Forman: The Social Life of Shakespeare's Age." Explores and interprets Forman's Case Books. Talk written and read by. BBC Radio 3, April 4, 1974. See also D568.

F316. *Kaleidoscope.* Discussion about *Simon Forman: Sex and Society in Shakespeare's Age* by. BBC Radio 4, April 4, 1974. Repeated April 6.

F317. *Today.* Interviewed about his book *Simon Forman.* BBC Radio 4, April 5, 1974.

F318. *Kaleidoscope.* Victorian Townscape—participated in discussion on the work of Samuel Smith. BBC Radio 4, August 12, 1974.

1975

F319. *Discoveries.* Talks on a lifetime of historical research and writing. BBC Radio 4, April 10, 1975.

F320. *Man of Action.* Talks about his tastes in music. BBC Radio 3, May 2, 1975.

F321. *The World This Weekend.* Interviewed by John Parry about his book *Oxford in the History of the Nation.* BBC Radio 4, June 8, 1975.

F322. *Kaleidoscope.* Ronald Bryden reviews *Discoveries and Reviews from Renaissance to Restoration* by. BBC Radio 4, June 19, 1975.

F323. *Woman's Hour—Arts Notebook.* Interviewed by Sue McGregor about Elizabethan Fairs. BBC Radio 4, June 25, 1975.

F324. *Pick of the Week—Network.* Reviews *A Cornishman at Oxford* by. BBC Radio 4, July 25, 1975. Taken from BBC 2 TV, July 19.

F325. "The England of Jane Austen." Shortened version of an address to the Jane Austen Society given by. BBC Radio 3, August 21, 1975. Repeated September 18. See also B42.

F326. *Kaleidoscope.* *Golden Lads* by Daphne du Maurier. Reviewed by. BBC Radio 4, September 3, 1975.

F327. *Pick of the Week—Peninsula—Poet's Eye.* BBC Radio 4, October 17, 1975. Taken from BBC 1 TV, October 10.

F328. *P.M. Reports.* Interviewed by Barbara Myers about his book *Jonathan Swift: Major Prophet.* BBC Radio 4, November 3, 1975.

F329. *Kaleidoscope.* David Nokes reviews *Jonathan Swift: Major Prophet* by. BBC Radio 4, November 3, 1975.

1976

F330. *Eminent Historian: Great Man.* George Macaulay Trevelyan, O.M., born 100 years ago this month, is remembered by. BBC Radio 3, February 17, 1976.

F331. *The World This Weekend.* Interviewed about his book *A Cornishman Abroad.* BBC Radio 4, March 21, 1976.

F332. *Today.* Interviewed by Ludovic Kennedy about his just completed American lecture tour and Shakespearean discoveries. Also reads poem "The Choice." Filmed at Trenarren and Oxford. BBC 2 TV mid-April 1976.

F333. *Patterns of the Past.* Clive Jordan interviewed Dr. A. L. Rowse, Hugh Tait, and Dr. Peter French about the Elizabethan Dr. John Dee. BBC World Service, circa December 1976. See also F82.

1977

F334. *Any Questions?* Contribution by. BBC Radio 4, April 15, 1977. Repeated April 16, 18.

F335. *Desert Island Discs.* Celebrity Guest. BBC Radio 4, August 13, 1977. Repeated August 16.

F336. *The World Encompassed.* In this film, A. L. Rowse retells the story of Drake's four-year voyage of circumnavigation. BBC 1—South West TV, September 23, 1977.

1978

F337. *Today.* Michael Wooldridge appeals for money for a statue for the Richard III Society. Contribution by. BBC Radio 4, January 18, 1978.

F338. *My Delight.* A. L. Rowse describes one of the pleasures of life. BBC Radio 4, February 24, 1978.

F339. *Any Questions?* From the Village Hall, Crafthole, Sheviock nr. Torpoint, Cornwall. Contribution by. BBC Radio 4, May 5, 1978. Repeated May 6.

F340. *Today.* Interviewed by Helen Palmer about *The Annotated Shakespeare.* BBC Radio 4, December 1, 1978.

F341. *Pebble Mill.* Interviewed by Donny Macleod about *The Annotated Shakespeare.* BBC 1 TV, December 5, 1978.

F342. *Round Midnight.* Interviewed about *The Annotated Shakespeare.* BBC Radio 2, December 29, 1978.

1979

F343. *On Location?* Includes interview contribution by. BBC Radio 4, January 3, 1979.

F344. *Sixth Sense.* Chaired by John Earle. Students from Mid-Peninsula Cornwall College of Further Education, St. Austell, talk to. BBC 1—South West TV, January 30, 1979.

F345. *Woman's Hour.* Guest of the week. Interviewed by June Knox-Mawer about his love for cats. BBC Radio 4, May 2, 1979. Repeated August 12, in *Weekend Woman's Hour.* See also F94.

F346. *Any Questions?* From Davidstow, Cornwall. Panel contribution by. BBC Radio 4, June 29, 1979. Repeated June 30.

F347. *Kaleidoscope.* *John Buchan and His World* by Janet Adam Smith. Reviewed by. BBC Radio 4, July 9, 1979.

F348. *On Location.* Interviewed by Tom Vernon on location at Fowey. BBC Radio 4, August 9, 1979.

F349. *P.M.* Interviewed by Gordon Clough about his book *A Man of the Thirties.* BBC Radio 4, August 14, 1979.

F350. *Zodiac and Co.* Guest contribution. BBC 1-South West TV, October 23, 1979.

F351. *Midweek.* Interviewed by Russell Harty as birthday guest—76 yesterday. BBC Radio 4, December 5, 1979. See also H69.

F352. *Leeds.* TV appearance with adversaries Malcolm Muggeridge and Bernard Levin. Mid-December 1979. See also H69.

1980

F353. *Michael Parkinson Show.* Guests: Dr. A. L. Rowse, Isla St. Clair, and Shirley Williams. BBC 1 TV, February 20, 1980.

F354. "Through My Window." Voices his thoughts as he considers the view from his window overlooking the South Cornish Coast. BBC Radio 4, May 25, 1980.

F355. *Kaleidoscope.* Reprints of Rebecca West's early books: *Harriet Hume, The Judge,* and *The Return of the Soldier.* Reviewed by. BBC Radio 4, July 22, 1980.

F356. *All about Books.* *Rupert Brooke His Life and His Legend* by John Lehmann. Reviewed by. BBC 1 TV, July 24, 1980.

F357. *Our Isaac.* Interviewed about Isaac Foot, 1880–1960. BBC 1-South West TV, September 5, 1980.

F358. *Kaleidoscope.* Reprints of Flannery O'Connor's books: *The Violent Bear It Away, Wise Blood,* and *Everything That Rises Must Converge.* Paul Bailey and A. L. Rowse talked about these reissues. BBC Radio 4, October 6, 1980.

F359. *Kaleidoscope.* *John Webster: Citizen and Dramatist* by M. C. Bradbrook. Reviewed by. BBC Radio 4, November 3, 1980.

F360. *The Book Programme.* Interviewed by Robert Robinson about *Women in Shakespeare* by Judith Cook. BBC 2 TV, November 12, 1980.

F361. *Midweek.* Interviewed by Ned Sherrin about his book *Memories of Men and Women.* BBC Radio 4, December 3, 1980.

F362. *London.* Radio broadcast for Australian Broadcasting Commission. Circa early December 1980. See also H72.

1981

F363. *With Great Pleasure.* Chooses poetry that reflects his love of his native Cornwall. Written and read by. BBC Radio 4, January 11, 1981.

F364. *Bookshelf.* Interviewed by Frank Delaney about Agatha Christie and his book *Memories of Men and Women.* BBC Radio 4, January 11, 1981.

F365. *Bookshelf.* Frank Delaney reports from Stratford-on-Avon. Interviewed about the Shakespeare industry. BBC Radio 4, April 19, 1981. Repeated in *Bookshelf Year,* December 20, 1981.

F366. *John Dunn.* Interviewed by John Dunn about his book *Shakespeare's Globe: His Intellectual and Moral Outlook.* BBC Radio 2, April 23, 1981.

F367. *Kaleidoscope.* Radio 3 production of *Gulliver's Travels,* pt. 1, *Voyage to Lilliput.* Reviewed by. BBC Radio 4, October 5, 1981.

F368. *Michael Parkinson Show.* Guests: Mel Brooks, Pamela Stephenson, and Dr. A. L. Rowse. Interviewed by Michael Parkinson about his book *A Life: Collected Poems* and reads from it "On Chaplin's 'Great Dictator.'" BBC 1 TV, October 7, 1981.

F369. *I Know It's Here Somewhere.* Talks about his search for Shakespeare's "Dark Lady." BBC Radio 4, November 5, 1981.

1982

F370. *Modern Biography.* Anthony Curtis asks why and how one writes new biographies of people who have been written about before. Interviewed about Shakespeare. BBC Radio 4, October 16, 1982. Repeated August 31, 1983 and May 31, 1984.

F371. *Modern Biography.* Anthony Curtis looks at autobiography and how far the author tells the truth about himself. Interviewed about his autobiographies. BBC Radio 4, November 13, 1982. Repeated September 28, 1983 and June 28, 1984.

F372. *The Poetry of A. L. Rowse.* Program of poetry compiled and presented by Frank Baker. Written and read by. BBC Radio 3, December 11, 1982.

F373. *Women of Mystery.* Jessica Mann investigates women crime writers. Interviewed about Agatha Christie. BBC Radio 4, December 22, 1982.

1983

F374. *By St. Thomas Water.* Contribution by. BBC Radio 4, September 7, 1983.

1984

F375. *London.* Radio interview about his cat Flippy. Circa February 18–22, 1984. See also H84.

F376. *The World at One.* Interviewed by Bill Turnbull about his New Modern English version of Shakespeare plays being published in the United States. BBC Radio, April 26, 1984.

F377. *The Colour—Supplement: Right to Reply.* Talks about his version of Shakespeare's plays. BBC Radio, September 9, 1984.

1985

F378. *Oxford.* Radio interview on Shakespeare. BBC World Service, circa February 2, 1985. See also H89.

F379. *Harty Goes to Oxford.* Interviewed by Russell Harty as he takes a trip down memory lane; visits old rooms at Christ Church; in the library at All Souls talks about modernising Shakespeare. Also talks of political influences such as Ernest Bevin. Ends by reading his poem "Peopled Sleep." BBC TV, March 30, 1985. See also H89.

1987

F380. *Trenarren.* Interviewed by Lord Althorp. *Today International,* NBC TV, March 5, 1987. See also H97.

1988

F381. *Thatcher: Longest Serving P.M. This Century.* Contribution by. BBC TV, January 3, 1988.

F382. *Book Choice.* Derek Parker reviews *Quiller-Couch: A Portrait of "Q."* BBC World Service, circa April 1988.

1989

F383. *A Cornish Inheritance.* Interviewed by James Mildren about his life. Filmed at Trenarren and on location in Cornwall. Approximately 25 minutes. BBC 1-South West TV, 1989.

1990

F384. *Today.* Allan Little interviews contributors on question "what does being British mean?" BBC Radio 4, April 21, 1990.

F385. *Mightier Than the Sword: Sir Arthur Quiller-Couch.* Film profile on the life of "Q." Contribution by. BBC TV, May 11, 1990.

F386. *Trenarren.* TV interview about Agatha Christie. Circa October 8, 1990. See also H105.

1991

F387. *Trenarren.* TV interview about Christopher Marlowe. Circa late March 1991. See also H108.

F388. *Trenarren.* TV interview about Marlowe versus Shakespeare–Homo versus Hetero. Circa mid-July 1991. See also H109.

1994

F389. *Ninety Not Out.* Interviewed by Ned Sherrin. BBC Radio 4, December 16, 1994. See also F136, H138.

1997

F390. *All Things Considered.* Obituary tribute by Marcia Brandwynne and Linda Wertheimer. Anchor program, National Public Radio (NPR), Washington, D.C., October 6, 1997.

G

References to A. L. Rowse in Books by His Contemporaries

G1. *Aspects of Biography* by André Maurios. Translated from the French by S. C. Roberts (1929)

Page 95: In chapter "Biography Considered As a Science," footnote: "For a Marxist theory of history see also A. L. Rowse's remarkable little book, *On History*."

Page 97: "Professor Trevelyan has written an essay, *If Napoleon had won the Battle of Waterloo.* The argument of Rowse and of the Marxist historians is that this victory would not have greatly changed the history of the world."

Page 170: "To get a truer idea of the importance and of the atmosphere of the Revolutionary and Napoleonic era," writes Mr. Rowse, "we must leave the historians for the novelists, we must read Tolstoy's *War and Peace* and Hardy's *Dynasts,* and it is almost true."

G2. *The Literature of England, A.D. 500–1946* by William J. Entwistle and Eric Gillett, second edition (1948)

Page 254: "A. L. Rowse has written extensively in various literary forms. His one book of essays, mainly on historical subjects, showing an admirable sense of perspective, is *The English Spirit* (1944)."

Page 265: "A sharp contrast to the urbanity and tolerance of Quiller-Couch's reminiscences is provided by another Cornishman, A. L. Rowse, in his deeply felt and occasionally querulous *A Cornish Childhood.*"

G3. *Fifty Years of English Literature, 1900–1950* by R. A. Scott-James (1951)

Page 78: "Also keenly interested in contemporary life is a younger historian, A. L. Rowse (born 1903) who has sought to rediscover the social life of the past as much through local evidences as from printed matter. In 1950 he produced the first volume of a work that promises to be a very thorough as well as stimulating and provocative study of the Elizabethan Age."

Page 205: "Of the younger historians the most promising is A. L. Rowse. . . . His book *The Spirit of English History* (1943) reveals that rare gift of imagination which is necessary if history is to be an art. His comprehensive study of the Elizabethan age (the first volume of which, highly original and provocative, appeared in 1950) will owe as much to his personal examination of local relics and records as to the printed material."

G4. *Aspects of Culture* by Harry L. Shapiro (USA) (1956)

In the 1956 Brown and Haley Lectures at the College of Puget Sound, Tacoma, Washington, no. 2, under "Culture Conflict in Ireland" (pp. 75–89), extensive reference is made to *The Expansion of Elizabethan England* (1955) by A. L. Rowse.

G5. *John Buchan: A Biography* by Janet Adam Smith (1965)

Page 225: Quoted as a regular undergraduate visitor to Elsfield.

Page 320: Rowse startled by Buchan looking in at his committee room to wish him well while campaigning as a Labour candidate for Penryn and Falmouth.

G6. Lytton Strachey: *A Critical Biography*, vol. 2, *The Years of Achievement, 1910–1932* by Michael Holroyd (1968)

Page 614: A. L. Rowse quoted discussing a Strachey book.

G6a. Troubled Loyalty: A Biography of Adam von Trott zu Solz by Christopher Sykes (1968).

Numerous important references: Beginnings of friendship with von Trott, pp. 36–37; visits von Trott in Berlin (1931), p. 53; introduces von Trott to All Souls and nature of their friendship, pp. 55–59; Rowse's condemnation of Hegelianism, pp. 56–57, 63; growing estrangement from von Trott, pp. 76, 90–91; breech between them, p. 110; subsequent relationship, pp. 152, 247–248, 261.

G7. T. S. Eliot: A Memoir by Robert Sencourt (1971)

Page 100: Rowse supports Eliot for a Research Fellowship at All Souls.

G8. *Cecil Roberts: The Pleasant Years*, fifth book of autobiography (1947–1972) by Cecil Roberts (1974)

Numerous references of great interest and insight:

Page 217: "My first visit was to Oxford for the Encaenia, as the guest of my friend Dr. A. L. Rowse, at All Souls College. . . . Margot Fonteyn and Sir Robert Menzies, the Australian ex-Premier, received degrees. My friend had a beautiful suite of rooms in the second court at All Souls, whose windows looked on to the long facade of the Codrington Library. . . . His suite in All Souls College had a large, light sitting-room, the width of the wing, with a great lawn in front and a small garden behind. Here, a prodigious worker, he wrote the books that made him the foremost Elizabethan scholar of the day. . . . Leslie, volatile, omniscient, was a compulsive talker. His positiveness enraged many but woe to them if they challenged him. He flourished a battle-axe of learning over their heads, exulting in the fray. I envied not his brilliant mind but his large writing-desk."

Page 225: "In August I left to spend the week-end with Leslie Rowse at his home, Trenarren, at St. Austell, Cornwall. He had a stately Georgian house, stone built, at the summit of a deep combe, umbrageous with chestnut trees, that fell swiftly towards the sea. . . . We often walked on the rocky seacoast headlands. He took me one day to Mevagissey. . . . For some elusive reason we both had a fit of the giggles. . . . With a huge public in the U.S.A., where the Shakespeare industry flourishes, he was now high in the top-earning category of the Society of Authors' poll. Prosperity had neither dimmed his industry nor his combatant sense of humour. What would our American audiences have thought of us, seeing two elderly authors, swaying giddily with mirth in Mevagissey?"

Page 226: "One day I fell flat on my face outside All Souls College, tripped up in a storm of laughter that some remark of his had provoked. 'You know this sort of thing is fatal to our reputations,' he warned. 'The public is impressed by the solemn owl, and Oxford is its nest.' Our friendship had begun many years ago when I had written to him pointing out some grammatical errors in one of his books. I feared he might be angry. Not at all. We visited each other. One day a letter came from him addressed 'Cecil Roberts, KCMG.'

I asked what he meant by that. 'Kindly Correct My Grammar' he replied."

Page 250: "At the beginning of August I went to stay with Leslie Rowse at Trenarren, at St. Austell in Cornwall. We always had an amusing correspondence. . . ." Followed by a full quote of a letter from Rowse to Roberts, explaining why Rowse had referred to him as Cyril Roberts.

Page 251: "So to Trenarren I went. He sent me to bed at ten o'clock because he wanted to retire and get on with his book. . . . Each day we walked and talked and went again to Mevagissey, and giggled there as before. Is the air there full of laughing gas?"

Page 274: "I went to stay with Leslie Rowse at All Souls College. He gave a lunch party for sixteen. . . . Beaming Agatha Christie was there. . . . Later my host wrote: 'You are a prize guest and a great charmer. You always pull something out of the bag.'"

Page 282: Roberts relates an experience with Evelyn Waugh in Rome when he was snubbed in his hotel: "When I narrated this incident some weeks later to A. L. Rowse, he said, 'My dear fellow, you should not be surprised. He's a writer of some genius, but we all know that he's paranoiac!'"

Page 315: "We went on to Oxford, to lunch with Leslie Rowse. He had just returned to All Souls College from his winter sojourn at the Huntington Library in California. . . . He had written a book on the Earl of Southampton. (1965). On his table I was surprised to find the proofs of one on the battle of Bosworth Field (1966). . . . Leslie, as always ebullient and industrious."

Page 320: Again at All Souls . . . "Inside the gate of All Souls College all was tranquil. My friend Rowse was still busy with the anatomy of the Great William. With what gusto he swept down Elizabethan corridors, opening new doors on history!"

Page 331: Again visiting Rowse at Trenarren. "My host was, of course, busy with the Great William, and after settling the question of 'Mr. W. H.' he would attend to his Dark Lady friend, and disinter her from the shadows; a phenomenon in pertinacity and research."

G9. *The Door Wherein I Went* by Lord Hailsham (1975)

Page 34: References to his friend "Leslie Rowse" and their concurring views about Shakespeare and his works.

G10. *Ottoline: The Life of Ottoline Morrell* by Sandra Jobson Darroch (1975)

Page 247: "Another was A. L. Rowse. He was taken to dinner at Garsington by David Cecil, another of Ottoline's favourites, and evidently made something of a hit with his hostess. Later he was invited out alone to lunch and she took him to meet Siegfried Sassoon, who was one of his heroes. But Rowse later looked back on those visits with a tinge of regret and remembered having made a bit of a fool of himself one day by pacing up and down the yew hedge walks harranguing Desmond MacCarthy on the Marxist approach to history."

G11. *The Road to 1945: British Politics and the Second World War* by Paul Addison (1975)

Page 49: "A. L. Rowse, a young Labour intellectual who stood unsuccessfully for parliament in 1935, wrote a book to prove that Keynes's General Theory gave Labour the method for achieving all its goals: but he was remarkably in advance of his time."

Page 101: "A point of interest to historians, perhaps is that A. L. Rowse wrote to *The Times* in support of a Halifax government."

G12. *Mallowan's Memoirs* by Max Mallowan (1977)

Page 294: About his time at All Souls: "Another sympathetic friend was that renowned historian, A. L. Rowse, for whom everybody that had ever mattered in the Shakespearian scene was still alive. In conversation he could, like a magician, conjure to life these domestic images of the past and bring them into the room."

G13. *The Inklings: C. S. Lewis, J. R. R. Tolkien, Charles Williams, and Their Friends* by Humphrey Carpenter (1978)

Page 230: Regarding C. S. Lewis's contribution to the Oxford History of English Literature (*English Literature in the 16th Century—Excluding Drama*, 1954), "A. L. Rowse called the book 'magnificient' and that it showed 'such intellectual vitality, such sweep and imagination, such magnanimity.'"

G14. *Leonard Woolf: A Political Biography* by Duncan Wilson (assisted by J. Eisenberg) (1978)

Page 241: Woolf "accused by A. L. Rowse in 1940 for being too gentlemanly towards Baldwin."

G15. *W. H. Auden: The Life of a Poet* by Charles Osborne (1979)

Pages 33, 35, 38–39, 253: telling of Auden's attempted seduction of Rowse in his rooms at Christ Church.

G16. *John Buchan and His World* by Janet Adam Smith (1979)

Page 82: "The historian A. L. Rowse, who in his early left-wing days was a regular visitor to Elsfield, was much struck by the 'extraordinary catholicism' of Buchan's political sympathies. 'In fact, I believe it was a special recommendation with him that one was on the other side.'"

G17. *The Tale Bearers: Essays on English, American, and Other Writers* by V. S. Pritchett (1980)

Pages 177–183: *Jonathan Swift, The Infantilism of Genius*, a review of *Jonathan Swift, Major Prophet* (1975) by A. L. Rowse.

G18. Change and Fortune: A Political Record by Douglas Jay (1980)

Page 42: Recollections from All Souls: "I then found myself sitting next to A. L. Rowse, whose intense love of Cornwall and naive interest in economics, both immediately exhibited, were agreeably reassuring. . . . To Rowse I was at once sympathetic partly because he was an avowed supporter of the Labour Party—then not so common in Oxford."

Page 179: "My familiarity with A. L. Rowse enabled me to ignore the outrageous verbal antics."

G19. *The Letters of Evelyn Waugh*, edited by Mark Amory (1980)

Page 528: Waugh in a letter dated October 2, 1959, to Margaret Waugh: "Did I tell you we went to luncheon at Dunster on Sunday? It was to meet a reformed socialist fellow of All Souls named Rowse."

G20. *W. H. Auden: A Biography* by Humphrey Carpenter (1981)

Pages 49, 59, 78, 83.

G21. *Winston Churchill: The Wilderness Years* by Martin Gilbert (1981)

Page 178: Rowse offers support to Churchill, as a Labour candidate and convinced radical: "'I have often been tempted,' Rowse told Churchill, 'to write to say that, although on the other side of politics, I am strongly in agreement with your views on the organization of peace in Europe, and menace of German armaments and the necessity of our own rearmament.'"

G22. *The Backbench Diaries of Richard Crossman*, edited by Janet Morgan (1981)

Page 725: Diary entry for Tuesday December 16, 1958: "I should perhaps here put a note in about the publication of : *The Charm of Politics*, . . . the Times Literary Supplement last week had a wonderful catty piece, which I now conclude must have been written by my dear old poison-pen pal Rowse of All Souls." [Note: This review was unknown to Rowse.]

G23. *Harold Nicolson: A Biography*, vol. 2, *1930–1968*, by James Lees-Milne (1981)

Page 260: Chapter 1952–1954: "He spoke at the Presidential debate at the

Cambridge Union on the subject of good government being better than self-government, and was bitterly attacked by A. L. Rowse. Harold was hurt by what he considered the unnecessary scolding Rowse submitted him to, but was gratified that the undergraduates witnessed his calvary in stone, disapproving silence."

G24. *The List of Books: A Recommended Library of over 3,000 Works* by Frederic Raphael and Kenneth McLeish (1981)

Page 89: Chapter History/British: "A. L. Rowse: *The England of Elizabeth* (1950). First and best of a series of studies of the Elizabethan age. Better on aristocrats than on what he calls 'the idiot people' especially the Puritans. Furious fun."

G25. Attlee by Kenneth Harris (1982)

Page 181: In a letter during the Blitz: "I saw Rowse the other day at Oxford. He is maturing a bit, but should certainly stick to history."

Page 495: "I've also read Rowse's last book—very good in parts with curious little strokes of egotism coming in."

G26. *The Life and Crimes of Agatha Christie* by Charles Osborne (1982)

Page 181: "'There is nothing immoral in my books, only murder,' Mrs Christie once said to A. L. Rowse."

Page 207: "She told her friend A. L. Rowse that she found the work fascinating, (a script for American T.V. based on Dickens's *Bleak House*), but that the constant interference of others had given her: 'headaches from worry over her work,' which never happened to her in the past."

Page 233: "When A. L. Rowse sent her a copy of his book about his cat, *Peter: The White Cat of Trenarren,* Agatha Christie wrote: 'I enjoyed your book about the White Cat so much that I really must ponder seriously about your suggestion of a little book about my cats and dogs.'"

G27. *Brothers and Friends: The Diaries of Major Warren Hamilton Lewis 1895–1973* (1982)

Page 216: Diary entry for Sunday December 21, 1947: "Whilst at Malvern I picked up and read A. L. Rowse's *A Cornish Childhood*: well written, interesting, and intolerable, it might except for less covenances have as its sub-title, 'Self Portrait of a Shit.' It is the best bit of self revelation that has come my way since Pepys, and, gosh, what a man it reveals! The only excuse for the fellow is the terrible loneliness which is the price he paid for emerging from the working class into academic Oxford, and which has left him brutal, arrogant, and intensely conceited—modesty, he says, is a vice, not a virtue."

G28. *The History Men: The Historical Profession in England since the Renaissance* by John Kenyon (1983)

Pages 207, 228, 232, 258, 283.

G29. *Cyril Connolly: Journal and Memoir* by David Pryce-Jones (1983)

Page 160: In his journal, Connolly refers to having received a letter from Rowse about one of his articles.

G30. *Shakespeare and Others* by S. Schoenbaum (USA) (1985)
Essays, lectures, and reviews Schoenbaum feels most worth preserving.

Pages 54–79: Part 1, "Shakespearean Themes," chapter 4: "Shakespeare, Dr. Forman, and Dr. Rowse." (1) "New Light on a Dark Lady," review of *Shakespeare the Man* (1974); (2) "Dark Secrets," review of *Shakespeare's Sonnets: The Problems Solved* (1973); (3) "Looking at the Underside of the Time," review of *Simon Forman: Sex and Society in Shakespeare's Age* (1974); (4) "Shakespeare's Dark Lady: A Question of Identity," a piece referring to Rowse's discovery of the Dark Lady at the Bodleian Library in the case books of Simon Forman.

G31. *Hugh Dalton* by Ben Pimlott (1985)

Page 251: Reference to A. L. Rowse as "amongst the Labour Party intellectuals in Britain."

G32. Stephen Spender: Journals, 1939–1983, edited by John Goldsmith (1985)

Page 107: Journal entry for December 4, 1951: "Dined with the very effete French aristocrat, Ann de Biéville, who can sometimes be very amusing. He told me that he had just been to Oxford, where he had lunched with A. L. Rowse. Rowse had told him how he hated and despised human beings—idiots, fools, hideously ugly, contemptible, etc. Ann said, 'Oh, but my dear, what a terrible time you must have every morning shaving.'"

G33. *The Englishman's Room*, edited by Alvilde Lees-Milne and photographed by Derry Moore (1986)

Pages 126–129: A. L. Rowse/Cornwall.

G34. *T. S. Eliot As Editor* by Agha Shahid Ali (USA) (1986)

Pages 20, 67–68, 79–82, 84, 86, 98: References in relation to Eliot's editorship of *The Criterion* (1921–1939).

G35. *The Fifties: Edmund Wilson: From Notebooks and Diaries of the Period,* edited and introduced by Leon Edel (1986)

Page 106: Diary entry for January 9, 1954: "We went to Folkestone for lunch with the Connollys. . . . He is evidently pleased that someone, in a recent review, had spoken of him as 'a great writer' (but later A. L. Rowse of All Souls wrote in to the paper to protest against this)."

Page 135: Diary entry for January 20–21, 1954: "At All Souls, in the darkened and vaulted room, they suddenly descended on us and stripped the table of its tablecloth, replacing the candlestick; then shoved at A. L. Rowse, the presiding don, the apparatus for the port and the claret."

G36. *Gardens of the Heart* by Susan Chivers and Suzanne Woloszynska. Photographed by Peter Woloszynski (1987)
Pages 40–43: A. L. Rowse in Cornwall.

G37. *Rebecca West: A Life* by Victoria Glendinning (1987)
Page 183: "Rebecca did not accept what she saw as her 'sexual deprivation' easily. She wrote to the Elizabethan scholar A. L. Rowse, of whom she was very fond, that 'I have never been able to write with anything more than the left hand of my mind; the right hand has always been engaged in something to do with personal relationships.'"

G38. *British Writers of the Thirties* by Valentine Cunningham (1988)
Page 135: In a list of dons at Oxford in the 1930s: "Not far away was Stephen Spender at University College. Harold Acton, David Cecil, Lord Longford, A. L. Rowse (making much of his poor origins in Cornwall at the same time as energetically altering his West Country accent to suit the new habitat), Brian Howard, Henry Green, Auden, Driberg were all Christ Church men."
Page 136: "The snobbery of entitlement to wear bourgeois England's Old School Tie . . . the insignia which even rebels as we've seen, chose to wear, and latecoming adoptees, scholarship boys like A. L. Rowse, couldn't fasten about their necks fast enough."
Page 137: "A. L. Rowse became the epitome of All Soulishness."
Page 211: "The then Leftist A. L. Rowse, referring to the *Manifesto* as one of the great classics of political thought, quotes a passage in a 1929 *Criterion* essay on Communism."

G39. *Young Betjeman* by Bevis Hillier (1988)
Page 141: Reference to Rowse remembering Bowra. Also p. 171.

G40. *Never Despair: Winston S. Churchill, 1945–1965* by Martin Gilbert (1988)
Pages 1149–1151: Substantial quote from Rowse's diary notes of his visit to Chartwell for lunch on July 11, 1955.
Page 1190: Regarding Rowse's assistance given with Churchill's *History*: "'Your comments are most valuable,' Churchill wrote to A. L. Rowse on April 12, 1956, 'and it is very good of you to have devoted so much time to my affairs.'"
Page 1269–1270: Regarding Rowse at Blenheim as a guest for a celebratory weekend for the fiftieth anniversary of the Churchills' engagement.

G41. *The Life of Graham Greene,* vol. 1, *1904–1939,* by Norman Sherry (1989)
Pages 148–149: Mentions of Rowse, as amongst poets who participated for a simultaneous broadcast of their poems in 1925.

G42. *Sotheby's Catalogue: English Literature and History, "Dolphin"* (December 13, 1990)
Page 197: Lot no. 285: A. L. Rowse, autograph manuscript, with autograph corrections and revisions of *A Cornish Childhood,* circa 360 pages; estimate: £2,000–2,500.

Page 196: Facsimile illustration of one of the manuscript pages. (item withdrawn prior to sale).

G43. *Winston Churchill: His Life As a Painter* (1990)

A memoir by his daughter Mary Soames.

Page 198: "Among the visitors who saw him at his best was Dr. A. L. Rowse, the historian, with whom he had a long and fruitful session."

G44. *A Sparrow's Flight: The Memoirs of Lord Hailsham of St. Marylebone* (1990)

Page 83: Recalls A. L. Rowse at All Souls, while he was on an All Souls fellowship: "Leslie Rowse in particular was extremely kind to me. . . . Incidentally, his life may have been saved by another fellow, somewhat senior to me, himself without medical qualifications but a specialist in the study of ancient Greek medicine. Leslie was looking and feeling extremely ill, and Reginald Harris claimed to recognize in him the so-called 'hippocratic face' which the ancient Greek practitioner asserted was an infallible mark of imminent fatality. Reginald took Leslie at once to the hospital, where he was found to be suffering from a perforated duodenal ulcer. He was just in time. Thus a doctor of the fifth century BC was able in the early thirties of the twentieth century AD to effect by proxy his latest and probably his last cure from what might have been a fatal illness."

G45. *C. S. Lewis: A Biography* by A. N. Wilson (1990)

Pages 243–244: Wilson details Rowse's review of C. S. Lewis's *English Literature in the Sixteenth Century Excluding Drama:* "Rowse and Lewis had known each other since 1926, when Lewis had Rowse to dinner at Magdalen. They had never been much one another's 'type' and over the years their views diverged. . . . Lewis was touched by Rowse's kind review and came up to him in a train to thank him. As they sat down together in the compartment, Rowse said, 'I did enjoy the book very much, and I think it was a good book. But now that I have got you in person, let me tell you some of the things which were wrong with it.'"

G46. *Letters of Leonard Woolf,* edited by Frederic Spotts (1990)

Page 306: Letter from H. G. Wells to Leonard Woolf dated March 7, 1932, demanding to know who his more brilliant of the younger critics was who allegedly said of him that he, Wells, was "a thinker who cannot think."

Page 307: Letter from Leonard Woof to H. G. Wells dated March 11, 1932, explaining that "the writer to whom I referred is A. L. Rowse, the young Oxford economist who is now at the London School of Economics." Woolf further suggests he thought he had read the offensive remark in Rowse's *Politics and the Younger Generation,* but on second thought remembers, "It was in an article which he submitted to me for the Political Quarterly and which I could not accept."

Page 307: Letter from H. G. Wells to Leonard Woolf dated March 13, 1932, pursuing the argument over the remark: "On the face of it, it looks as though you wanted the thing said and hadn't the guts to say it on your own."

Page 308: Letter from Leonard Woolf to H. G. Wells dated March 19, 1932, suggesting he could write a letter to the editor of the *New Statesman* explaining the position but that it might make him look slightly ridiculous.

Page 308: Letter from H. G. Wells to Leonard Woolf dated March 23, 1932, dictating the type of letter he wants printed as an apology, including, "and I tender now my sincere apologies both to Mr. Wells and to the rising young economist to whom, in the first excitement of being challenged, I ascribed it."

Page 309: Letter from Leonard Woolf to H. G. Wells dated March 25, 1932, stating he has written to the *New Statesman* explaining the facts and adding, "I had read it in the last six weeks. I was apparently wrong in thinking it was by Rowse."

Page 309: Letter from H. G. Wells to Leonard Woolf dated March 27, 1932, persisting with the matter and claiming he finds it a little difficult to accept this new "young writer on politics . . . who now appears in the place of Rowse. I gather you have still to find him."

Page 310: Letter from Leonard Woolf to H. G. Wells dated April 4, 1932, stating he, Woolf, had received a letter from Rowse in which the air is cleared and "that Rowse had told H. G. Wells that it was his remark, and, that H. G. Wells had apparently kept this knowledge from Woolf."

Page 311: Letter from H. G. Wells to Leonard Woolf dated April 2, 1932 (this letter crossed that of Woolf as Wells was in France), in effect letting the matter rest: "having worried you as much as I can . . . it seems you didn't mean it."

Page 426: Long letter from Leonard Woolf to A. L. Rowse, dated May 24, 1941, thanking him for his letter and words of sympathy (Virginia Woolf had drowned herself on March 28, 1941) and discussing an article Rowse has submitted to him for the *Political Quarterly:* "Your article is a terrific indictment of Baldwin." Note: Printed in the July-September issue and reprinted in *The End of an Epoch* (1947).

G47. *Shakespeare Survey Number 42,* edited by Stanley Wells (1990)

Page 186: "A cause célèbre from an earlier, hardly less controversial 'reading' of Shakespeare's life, has resurfaced. Roger Prior has revived A. L. Rowse's suggestion that the 'Dark Lady' of the Sonnets was Emilia Lanier (née Bassano). Stanley Wells seriously undermined Rowse's case by pointing out that a phrase in a manuscript which the latter had read as 'very brown in youth' actually said 'very brave in youth.'"

G48. *Barbara Pym: A Reference Guide* by Dale Salwak (1991)

Writings about Barbara Pym (1950–1990)

1977: *Punch,* October 19, pp. 732–734; A. L. Rowse review: "Excellent Women" and "A Glass of Blessings"

1982: *Spectator,* December 18, p. 45; A. L. Rowse in "Books of the Year" cites *A Few Green Leaves.*

1984: *Financial Times,* December 1, p. 14; A. L. Rowse, "My Book of the Year," cites *A Very Private Eye.*

1987: *The Life and Work of Barbara Pym,* edited by Dale Salwak, pp. 64–71; A. L. Rowse, "Miss Pym and Miss Austen," chapter 9.

G49. *Will This Do?: An Autobiography* by Auberon Waugh (1991)

Page 129: "Of the few Oxford contemporaries who have distinguished themselves in later life—Peter Jay, David Dimbleby . . . all went off to the worlds of newspapers and television. Most were the sons of famous parents . . . Alasdair Clayre, thought to be the most brilliant young Fellow of All Souls since A. L. Rowse, sang protest songs in cellar cafés . . . slipped off the mental coil under a train."

G50. *Sotheby's Catalogue: English Literature and History, "Aurevoir"* (December 14–15, 1992)

Page 171, lot no. 370: A. L. Rowse, autograph manuscript of his first book, *On History: Present Tendencies,* 45 pp. folio, 1925; estimated: £100–150. Donated by the author for the London Library 150th anniversary appeal. Purchased on behalf of the bibliographer by Hinda Rose of Maggs Bros.

G51. *Shakespeare: An Annotated Bibliography* by Joseph Rosenblum (USA) (1992)

Pages 29, 292: Annotations on A. L. Rowse's *William Shakespeare* (1963); *Shakespeare's Sonnets: The Problems Solved* (1973); *Discovering Shakespeare: A Chapter in Literary History* (1989)

G52. *Shakespeare Index: An Annotated Bibliography of Critical Articles on the Plays, 1959–1983,* edited by Bruce T. Sajdak (USA) (1992)

Pages 4, 18, 130, 746 list articles and sources relating to A. L. Rowse contributions.

G53. Selected Letters of Philip Larkin, 1940–1985, edited by Anthony Thwaite (1992)

Page 330: Reference to A. L. Rowse in a letter dated June 1, 1961, to Robert Conquest: "Talking about O. W. [Oscar Wilde], Betjeman's new record of his poem re. the arrest of same [Betjeman's "The Arrest of Oscar Wilde in the Cadogan Hotel"] is v. poor. He puts on a special voice for the dialogue bits & makes O. W. sound like A. L. Rowse."

Page 435: Reference to A. L. Rowse in a letter from All Souls College, Oxford, dated January 16, 1971, to Douglas Dunn: "I've managed to avoid giving any readings, usually just by refusing. A. L. Rowse is rather over-friendly to a brother bard, but better than underfriendly, I suppose."

Page 437: Reference to A. L. Rowse in a letter dated April 14, 1971, to Anthony Thwaite: "I'm through with All Souls now: Cinderella is back in the kitchen, waiting for the princess to, I mean the prince to come along and say whose hands are small enough to fit this tiny typewriter? Rowse and Sparrow as the ugly sisters."

Page 509: Reference to A. L. Rowse in a letter dated June 5, 1974, to Barbara Pym: "Thank you for asking after my mother: she seems to have stabilized at a fairly reasonable level of debility, gets up & dresses (or is dressed) daily, reads The Daily Telegraph and cuts out bits for me (about Duke Ellington and A. L. Rowse, odd pair)."

G54. *Leonard and Virginia Woolf As Publishers: The Hogarth Press, 1917–1941* by J. H. Willis Jr. (USA) (1992)

Page 239: under chapter "Pamphlets and Politics," A. L. Rowse's *The Question of the House of Lords* (1934).

G55. *G. M. Trevelyan: A Life in History* by David Cannadine (1992)

Page 11: "According to A. L. Rowse, the family was "apt to think that there were Trevelyans—and then the rest of the human race.'"

Page 18: "Trevelyan . . . attended the first series of lectures (The Trevelyan Lectures) given in 1958 by A. L. Rowse."

Page 46: "Nor do the evocations of him by others give much away: among those who have set down their recollections of him in print, neither J. H. Plumb nor A. L. Rowse seems to have known him all that well. Both draw attention to his 'bleak surface', to his 'guarded heart', and to the 'impersonal front' he presented to the world."

Page 52: "Trevelyan . . . encouraged young scholars like Arthur Bryant . . . A. L. Rowse."

Page 195: "For as A. L. Rowse has remarked, Trevelyan was a consummate literary craftsman, who was 'possessed' by the idea of writing."

Page 223: "Trevelyan told A. L. Rowse that he 'disliked practically everything since the Industrial Revolution.'"

G56. *Shakespeare, the Evidence: Unlocking the Mysteries of the Man and His Work* by Ian Wilson (1993)

Numerous references to A. L. Rowse, covering the wide range of his Shakespeare discoveries and interpretations: pages 25–26, 41, 85, 92, 94, 95, 100, 126, 138–139, 146, 154–155, 158, 161–162, 193, 201, 209, 243, 281, 286, 302, 317, 337, 345, 349, 357, 370, 373, 393, 408, 410.

G57. *The Essential Shakespeare: An Annotated Bibliography of Major Modern Studies* by Larry S. Champion (USA) (1993)

Pages 16, 108: annotations on A. L. Rowse's *William Shakespeare: A Biography* (1963) and *Shakespeare the Man* (1973).

G58. *Oliver Franks: Founding Father* by Alex Danchev (1993)

Page 21: Quotes Rowse on his early education.

G59. *Philip Larkin: A Writer's Life* by Andrew Motion (1993)

Page 104: "Larkin was taken to his first dinner in college (All Souls), by the historian A. L. Rowse, who along with the Warden John Sparrow, Monteith, and other Fellows such as Alasdair Clayre, became a frequent albeit much criticized—companion. As they eyed up the new arrival, one or two people found some of his habits disconcerting. Rowse, for instance, was alarmed by the amount he drank. ('It's odd that he should have been so pernickety and yet so undisciplined in that respect.') . . . 'Falling over backwards to be philistine,' Rowse says, 'it's an undergraduate attitude which he perpetuated into adult life.'"

G60. *Daphne du Maurier* by Margaret Forster (1993)

Page 190: About her book *The King's General,* which she wanted to base on the history of Menabilly and the Rashleigh family, "A. L. Rowse, who lived nearby, also advised her on which books to consult. He had been introduced to Daphne by the Quiller-Couches two years before and was greatly impressed, describing him to Tod as 'about to be the leading historian in England.'"

G61. *A. J. P. Taylor: The Traitor within the Gates* by Robert Cole (1993)

Pages 195, 201: About Taylor's book, *The Origins of the Second World War,* Rowse joins other historians in criticizing this work.

G62. *The Oxford Book of Schooldays,* edited by Patricia Craig (1994)

Pages 245–246, 332–333, 407–408: Quotes three separate passages from *A Cornish Childhood* (1942).

G63. *John Betjeman: Letters,* vol. 1, *1926–1951,* edited and introduced by Candida Lycett Green (1994)

Page 353: About his first acquaintance with A. L. Rowse in 1945.

Page 373: A. L. Rowse quoted from a letter to the compiler about Betjeman's love for Cornwall and their time visiting churches and monuments there.

Page 402: To Lionel Curtis (1946) stating that like Rowse he has thoroughly enjoyed his poems.

Page 485: To Anne Barnes (1949) telling her while in Cornwall he went to see Gerald Berners, staying with Rowse in a small house outside St. Austell and near St. Just-in-Roseland.

Page 523: To Anne and Arthur Bryant (1950) stating: "Most of the history I have read by modern writers (always excepting Leslie R.) is unreadable." And, commenting on an intended review, "I know of no reviewer (except A. L. Rowse who is probably bespoke for a high fee) capable of doing justice."

G64. *A Vowed Intent: An Autobiography of Lord Longford* (1994)

Page 7: "My illustrious friend (Professor) Leslie Rowse told my daughter Antonia on one occasion that he was very fond of me but regretted that I had not had any homosexual experience. He was no doubt contrasting me with a number of the famous intellectuals who were at Oxford in my time."

Page 27: "How far were the Aesthetes of that time practising homosexuals? No one, perhaps, will make a just assessment, least of all someone like myself who, as Dr. Rowse has already been quoted as saying: 'has lacked homosexual experience.'"

G65. *A. J. P. Taylor: A Biography* by Adam Sisman (1994)
Numerous references: pages 60, 131, 133–134, 152, 217, 246, 294, 297, 345–346.

G66. *John Betjeman: Letters,* vol.2, *1951–1984,* edited and introduced by Candida Lycett Green (1995)
Page 326 (1966): "Your A. L. Rowse poem is splendid. He is a very strange character. I enjoyed his *Cornish Childhood.*"
Page 482 (1974): "That book of A. L. Rowse and yours truly on old Cornwall needs better and bigger photographs."
Page 573: On A. L. Rowse's contribution of a poem to John Betjeman's 75th birthday: "A Garland for the Laureate" (Celandine Press, 1981), via Roger Pringle (founder) 350 copies.

G67. *Country Life 1897–1997: The English Arcadia* by Roy Strong (1996)
Page 128: "On 24th August 1940, when the Battle of Britain was being waged, an issue was dedicated to the 'core of the English spirit,' highlighting in its pages 'something of the face of the land that her sons and grandsons are now mustered to defend.' . . . A. L. Rowse on 'The English Spirit' ('Happy contentment, the secret compact . . . with nature, pride, courage, tenacity.')"

G68. *The Roy Strong Diaries, 1967–1987* by Roy Strong (1997)
Page 51: "The ultimate compliment was to be attacked by A. L. Rowse in a review verging on hysteria in *History Today.*" (See D460.)
Page 303: Regarding the death of Pamela Hartwell, January 1982: "She could be appallingly rude. Once at Oving she asked A. L. Rowse to lunch and placed him to her right. There was a terrible fracas between them and he left immediately after."
Page 342: "Dear A. L. Rowse was so touched to have my book *The English Renaissance Miniature* [published in 1983 with dedication "For A. L. Rowse"— the review in the *Standard* not yet found] dedicated to him and gave it a rave in the *Standard.*"

G69. *Enchantress: Marthe Bibesco and Her World* by Christine Sutherland (1997)
Page 299: "At Tullimaar where she could entertain her English friends. 'She was a great woman, such courage,' the historian A. L. Rowse, a neighbour, told me when I asked how he remembered Marthe. 'She never complained and spoke of the riches and grandeur she lost; she adored life and was determined to maintain standards at all costs. I thought she was simply magnificient.'"

G70. *Cyril Connolly: A Life* by Jeremy Lewis (1997)
Page 101: Regarding ALR's contribution to *Oxford Poetry 1924,* which omits work by Connolly.
Page 104: Regarding ALR and F. F. Urquhart.
Page 133: On ALR gaining a first in history at Oxford.

Page 371: On Lord Astor thinking ALR: "A militant atheist."

Pages 372, 443: Mentioned as reviewer for the *Observer* and the *Sunday Times*.

G71. *The Players: A Novel of the Young Shakespeare* by Stephanie Cowell (1997)

Dedication page: "For my husband Russell and A. L. Rowse."

Page 240: The story of the sonnets and their triangle: "Anything more truly intimate has never been written," commented the Elizabethan historian A. L. Rowse of the 154 sonnets, very likely composed in the years 1591–1595 by Shakespeare to the young Lord of Southhampton, his patron.

Page 241: Historical notes: "With Dr. Rowse I do believe that the love triangle between the poet, his mistress, and his patron was the great crisis of Shakespeare's life. . . . Of the identity of the Dark Lady of the Sonnets, there is rather more dispute. I have chosen for this novel the Italian musician Emilia Bassano."

Page 251: Acknowledgments: "I am most indebted to Dr. A. L. Rowse for his several suggestions and encouragement . . . and for his lifelong work on the Elizabethans and Shakespeare, whose gentle creative character he delineated so remarkably."

Note 1. Back of dust jacket: Praise for Stephanie Cowell's previous novels has five-line quote by A. L. Rowse for *Nicholas Cooke.*

Note 2. See also *Biblio,* April 1997, pp. 50–55; "Romancing the Tome: The Making of a Novel on the 400-year-old Love Triangle of Shakespeare's Sonnets" (article by Stephanie Cowell).

G72. *Phillips Catalogue: Items from the Estate of the Late Dr. A. L. Rowse,* Sale no.: P435, July 2, 1998, held at Cornubia Hall, Par, Cornwall.

H

Manuscripts and Letters

All the original manuscripts and letters documented in section H are entirely in the holograph/autograph of A. L. Rowse and are all the property of the Sydney Cauveren Collection.

The poems are original drafts in various stages of completion and refinement. References are given to the books and periodicals in which they were printed. Some of the poems were published under a different title from that given in the draft version, while others without title, or part poems, were either not located—or unpublished—at the time of final preparation.

To assist researchers, unplaced poems are collated quoting the opening lines verbatim. Where poems have been written on versos of scrap paper or old correspondence, a brief description is provided to illuminate the author's spontaneity and method of work.

The letters section constitutes the complete correspondence 1976–1996. Substantial extracts are quoted from them for the purpose of collating them here.

Note. For details on other original A. L. Rowse manuscript locations, refer to the following:

1. A. L. Rowse Archive, deposited at the Exeter University Library;
2. *Location Register of Twentieth Century Literary Manuscripts and Letters,* vol. 2, *The British Library* (1988) p. 811, Rowse, A. L. (1903–); eleven entries of known deposits of his original correspondence include the BBC 1932–1962; to Nancy Astor; Gerald Duckworth and Co.; Keats House; Lord Cherwell; and Basil Liddell Hart;
3. A. L. Rowse in a letter to Sydney Cauveren dated July 10, 1996: "The fullest file of letters to Publishers would be with Macmillans, London— but they handed over their letter files to some University" [Reading]. "My letters to Lady Astor are among the Astor Papers at Reading University

Library. Rebecca West's letters to me are among my papers at Exeter University Library."

BOOKS

H1. *On History: Present Tendencies*

The author's first book. Original holograph manuscript with autograph corrections, deletions, and revisions, 45 pp, folio, written in dark blue ink, bound in dark blue cloth hardcover, only slightly worn.

On title page, inscription in black biro: "Autographed for the London Library Appeal 1992 A. L. Rowse 1925."

Lot no. 370 in Sotheby's literature catalogue, December 15, 1992, London. Purchased on behalf of the bibliographer by Hinda Rose of Maggs Bros., London.

A. L. Rowse considered this essay on historical materialism the blueprint to his career as a historian and a summing up of his strenuous experience of reading the History School at Oxford.

In *A Cornishman at Oxford* (1965), p. 262, he mentions an offer from C. K. Ogden to write a little book for his Psyche Miniatures series. Rereading it twenty years later, in preparation for his follow-up book, *The Use of History* (1946), he found that "luckily I still agreed with it all."

On History: Present Tendencies was first published by K. Paul, Trench, Trubner, London 1927, as no. 7 of the Psyche Miniatures General Series.

H2. *The Use of History*

Original holograph manuscript with autograph corrections, deletions, and revisions, 202 pp, quarto, bound in blue boards with black leather label on spine with gilt lettering.

Title page: three lines in biro. Pp. 1–154 in ink; pp. 155–159 in pencil; pp. 160–162 in ink; p. 163 two and part lines in ink only, rest in pencil; pp. 164–202 in pencil; p. 186 "Chapter VIII" and title, only in ink; p. 158 out of sequence: between pp. 150 and 151; p. 185 put in back to front; p. 202 on final page, author dates completion of manuscript as "Oct. 24/ 1945."

Manuscript was given to the bibliographer as a present by A. L. Rowse while on a visit to his home at Trenarren in Cornwall, on Friday September 10, 1993, as it was his wish that it should be reunited with the holograph manuscript of *On History: Present Tendencies,* whose successor this book is.

On pp. 58–59 of the book, (pp. 49–50 of the ms), the author reveals a time capsule as to the writing instrument he was using at the time of writing. At the beginning of chapter 3, "What History Is About," he writes: "This particular nib is a 'Relief nib,' No. 314, made by R. Esterbrook and Co. in England, who supply the Midland Bank with pen-nibs, from whom I got it—a gift, I may say. But behind this nib there is a whole process of manufacture."

In *A Cornishman at Oxford* (p. 262) A. L. Rowse says that this book "developed the position (on history) more fully and said what I thought about the subject after the experience of writing history." The *Use of History* was first published by Hodder & Stoughton for the English Universities Press in May

1946 and forms the key volume in the Teach Yourself History Library, all edited by A. L. Rowse.

H3. *Historians I Have Known*

Original holograph manuscript with autograph corrections, deletions, and revisions.

342 pages on 306 leaves. Various page sizes: pp. 56 folio, pp. 177 large quarto, pp. 23 standard quarto, and, pp. 50 small quarto. The holograph manuscript comprises 26 essays—Sir Lewis Namier twice. One of these essays is unpublished. (Sir Maurice Powicke and H. R. Trevor-Roper are missing.) The other 24 essays are of the following historians: G. M. Trevelyan, Sir Charles Firth, Sir George Clark, Sir Keith Feiling, Sir Arthur Bryant, H. A. L. Fisher, Sir Charles Oman, A. H. M. Jones, K. B. McFarlane, A. F. Pollard, Sir John Neale, Garret Mattingly, R. H. Tawney, Christopher Hill, C. V. Wedgwood, A. J. P. Taylor, Richard Pares, Samuel Eliot Morison, Allan Nevins, Sir Reginald Coupland, Sir Keith Hancock, Sir Michael Howard, Denis Mack Smith and Barbara Tuchman.

The collection of essays was a present from A. L. Rowse at Trenarren, Friday, April 19, 1996, who considered this the companion volume to both *On History: Present Tendencies* and *The Use of History.*

The 306 leaves are uniformly contained within 205 + 2 large quarto Marbig Copy Safe 25100 clear transparent sleeves. Bound together in one white-cover Bantex 4 clip folder. Lettering horizontally along spine: A. L. ROWSE / 'HISTORIANS I HAVE KNOWN' / ORIGINAL MANUSCRIPT.

The irregularity of page sizes catches the spontaneity of the writer at work, as he utilizes the backs of old proof sheets, correspondence backs, and even versos of deleted accounts. A rare glimpse into the working method of an urgent man of letters in the creative process. Even more remarkable considering the author was then in his ninety-first year!

Historians I Have Known was first published by Duckworth, London, September 1995, as 27 essays, each constituting a chapter.

POETRY

H4. "Sunday Afternoon in Hartford, Conn."

2 pp. recto and verso in black biro with traces of pencil draft underneath. Last line of published version missing.

Printed in *The Road to Oxford* (1978), p. 58; *A Life: Collected Poems* (1981), pp. 258–259; Transatlantic (1989), a reading by author on cassette.

H5. "Modernist Poetry"

1p. in black biro. Printed as "Modernist Verse" in *The Road to Oxford* (1978), p. 74; *A Life: Collected Poems* (1981), pp. 340–341.

H6. "Suburbia"

1p. in black biro. On verso of an Oxford social committee report for 1977. "Suburbia (Reading) Ears Have They." 2 pp. recto and verso in black biro.

Printed as "Suburbia" in *A Life: Collected Poems* (1981), pp. 379–380; *Transatlantic: Later Poems* (1989), p. 39.

H7. "Reproaches"
1p. in black biro. On free-end paper of a book or booklet. Printed in *A Life: Collected Poems* (1981), p. 398.

H8. "In the Street"
1p. in black biro. On free-end paper of a book or booklet. Printed in *A Life: Collected Poems* (1981), pp. 398–399.

H9. "The Conveyor-Belt"
1p. in blue biro. Printed in *Transatlantic: Later Poems* (1989), p. 1.

H10. "The Road by Penrice"
1p. in black biro. Printed *Transatlantic: Later Poems* (1989), p. 21.

H11. "Whose is that spirit moving over the Moor" (first line)
2pp. recto and verso in black biro. Title missing. Printed as "Marika at Maidenwell" in *Transatlantic: Later Poems* (1989), p. 24.

H12. "The Years"
2pp. recto and verso of small pocket book page, in black biro. "The Years" 1p. in black biro. Printed in *Transatlantic: Later Poems* (1989), p. 53.

H13. "To Ld David Cecil"
2 pp. recto and verso, in black biro with some changes in pencil. Printed as "To David Cecil on His Eightieth Birthday" in *Transatlantic: Later Poems* (1989), p. 54. Transatlantic (1989) a reading by author on cassette.

H14. "Christ Church Meadows"
1p. in blue biro on verso of Sotheby's European Newsletter postal wrapper. Printed in *Transatlantic: Later Poems* (1989), p. 55.

H15. "Peopled Sleep"
1p. in black biro. Printed *A Life: Collected Poems* (1981), p. 375.

H16. "Bank Holiday"
1p. black biro. Printed in *Transatlantic: Later Poems* (1989), p. 63.

H17. "Boy Drowned"
1 p in black biro. Printed in *Prompting the Age* (1990), p. 13.

H18. "Carrickhowel"
1p. in blue biro. Printed in *Prompting the Age* (1990), p. 17.

H19. "The Rooks Come Home"
1p. in blue biro. Printed in *Prompting the Age* (1990), p. 24.

H20. "O That It Might Be So!"
1p. in blue biro. Printed in *Prompting the Age* (1990), p. 26.

H21. "The Trees"
1p. in black biro. Printed in *Contemporary Review,* September 1989, p. 157; *Prompting the Age* (1990), p. 46.

H22. "Trafalgar Square"
4 pp. in black biro with several stanzas redrafted. Printed in *Transatlantic: Later Poems* (1989), pp. 33–34; *Selected Poems* (1990), pp. 66–67.

H23. "At Charlestown (for David Treffry)"
1p. in blue biro on verso of telemessage dated April 1, 1987. "On the Cliff at Charlestown." 1p. in blue biro. Printed as "At Charlestown (for David Treffry)" in the *Cornish Scene,* July–August 1987, p. 16. With a photographic illustration of Charlestown Harbour. *Transatlantic: Later Poems* (1989), p. 22.

H24. "At Bowdoin College"
1p. in black biro on verso of National Portrait Gallery flyer for a function on June 13, 1984. Printed as "At Bowdoin College, Maine" in *Transatlantic: Later Poems* (1989), p. 5.

H25. "Politics"
1p. in green felt-tip pen with corrections in pencil. On verso of p. 56 carbon copy of *Peter: The White Cat of Trenarren.* Printed in *Prompting the Age* (1990), p. 38.

H26. "The Spirit of the House"
2 pp. in blue biro, the first on verso of roneo letter from Victoria and Albert Museum dated June 15, 1987, and the second on verso of letter from Newlyn Art Gallery, Penzance, dated October 27, 1988, regarding arrangements for a poetry reading at the gallery for 1989. Printed in the *Cornish Scene,* n.s., Autumn 1989, p. 95; *Prompting the Age* (1990), pp. 37–38; Transatlantic (1989), a reading by the author on cassette.

H27. "Trenarren towards Christmas"
1p. recto and verso in black biro. 1p. recto and verso in blue biro "Latticed shadows on white gravel" on recto, with first four lines of poem on verso. Printed in *A Life: Collected Poems* (1981), pp. 392–393.

H28. "The Pavements of Pasadena"
1p. in black biro. On verso of first page of minutes of the 157th annual general meeting, June 15, 1981, of the Athenaeum. Printed in *Transatlantic: Later Poems* (1989), p. 8.

H29. "Monmouthshire Bus"
1p. in blue biro. Printed in *Prompting the Age* (1990), p. 29.

H30. "Last of the Line"
1p. in black biro. On verso of roneo notes from the Devon and Cornwall Record Society for their meeting on October 5, 1984. Printed in *Transatlantic: Later Poems* (1989), p. 29.

H31. "L. M."

1p. in blue biro. On verso of bright yellow roneo fullscap page giving biographies on two candidates "submitted by the fellowship standing committee." Printed as "Louis MacNeice" in *A Life: Collected Poems* (1981), p. 382.

H32. "All Souls Day"

2 pp., three sides in black biro. Printed in *Transatlantic: Later Poems* (1989), pp. 44–45; *All Souls in My Time* (1993), pp. 203–205 (1960s, author's note).

H33. "On Lady Strong's Cat"

2 pp. in black felt-tip pen. On versos of roneo memo from Skidmore Theatre News, Skidmore College, Saratoga Springs, New York, April 21, 1983. Publication is unknown, but Sir Roy Strong in *Country Life* (January 17, 1991, p. 37), "A Week in the Country," in his concluding paragraph makes mention of this poem: "and he [the Rev. Wenceslas Muff] has been basking in the glory of a many-versed poem: 'On Lady Strong's Cat,' by the redoubtable A. L. Rowse."

H34. "Winter in Stratford Church"

2 pp., both recto and verso in half black and half blue biros each both with additions and corrections of two versions. Printed in *The Road to Oxford* (1978), pp. 53–54.

H35. "Hot Weather in the Meadows"

1p. in blue biro. Printed as "Eros in the Parks" in *Prompting the Age* (1990), p. 10.

H36. "Shadows" (another title, "The Cloister," has been crossed out)

1p. in blue biro. Printed as "Magdalen Grove" in *Prompting the Age* (1990), p. 26.

H37. "Trenarren"

1p. in blue biro. Printed in the *Cornish Banner,* August 1993, p. 13.

H38. "St. Dennis"

1p. in blue biro, recto, with final four lines on verso. Written in tribute to his elder brother George on the occasion of his funeral. Printed in the *Cornish Banner,* August 1993, p. 23.

H39. "John Sparrow"

1p. in blue biro with "urgent" in top right corner. A tribute written upon the death of John Sparrow (1906–1992), former warden of All Souls College. Printed in *All Souls in My Time* (1993), p. 199.

H40. "Jock"

"This is all I live for," said the boy." Twenty lines, 1p. in blue biro. On verso of letter from the secretary of the Athenaeum, dated February 10, 1992, inviting A. L. Rowse to give a talk on "The Dark Lady in Shakespeare."

H41. "Ghostly Inhabitants"
"The cows like cats stand up on the horizon." Fourteen lines, 1p. in black biro. On verso of roneo page regarding seating reservation for a function.

H42. "Now the chores of motherhood hung heavy."
Eight lines, 1p. in black biro. On verso of part of a letter regarding an invitation to an investment seminar of the Sun Life Marketing Group, West Cornwall Branch. Possible continuation of "Ghostly Inhabitants."

H43. "At Bournemouth"
"Here I my silly seaside face assume." Twenty-six lines, 1p. in blue biro, with last two lines on verso.

H44. "Modern Love"
"A cold wind from Canada comes across." Nineteen lines, 1p. in black biro. On verso of letter from Chartered Accountants Wenn Townsend, dated May 21, 1984.

H45. "A Cold Wind from Canada."
Twenty-two lines, 1p., typescript with several autograph corrections, including "from Canada" added to the original typed title: "A Cold Wind."

H46. "Plymouth"
"Look at all the f—— hutches." Seventeen lines, 1p. in blue biro. On verso of Francis Edwards Limited notice.

H47. "Old Man"
"An old man, I have become my mother." Eleven lines, 1p. in blue biro. On verso of bottom part of a letter.

H48. "Writing It Down (Or, was Philip Larking?)"
"What a view of life, what a view!" Fourteen lines, 1p. in blue biro. On verso of Sotheby's lecture evening invitation.

H49. "The Question Mark"
"A rind of moon is hung in the trees." Twelve lines, 1p. in blue felt-pen.

H50. "Pauli Was a Wykehamist"
"The facts of life he would have known" Probably a continuation of a poem. Twenty-six lines, 1p. in blue biro.

H51. "Desire is dead; no longer the alert / Of eye and heart at what passes."
Twenty-five lines, 1p. in black biro. On verso of typed proof page about Hugh Peter.

H52. "Poor Old Nancie"
"Poor old Nancie / She was not my fancie." Sixteen lines, 1p. in black biro. On verso of part of a John Major reelection spiel.

H53. "Half-Mast"

"When a king dies the West End / puts flags at half-mast." Sixteen lines, 1p. in blue biro. On verso of part of a letter thanking the author for a talk.

H54. "Chancery Lane"

"The released sun in glory / leans down from the roofs." Thirteen lines, 1p. in blue biro. On verso of the bottom part of the above letter (H53).

H55. "The Dark Bay"

"O, starlight and moonlight and boatlight over the bay / A crimson band in the east to tell me it is day." Eighteen lines, in black biro.

H56. "No Spring Is Here"

"The purple day warm in bursting buds / beneath the cold architecture of trees." Twenty lines, 1p. in blue biro. On verso of Eton College Collections letter dated February 7, 1989, thanking the author for gifts of his books and cassettes.

H57. "Larkin Gets His Answer"

"Laureate of lower middle class life / The thing to do is to keep out of it." Twenty-seven lines, 1p. in blue biro with pencil revisions.

LETTERS

All letters, of which excerpts are herewith given, are addressed to Sydney Cauveren and John Walde, referred to often as "S. & J."

H58. Trenarren, postmarked April 30, 1976; on letterhead of All Souls College, 1 p, 8vo

"Very nice to meet you some time when up in London—early June. . . . I shall be back at Oxford early July, if you would like to see over All Souls College. . . . I well remember the courtesy and charm of the stewards on Qantas coming from New York—the nearest I have got to Australia." Signed: "Best wishes, A. L. Rowse."

H59. Trenarren, undated, but written shortly after our afternoon tea—first meeting—at the Athenaeum on June 2, 1976. On letterhead of All Souls College, 1 p, 4to

Rowse offers advice for classes in the autumn on writing and literature at the Regent Polytechnic or any Workers Educational Association classes: "The important thing is that you, with your ability, should learn to write. . . . The same is true for John, who has more appreciation of history. . . . I am sending you mine [*A Cornish Childhood*], to show what a struggle I had when young." Signed: "Affectnte wishes to both, In haste, A.L.R."

H60. Trenarren, postmarked June 30, 1976; on letterhead of All Souls College; correspondence card

Invitation to lectures at Oxford: St. Peter's College, 12 noon on 12 and 13 July on Shakespeare, and, University College, 9 a.m. on 12 and 13 July on The Churchills.

Signed: "In haste, Best to both, A. L. Rowse."

H61. Trenarren, postmarked October 4, 1976; postcard of City Centre, Truro

"Delighted to hear of your classes. . . . Thank you for the lovely photos. This is to remind you of your naughty pilgrimage to Cornwall just when I was most pressed with work. . . ." Invitation to attend: October 7, Royal Institution, 7 p.m. Lecture. Signed: "Best to John, A. L. R."

H62. Trenarren, postmarked October 9, 1976; on letterhead of the Athenaeum, 1 p, 8vo

"I should like to use the photo of me alone—the head, with shirt open at the neck—on the jacket of my next book. I hope that will interest you." Signed: "Best to John, Yours Leslie."

H63. Trenarren, postmarked October 18, 1976; postcard of Duporth Beach, St. Austell

"Thank you for negatives . . . You shall certainly have acknowledgement of your expertise. How ambitious you are! Quite right—but you must equip yourself to fulfill it." Signed: "Leslie."

H64. Trenarren, postmarked November 8, 1976; note

Returning negatives: "I have instructed publishers to put your name to the photo." Signed: "Best to both you & John, Yrs, Leslie."

H65. Trenarren, postmarked January 14, 1977; on letterhead of Trenarren St. Austell; correspondence card

"You will find your name prominent on the jackets of 2 books! The re-issue of my Sir Richard Grenville (Cape) & the forthcoming Shakespeare the Elizabethan . . . You should be pleased." Signed: "Best of Luck to both for 1977, Leslie."

H66. Trenarren, postmarked April 8, 1977; on letterhead of All Souls College, Oxford; correspondence card

"You will also find your name blazoned on the jacket of Milton The Puritan (Macmillan June). . . . I hope you will see to it in Australia that the public libraries & best bookshops stock my books. If you would angelically suggest them." Signed: "Affec wishes to you & John, Yrs Leslie."

H67. Trenarren, postmarked July 18, 1977; letter

"You and John are perfect dears to me, if not Angels. . . . I have been busier than ever: a little lecture tour in U.S., followed by another to Swiss Universities. Endless T. V., including a film for the Quartercentenary of Drake's Voyage round the World. . . . Then lectures at Oxford—at the end I had to autograph 50 or 60 copies of my books. This does not please the London intellectuals. . . .

I ought to visit Australia one day, but surely am too OLD." Signed: "Much affectn to You both Leslie."

H68. Trenarren, undated/unpostmarked; received March 10, 1978; letter
"I am much interested by your idea of settling with John in a resort area in Britain. . . . I am prejudiced in favour of the S-West for climatic reasons. . . . I adore Devon and Dorset. . . . South coast of Devon heavenly . . . Thank you again for your kind puff of your poor old friend. Marks & Spencer ordered 30,000 of my Heritage of Britain, sold out before Xmas, & have ordered another 30,000! . . . If only I could save my earnings from the tax-hounds, I'd be able to bail you out when you go bust." Signed: "Affectly Leslie."

H69. Trenarren, December 1, 1979; letter
"You may be surprised, but I have written an Australian article—a very appreciative one about Judith Wright, to appear in Blackwood's Magazine. . . . I shall be sorry to miss you in London—I am there 4–6 December for BBC interview on my birthday, then Leeds for a grand T. V. panjandrum with celebrities who are rather enemies—Muggeridge and Levin. . . . Have been in US on a T. V.—radio tour—and just published A Man of the Thirties—ante—penultimate volume of autobiography." Signed: "Affectionate greetings to you and John, Leslie."

H70. Trenarren, February 1, 1980; letter
"I am sorry to hear about your nose. If you have to leave the air the best thing you could do would be to set up a bookshop." Signed: "Best of luck for that, A. L. R."

H71. Trenarren, September 2, 1980; letter
"Many congratulations! Delighted to see that you have made a success of it with that article. . . . You should now collect the odd stories from your passengers and write them up. . . . To London to a dinner Sir James Goldsmith is giving to celebrate the new magazine 'Now' with Mrs. Thatcher as guest of honour." Signed: "Best of Luck always, Leslie."

H72. Trenarren, December 14, 1980; letter
"Last week up in London, and did half an hour interview on Australian B.C., you may hear it some time." Also discusses watercolor painting by Andrew Freeth, R. A., which hangs on the staircase at Trenarren: "I think very good. . . . He did another of me looking very angry & irritable, because a Lady (Osborne) was banging away at my outer door to get in & I wanted him to finish and get it over." Signed: "Good Luck to Both for 1981, Leslie."

H73. Trenarren, December 27, 1981; letter
Tells he has been reading Patrick White's autobiography (*Flaws in the Glass*) and that he would like to read his short stories—a paper back, not too expensive in the post! Goes on to critizise the book for White's meanness towards the Queen: "she does her duty nobly, without liking any of it. White ought to

have the imagination to realise what a strain it is on her. . . . He seems rather a nasty nature, full of spleen. . . . The only thing that has gone right with him is his relationship with his Greek friend. Lucky there." Signed: "Best of Luck for 1982, A. L. Rowse."

H74. Trenarren, February 14, 1982; letter

Expresses thanks for Patrick White stories but has been "so shocked by the sheer silly superfluous filth of The Twyborn Affair. I have written a regular exposure of it for a book to come from Hodder & Stoughton. You are right to object to his attack on divine Joan Sutherland; he also attacks Sidney Nolan, a former friend. Nasty—all because his mother didn't love him as a child. Who could? . . . Of course White would never have got a Nobel Prize if he had not been (a) an Australian (b) a Leftist. It could have gone more worthily to Judith Wright, a great woman." Signed: "Best of Luck for 1982 & especially to John, Leslie."

H75. Trenarren, September 30, 1982; letter

"The Royal Society of Literature are awarding me their Benson Medal for services to Literature. Presentation December 9. . . . I don't think they have awarded it before to a historian, but you know I have always been ambivalent between history and literature. I am particularly pleased with the wording because you know that I am so categorised as historian that people overlook my literary work, esp. my poetry. . . . I regard my: A Life: Collected Poems as my most important book, for it is the register of my inner life (and my secrets) where the history books contain the outer interests. . . . I am just off to Washington to lecture on my project of Modernising Shakespeare. . . . President Reagan wrote me a charming personal letter, saying that he was in favour of making Shakespeare more accessible." Signed: "Best to you & John, Yours Leslie."

H76. Trenarren, November 28, 1982; letter

"Yes, I will keep free for lunch at Athenaeum. . . . on December 10, 1p.m. . . . I will wait for you, but don't make it too late or the lunch vanishes. Better still if you can arrive 12:30. . . . Much to tell you when we meet. I have been in Oxford entertaining President Reagan's son and daughter in law, with a whole squad of secret service agents." Signed: "Affectionate wishes to both you and John, Yours Leslie."

H77. Trenarren, February 7, 1983; letter

"What an enjoyable visit to the Athenaeum, nearly ordered out by the management for laughing so much. And giggling like drunks—this T T—along the pavements of Piccadilly, and losing my reputation in the basement of Hatchard's! . . . I want the biog. of Bob Hawke, because he's Cornish. . . . I leave for US about March 5. . . . Delighted and relieved John has made a good recovery. . . . I hope you are saving on the CAT." Signed: "Yrs affec. Leslie."

H78. Trenarren, May 24, 1983; letter

Gives thanks for Bob Hawke biography: "Bob Hawke's characteristics are as Cornish as Australian. I know them well: the aggressive individualism, the egoism, the touchiness, the liability to resentment, even a touch of vindictiveness." Signed: "Yrs A. L. R."

H79. Trenarren, July 4, 1983; letter

"Yes—I have found a last copy of A Man Of The Thirties and inscribed it for you. . . . Also Sunday July 24—if you are in London—I give a Shakespeare lecture at Victoria & Albert Museum at 3 p.m. . . . Again at Sutton Place, Guildford, August 13. . . . Thank you about intervening about Bob Hawke. . . . some people's egos are more interesting than other's—and his is not really a very interesting one: so common, vulgar and Philistine; no interest in the arts or things of the mind. Just what a Cornish Nonconformist would turn into, going into politics. Menzies was much more my man—a distinguished personality." Signed: "Affectly to you & John, Yrs Leslie."

H80. Trenarren, September 22, 1983; letter addressed to "Dear Colonel"

"I hope to be at Athenm Oct. 21—to speak at a School dinner that evening. And Nov. 30—to lecture at Victoria & Albert Museum 7.30 to help to save Shapespeare's Southampton's (patron, not boy-friend) Armour for this country." Comments on Bob Hawke, who has failed to answer Rowse's letter to him: "If the President of the United States (let alone the Colonel) can reply to a letter of mine, the PM of a second rate country, or 3rd rate, should do so too. Hawke must have known about me from Oxford days—I was a friend of his tutor, Ken Wheare, & also of Colin Clark whom he quarrelled with." Comments on my impression of the early portrait on the back cover of *A Man of the Thirties*: "Beautiful hands?—worn-out with writing to you. Beautiful eyes, too?—Ditto. Any thing else you fancy? . . . Stop spoiling that cat! And spoil me." Signed: "Love to both—Leslie."

H81. Trenarren, All Souls day, 1983. Postmarked Plymouth, November 3, 1983; letter

"Bob Hawke—No Bastard. He has sent me a nice letter giving me his Cornish ancestry. . . . I dare say I owe this information to your intervention, whose charm can charm a bird off a tree. . . . But then, your kindness to your poor old friend! What have you left for me at the Athenaeum? I cannot Imagine. . . . You needn't wear out my—tape. . . . I am expecting another of Cornish Stories & Poems, and a whole lecture on The Elizabethans & America. . . . I do hope you may be free for my Lecture at Victoria & Albert, Nov. 30 about 7.30." Signed: "Yours faithfully, Leslie."

H82. Trenerran, December 6, 1983; letter addressed to "Colonel"

"Have I thanked you for your surprising present of a little kangaroo? [in fact a koala] He sits up on a table in the library, keeping order among the numerous birthday cards, and is called Archie. . . . That was the name of John Betjeman's bear, whom he took to bed with him into his married life. One day his wife threw Archie out of the bedroom window—there was nearly a divorce. . . . I have just read Jim Faull's little book . . . The Cornish in Australia . . . I wish you would, as an honorary Cornishman, get in touch with Jim Faull, Cornish name, and tell him that I appreciate his book. . . . I have been rather over-whelmed by Birthday celebrations (80th birthday), & today broadcasting about Shakespeare to Liberia! . . . Thank you also for a whole cargo of tea. . . . I greatly admire John for his courage with which he conquered his illness, and you for your spirit, vivacity, intelligency, gaiety (dare I use the word?) and kind-ness, esp. to your poor old friend. . . . We had an orgy of a celebration at a beautiful historic mansion, Cotehele . . . near Saltash . . . large birthday cake and autographing scores of my books. . . . I told everybody I was 63." Signed: "Affectionately—Leslie."

H83. Trenarren, January 3, 1984; letter addressed to "Dear Commodore"

Gives thanks for photographs of home in Sydney, plus Marlene, the cat, "oc-cupying the best seat, no room for me. . . . I admire the tasteful apartment, esp. the books, in such beautiful virginal, condition, like the proud author." Dis-cusses the cassette tapes done by Sentinel Records at Penzance, of his lectures and poetry readings and asks if Australia may be interested: "They seem to be very much appreciated by grandies, persons of taste & cultivation, in US. . . . I sent one to Bob Hawke's Secretary to put on for him. . . . But are they per-sons of taste and cultivation? . . . I have to go to US again later in March & most of April. . . . Best of Luck for 1984—I hope to make it a Shakespeare Year with 3 books." Signed: "Affectionate wishes to Both & tickle Marlene for me. Yrs L."

H84. Trenarren, Candlemas Day 1984; postmarked February 3, 1984; letter addressed to "Your Reverence"

"To be practical: I have to be in USA mid-April to mid-May, so I shall miss you there. I shall be at All Souls mid-July, if you want to hear a lecture. Fancy your never having heard the best lecturer in England—now that Kenneth Clark is dead. . . . If you are here between May 29–June 7, when I shall be here, we might call & see them (Sentinel Records), at Penzance—I've never been there. . . . What a globe trotter you are, lucky dog—Greece—I've never been to Greece. . . . You were very kind to contact Jim Faull and also to jolly up the Prime Minister. . . . I suppose you are by way of becoming honorary Cornish. . . . Yes—Archie is very much at home. . . . I hope he doesn't get stuck up like that spoiled cat. I suppose you know that I am very jealous of Marlene. . . . In London 18–22 Feb. I have to do an Interview—Radio—about my cat Flippy." Signed: "Your uncle Leslie."

H85. Trenarren, March 22, 1984; letter addressed to "The Rt. Revd"

"I have obeyed your command and inscribed May 30 in my Calendar and shall hope to conduct you to 2 or 3 historic houses, which you ought to see, as well as Penzance." Makes mention of his impending U.S. trip and *The Contemporary Shakespeare*: "I am sticking to every line of Sh's texts but removing difficulties. . . . Delighted that you like my tapes—very clear to me; but I haven't got a machine to hear them! Just done one on 'Famous People I Have Known'—Churchill, Agatha Christie, Rebecca West, T. S. Eliot, Attlee, Bevin etc. Also Shakespeare's Self Portrait. . . . Macmillan have just produced my final & definitive edition of the Sonnets. . . . Look forward to showing you more of Cwll." Signed: "Love to you & J. Your Uncle Leslie."

H86. Oxford, July 14, 1984. on letterhead of All Souls College, Oxford, 2 pp, small 4to
Gives thanks for photographs taken during Cornwall visit: "Yes—after your delightful introduction to the fleshpots of the Pier House (in Charlestown), I gave a little dinner there before coming up to Oxford. . . . I hope you remember your poor old Uncle's recommendations before he is dead and gone:—(1) Health comes first. . . . (2) Money comes second. . . . (3) . . . if Adelaide is better for your health, you might think of starting a bookshop there. . . . that would feature and tie in with your other activities, autographs, mss collecting, photography & illustrations, tapes both audio & visual. . . . I'm busy here at Oxford. Gave the annual Claydon Lecture on 'What Kind of Man was Wm. Sh.?', out at wonderful Claydon House, Bucks. . . . Monday I open the English Speaking Union Summer Conference, as for 12–15 years past. . . . We had a few nice days together." Signed: "Yrs Leslie."

H87. Trenarren, October 3, 1984; on letterhead of All Souls College, Oxford. 2 pp, small 4to; addressed to "My Dear Lord Charlestown"
"I never go down to dear Charlestown without thinking of you, you have left such an imprint on the place. It remembers you. . . . What a chumb you are to remember your old teetotaller with Tea!. . . . And I have a present for you—a lovely book of short stories (*Night at the Carn*). . . . Very best wishes to you and John on your birthdays, young things. Both of you added up don't advance to the years of your poor old friend. . . . Fretting and fuming at the way things are going down the drain here, and Australia!—the PM's daughter a heroin addict, silly little bitch. I've no patience with such." Signed: "Yours L."

H88. Trenarren, October 26, 1984; letter addressed to "Dear Lord Charlestown"
Gives thanks for introduction to a possible house keeper to assist Phyllis, his permanent help: "Thank you too for tea—I called in at the Old Folks Home (Athenaeum!), and picked up the package, before going on to lunch with the Duke and Duchess of Portland. . . . Just back from Oxford. . . . talking Shakespeare to a group of American Managers. And stopping with the beautiful Lady Hesketh in Northants. . . . I may have to add a 4th Cat to my book for a paperback: A Quartet of Cornish Cats!" Signed: "Yours gratefully Leslie."

H89. Oxford, February 2, 1985—Candlemas Day; letter addressed to "The Rev"

"Thank You Your lordship . . . for lovely gift of tea. You are kind to your poor old friend. . . . I've been up here for BBC World Service, half an hour on Shakespeare. . . . Lecture at Purcell Room, gloomy great hall well filled—I missed you there, but got a warm reception the moment I appeared. . . . I have to come back here Feb. 10–17 for a lot of T.V. about Oxford. . . . anybody would think I was John Betj., I am so Badgered. No more—I must catch the train to Cwll." Signed: "Love to you Both, Leslie."

H90. Trenarren, postmarked June 28, 1985; addressed to "Col"

"Much relieved to have your letter. I was worrying about you. With my suspicious Cornish nature. . . . Alas, July 7 onwards I have to be at All Souls—and Sunday the Athnm is closed. . . . Since back from USA desperately busy—Oxford & London, lecturing at Sutton Place near Guildford. . . . then Hastings, a Royal Academician wanted to paint my portrait—modern, pretty awful. . . . Sad about Marlene—it does go to one's heart; I think every night of my poor little Flip, such a dear cat and so loving. . . . And of course I think of your lordship at Charlestown. . . . Thank you again for your kindness to your." Signed: "POF Leslie."

H91. Trenarren, August 7, 1985; letter

"Dear Lord Charlestown. . . . I write by air at once, in case you feel lonely without J. and Marlene. . . . And to thank you for your thoughtful kindness in Tea. . . . In return I am sending Glimpses for you to pick up at the Athenaeum, since you are almost a member, and must come to lunch or dine when we next coincide in Ln. . . . Keep out of trouble and me in mind." Signed: "Affect. Leslie."

H92. Trenarren, January 16, 1986; letter

"Dear Ld Charlestown. . . . You have a rival. Just had such a warm, enthusiastic letter from John Spender, MP. for North Sydney. The great historian Gibbon was proud to think that his books were read 'on the banks of the Wolga'. I am proud to think that mine are read on the banks of—what is your river called? . . . I dare say You roped him in. . . . I have finished a book about William Colenso. . . . The Controversial Colensos. Very recognisable Cornish temperament, though personally I don't like controversy—I prefer agreement. . . . You know that there is nothing controversial about my discoveries about Shkspre—they are just plain commonsense, only unanswerable. It is just envy on the part of the 3rd rate that I made them." Signed: "Love & Good Luck for 1986 to Both. L."

H93. Trenarren, May 5, 1986; letter

"Can you tell me anything about the beautiful Germaine Greer? Is she beautiful? . . . Why did she leave Australia? Why is she so dissatisfied and nasty?

Can't get anybody to love her? I know she is an aggressive feminist. . . . Her book is called The Female Eunuch. . . . Just back from US, in bed with phlebitis in my right leg. . . . I got bad hay-fever in Washington & couldn't go to Florida, which put on a fine production of my modernised Hamlet. Nor to Stratford, Conn. But I did get to Dallas. And gave a Shkspre lecture at the Folger. Last week NY Times gave a lunch party for me. They are producing my article on Venice in their Travel Supplmt—keep an eye open—I lectured there in March. . . . Always think of you in connexion with air stewards. . . . But all these flights are not good for me. . . . Thank you kindly for tea. Actually I prefer Earl Grey always." Signed: "Best from Bed to Both, Leslie."

H94. Trenarren, September 19, 1986; letter

"This is only a word of consolation for future family trouble. You cannot expect to keep your parents for long, and must steel yourself against the inevitable loss. Thank goodness you have John. . . . and don't suffer too much from my disease—Cat fixation. . . . I am noting October 20 & 21 in case I shall be in London. . . . a publisher wants to do a 'Rowse's Cornwall' . . . I may have to tour round with the photographer. . . . May see you, with tie on, at Athenm. . . . Love to you both—a fan has just arrived with a load of books—I have sent her off to have tea on the terrace with Phyllis." Signed: "Affectly Leslie."

H95. Trenarren, October 21, 1986; on letterhead of All Souls College, Oxford, 2 pp, 8vo

"Sorry not to have been able to be in London when you were there. I had several lecture engagements down here—one to the RN Engineering College at Plymouth, another for Exeter University. . . . Could you please forward the enclosed letter to Judith Wright? She has changed her address—nuisance—and it is beyond the capacity of the Australian P.O. to track the country's most famous woman. Democracy! . . . Why are people such (a) fools, (b) so slack? I hate them for it. Unlike you & Yours." Signed: "Affectn to Both you & John, Leslie."

H96. Trenarren, March 5, 1987; letter

"Alas, I am going to be in London April 1–3. Pity I shall miss you—lecturing to London Cornish April 2. Evening at Reform Club. And The Poet Auden: (Methuen) April 3 pub. . . . Every minute I expect Lord Althorp with T. V. team to do me for Today International, NBC. . . . Yesterday photographed in bed for Sunday Times Mag. feature. . . . Last week for front p. of N.Y. Times and article in House & Garden. . . . Keep your eyes open for I never see a thing." Signed: "Love to both, Leslie."

H97. Trenarren, Easter Saturday, 1987; letter addressed to "Colonel"

"I have been desperately engaged in drudgery—proofs of the revised edition of Shakespeare the Man. Practically a quarter new. . . . Also proofs of the last five plays, to complete the Contemporary Shakespeare. . . . And have been being photographed and televised to bits. The latter by very handsome, tall young Lord Althorp. I see where the Pcess of Wales gets her looks from. He was very intelligent & had done his homework. . . . So you now have another rival in the peerage, dear Lord Charlestown. . . . Another photographer has been down here for 'Rowse's Cornwall' which I have written—mostly in bed, where I work." Signed: "Affectionately, Leslie."

H98. Trenarren, March 15, 1988; letter addressed to "Colonel"

"What a remarkable bibliographer you are! . . . Fancy finding that book in low-brow Australia . . . [*Oxford Poetry 1925*]—containing two early poems) . . . Glad you liked my little Auden. . . . It was attacked by the envious third-rate Carpenter, who never knew Wystan. . . . I have been briefly to London. . . . grand dinner the Prime Minister asked me to at 10 Downing st., for my old friend Caspar Weinberger. A Falklands Islands affair. . . . On my right Lady Pym highly intelligent, had read all Barbara Pym, knew my books, a pleasure to talk to. On my left the wife of an Air Marshal, had read N O T H I N G , lived in Norfolk. . . . had never been to Felbrigg or Holkham, or had heard of any Norfolk writers. She turned out to be NZ. . . . I hate a low brow—such Bores—Nothing to talk to them about." Signed: "Love to Both, L."

H99. Trenarren, May 19, 1988; letter

"Angel to send me lovely Australian tea. . . . I am reciprocating with Q—very Cornish book. . . . up to my eyes with T. V. I have done the Armada, now 3 days hard labour about ME and Cornwall. . . . ALR's Cornwall comes out next month . . . but the great photographer Prof Hedgecoe . . . has had his way with me so much that it is more likely to turn out HEDGECOE and Rowse's Cornwall. Photographs of Sheep on Bodmin Moor—not me at all. . . . My little book on the great historian Froude is out. . . . Charlestown comes into my T. V. film—every time I see the Rashleigh Arms I think of you. I have my hair cut by the ladies just across the road." Signed: "Affection to Both, Leslie."

H100. Trenarren, undated; received December 6, 1988; note, with package containing tape of *Cornish Stories & Poems*

"Best of Luck to Both for 1989. . . . Much thanks for tea. Mixed up with Mrs. Eliot's. Do you mind being Mixed Up with Mrs. T. S. Eliot?" Signed: "Affectly, Leslie."

H101. Trenarren, November 24, 1989; letter addressed to "Dearest Nephews"

"Delighted that Sydney is retiring from his air-career." Goes on to advise on alternative careers like going to university or starting a bookshop. "I have sent the National Library, Canberra, my new Cornish book, The Controversial Colensos. . . . Chief Buthelezi of Natal is very interested. . . . Bishop Colenso is a hero to the Zulus whom he spoke for. . . . Yes, do get my new book, Discovering Shakespeare. . . . And send me a Guide to NZ with maps. . . . Often think of you at the Rash. Arms—we lunch there nearly every week." Signed: "Affect, Leslie."

H102. Trenarren, Christmas 1989; letter

Expresses thanks for NZ books. "Just what I wanted. . . . What a beautiful country! More beautiful than Australia? . . . I should be willing to pay for Sir Keith Hancock's last book—about the beauty of the country along the Murray River and those hills. . . . Snaky country. . . . I am being painted in bed—I know you don't like me in bed—being photographed, I mean. But I have been painted so often that this makes a different pose. I have come out looking like an old parson." Signed: "Much love and Good Luck to my two nephews down under. Yours, Leslie."

H103. Trenarren, February 9, 1990; letter

"Tomorrow I shall at last have more Colensos and will send you yours. Fancy your not being au fait with everything about Sir Keith Hancock—Australia's leading historian. Fellow of All Souls. . . . I want his last book about the Murray River country." Goes on to discuss further educational opportunities: "You should study British and Dutch history and literature. . . . John should study British and Scandinavian history. Both Scandinavia and the Netherlands are intimately bound up with Britain's history, literature and art. . . . I suppose Sydney NSW was named for you?" Signed: "Love to Both, Leslie."

H104. Trenarren, June 9, 1990; letter

Expresses thanks for photographs of the Huntington Library in California: "Funnily enough, a lot of people on the East Coast in USA do not know about it, and are snooty about the West Coast. . . . You may have missed a lovely article of mine on the Oxford & Cambridge Gardens, in New York Times, Travel Supplement, last week, June 3. Do look it up. . . . I have a couple of books in the press: Selected Poems . . . and a new volume: Prompting the Age: Poems Early and Late. . . . Meanwhile, putting together a fat volume of: Note Books of ALR following the example of Samuel Butler. . . . I am so pleased that your Manuscript enthusiasm has opened up so many paths for you. . . . Can't tell you how much the Left intellectuals hate me over here, and the academics. But they don't hate me half as much as I do them—and despise them. Just been reading how much Tennyson had to put up with from them, because he was the goods and also popular. Just envy. . . . Charlestown has been bought for development and is being spoiled. Like everywhere in the filthy modern world." Signed: "Much affectn to Both, Leslie."

H105. Trenarren, October 8, 1990; letter

"I had no high opinion of P. White as a writer. Certainly not a great writer, he was given the Nobel Prize only because he was an Australian. Plenty of second-rate writers get the Nobel Prize. . . . Now a contemporary novelist whom I greatly admire is Barbara Pym. . . . look under her petticoats and you will see how subtle she is. Also how true and real and sympathetic. . . . I find

P. White an unsympathetic man. . . . Nor do I find Bob Hawke sympathetic . . . recognisably Cornish in his boastfulness and being full of himself. Just like the Rowses. . . . Joan Sutherland is much more my cup of Earl Grey. Also Judith Wright. You will think I have gone over to the ladies. . . . I have just had to do a tape record about Agatha Christie—wouldn't go up to London to do T. V., don't mind doing it down here." Signed: "Love to you & John, Yours Leslie."

H106. Trenarren, December 1, 1990; letter

"O—You—Clever—Young—Man to spot the Sotheby item. But of course you are a professional. I put it on sale as a trial, to see how my things would go (The Mss of A Cornish Childhood). What I would really like would be to sell my Archive, mss etc to a good American university for a quarter of a million or so. I'd rather have them over there for scholars . . . also safer. . . . they would be better looked after. . . . If I sold them bit by bit through Sotheby's say, it would pile up money for the beastly tax people to take. . . . I have nearly finished My Books: A Testament, 40 or 50 chapters about the books, intention, reception. Also my Note Books . . . There remain all the unpublished Diaries, Journals and Pocket Books, mostly in type now. Enough to keep a Rowse Industry a la Boswell or Horace Walpole going next century. . . . Forgive all this about me—but you are an authority on the subject. Keep my flag flying when I am gone." Signed: "Love and Good Luck to Both, Yours, Leslie."

H107. Trenarren, February 11, 1991; letter

"So glad the Shakespeare book got through to you. . . . It is very good of you to see the whole point of my Shakespeare work as few professors do. . . . There is a strange and very interesting silence from them, as if they are stunned. . . . It may very well be that they are waking up to the facts. . . . What is rather paradoxical, and I think befogged conventional people in their rut has been that all my work is one way revolutionary, but in another quite conservative, in complete keeping with tradition. . . . Third-rate minds find it difficult to grasp that. They should be more open-minded, like you." Signed: "Much love to Both, Yours, Leslie."

H108. Trenarren, March 25, 1991; on yellow sheets 4 pp, 8vo

"What an excellent scholar you have become! I am delighted too that you are writing and publishing. You will be quite an authority on your poor old friend in time to come. . . . Thank you for your advice about keeping my Archives together . . . it is so huge . . . I would prefer my things to be in US—they look after them more carefully. I am half inclined to give them to friendly Georgetown provided that they pay for transport [in the event, the archive was given to Exeter University Library]. . . . Yesterday I was photographed on the terrace for an article on Mid-Cornwall for The Field for May. . . . Have also done T. V. on the terrace about Marlowe. . . . They kept on pressing me about his and Edward II's homosexuality—all that people are interested in to judge from the newspapers and media. So silly—as if just discovered. When a simple everyday fact of life—even common on jets and air-liners . . . Publishing is very topsy-turvy—publishers ruining themselves by vast handouts to popular journalists. All they want is the low-down on the sex life of public figures. . . . I believe even buster Hawke has appeared in that guise. . . . Do you love Mr. Hawke? My fan is Mr. Spender." Signed: "Love to you & John, Leslie."

H109. Trenarren, July 18, 1991; letter

"The English papers have been more than generous to the dear departed Patrick White, horrible man, and to the biography of him. . . . Of course it is a great joke that the very masculine, hetero Aussies should have produced as their leading writer an aggressive preaching homo. . . . But how good a writer was he? All the English papers treat him as a great novelist. But was he? The only novel I read—a transvestite one was muddled and unconvincing. . . . But I was prejudiced against his nastiness. . . . Like most intellectuals, his thinking was childish. . . . So—if you come across a cheap paperback . . . Voss?—do send . . . to your apt pupil always willing to learn. . . . Now I have just had to do a new T. V. piece: Marlowe versus Shakespeare. Homo versus hetero-sexuality. I hope you approve of that—it gets both bulls' eyes." Signed: "Love to both, Yours Leslie."

H110. Trenarren, August 6–7, 1991; on letterhead of The Towers—The Waldorf Astoria, New York, 2 pp, small 4to

"What a kind good heart you have—and a distinguished mind too! One can tell from the beautiful home you have constructed and the original fabric you have made of your life, with its intellectual interests. . . . All the same I disapprove of P. White's appalling manners. He was born a gent. . . . I was not . . . but know how a gent should behave. So too William Shakespeare. A propos him—thank you for standing up for me. You know the Left, dominant in intellectual, literary and academic life, exercised a tacit censorship against Roy Campbell. . . . So they have done with me. They have kept me out of everything all they can. Out of BBC, British Council, Arts Council, TLS, the media. My All Souls friend, Charles Monteith, took the decision at Faber's to discontinue publishing my poetry. No doubt it did not sell. But they continued to publish third-rate people. . . . If my poetry was good enough for Eliot to publish—he did, and wrote the blurbs for the first three vols—it was certainly good enough for the third raters. . . . Of course they hate me for saying that sort of thing. . . . A Swiss fan of mine noticed quite independently that they do not quote my books, the academics notably. But they can't answer them. . . . I can't get my books reprinted in London. So, undefeated, I get them reprinted in Cornwall. It has all made me work all the harder. . . . And you help me bravely." Signed: "Love to both, Leslie."

H111. Trenarren, August 11, 1991; letter

"Thank you for Voss, which I have now read with care. It is an original book which makes a powerful impression. People will read it as an epic of Australia and a picture of Victorian life in Sydney. . . . Interesting too about the Aborigines—makes one want to know more about the history of the extraordinary land. What I hate is the way White writes. Far too long-winded. Everything is exaggerated and pointed up with pretentious comments, which he thinks profound, but are either platitudes or perverse. . . . Intellectually he was not up to his pretentions, and 'thought' a lot of sheer nonsense. . . . He would not have got away with that in the Victorian age, the age of George Eliot or Henry James, real brains. White was uneducated and mentally undisciplined—thought he knew when he didn't. His gifts were otherwise. He had imagination and an understanding of human beings and character, if a distorted one. So—not a great writer, but a remarkable one." Signed: "Love to both, Leslie."

H112. Trenarren, August 29, 1991; letter

"Voss would be a better book if cut down by a quarter—all the passages that White thought profound thinking were either dressed-up platitudes or simple perversities. He was not a thinker. Unlike Keith Hancock: I wonder if they knew each other. Then White quarrelled with everybody—his friend Nolan for instance. He admired maleness, several times writes of the hairy man's chest, arms, wrists . . . in another novel describes the pain of being buggered. So I suppose he liked things that way. . . . Personally I prefer Judith Wright." Signed: "Love to both, Leslie."

H113. Trenarren, September 19, 1991; on letterhead of Trenarren-St. Austell

"Rare book & lovely tea just this minute arrived [Sir Keith Hancock, *Discovering Monaro*]. . . . I send you a rare book in return [Rowse's *The Cornish in America*]. . . . A Bassano–Dark Lady Exhibition for 1992 is preparing for Richmond—Virginia and Bassano near Venice. It seems that my Shakespeare work is gradually getting across. . . . The third-rate academics defend themselves by saying it is 'faulted'—but there is not a single fault they can find. Bugger them. But I'd rather horsewhip them." Signed: "Love to both, Marlene R, Le."

H114. Trenarren, September 20, 1991; 4 pp, large 4to

"Keith Hancock was the most eminent historian Australia has produced. . . . When I won a Prize Fellowship at All Souls very young, at 21, he was kind and took me up. When he went back to Australia he arranged for me to look after his interests and keep him in touch with English affairs. . . . I may be wrong about this. But Hancock may have disliked the way I chose as a writer. His standards were highly academic in favour of suppressing the personal. . . . What is the point of writing an autobiography if you are selfconscious and cagey, and suppress the personal? . . . I dare say that Hancock disliked the way that I always featured the personal element in my writing. The academics did. But they didn't know that this was the way to make a book live—even history: witness the greatest historians, Gibbon and Macaulay. . . . It may be that Hancock didn't like the way his junior and protégé developed way beyond him, became far more famous and sold in hundreds of thousands. He could never

have done that. . . . But Hancock was a first-class writer and a first-class scholar.
. . . I am sad that I got out of touch with Hancock. I blame myself, but feel
that he must have disapproved of me—though I became far more successful
and fulfilled than he. He remained academic." Signed: "Leslie."

**H115. Trenarren, September 22, 1991; on letterhead of the University of
Wisconsin, Madison 6, Department of History, Bascom Hall, 4 pp, 4to,
onion paper; addressed to "Dearest S— and J."**
"The Hancock book has made me fascinated with Australia." Continues, at
length, to describe the Australian experiences and failures of his brother
George—5 years his senior, who got a soldier's grant of 100 acres to break into
cultivation and grow wheat in Western Australia. "At the same time married a
girl he had taken up with. . . . Fancy being such an ignorant working class fool
as to take on two gambles in one. . . . I was too young to know, just starting at
Oxford and had problems enough of my own. . . . When their baby arrived—
called Leslie after me—his wife Dossie opted for the child and completely
turned against the husband. . . . The bottom fell out of the wheat market at the
same time. George sold his lot and packed up. A double failure. . . . He arrived
on me, in the grandeur of All Souls by then, just like a returned remittance man.
I was not pleased by the spectacle . . . really furious that nobody in our ignorant working class family could make a success of anything. . . . He always
remained a decent honest fellow, of no interest to me . . . would come down
to this manor house to shoot the pigeons, never give me a hand in the big garden. . . . Somewhere in Western Australia there is a Leslie Rowse. . . . But all,
or nearly all, my silly working class relations, in Canada my sister's family,
have an inferiority complex about me. O.K. by me. I don't want to know about
the Australian Leslie Rowse—of no interest." Signed: "Love to both, Leslie."

**H116. Trenarren, December 1, 1991; on letterhead of the Connaught,
Carlos Place, London, W1Y 6AL; 2 pp, 8vo, blue notepaper**
"I wonder if there isn't a convenient paper back History of Australian Exploration? I should like to read about the opening up of the continent, the heroic
journeys, the gradual settlements, the aborigines. . . . Thank you for your kind
Birthday message, you dear ones. Hope my book gets through the Xmas post
safely to you with my love." Signed: "Leslie."

**H117. Trenarren, February 19, 1992; on letterhead of Trenarren, St.
Austell, 4 pp, 8vo**
"You may be surprised, but I cannot claim to be in love with Bob Hawke. But,
yes, I shall be glad to read his Memoirs. . . . You are right as usual about the
Illustrations Book [A. L. Rowse's *Cornwall*]. . . . Since we were to go 50-50
on it I had to give way to the bossy Professor Hedgecoe. Do you think that I
wanted sheep-faced sheep farmers on Bodmin Moor? . . . I should have liked
more historic buildings, but the Professor was bent on illustrating contemporary life. And you know how much I like that! . . . I dare say Lord Charlestown
should be in. . . . I have succeeeded in stopping a new road across lovely

Luxulyan Valley. Though there is going to be a beastly new road across the top end of Charlestown. All due to the filthy population explosion. . . . I fear I am not much in sympathy with the democratic way of life, of which Australia provides such a beautiful specimen and to which Bob Hawke has sucked up so successfully—Ugh! . . . Alas, no, we have never got a successor to dear loving little Flippy, though I think of him every night when I go to bed. And sometimes say a prayer to him." Signed: "Love to both—Leslie."

H118. Trenarren, February 22, 1992; 4 pp, 8vo, torn from writing pad, in purple biro

"Thank you again & again. Blainey is just the book I needed to understand Australia. I was so fascinated that I read it all in one day—yesterday. . . . Only once does he mention snakes. The aborigines, naked as they were, must have had a high mortality from snake-bite. . . . Curious that I should have this fascination for Australia, when I have no liking for brash, democratic society. . . . From my reading of Blainey I portend that Queensland may become the most important of the provinces in the future." Signed: "Much love & gratitude, Leslie."

H119. Trenarren, May Day 1992; on letterhead of Trenarren, St. Austell, 4 pp, 8vo

"Thank you for lovely tea and Blainey, good book. . . . Delighted that the Queen gave Judith Wright the Gold Medal for Poetry. . . . I enclose my review of Ted Hughes for my file at St. John's Road. . . . In London they think poor Ted Hughes has taken leave of his senses—and his book even crazier than I said. . . . I don't wonder, for he is under constant persecution by the Sylvia Plath–maniacs. They have made a cult of her, teach her second rate verse in all the Eng. Lit. departments. . . . No wonder Hughes left her—now they make him responsible for her suicide. . . . Poor Hughes should never have married her, but you know what mugs young heteros are about women. Hormones!—they can't help themselves. Now he wants to come down and see me. . . . Tomorrow I lunch at your Rashleigh Arms with the Cornish publisher who is re-publishing The Little Land of Cornwall." Signed: "Much love to both, Yours, Leslie."

H120. Trenarren, August 29, 1992; letter

"You wouldn't find that Keith Hancock kept any of my letters, though I kept his. . . . He used me to keep him in touch with things, and to get things of his published, like his essay on Pitcairn. But I expect he disapproved of my youthful Politics and the Younger Generation, and of the way I went, stuck my neck out about politics, made myself notorious with my campaign against Appeasement. . . . When he wrote an autobiography it was attacked in the Times Literary Supplement. He probably thought that was me. It wasn't, but by my friend Ken Wheare, who disliked Hancock . . . couldn't bear Hancock's closed up, cautious reticence—nobody was a close friend. He was the son of an Archdeacon of Melbourne, prim and prude. . . . What is the point of writing an auto-

biography and being so selfconscious you dare not be frank and outspoken?"
Signed: "Love, L."

H121. Trenarren, New Year 1993 (postmark January 6, 1993); letter

"Delighted that that early Ms of mine has found such a good home. . . . I have
just had a request from the Ukraine, for All Souls and Appeasement, and, A
Man of the Thirties. I have not got a copy, nor of: The End of an Epoch. Can
you help? . . . Fancy your poor old friend being wanted in the Ukraine! The
two volumes: The Elizabethan Renaissance, have been translated into Polish.
. . . Many of my books are on tape in US. . . . Books on Tape. . . . They have
just sent me the whole book: A Man of the Thirties. Fancy that! Unobtainable
in this bloody country. What matter in such a filthy society? I watch it with
interest, but no sympathy, going down the drain. . . . I have written you a couple
of letters during the past few months not neglecting my young friends." Signed:
"Good Luck for '93, Leslie."

H122. Trenarren, May 9, 1993; letter

"I wish you were Prime Minister, instead of Keating. But Democracy—I just
couldn't bear Australian democratic society. No wonder Patrick White couldn't,
in spite of his callous Leftism. I suppose his private tastes were hardly in keeping with those of the Idiot People. And fancy wanting a squalid Republic—of
Clintons and Majors. . . . No sense of history, no sense of the glories of the
past; I like a touch of romance and poetry. As when, in Westminster Abbey, I
watched the Queen's coronation, her dedication to duty. I thought of all the
coronations on that spot, Elizabeth I and right back to William the Conqueror.
And somebody said there was only one other such spectacle in the modern
world—St. Peter's at Rome. Fancy preferring a lot of proxy politicians. . . .
Did I tell John that I once went to the theatre with the former King of Sweden
incognito. . . . He told me that he didn't go in for ceremony, but did give a reception for both Houses of Parliament." Signed: "Affectionately, Leslie."

H123. Trenarren, May 25, 1993; letter

"Society is breaking up everywhere in every country. Filthy democracy, inevitable, but everywhere the Idiot People are out of hand. Here the Queen, Queen
Mother, Philip, Prince of Wales . . . all work hard at doing their duty and making
the monochrome of demotic society more colourful and interesting. But it is
the historical side of it that I care for. . . . They are let down by the young
people—like young people everywhere. Fergie is a fool and an empty head. . . .
Andrew was a fool to marry her, but she was beautiful and, since he has lots
of it, he needed a good f——. Can you understand it? He does his duty, she
wouldn't. Diana does her duty, works hard, but is neurotic, very beautiful, but
stupid and far too young for Charles. He is intelligent—one of us, a book collector, and works very hard—too hard—at his job. He is highbrow, like you
and me, and ought not to have married a low-brow he finds a bore. . . . But
they had difficulty in finding a virgin with no past—these days! . . . Anyhow
she has produced two good kids for the succession. Perhaps she thinks that's

enough—wouldn't you?—and doesn't like the Family, who are rather German.
. . . Three books in the press in my 90th year!" Signed: "Love to Both, Yours
Leslie."

H124. Trenarren, June 5, 1993; letter

"Of course people with no historical knowledge or imagination do not appreciate Monarchy. But you can imagine what I felt in Westminster Abbey, looking down on the Coronation of the Queen, on the spot where they had all been
crowned. . . . I watched Churchill saying farewell to it all. . . . Actually, the
Queen—who is just straight and simple and sincere—doesn't like Ceremony.
But she accepts her duty. And it lends colour and romance to the common
monotonous grey of ordinary 20th century life. . . . Abroad, in France and
Germany, people envy our monarchy, as a great many people do in USA, who
would change it for the Hollywood vulgarity of Clinton's White House, or the
shirt-sleeves and jeans of Bob Hawke and Keating? Of course, the poor Queen
has been let down by some of the younger generation—like the young people
everywhere in the breakdown of modern society. Myself, I don't care what happens to it, as it goes down the drain everywhere, more terrorism and violence,
more bombs, more drugs, more Aids—Let them have it all. Now bombing the
art galleries with the grandest collections of past culture and civilisation."
Signed: "L."

H125. Trenarren, June 21, 1993; letter

"Thank you, Thank you, dear boys, for lovely tea. Lovely smell. You know that
Dr. Johnson was a terrific guzzler of Tea—so what more appropriate for
Bookmen like Us? I am no less delighted by news of your bibliophilic engagement [reference to two lectures given at the State Library of NSW]. . . . Two
of the three books of this, my 90th, year are on the way to you. The third book
has been a secret. Duckworth's asked me to write: All Souls In My Time, and
I have just finished proofs. . . . Just thought of a good bibliographical idea. I
will send you a batch of mss Poems—corrections and all—for the great
Cauveren Collection. . . . I am so glad you are lecturing. I expect you have the
gift to make your lectures interesting. Whatever critics say (take no notice of
them!)—it is the personal element that gives life to what one writes." Signed:
"Much love & Thanks, Leslie."

H126. Trenarren, August 22, 1993; letter

"What a scolard you are! Do be careful, or you'll end up a professor. . . . I have
attended to your (proper) suggestions and have a lock of hair and a pair of spec-
tacles waiting for when you turn up. . . . I have finished a book on the Regicides, which Duckworth suggested to me. It makes a proper sequel to my:
Reflections on the Puritan Revolution—same tone & temper, which so provoke
the pro-Puritan Leftists. I enjoy teasing the humbugs. . . . Another publisher
asked me to update: The Spirit of English History, with an additional chapter
to cover 1943–1993. So I have done that too. Plenty to occupy you when I get
it all across to you. Delighted you like the Caroline Portraits. Hardly at all re-

viewed—though they review all the topical trash of the third-rate and all the boring Sex scandals. . . . The fact is, the Politically Correct don't like me—I am their Enemy No 1—and I enjoy provoking and teasing them." Signed: "Love to Both—Leslie."

H127. Trenarren, September 13, 1993; letter

"The heavens have wept at your departure, rain has poured down, the trees have raged and tossed, the magnolia slashed against my window, the whole of Cornwall is angry, electricity cut off. Good thing you are not here for lunch today—no heating. You see how you are missed and what an impression you made—a disturbance all over Cornwall—you raised a storm. . . . Yesterday morning we thought of you still at Charlestown, sorry you did not meet David Hill & David Treffry. . . . Glad that you met the Hon. Robert Eliot and fell for the peerage. . . . I shall hear from him no doubt!! . . . Thank you for a lovely visit." Signed: "Much Love to you & J., Leslie."

H128. Trenarren, September 17, 1993; letter

"In the Elizabethan Age it is well known that witches raised up storms. Today you must be the most powerful wizard, considering the storm you called up on leaving. We had three big trees blown down, any amount of rhodos and fuchsias flattened the gravel and paths all strewn with leaves. Or, if it wasn't you, perhaps Cornwall was raging and protesting at your departure. It shows what an impression you made! . . . Well, Phyllis and I enjoyed seeing you again, and now that the whirlwind is over, and all is quiet, we miss you. Didn't we put our time to good use? The young man full of wizard energy quite wore the P.O.M. out." Signed: "Much love to John & You, Leslie."

H129. Trenarren, October 1, 1993; letter

"Nice to think that the poor old country has been visited by two important Australians: Mr. Keating at Balmoral, Mr. Cauveren at Trenarren. What fun and interesting chat we had! I don't suppose the poor Queen had with Mr. K.— just another boring politician she had to do duty and go through with. . . . I was much amused by your expecting the young Cornishman in the bus to know my name and to have heard of: A Cornish Childhood. Of course not. The Idiot People don't buy books. In USA 60per cent of people don't; same in Spain. . . . I don't expect any thing from them. This is why ordinary people are so boring (apart from sex)—not worth talking to. . . . Nothing but bad weather since you left. You disturbed the elements. The heavens raged and poured." Signed: "Much love to S & J, Leslie."

H130. Trenarren, November 10, 1993; letter

"I am writing at once, the moment I got your letter about J. I pray all goes well—you may not know that Mrs. Simpson, Duchess of Windsor was operated for cancer of the bowel, and completely recovered to give trouble to everybody. . . . I hope the doctors have removed every bit of the trouble. As for pain, at the worst moment after the last of my four stomach operations, I was given heroin. The only time I have experienced it—and it was heaven. But one mustn't become an addict! I am rushing by air a book of the most beautiful colour productions of Cornwall I know—specially for John. . . . I have now been interviewed and photographed by three papers—Guardian, Independent and Telegraph. The first was excellent, by their Terry Coleman, who interviewed me 30 years ago at All Souls. . . . I always read a lot in hospital." Signed: "Much love to Both, Leslie."

H131. Trenarren, November 26, 1993; letter addressed "Dearest John"

"I am thinking of you, and this is advice especially for you. I am an old hand at operations—4 stomach ops, peritonitis twice (a narrow escape), and now ninety. When you go in to hospital you must take a lot of books and do all the reading you can, to take your mind off yourself. . . . I want you to pass your other examination first class. I know that an internal interference takes more out of one than one expects. . . . Drugs are much better nowadays than in my time to help with pain, and sleep all you can. . . . Thank you both for lovely tea and do your best to co-operate as I have always done in hospital, where I've spent a lot of time usefully." Signed: "Much love to Both, Leslie."

H132. Trenarren, Xmas 1993; postmarked December 29, 1993; letter

"I am now most anxious to know how dear John is going on, and pray that all is going well. . . . You—naughty boy—woke me up on my birthday. But I managed to stop people that evening by never answering. Busy people in my generation don't like the telephone. Quiller Couch never answered it. . . . I have been snowed under—newspaper interviews too. One of them dredged up absolute lies from the gutter. I will alert you later." Signed: "Please Both Keep Well. Love and Good Luck for '94, Leslie."

H133. Trenarren, January 7, 1994; letter

"O God, now I am dreadfully worried about your house—and so is Phyllis. I hope and pray the fires have not reached Glebe and destroyed your house. . . . God, what a country—democracy, Keating and all, now burning. Even Cornwall, cold and rainy, is better. And I pray all is going well with John. Let me know by letter, not telephone. That alarms me. . . . Sisman in the Independent grubbed up absolute lies from the gutter about my Oxford life. Quite untrue. They don't care what they say, and can't tell what is true or false, what is right or wrong. That is what ordinary humans are like—that is democracy—and I prefer Cats." Signed: "Love & Good Luck, I pray, for '94, Leslie."

H134. Trenarren, February 23, 1994; letter

"I pray that all is going well with John, and not too much pain. . . . I was much relieved to hear that the fires had escaped you and your home was safe. . . . You have both been much in mind, but I have been kept busy with reviews, interviews, articles and can't keep up with it all. . . . Now I am expecting final proofs of: The Regicides. Weidenfeld jumped the gun and reprinted a large edition of my illustrated: Story of Britain, without consulting me or a word to let me know! That was a worry, but anyhow they are paying up. . . . In New York my fan Jacqueline Onassis has joined John's club—I do hope she will be all right. The three or four women who had breast cancer all recovered—so too a Cornish clay worker who had one testicle removed." Signed: "Much love to both, Leslie."

H135. Trenarren, June 9, 1994; letter addressed to "The Reverend"

"Of course I have been thinking of you, esp. of J., hoping that he is free of pain and taking proper rests. Yes, I am sad about Jacqueline. She was such a nice woman—one of us, a devoted book woman, worked in Doubleday's, editing art history books. She was European in her tastes and beautiful handwriting and voice—talked in a soft voice just above a whisper. She collected my history books, had about a dozen in her pretty library at 1012 Fifth Avenue. As for all the public brouhaha, she said to me, 'It doesn't affect me—it's all out there,' pointing to the window overlooking the lake in Central Park. At lunch I said that I had never been further up in Fifth Avenue. She said, 'You had better not, you might be mugged.' . . . I have several letters from her. Also from Mr. Nixon, who used to send me all his books, gave a dinner party in his NY house for me. . . . Pity he had such a split personality—a fine world statesman on one side, but a raging hatred of the Left intellectuals & media. . . . Now your friend Robert Eliot has gone too. Has had a fine send-off down here." Signed: "Much Love to Both, Leslie."

H136. Trenarren, August 2, 1994; letter

"Delighted that John is taking time off. When he comes back you must make him rest regularly every day. You too. I do it 2–4. The great Queen Elizabeth I, 5–7. But she stayed up at night, dancing etc at Court. . . . You must take no notice of what the Third Rate write about me. Just destroy it. The poor fools genuinely can't understand, and being Third Rate don't know their place. In modern democratic society it is the habit to write everything and every body down. Lop the tallest. . . . Yes—if no trouble to you, I should like a Xerox of my lrs for Ollard. . . . My Homo book is just going on tape in US." Signed: "Affectly, Leslie."

H137. Trenarren, September 12, 1994; letter

"It is a pity Bob Hawke is so vulgar, but that is the way he has won his success by always playing to the gallery, the Idiot People. Also exceptionally egoistic. . . . It is also a rather Cornish trait, as I well recognise. How superior Keith Hancock is to these boring politicians. Politics, especially demo politics, are so trivial, so ephemeral, not worth wasting time to read the newspapers. . . . But I see you are getting trouble from your Asian immigrants as we are from our blacks. No business to have imported so many. I would allow in only those who pass a beauty test (male), to improve the general looks. . . . I have been made to write: Historians I Have Known, in which I have given Hancock a good write-up. . . . And have been reading your poets—I do like Judith Wright, though so feminine. Femininity is a Bore. Like Politicians." Signed: "Love, Leslie."

H138. Trenarren, New Year 1995; postmarked January 18, 1995; letter

"Most of all, delighted to hear good news of J. Good Boy! Correspondence I prefer to maintain by telepathy. For of course I think of you at proper intervals, and gratefully for tea to keep my poor old brain working. But just think— I can't answer all the lrs that flow in on me. What I need is a nice young person. . . . the Daily Telegraph says that there is a 'Rowse renaissance' on. I think there is. I should have sent you the important article I wrote for them, to start the Shkspre season in Ln, on Sh's Language Today. . . . I had a most successful interview with Ned Sherrin on radio. Now every body has heard of it and badger me for a tape. Bugger them—they should listen in themselves, not miss it—and then write to bother me. Bob Hawke is making a great fool of himself. What a vulgarian he is—but well geared to Australian democracy, no doubt." Signed: "Best of Luck, Love L."

H139. Trenarren, March 12, 1995; letter

"Did you ever meet Christina Stead? . . . I have just read Hazel Rowley's biography of her. . . . Miss Stead had a lifelong crush, part fantasying, on my former Communist friend Ralph Fox, who was killed in the Civil War in Spain. . . . obey Party orders and go out to be killed, along with John Cornford, Julian Bell and other young University fellows of great promise whose lives were thrown away. In vain. . . . He was a few years my senior at Oxford. I used to argue with him fiercely how foolish it was of the Communists to attack the Social Democrats—it would only let in the Nazis and Hitler. As it did. Fox must have realised this in the end—it brought about his disillusionment with Communism. . . . Christina Stead fancied herself in love with Ralph. . . . he comes into her novels, esp.: For Love Alone. Patrick White admired her work. A suitable pair, for she was difficult and so was he, both riddled with their complexes, not grown up." Signed: "Love, Leslie."

H140. Trenarren, April 6, 1995; letter

"Phyllis and I are both touched by your constant kindness to us. And I have had you much in mind, having caught up with Chr. Stead's novel: For Love Alone. She is crazy for sex, quite sex-mad. . . . She was an authentic novelist, with her interest in people. But why do Australians have so many complexes?— like P. White. She had a perfect hatred for her father—no real ground for it, rather a remarkable man—she was lucky to have one such. I didn't. Then she had no distinction of style, such as writers I like, Barbara Pym, Elizabeth Bowen. . . . she should have cut out one-third, even a half. Then her profound thoughts, who wants those? She must have been influenced by D. H. Lawrence. One half of his thoughts were nonsense but the rest was genius. . . . She makes one understand the dreadful Germaine Greer. Think what we have missed from the likes of them. Stead was a battle-axe too. Her fixation about Ralph Fox was illusory. . . . My publishers are enthusiastic about my Historians book. . . . the Leftist academics are already attacking it. . . . The Garden here has never been more beautiful—mountains of red and white rhodos." Signed: "Love to Both, Leslie."

H141. Trenarren, April 8, 1995; letter

"Now P. and I have to thank you for lovely tea. You shall be promoted to Heaven for your angelic disposition. . . . You don't say whether you have read the horrid Stead. . . . I don't think much. She can't be better than P. White—and I don't think much of him. Keith Hancock, the historian, wrote better than either—a good stylist, which they are not. I have written him up in my Historians book— done him justice. The Leftist academics are already sharpening their knives for me. They hate me—naturally, for I stand for all they dislike and know that I think them second rate, when not third-rate. On the other hand, William Waldegrave (now a Cabinet Minister) writes me he is delighted that I have put in his proper place the 'over-estimated' T.V. historian, A. J. P. Taylor. I knew him well. . . . he is the sort they like, Leftist though bribed by Beaverbrook, totally irresponsible, in fact dishonest. What a lot! . . . the third-raters flock together. I gather they didn't like Geoffrey Blainey either—attacked him too. But what matter in today's filthy society anywhere? Look at USA, presided over by the Clintons. How low the Presidency has sunk compared with its prestige under Roosevelt! Or the monarchy here—when the Queen does a first class job." Signed: "Affectly, Leslie."

H142. Trenarren, June 4, 1995; letter

"I wanted to know what you thought of the Stead woman. But now realise that she is less good than P. White—and I don't think highly of him either. She was not a good stylist & dreadfully long-winded. So was he, neither of them really good writers, by the best standards. . . . Glad you have got an article in some-where. . . . One has to Push—the Pen rather than the Penis. I have wrapped up my Historians—You shall have your copy in the autumn. . . . But what bitches you grow in Australia! Germaine Greer is another." Signed: "Love to Both, Leslie."

H143. Trenarren, September 2, 1995; letter

"No—Neither the book nor tea has turned up. Where did dear J. dispatch it from? Australian airmail seems always reliable. Ordinary surface mail is not. Once a book I sent you went astray [*The Little Land of Cornwall*]. Bloody people. Many congratulations to John on his good fortune. Shows what a dear he is, and it will bring him near home. . . . Lovely to have you nearby in London. Better for your health. . . . look after your Health Insurance everything is expensive. Especially houses in Hampstead. . . . Good news. My Historians book comes out later this month, but a Book Club has taken 1,000 pre-publication. Duckworth's are 'thrilled,' they say. Blackwell's at Oxford are having a window display. Your old friend will be on the shelves, not on the shelf." Signed: "Much Love and All Luck, Leslie."

H144. Trenarren, September 13, 1995; letter

"Thank you for latest lovely tea just come. And I am sending Historians book by Air Mail, which is safer. . . . The book is portending a good reception. . . . I have been autographing 150 copies for Blackwell's, doing 5 Interviews for Germany; yesterday an Interview for the Independent. . . . No luck yet with the parcel from Sweden. . . . Lovely to have you over here. Don't leave it until I am up above or down below." Signed: "Much love to both, Leslie."

H145. Trenarren, September 25, 1995; letter

"I am writing at once to say that the parcel from Sweden has this moment arrived. So Sweden's postal honour is saved. . . . Thank you, John, for taking the trouble and for the sad but sweet note about your Aunt enclosed—evidently a dear woman, who knew what a good nephew she had. Thank heaven John that you have Sydney to console you—and that you have each other as a stout defence, a refuge against the cruelty of the world. I have not got that good fortune, and as a public target am under constant attack. . . . They resent my hating their filthy society and down-grading their media-icons, like A. J. P. Taylor. But private letters are quite different. The Chancellor of Oxford University, Lord Jenkins, has written to me warmly praising the book & agreeing with me about A. J. P. T. This is the price one has to pay for all the publicity—it will sell out the book and I shall cry all the way to the Bank." Signed: "Thank you for White and lovely tea, dearest young men. Yours, Leslie."

H146. Trenarren, October 10, 1995; letter

"When is John going to begin his long and serious campaign to get me a Nobel Prize? Why not? Cornwall has never yet received that recognition. And I am the representative writer. As a Cornish Bard my name in the old Cornish language Lev Kernow means The Voice of Cornwall. I know that the Nobel Prize does not go to historians. But there are . . . my life's work in poetry . . . my literary biographies . . . volumes of literary and social criticism . . . short stories . . . all my work on the Elizabethan Age and Shakespeare, solving the problems . . . making discoveries. . . . For Sydney I will keep the Ms of my Historians— expensive to send by Air and we cannot trust Surface Mail. . . . Perhaps you could take it when you come over to prospect for a house." Signed: "Much love to both, Yrs. Leslie."

H147. Trenarren, December 4, 1995 at 92! 2 pp, 8vo, recto & verso

"How kind to pep me up with tea—just had a cup to inspire me—I've been choking people off from telephoning me, silly nuisances, now going to take off the receiver. . . . I may send the mss before you come, but dreadfully busy. The Pr. of Wales came last week, wanted to talk to your poor old friend. I was most impressed, so friendly and nice and unaffected, intelligent and responsive, quick sense of humour, looks only half his age. The filthy media have never told the public how lucky we are in him. . . . Now he wants me to come up to Highgrove—beyond me . . . wants to come again. . . . Rather a fuss, an escort of nine, a nice policeman circling the house in case of bombs. What a life! . . . I share birthdays with the ghastly Carlyle and odd but amusing Butler of 'Erewhon' (NZ)." Signed: "Much Love to Both. Yours, Leslie."

H148. Trenarren, New Year 1996; postmarked January 13, 1996; letter

"Yes, John is quite right to have regular check-ups. It is wonderful what modern drugs can do. They have kept Phyllis going to 86. Now she had to give up & retire to a nursing home. I am miserable about it and shall miss her dreadfully. Also my eyesight is failing, so I can't put together the ms of the Historians book for you. Never mind—you shall have something else—probably the ms of the last book I shall write—My View of Shakespeare. It is done & now being typed. . . . Pray for me that one of the women neighbours here will be willing to come to my rescue. They say I am not a nuisance, but they mostly have their own dear families, with kids and dogs. . . . It will be lovely to see you here to cheer me up, and I hope I may be taken care of by then—though no one can fill Phyllis' place for me." Signed: "Love to Both, Leslie."

H149. Trenarren, March 25, 1996—Lady Day; letter

"Yes, I am looking forward to seeing you in the week after Easter. I am saving some mss for you. . . . there was so much upset when Phyllis was leaving. She is now well installed in a little warm & cosy flat, Prince Charles House . . . St. Austell . . . Only a road or two away from the little shop where I was born. I have moved to the downstairs study where I have my bed, more convenient for everybody. . . . I have sent off my book: My View of Shakespeare. I hope I may be able to dedicate it to the Prince (not the Princess) of Wales. That will annoy the Leftists and Politically Correct. He is Politically Incorrect, like your old friend Leslie." Signed: "Much love to both and lovely to see you, Leslie."

H150. Trenarren, April 28, 1996; on letterhead of All Souls College, Oxford; 2 pp, small 4to.

"Lovely to see you, looking so well—but too young. I want you to look more your age and make them take you as a serious authority. I have known several young dons at Oxford who made themselves out to be and act much older, in order to get on. Can you believe it? . . . You were very good to take it rough and rude—but I am twice your age, and am ambitious for you. . . . Friday I had to record a reading of my poems—I held out, my voice did very well. . . . I'm sure you'll put the Eng. Historians mss. in order, & if any more turn up I will send them, along with some more pieces. . . . You are wrong about Brooks's, appreciated by all the right people for its historic associations." Signed: "Love, Leslie."

H151. Trenarren, May 15, 1996; letter

"Many thanks for Blainey's book [*A Shorter History of Australia*]. Tell him it is simply first class, just what I needed. And I so much agree with his approach, his inflexion and his views. It is curious that I have a bit of a fixation on Australia—I don't know why, except that it is both fantastic and fascinating. 'Homosexuals in History'—JKO's autographed copy has just fetched in her NY sale, US$5175. I am surprised. Just be careful of all your autographed copies. And now a Czech publisher is offering a large advance for a translation. . . . It was so nice seeing you and teasing you . . . my dearest Cornubophile." Signed: "Love, Leslie."

H152. Trenarren, July 10, 1996; quarto sheet, folded for 4 pp, 8vo
"Information for you." Sends names and addresses of agents and publications to assist in the compilation of his bibliography. "Enough to get on with, enough for your poor tired old friend. I send you the catalogue of Australian at Oxford, Alistair Crombie, a disappointed man, for the young Leftists at All Souls would never make him a Fellow. . . . he was a man of taste . . . top hat and all. . . . I was always friendly with him though a Roman Catholic and the History of Science was not my field. . . . In the end Trinity did make him a Fellow, glad to say, I hope he died happy. At Oxford it makes all the difference whether one is a Fellow or not. . . . Much enjoyed Geoff Blainey's book—most illuminating, it helped me to understand Australia. He's a top class historian, so superior to the third rate Leftists. Tell him from me. . . . Does John know educated people in Stockholm in touch with the Nobel Prize authorities?!" Signed: "Love to Both, Leslie." [This was the last letter in our twenty years of correspondence. A. L. Rowse suffered his major stroke thirteen days later and never recovered to write again.]

MISCELLANEOUS LETTERS

H153. Oxford; postmarked April 12, 1962; on letterhead of All Souls College, Oxford; correspondence card
To: Mr. Frank Waven Esqr: "Thank you for so appreciative a letter. Most critics are frightful asses and seek to show how much better they could have written the book than the author. In fact they don't because they couldn't." Signed: "A. L. Rowse." [Source: John Wilson, January 1991; £20.]

H154. Oxford; undated, circa late 1950s; on letterhead of All Souls College, Oxford, 1 p, 8vo
To: "Dear John . . . Plenary dispensation from reading this at present. But when you go abroad next take it with you. Very good for your French—she writes wonderfully. Apart from that I think you'll like her. It's funny to think she's a classic now." Signed: " Yours, Leslie." [Source: Purchased together with book *La Vagabond* by Colette at Truro Bookshop, April 17, 1996; £20.]

H155. Postmarked Los Angeles California, Terminal Annex, October 25, 1965; letter on letterhead of Henry E. Huntington Library and Art Gallery, San Marino, California 91108
To: Ava, Viscountess Waverley: "I left England on September 26—evidently you don't read the Times newspaper. . . . in New York . . . I was giving the

opening lecture for the autumn at the Ppt. Morgan Library. . . . I also learned that my: Shakespeare biography is nearing 200,000 in hard covers—it has made a nice fortune. Isn't the book 'singing like a bird' for me? And that my edition of the Sonnets is coming out in Harper's Perennial Classics with a first impression of 65,000. Isn't it shocking, especially to say so. . . . I'm having a month's lecture-tour across US, to minister to circulation and useful publicity, before settling down at the Huntington Library for a winter's work on the next book but two." Signed: "Yours Affectly, Leslie." [Source: Sophie Dupré, December 1987; £15.]

H156. Undated but circa early 1967; on letterhead of Henry E. Huntington Library, California; 2 pp, 8vo

To: "Dear Richard" . . . (Richard Church) . . . Concerning a possible offer for his library from the Huntington: "which is interested in English literary mss (& possesses the finest—the Ellesmere Chaucer!). . . . If you have a considerable archive, I think they would make as good an offer as any. (They are after mine too)." Signed: "Affectntely, Leslie." Richard Church has added a note at top right: "Acld, 18/3. Told of Texas." [Source: One of series of three, Bertram Rota, London, December 10, 1982.]

H157. Oxford, May 3, 1967; on letterhead of All Souls College, Oxford; 2 pp, 8vo

"Dear Richard" [discussing his poetry] "I haven't dried up, as so many of the fashionables have done—e.g. Spender, even the later Auden isn't poetry at all: mere words. . . . I suppose they think one is too successful already as an historian." Signed: "Affectntely, Leslie." [Source: One of series of three, Bertram Rota, London, December 10, 1982.]

H158. Oxford, June 2, 1967; on letterhead of All Souls College, Oxford; 2 pp, 8vo

"Dear Richard" [stating that he (Richard Church), should be poet laureate] "I shall never repay your kindness. . . . think what treatment I might have received at your colleague's hands! And yet I should have thought: Cornish Stories, right up Geoffrey's (Grigson!) street—one of them he himself told me. . . . it has sold nearly 3000 in a month without a review!" Signed: "Love to you & much happiness to you both. Yrs—Leslie." [Source: One of series of three, Bertram Rota, London, December 10, 1982.]

H159. Trenarren, undated, circa late 1982; on letterhead of All Souls College, Oxford; correspondence card

"Dear Mr. Martin . . . If down this way, come & see me—marooned on my headland till March-April in US." Signed: "Good Luck for 1983, Yours A. L. R." [Source: Bertram Rota, London, September 1993.]

H160. Trenarren, June 20, 1986; letter

"Dear Mr. Goyen . . . Yes, my mother's mother was Elizabeth Goynes—they came from Duloe parish near Looe. But since they were only working people they didn't know anything about their origins, or much else. . . . The name reminds me of the French town, Guines, near Calais." Signed: "Best of Luck with your researches, A. L. Rowse." [Source: Sent to me by A. L. R. as an example of the "Slackness of people." The letter has been heavily marked over by redirections through the post, and back to Cornwall, before being sent on to me as an autograph!]

H161. Oxford, dated Monday, postmarked February 18, 1975; on letterhead of All Souls College, Oxford; 1 p, 8vo
"Dear Phyllis . . . I had a good journey up yesterday. . . . Enjoyed my picnic on a hill overlooking Swindon. . . . What a nice time we had, gardening & everything. Thank you for looking after me." Signed: "Yrs ever, A. L. Rowse." [Source: Present from Mrs. Phyllis Cundy, housekeeper to A. L. Rowse.]

H162. Lynchburg College, Lynchburg, Virginia, USA, April 3, 1982; letter
"Dear Phyllis . . . Yesterday I had a beautiful day across the mountains to lecture to another university—wonderful drive, the hills rather alarming, but lovely along the James River. . . . While in Georgetown I have to lecture at the University next door to Mr. Treffry's, and where Lord Caradon lectures every year. . . . We all have to earn our living off the Americans, and everywhere I go I have to sing for my supper." Signed: "Yours, A. L. R." [Source: as above.]

H163. Lynchburg, April 10, 1982; letter
"Dear Phyllis . . . Only 10 more days here & I leave for 4 days with Mr. Treffry before homeward bound. . . . I must say I have been missing the fresh open air in the garden and am longing to be up in the Wilderness with morning coffee/cocoa on the hedge. . . . You would laugh to see me in my kitchen, where I make tea but can't use the new fangled tin opener—I prefer the old sort. . . . The Americans are all very kind and helpful. . . . I have been very careful and managed to keep well, though flu & colds about. And got over my ear infection." Signed: "Yours, A. L. R." [Source: as above.]

H164. Washington, D.C., March 27, 1986; letter
"Dear Phyllis . . . the POM (Poor Old Man!) has arrived safely in one piece. . . . A couple of kind friends met me at Washington airport . . . off to see the wonderful exhibition of Treasures from English Country Houses. . . . Love to you and both Jacks & all the family [Jack, the gardener, and one other!]." Signed: "Your P O M." [Source: as above.]

H165. Lynchburg, Virginia, April 13, 1986; letter
"Dear Phyllis . . . Over here I have been photographed to bits, some of last year's photographs have come out well, and they are giving them to us. . . . I hope you had some company—Jack G. and Valerie and that Jack B. is recovering from his op. . . . Ops are wonderful nowadays. But no cure for the common cold." Signed: "Affectly P O M." [Source: as above.]

Index

The aim of this index is to be thorough and user-friendly.

References are to item numbers in the bibliography. Contributions to books by A. L. Rowse in section B are listed by author, title, and type of contribution, i.e., (foreword). Similarly, all books reviewed by Rowse are listed by author (or editor), title, and review. Books edited by Rowse are identified as such to avoid confusion with books indexed under the name of the editor. For reasons of space, the extended titles of books are partly reduced by ellipses.

All articles by A. L. Rowse in section D are indexed under the title, which is cross-referenced to publications and also to names of interest relevant therein. Letters to the editor are grouped under that heading and are similarly cross-referenced. Poems and short stories are indexed under publications only. Sections E, F, G, and H are indexed through names significant elsewhere.

Names of reviewers and reviews of A. L. Rowse's books are listed only if they merit wider significance elsewhere in the A. L. Rowse canon of work.

Allen, J. W., *English Political Thought, 1603–1660*, vol. 1 . . . (review), D141
Allen, P. S., *Erasmus: Lectures and Wayfaring Sketches* (review), D75
Allen, William, Cardinal, D71
"All Hail to Q" (article), D1051
"All Souls" (article), D273; F2
All Souls and Appeasement, A31; D368; H121
All Souls in My Time, A102; F126; H125
"All Souls Stories" (article), D895
"Alltyrynys and the Cecils" (article), D357
A. L. Rowse's Cornwall: A Journey Through Cornwall's Past and Present, A93; H94, 97, 117
"An Alternative All Souls" (article), D894
"Always True to Cornwall" (article), D979a
American Heritage (journal), D348, 349, 352, 353, 355, 387
American Mercury (journal), D316
Amis, Sir Kingsley, A92
AMS Press (publisher), A24
Andrews, K. R. (editor), *English Privateering Voyages to the West Indies, 1588–1595* (review), D369
———, *The Last Voyage of Drake and Hawkins* (review), D528
Andrews, Martin, *Canon's Folly* (foreword), B39
Anglia w epoce elzbietanskiej (Polish trans. of A19, 25), C11
Anglo, Sydney, *Machiavelli: A Dissection* (review), D447a
Annenberg School Press (publisher), A47
Annenberg, Walter H., A47
The Annotated Shakespeare, A69, 80; F87, 92, 340–342
Anstruther, Godfrey, *Vaux of Harrowden* . . . (review), D317a
Antaeus (journal), D949
Anthony Mott (publisher), A10, 36; B50

Antique and New Art (journal), D1055
Appeasement: A Study in Political Decline, 1933–1939, A31; E8
"Are We Playing Germany's Game?" (article), D63
Arnold, Matthew, A41; D297, 492a; E28
Arrow Books (publisher), A10
"Arthur Symons: The Symbolist Movement in Literature" (article), D1006
Artus (publisher), A65, 72
Ashe, Dora Jean, *Four Hundred Years of Virginia, An Anthology* (foreword), B52
———, *A Maryland Anthology, 1608–1986* (foreword), B58a
Ashley, Maurice, A19, 36
———, *Louis XIV and the Greatness of France* (edited by ALR), B71
———, *Oliver Cromwell and the Puritan Revolution* (edited by ALR), B100
———, *The English Revolution: Oxford Royalist Notebooks* . . . (review), D672
Ashton, Robert, *The English Civil War* . . . (review), D733
———, *The City and the Court, 1603–1643* (review), D746
"As I Saw It: Once More on the Campus Trek" (article), D473
Aspects de la Biographie (*see* Maurios, Andre)
Aspinall-Oglander, Cecil, *Admiral's Wife: The Life and Letters of Mrs. Boscawen, 1719–1761* (review), D178
"Assessing Elizabeth I on Her 450th Birthday" (article), D854
Astor, Nancy (Viscountess), A74; D402, 764a; E31; F32
Astor, William Waldorf (later Viscount), D309
"At Home with History in London" (article), D918
Atmosphere Publishing (publisher), B63

Byrne, M. St. Clare (editor), *The Lisle Letters* (reviews), D796, 800, 847, 865

Byron, Lord, D567, 574, 578; E28

"Byron's Friends, Bankes: A Portrait" (article), D618

The Byrons and the Trevanions, A67

Camden, Carroll, *The Elizabethan Woman* (review), D312a

Campbell, Lily B. (editor), *The Mirror of Magistrates* (review), D157, 159

Campbell, Mildred, *The English Yeoman under Elizabeth and the Early Stuarts* (review), D262a

Cannadine, David, *G. M. Trevelyan: A Life in History* (review), D1027a

Cannan, May Wedderburn, *Grey Ghosts and Voices,* (review), D650

Cannon, John (editor), *The Letters of Junius* (review), D705

Canny, Nicholas, *The Elizabethan Conquest of Ireland . . .* (review), D675

Capp, Bernard, *Astrology and the Popular Press . . .* (review), D741

Capp, B. S., *The Fifth Monarchy Men* (review), D507

Carcanet Press (publisher), B46

Cardinal by Sphere Books (publisher), A10, 19, 25, 44, 45, 48

Carew, Sir Peter, A89

Carew, Richard, A89

Carey, John, *The Intellectuals and the Masses* (review), D1025a

Carlson, L. H., *Martin Marprelate, Gentleman . . .* (review), D866

Carlton, C., *Charles I* (review), D853

Carlyle, Alexander, *Anecdotes and Characters of the Times* (review), D557

Carlyle, Thomas, A13; D782, 1066; H147

"The Caroline Country Parson: George Herbert's Ideal" (article), D227a

Carpenter, Edward, *The Protestant Bishop* (review), D330f

—— (editor), *A House of Kings* (review), D418a

Carr, E. H. *Michael Bakunin* (review), D143

——, *The Twenty Years' Crisis, 1919–1939* (review), D206

Carr, Raymond, A94, 102, 104

——, *Spain, 1803–1939* (review), D418b

Carroll & Graf (publisher), A61

Carswell, John, A26

——, *The South Sea Bubble* (review), D371

The Case Books of Simon Forman: Sex and Society in Shakespeare's Age, A51 (*see also* Forman, Simon)

Cather, Willa, A74; D897

Cats and Dogs (theatrical review of Cats), D793

Catto, J. I. (editor), *The Early Oxford Schools . . .* (review), D879

Causley, Charles, A10, 92

Cecil, Lord David, A94

——, *The Cecils of Hatfield House* (review), D550

——, *Lady Ottoline's Album,* introduction (review), D667

——, *A Choice of Robert Bridges' Verse,* introduction (review), D941

Cecil, William, *Lord Burghley,* D67

Cell, G. T., *English Enterprise in Newfoundland, 1577–1660* (review), D508

——, *Newfoundland Discovered* (review), D891

Chambers, Sir E. K., *Sir Henry Lee* (review), D114

Chaney, Edward, and Ritchie, Neil (editors), *Oxford, China, and Italy: Writings in Honour of Sir Harold Acton on His Eightieth Birthday* (essay), B51

Chapman, Hester W., *Anne Boleyn* (review), D560a

Chapman, W., *The Last Tudor King: A Study of Edward VI* (review), D344

Charles, B. G., *George Owen of Henllys: A Welsh Elizabethan* (review), D638

Charles, H. R. H., the Prince of Wales, A105; F142, 147; H147, 149

The Later Churchills, A27; F263
Lavrin, Janko, *Pushkin and Russian Literature* (edited by ALR), B78
Lawrence, D. H., A20, 41; D1070; H140
Lawrence, T. E., D642a
"Lawrence of Oxford" (article), D1070
Lee, Charles, *Cornish Tales* (review), D217
Lees-Milne, James, *Prophesying Peace* (review), D687
——, *Caves of Ice* (review), D836
——, *People and Places . . .* (review), D1027b
——, *A Mingled Measure: Diaries, 1953–1972* (review), D1051b
Lefranc, Pierre, *Sir Walter Ralegh ecrivain . . .* (review), D461
Legg, L. G. Wickham (editor), *The Dictionary of National Biography, 1931–1940* (review), D292
Leggatt, Alexander, *Shakespeare's Comedy of Love* (review), D584
"Leisure Must Be Shared" (article), D46
Le Quesne, A. L., *After Kilvert* (review), D728
L'esprit de l'histoire de l'angleterre (French trans. A11), C5
"A Lesson from the Past" (article), D474
"Let's Be Fair to Edward and Wallis" (article), D930
The Letters of Marsilio Ficino . . . (review), D967
Letters to the Editor:
D1, 2, 17, 18, 61, 66, 103, 129, 130, 142, 159, 163, 171, 174, 182, 229, 230, 256, 258, 265–267, 271, 275, 275c, 283–285, 287–289, 295, 298, 300, 304, 307–309, 311, 313a, 314, 320, 323, 331, 332, 338, 347a,360, 361, 364, 367, 368, 370, 376–379, 382, 384, 390, 397, 398, 401, 402, 409, 416, 419, 430–432, 444, 445, 448, 450–453, 456, 459, 464, 468, 470, 488, 496, 506, 518, 520, 525, 530, 531–534, 537, 563, 570, 703, 707, 713, 755, 761, 762, 765, 775, 778, 780, 784, 785, 792, 794, 882, 910, 913, 931, 947, 968, 1018, 1049, 1053, 1058, 1073

Leveson-Gower, Sir George, and Palmer, Iris (editors), *Hary-O: The Letters of Lady Harriet Cavendish, 1796–1809* (review), D186
Levi, Peter, A81; D882; F117–120
Lewis, Alun, A20
——, *In the Green Tree / Letters from India* (preface), B13
Lewis, C. S., A82, G13, 45
——, *English Literature in the Sixteenth Century . . .* (review), D326b
Lewis, Michael, *The Spanish Armada* (review), D362
——, *The Hawkins Dynasty* (review), D461a
Lewis, Warren Hamilton, G27
Lewis, W. S. (editor), *Selected Letters of Horace Walpole* (review), D586
—— (editor), *Horace Walpole's Correspondence . . .* (review), D629
"Liberalism No Remedy" (article), D38
Liebman, Marcel, *The Russian Revolution* (review), D462a
A Life: Collected Poems, A76; B3, 38, 48, 63; F368; H75
Lindsay, A. D., *The Essentials of Democracy* (review), D16
Linklater, Eric, *The Royal House of Scotland* (review), D464a
Lisle, Lady, A89
Listener (journal), B48; D67, 68, 70, 71, 87, 88, 91,92, 101, 112, 126, 162, 169, 205, 208, 213, 218, 228, 232, 237, 238, 246, 251, 262, 263, 274, 281, 312, 329, 344, 345, 347, 351, 354, 356, 359, 362, 385, 412, 417, 418, 469a, 531, 534, 568, 778, 784, 785
Literary Digest (journal), D3
Literary Guild (publisher), A49
Literary Review (journal), D774
"Literature As Pleasure" (article), D949
Little, Bryan, *The Life and Work of James Gibbs, 1682–1754* (review), D329a
——, *The Monmouth Episode* (review), D332a

Mr. Keynes and the Labour Movement, A6; G11

"Mr. Keynes and the Labour Movement" (article), D110

"Mr. Keynes on Socialism: A Reply" (article), D37

Mr. W. H. (*see* Harvey, Sir William)

"The 'Mr. W. H.' of Shakespeare's Sonnets—and his Tomb" (article), D447

Muir, Kenneth, A33, 34

———, *Shakespeare Survey 24* (review), D493

———, *Shakespeare the Professional* (review), D526

——— (editor), *Shakespeare Survey* (review), D695

———, *Troilus and Cressida* by William Shakespeare (review), D845

Mullen, Richard, A96, 102, 104

———, *Anthony Trollope: A Victorian in His World* (review), D1002

Murray, Charles Augustus, A71; D732

"Mushroom Universities . . ." (article), D605

My Books: A Testament, A105

"My Perfect Weekend" (questions/ answers), D1020

"My Time of Life/80s" (contribution), D939

My View of Shakespeare: The Shakespeare Revolution, A105; E25; F144; H148, 149

Namier, Sir Lewis, A104

———, *In the Margin of History* (review), D170

National and English Review (journal), D294, 296, 297, 299, 301, 303, 305, 315, 325

"The National Government in Decline" (article), D56

National Review (journal), D286, 291– 293

Neale, Sir John E., A7, 19, 104; F25, 32

———, *The Age of Catherine De Medici* (review), D250a

———, *Elizabeth I and Her Parliaments, 1584–1601* (review), D334a

Nelson, Horatio (later Lord), D240a

Nevins, Allan, A31, 104

"New and Kind Light on George III" (article), D363

New Clarion (journal), D32, 35, 38– 41, 43, 44, 46, 48, 49, 51, 52, 55, 59, 60

Newdigate, B. H., *Michael Drayton and His Circle* (review), D223

A New Elizabethan Age?, A21

New English Library (publisher), A33

"New Light on Shakespeare" (article), D850

Newman, A., *The Stanhopes of Chevening* (review), D444a

Newman, Peter C., *Company of Adventurers . . .* (review), D922

———, *Caesars of the Wilderness . . .* (review), D960

New Oxford Outlook (journal), A3; D86a

New Republic (journal), D347a

The New Standard and *Evening Standard* (newspapers, UK), D789, 956a, 1008a–b, 1011a, 1020a, 1021a, 1022a, 1025a, b, c, 1027a–b, 1030, 1031a, 1035a–b, 1036a, 1038a, 1040a, 1042a–b, 1051 a–b, 1052a, 1057a, 1064a, 1066a, 1067a, 1071a, 1075a

New Statesman and Nation (journal), D7, 13, 27, 29, 74, 83, 94, 99, 128, 157, 177, 181, 183, 187, 215, 216, 219, 221–223, 226, 236, 240, 243, 248–250, 252, 254, 257, 264, 272, 284

New Yorker (journal), A33; 49; D366

New York Times (newspaper), D363, 365, 372, 399, 401, 416, 474a, 478a, 824, 838, 854, 870, 875, 883, 897, 907, 913, 918, 926, 930, 935, 990, 999, 1004, 1042

Nicholl, Charles, *The Reckoning* (review), D1025, 1042

Nicolaievsky, B., and Maenchen-Helfen, O., *Karl Marx: Man and Fighter* (review), D121

About the Author

Sydney Cauveren was born in Amsterdam in 1947. While in high school in Adelaide, South Australia, he first became acquainted with the writing and scholarship of A. L. Rowse, when he read *The England of Elizabeth*. This triggered a lifetime passion for the author's work.

Cauveren is a former senior crew member for QANTAS, the Australian international airline. In 1976 he had a posting in London and happened to view a television interview with A. L. Rowse, which prompted a letter of appreciation. This developed into a twenty-year friendship with A. L. Rowse that ultimately yielded this "labor of love" bibliography.

Now a Sydney-based freelance writer and researcher, he has published several articles on A. L. Rowse, including his obituary/tribute in the national paper *The Australian*.